NETWORKING UNIX

Salim Douba

SAMS
PUBLISHING

201 West 103rd Street
Indianapolis, Indiana 46290

To my parents

Copyright © 1995 by Sams Publishing

FIRST EDITION

All rights reserved. No part of this book shall be reproduced, stored in a retrieval system, or transmitted by any means, electronic, mechanical, photocopying, recording, or otherwise, without written permission from the publisher. No patent liability is assumed with respect to the use of the information contained herein. Although every precaution has been taken in the preparation of this book, the publisher and author assume no responsibility for errors or omissions. Neither is any liability assumed for damages resulting from the use of the information contained herein. For information, address Sams Publishing, 201 W. 103rd St., Indianapolis, IN 46290.

International Standard Book Number: 0-672-30584-4

Library of Congress Catalog Card Number: 94-69266

98 97 96 95   4 3 2 1

Interpretation of the printing code: the rightmost double-digit number is the year of the book's printing; the rightmost single-digit, the number of the book's printing. For example, a printing code of 95-1 shows that the first printing of the book occurred in 1995.

Composed in AGaramond and MCPdigital by Macmillan Computer Publishing

Printed in the United States of America

Trademarks

All terms mentioned in this book that are known to be trademarks or service marks have been appropriately capitalized. Sams Publishing cannot attest to the accuracy of this information. Use of a term in this book should not be regarded as affecting the validity of any trademark or service mark.

Windows NT is a trademark of Microsoft Corporation.

Publisher	*Richard K. Swadley*
Acquisitions Manager	*Greg Wiegand*
Development Manager	*Dean Miller*
Managing Editor	*Cindy Morrow*
Marketing Manager	*Gregg Bushyeager*

Acquisitions Editor
Rosemarie Graham

Development and Technical Reviewers
Larry Schumer
Chris Negas

Production Editor
Cheri Clark

Editorial Coordinator
Bill Whitmer

Technical Edit Coordinator
Lynette Quinn

Formatter
Frank Sinclair

Editorial Assistant
Sharon Cox

Cover Designer
Tim Amrhein

Book Designer
Alyssa Yesh

Production Team Supervisor
Brad Chinn

Production
Angela D. Bannan
Charlotte M. Clapp
Jeanne Clark
Mary Ann Cosby
Mike Dietsch
Mike Henry
Ayanna Lacey
Paula Lowell
Donna Martin
Casey Price
Brian-Kent Proffitt
SA Springer
Tina Trettin
Susan Van Ness

Indexer
Cheryl Dietsch

Overview

Contents

Acknowledgments

The author would like to thank all the people who were involved in developing this book. My first thanks go to my wife, May, and son, Nadeem, for their relentless support and continued encouragement. They had to put up with the long hours that went into writing this book, and had to compromise the time we were used to spending together, which made a long Canadian winter even longer. Thanks again.

The development and technical editors, Chris Negas, Dean Miller, and Larry Schumer, have helped in keeping the covered material accurate and the flow logical. Thank you for your contribution.

Special credits go to the extraordinary friends Andrea Mills and Patrick T. Gilligan. They both volunteered to support this work. Andrea put up with the long hours it takes to edit the manuscript for better readability. Patrick contributed, with enthusiasm and academic curiosity, by writing the Windows NT section in Chapter 17. Thanks to both of you.

Cheri Clark's meticulous work in editing the manuscript made a significant contribution to the consistency of the material presented in the book and its final form. Thank you for the fine work.

About the Author

Salim M. Douba is a senior network consultant mainly specializing in UNIX, NetWare, and mainframe connectivity. He is also an independent Certified NetWare Instructor (CNI), teaching NetWare operating systems and advanced courses. He holds a master's degree in electrical engineering from the American University of Beirut. His experience and main career interests have primarily been in Internetworking and multiplatform integration.

Salim has coauthored the textbook *UNIX Unleashed* for Sams Publishing.

He is reachable on CompuServe on 70573,2351.

Introduction

Over the past few years, computer networks underwent an explosive growth rate as users began to realize the benefits they can derive from them versus the old-style standalone environments. Besides basic file and print resources that users can transparently share, networks allowed them to use an ever-expanding suite of other productivity tools such as electronic mail and calendering applications—tools that resulted in an ever-increasing dependence on networks to the point where in many environments, a fatal network failure can easily mean a total loss of one or more business days of productivity.

Another important factor for the increase in dependability on computer networks is the Internet. For many organizations, the Internet provided them with the backbone to connect remote office networks together. For others, the Internet provided them with yet another business vehicle that they can use to promote their productivity and market reach.

Implementing and maintaining networks that can meet the ever-increasing user demands on networked resources and productivity tools are becoming increasingly challenging tasks. UNIX networks are no less challenging than others. If anything, they are more complex to deal with. The complexity stems from the nature of protocols that underlie UNIX networks, namely the Transmission Control Protocol/Internet Protocol (TCP/IP) suite. TCP/IP LAN administrators cannot possibly do a good job without gaining an insight into this protocol suite and dealing with its intricacies.

This book is about networking UNIX environments. It is written to provide the knowledge and practical skills that network professionals need to have in order to deal with TCP/IP from the UNIX perspective. The audience of this book includes network professionals who have the need to understand TCP/IP and the issues pertinent to implementing and maintaining it on UNIX platforms. *Network professionals* is a broad term used to include network managers, administrators, and consultants. Also, among the audience the book is intended for are the curious users who want to learn more about this technology that governs important aspects of their production.

The book is written in two parts. Part I introduces the concepts governing TCP/IP. No prior knowledge on behalf of the user is assumed. Readers with no conceptual understanding of TCP/IP should read this part first before pursuing Part II. Part I is also intended for MIS managers who need to know of the capabilities and limitations of TCP/IP without engaging in the how-to details.

Part II covers the practical side of implementing UNIX networks using the TCP/IP suite. It starts with a chapter on network planning—a necessary phase for ensuring a successful implementation. Subsequent chapters mainly deal with the actual implementation right from installing TCP/IP to setting up Domain Name Services and Network File Systems, among other network services. A chapter on network troubleshooting is also included to familiarize the reader with some of the troubleshooting methodologies that can be adapted to suit situations that the reader might be dealing with in the future.

Part II closes with a chapter on UNIX in a multiplatform environment. The chapter is meant to provide only a conceptual overview of how different vendors have dealt with issues relating to interconnectivity between hybrid operating systems and networks.

It is the author's conviction that learning is best achieved if discussions are coupled with practice. The book is enriched with examples based on real-life scenarios and examples supported by actual walk-throughs through the necessary configurations and usage of some of the most pertinent commands. In short, the book is a balanced mix of both theory and practice.

A final word about the prerequisites to reading this book. Readers are expected to be familiar with computers and must be comfortable using UNIX. You do not need to be a UNIX wizard to understand the covered concepts. But you need to know how to use a UNIX text editor, for example, to implement the configuration files being described. You also need to know how to use the man pages and how to find your way around the UNIX file system.

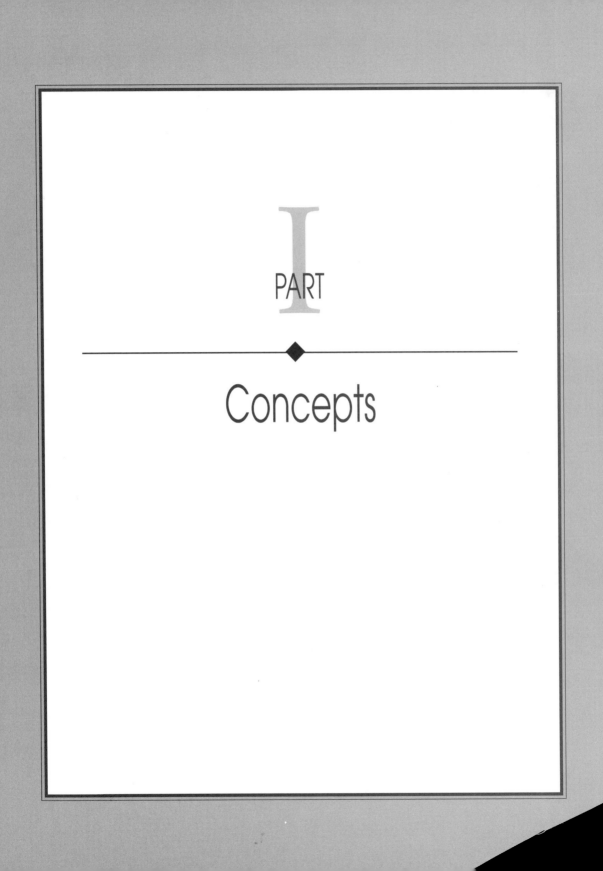

I

PART

Concepts

CHAPTER

Overview of Data Communications

Introduction

Before you can use any technology, you should understand the terms, concepts, and models that represent it. Data communications is no exception. The Open System Interconnection (OSI) model of data communications is the frame of reference most commonly used by people working in this field to describe the inner workings and architectural structures of communication protocols. This chapter introduces the concepts and frame of reference that underlie the topics covered in all the upcoming chapters.

Elements of Data Communications

A good place to start is to ask the question "What is data communications about, and what is involved?" To make the question clearer, the first part might have to be put this way: "What are the *ultimate* communicating entities, when data is transferred across the wire?" The author has received all kinds of answers to this question except for the most applicable one: *processes that are representative of user applications,* without regard to the platforms on which they run. However simple this answer might sound, it hides complexities that will unfold as this discussion attempts to answer the second part of the original question ("what is involved?").

It is important that you keep this answer in mind as the discussions in this chapter and the subsequent ones evolve. Data communications' concern is not to allow two computers to communicate per se; the concern ultimately is to allow users access to information that is kept somewhere on a network of data repositories. This concern should be taken care of, as well as shielded from users, by the previously mentioned representative processes.

The answer to the "what is involved?" part of the question lies in defining the concerns that would be encountered in the process of the data exchange between user applications. The following discussion highlights some of those concerns, with the objective being, aside from raising the reader's awareness of these concerns, to justify the need for a so-called "layered solution" to the communications puzzle. This justification will be presented later in this chapter, as a prelude to discussing the Open System Interconnection model of data communications.

Physical Data Encoding

This concern deals with ways by which data is physically represented on the wire. Data is carried on the wire by means of electrical signals that assume certain patterns. Those patterns can be characterized by changing voltage levels, current levels, frequency of transmission, phasal changes, or any combination of these factors to reliably convey data from point A to point B. To be able to communicate across the wire, both computers, A and B, should have compatible implementation of physical data representation, which is referred to as data encoding. Encoding not only defines the levels that electrical signals can assume, but also defines how the level changes should be interpreted by the communicating devices. To understand the last statement, consider two examples of data encoding: bipolar encoding and the non-return-to-zero encoding (NRZI).

In bipolar encoding, binary data is simply represented by the actual signal level, in which a binary 1 is encoded using a fixed positive voltage (for example, +5V) and a binary 0 is encoded using a negative voltage level (for example, –5V). Figure 1.1 shows two computers involved in the exchange of a train of bipolar-encoded, data-carrying electrical signals and the equivalent binary data.

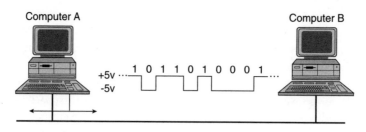

Figure 1.1. Bipolar data encoding.

On the other hand, although NRZI also defines only two (positive and negative) voltage levels that the data-carrying signal can assume, data itself is encoded in the presence or absence of voltage transitions at the beginning of each bit undergoing transmission. This technique encodes a binary 0 by forcing a transition, from one voltage level to the other, at the beginning of the transmission cycle, in which a binary 1 is represented by the mere absence of the transition. Figure 1.2 shows two computers involved in the exchange of a train of NRZI-encoded, data-carrying signals pertaining to the same binary equivalent depicted in Figure 1.2. Notice, in particular, how a train of contiguous 1s generates a sustained signal level on the wire, whereas a train of 0s generates alternating signal levels.

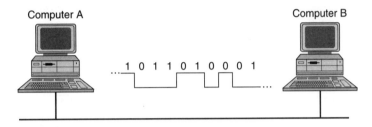

Figure 1.2. *Non-return-to-zero data encoding.*

Transmission Media

This concern deals with the type of media (fiber, copper, wireless, and so on), which in turn is dictated by the desirable bandwidth, immunity to noise, and attenuation properties. These factors affect the maximum allowable media length while still achieving a desirable level of guaranteed reliability of data transmission.

Data Flow Control

Data communications processes allocate memory resources, commonly known as communications buffers, for the sake of transmission and reception of data. A computer whose communications buffers become full in the process of receiving data from the wire runs the risk of discarding extra transmissions and losing data unless it resorts to data flow control techniques (see Figure 1.3). Proper data flow control techniques call on the receiving process to send a "stop sending" signal to the sending computer whenever it cannot cope with the rate at which data is being transmitted. The receiving process later sends a "resume sending" signal as data communications buffers become available.

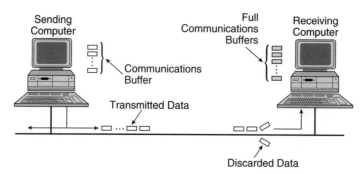

Figure 1.3. *The receiving computer risks losing data whenever its communications buffers become full, unless data flow control techniques are used.*

Data Frame Format

As computers communicate, they need to make certain decisions about various aspects of the data exchange process. Figure 1.4 shows a flowchart representation of a simplified receive algorithm. This flowchart demonstrates the kind of decisions a receiving end might need to make in the course of recovering data from the wire.

Following is a summary of some of those decisions a receiving end might need to make, following the order in which they take place in Figure 1.4:

1. As computers listen to the wire to recover messages sent to them, they require a mechanism by which they can tell whether to treat signals they detect as data-carrying signals or to discard them as mere noise.

2. Assuming that what are on the wire are data-carrying signals, the second decision that might have to be made is whether the *listening computer* is the intended party or whether the transmission is intended for other computers on the network.

3. If a computer engages in the process of recovering data from the wire, how is it going to tell where the message ends? After it determines where the message ends, it can discard all subsequent signals unless it can determine that they belong to a new, impending transmission.

4. When data reception is complete, how can the receiving end trust that data withstood corruption from noise and electromagnetic interference? How is it going deal with data corruption if that occurs?

To accommodate these concerns, among other concerns that will be discussed in due course, data is exchanged in units called *data frames*. In addition to user data, a data frame includes enough information to help both ends of the communication channel reach the desirable decisions. Figure 1.5 shows an example frame format pertaining to the IEEE 802.3 Ethernet data link technology. When an Ethernet frame is transmitted, the preamble field is sent out first. It consists of a sequence of alternating 0s and 1s with the last bit being set to 0. Because it is extremely improbable that such a uniform pattern can be generated by noise on the wire, the preamble field serves as the attention-getting signal to alert the participating computers on the network about an impending transmission event.

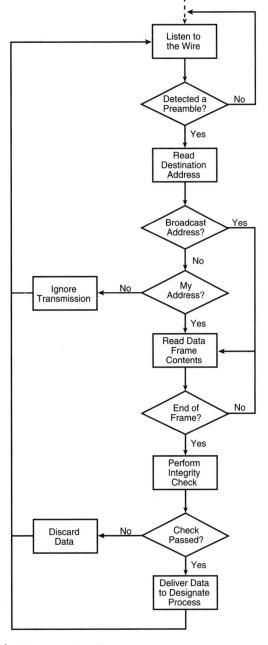

Figure 1.4. *An algorithm depicting a generic receive process.*

Preamble (8 bytes)	Destination Address (6 bytes)	Source Address (6 bytes)	Length (2 bytes)	Information	FCS

Figure 1.5. *IEEE 802.3 Ethernet data frame format.*

The next field is the destination address field, also known as the *data link address* or the *medium access control* (MAC) address. This field assists the computer in determining whether the impending transmission belongs to it. This determination is based on a comparison that the receive process makes between the transmitted address and the one that is hardwired on the network interface card (that is, the communication interface). The address is guaranteed to be unique by communications products vendors in partial compliance with worldwide adopted standards (most notably the IEEE and OSI standards). A receive process is normally "educated" about two addresses: that of its own and a broadcast address, which is normally taken to be a field with all bits set to 1. In both cases, the receive process is allowed to recover data on the wire. The source address field tells the recipient who the sender was.

The fourth field describes the length of the information field and therefore helps in answering the third point raised previously. It tells the computer when transmission of the current data unit (that is, frame) comes to its end.

The last field, the frame check sequence, is a 32-bit cyclic redundancy check character that serves the ultimate goal of determining whether transmitted data preserved its integrity. The receive process compares the contents of this field with the outcome of an integrity check routine it invokes, which acts on all fields in the data frame except for the preamble and FCS. If the comparison is favorable, data will have passed the check, and the information field is submitted to some other process for subsequent processing. Otherwise, the entire frame is discarded.

It is important to realize that the primary concern of the receive process just described is the reliable recovery of the information embedded in the information field, with no attention paid to the nature of the actual contents of that field. Instead, processing the data in the information field is delegated to another process as the receive process reverts to listening mode to take care of future events from the wire. These two realizations, as you will see later in this chapter, underlie the layered architecture of the data communications solutions.

Link Management

Network cables are the highways through which data travels. These data highways have limited data transmission capacity, measured in kilobits or megabits per second. Unlike when you drive your car on a highway, however, a network interface card cannot drive its data on the wire at ranging rates up to the limiting transmission rate. Instead, data is always driven at the rated speed (for example, 10 Mbps in the case of Ethernet, and 16 Mbps in the case of the Token-ring). Another characterizing aspect of any networking technology is whether more than one station is allowed to transmit simultaneously. If so, the transmission is referred to as broadband transmission; otherwise, it is baseband transmission, in which case only one station can send data at a time.

Taking baseband transmission as an example, it is conceivable that at times, more than one computer will want to attempt transmission—hence the need for data *link management.* Among other things, a data link management process determines when it is appropriate to seize the link and transmit data, and for how long. Link management is achieved differently by different networking technologies. In the case of Ethernet, link management and control is more the individual responsibility of each computer independent of all others, whereas in the case of Token-ring, it is a collective responsibility shared by all computers. For further details on both link management and control methods, refer to Chapter 3, "The Network Access Layer."

The Routing Problem

One of the problems that the networking technology had to address is how to handle data traffic on an internetwork (that is, a network of networks). The internetwork can be connecting networks belonging to the same campus or spanning geographically dispersed locations. Figure 1.6 depicts one such internetwork. Each line in the diagram represents an independent network, and each solid circle represents a connectivity device attaching several networks together, thus enabling stations on different networks to communicate with each other.

Assuming that workstation X on network 1 wants to send a message to workstation Y on network 5, a question comes to mind: "How will this data be handled by the intervening connectivity devices?" The industry has responded with two solutions to this question: bridging and routing. However, because a more precise distinction between both approaches can be made after a thorough examination of the OSI model, only the "routing" approach will be handled. The connectivity devices shown in Figure 1.6 will, from now on, be called *routers.*

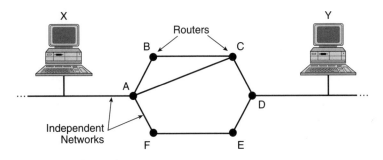

Figure 1.6. *An internetwork of networks.*

The routing approach calls on the implementation of various cooperative processes, in both routers and workstations, whose main concern is to allow for the *intelligent* exchange of data. Data exchange can take place between any two workstations, whether or not both belong to the same network. In the following sections, the main functions and features that characterize the routing process are described.

The Network Address and the Complete Address

Aside from the data link address, which should be guaranteed to be unique for each workstation on a particular physical network, all workstations must have a higher level address in common. This is known as the *network address*. The network address is very similar in function and purpose to the concept of the street name. A street name is common to all residences located on that street. When mail is delivered to your office or residence, the postal carrier is initially more concerned about finding the street where the residence belongs than the exact identifying residence number. Only after finding the named street, which is part of the address, does the carrier pay attention to the actual residence number to ensure that the correspondence is delivered to the designated recipient.

Unlike data link addresses, which are mostly hardwired on the network interface card, network addresses are software configurable as part of network installers' or network administrators' responsibilities. It should also be noted that the data structure and rules of assigning network addresses vary from one networking technology to another. This book concerns itself only with IP addressing schemes, which are detailed in Chapter 4, "The Internet Layer and Routing."

For the time being, and for the purpose of illustration, this discussion assumes that the networks shown in Figure 1.7 are assigned the encircled numerals as network addresses. It should be obvious that to aid in the process of data routing, the *complete* destination and source addresses should be embedded somewhere in the transmitted frame. The complete address should include enough information to assist in determining both the network address (which is like the street name) and the data link address (which is like the residence number). It is of the utmost importance that you do not confuse complete destination and source addresses with the data link or MAC addresses discussed earlier in the context of data frame formats. As you will see later, the complete addresses designate the ultimate communicating partners on the internetwork, whereas the data link addresses can designate intermediate devices (such as routers and workstations). Should the ultimate communication partners belong to the same network, however, there will be a one-to-one correspondence between the complete addresses and the data link addresses.

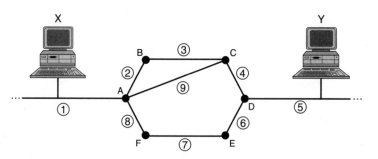

Figure 1.7. *Networks are assigned addresses. The diagram shows a hypothetical network, in which encircled numerals represent network addresses.*

You might wonder where the complete addresses are hidden in the transmitted data frame. To answer the question, look back at the data frame format shown in Figure 1.5. Remember that all but the information field were significant only to the receive process, with each field serving a completely different purpose. Those fields represent overheads that are necessary to achieve a minimum level of reliability in delivering the data carried in the information field of the data frame. It was also mentioned that when the data frame is recovered, and the integrity check is passed, the receive process submits the information field and delegates the responsibility of processing it to another process, which is the routing process. While doing so, the receive process does not care about the actual contents of the information field.

Like the data frame, the information field is also formatted. However, it is formatted in order to serve entirely different objectives than those served by the frame format. As the routing process takes hold of the information field, details that were hidden in that field from the receive process start to reveal themselves at this level of processing. Most technologies refer to the information field at this level of processing as a data *packet*.

Figure 1.8 illustrates the relationship between the data frame format and the packet format. The figure also shows the packet format pertaining to the routing process only, and it highlights the parts that bear local significance to the routing process. The packet format in Figure 1.8 is hypothetical and is used in the next few sections for the purposes of illustration. Notice how the complete addresses designating the ultimate communicating partners are assigned fields in the packet. The shaded part of the packet represents fields taking care of concerns that won't be addressed at this point. It should also be clear to the reader's mind that the information field of the data packet bears no significance to the routing process (except in very special cases, which are discussed in Chapter 4).

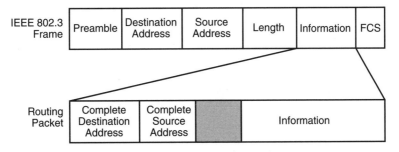

Figure 1.8. *The relationship between the data frame format and the packet format.*

Assuming that complete addresses are represented following the *network address:data link address* notation, Figure 1.9 illustrates the contents of a data frame as it emerges out of workstation X on network 2 (see Figure 1.7). According to this frame, the MAC destination and source addresses correspond to the sending workstation X and router A, respectively. The complete addresses, however, indicate that the ultimate communicating partners are X on network 1 and Y on network 5, the latter being the destination party. Accordingly, this frame should be interpreted in the following way: workstation X is addressing router A to help in the delivery of data to workstation Y on network 5. This is very similar to your delivering correspondence to the post office for subsequent handling and delivery to the ultimate addressee identified on the envelope. How the post office is going to handle your mail is more of a concern local to the mail-handling system than to you. In like fashion, how the router is going to handle data delivered to it for subsequent delivery to the ultimate partner becomes a concern that is local only to the routing capability, which is discussed next.

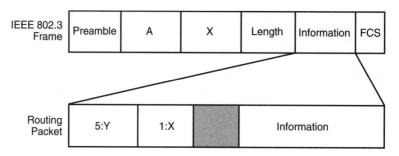

Figure 1.9. Contents of a data frame as it emerged from workstation X. Route addresses indicate that workstation Y on network 5 and workstation X on network 1 are the ultimate communicating partners.

The Routing Table

The routing process should be equipped with a route discovery capability that is responsible for the routine maintenance of the "road map" of the internetwork. Thus, it is the mandate of the routing process to ensure that it has all the answers as to who belongs where on the internetwork and how far (which is normally measured by the number of intervening routers). Two generic road maps, called routing tables, are shown in Figure 1.10. The additional Output Port column in these tables represents labels identifying the communication interfaces that connect the workstation or router to the networks. A1 and A2, for example, represent the communication interfaces that connect the router to networks 2 and 9, respectively.

Taking the first entry in router A as an example, it should be interpreted in the following manner: Router A is two routers away from network 5 (the intervening routers being, in this case, routers C and D). Furthermore, if router A is required to deliver data destined to network 5, it should seek the assistance of router C (see the Next Router field) by delivering the data directly to it, out of output port A2, which connects A to network 9. Although the routing table of workstation X provides different information about the reachability of the same network (network 9), it remains consistent with the information maintained by router A.

Path Selection

Routers should be capable of selecting the shortest path connecting two networks. Reflection on Figure 1.10 shows that more than one route connects networks 1 and 5. Router A's table, as shown in the figure, includes only one path. If you were to consider the number of intervening routers as a measure of the separating distance, the included path is indeed the shortest one.

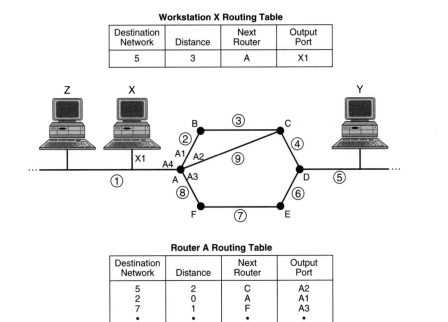

Workstation X Routing Table

Destination Network	Distance	Next Router	Output Port
5	3	A	X1

Router A Routing Table

Destination Network	Distance	Next Router	Output Port
5	2	C	A2
2	0	A	A1
7	1	F	A3
⋮	⋮	⋮	⋮

Figure 1.10. Routing tables of both workstation X and router A.

How do routers discover the road map of the internetwork? They do it either by dynamically exchanging routing information among themselves or by being statically configured by network installers—or both. The dynamic exchange of routing information is handled by yet another process besides the routing process itself. In the case of TCP/IP, IP (that is, the *internet protocol*) handles the routing process, whereas RIP (that is, the *routing information protocol*) handles the route discovery process. The IP protocol is discussed in Chapter 2, "Overview of TCP/IP," and Chapter 4, "The Internet Layer and Routing." RIP is also discussed in Chapter 4.

Table 1.1 should help you visualize the previous concepts and the interaction that takes place between the various components of the routing process. The table depicts the changes in the frame (MAC) addresses and packet level (complete) addresses as data that emerges from workstation X and crosses routers A, C, and D to end up being delivered to workstation Y. It is left to the reader to justify the address changes. The table should be interpreted in association with the hypothetical network shown in Figure 1.10. Note that the first column refers to the address of the actual network that the packet is crossing as part of the path leading to workstation Y.

Table 1.1. Changes in frame and packet level addresses in the data frame transmitted from workstation X to Y in Figure 1.10.

Data on Network	MAC Destination Address	MAC Source Address	Complete Destination Address	Complete Source
1	A	X	1:X	5:Y
9	C	A	1:X	5:Y
4	D	C	1:X	5:Y
5	Y	D	1:X	5:Y

Section Summary

The routing problem, as defined by data communications and networking technologies, addresses the concern of the intelligent delivery of data from point A to point B on an internetwork of distributed networks. Routers are the devices that deliver this service. Intelligent path selection implies that routers should be able to route data using the shortest path connecting any two networks, in which distances are commonly measured by the number of intervening routers.

To deliver the routing service, routers maintain a routing information table, which serves as the road map of the network. The routing information table (RIT) includes one entry for every destination network the router is aware of. The included entry provides details regarding the shortest path connecting the router to the network in question. You were presented in Figure 1.10 with a would-be routing information table pertaining to a hypothetical technology. The concepts of network addresses and complete addresses were also introduced, with the former being an address that all workstations on the same network have in common. The complete address is an address that provides enough information to lead to the determination of the network address and the MAC address of the ultimate communicating partner.

Data Multiplexing/Demultiplexing

What has been discussed so far has dealt primarily with issues specific to the computer-to-computer data delivery process. In other words, the discussion was more concerned with how data can be communicated between computers than with processes that are representative of user applications. The ultimate purpose of data communications, however, as defined at the beginning of this chapter, is the exchange of data between user processes.

When data is finally delivered to its ultimate destination, a new concern surfaces: which process representing which user application should the data be submitted to? This concern especially applies to multitasking computer environments, where at times more than one such process might be communicating with its counterparts on the network. In other words, although necessary, it is not enough to have the data delivered to the machine described by the complete address. When the routing process on the ultimately destined machine decides that the data packet requires no further routing, it is required to deliver its information field to a higher level process that is aware of the actual identity of the communicating user process.

A process that is capable of delivering data to user processes must rely on some additional process-addressing conventions that can be easily associated with the actual communicating processes. Hence, once more, what you are going to see is that what used to be an insignificant information field to the routing process becomes structured data that includes, among other fields, the addresses of the destination and source processes. This process is similar in function and role to that of a mail reception desk in an office environment. After the postal service succeeds in delivering all the correspondence to the right address designated on the envelope, it becomes the mandate of the mail reception desk attendant to make sure that, based on the mail stop number, correspondence is internally delivered to the associated recipient. The previously described process is called *data multiplexing/demultiplexing*. Refer to Chapter 2, "Overview of TCP/IP," for more details on this concept.

Interprocess Dialogue Control

When two applications engage in the exchange of data, they are said to have established a session between them. Consequently, a need arises to control the flow and the direction of data flow between them for the duration of the session. Depending on the nature of the involved applications, the dialogue type might have to be set to full-duplex (that is, a two-way simultaneous mode of communications), half-duplex (a two-way alternate mode of communications), or simplex (a one-way mode of communication). Even after setting the applicable communications mode, applications might require that the dialogue itself be arbitrated. For example, in the case of the half-duplex mode of communications, it is important that somehow applications know when to talk and for how long.

Session Recovery

Another application-oriented concern is the capability to reliably recover from failures and at a minimum cost. This goal can be achieved through provision of a checkpointing mechanism that allows the resumption of activities since the last checkpoint. As an example, consider the case of invoking a file transfer application in order to have five files transferred simultaneously from point A to point B on the network. Unless a proper checkpointing mechanism takes care of the process, a failure of some sort during the transfer process might require the retransmission of all five files, irrespective of where in the process the failure took place. Checkpointing circumvents this requirement by retransmitting only the affected files, thus providing time and bandwidth savings.

Presentation Problem

Whenever two or more communicating applications run on different platforms, there arises another concern: that of differences in the syntax of the data they exchange. To resolve these differences, an additional process is required. Good examples of presentation problems are the existing incompatibilities between the ASCII and the EBCDIC standards of character encoding, terminal emulation incompatibilities, and incompatibilities due to data encryption techniques.

Section Summary

In this section, you were presented with a *partial* list of the problems and technical challenges that data communications and networking technologies have to deal with for the sake of the reliable and transparent exchange of data. The purpose of the preceding discussion was to raise your awareness of the complexity and sophistication that this technology has achieved, in addition to developing the feel of the inner workings of the various components that contribute to the overall framework. The underlying theme that governed the discussion, which the reader should bear in mind for chapters to come, is that the ultimate concern of data communications is to allow processes that are representative of user applications to talk to each other.

Categorizing the Involved Elements

The concerns addressed in the preceding section broadly fall into two categories:

- ◆ On-the-wire and end-system-to-end-system-oriented concerns, and
- ◆ Applications oriented concerns

The first category includes the following concerns:

- ◆ Data encoding
- ◆ Transmission media
- ◆ Data flow control
- ◆ Link management
- ◆ Routing

The objective they have in common is the computer-to-computer delivery of data. The processes required to address these concerns are not made aware of the nature or identity of the involved applications. Their collective mandate is to ensure link availability, to ensure physical representation of data, to make sure that the receiving end is never overwhelmed with a flood of data, and to make sure that data is routed intelligently between any two workstations on the network.

The second category includes the following concerns:

♦ Data multiplexing/demultiplexing

♦ Interprocess dialogue mode establishment and control

♦ Session recovery

♦ Data presentation-related concerns

After a computer successfully receives data from the network, on-the-wire specific concerns disappear for other application-oriented ones to surface. The concerns here have more to do with the nature of the communications mode that a dialogue session has to assume, whether received data conforms to the syntax supported by the receiving platform, differences in data encryption techniques, session maintenance, and many other concerns that do not lend any attention to what has happened, or to what is happening, on the wire.

The Need for Layered Solutions

Given what has just been discussed, it becomes easy to recognize the need for a *layered* solution to the data communications puzzle. Layering implies breaking the puzzle into its constituent components and dealing with them according to categories to which they were found to belong. Categorization must take into account the interdependency of some processes relative to others. At a *minimum*, given the two broad categories that were highlighted in the preceding section, it should be acceptable to rely on a two-layer solution. Figure 1.11 illustrates the concept. The figure shows two computers connected to a cloud representing some sort of a network, with the two-layer model implemented in both of them. Notice in particular the relative placement of the layers. The end-system-to-end-system-oriented layer is placed at the bottom because of its close intimacy to events on the wire. At least three advantages could be achieved in following the layered approach:

♦ *Specialization:* Solution developers will be able to specialize in one or the other category of problems, which, given the rate at which the technology is advancing, is more affordable than an approach based on integrating all problems into one category.

♦ *Minimal cost:* Using the layered approach, it will be easier for vendors to introduce changes, or even replace an entire layer while leaving others intact. In the case of the two-layer solution, a vendor will be able to develop better techniques for the purpose of transmitting and routing data without having to rewrite the code pertaining to the upper layer, which is taking care of entirely different set of concerns.

♦ *Freedom of choice:* As you will see later, users benefit from layering because it provides them the freedom to implement networks that can be tailored to meet their needs. For example, whereas Ethernet might be suitable to one environment, Token-ring might prove to be a better choice for another.

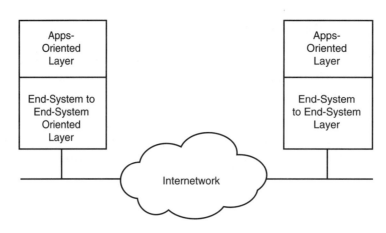

Figure 1.11. *Two-layer data communications model.*

An example of the benefits introduced by the two-layer approach is the ease with which network applications can be developed. The application developer does not have to know anything about how to reach the end system. Using a standard set of routine calls, he only has to provide the underlying layer with address and application designation in the right form. Furthermore, these applications continue to run regardless of upcoming changes that could be introduced to the lower layer—a time- and effort-saving feature.

The hypothetical two-layer solution, although simplistic, was introduced to build the case for layered solutions in general. The problems and concerns being addressed are distinctively too many to accommodate by employing two layers only. Hence the need for a communications model that resolves those problems and concerns into a more comprehensive set of logically interdependent layers. This brings us to the OSI (Open System Interconnection) model, which is discussed in the next section. But before going any further, the author owes the reader an answer to the question, "What is a protocol?" This question should have crossed the reader's mind due to the liberal use of the term in this chapter without formal introduction.

What Is a Protocol?

A protocol is set of mutually accepted and implemented rules, at both ends of the communications channel, for the orderly exchange of data. For example, in a lecture setting, a recognized and generally accepted protocol is that no two people can talk simultaneously. In addition, whoever wants to talk should raise his or her hand. Unless the protocol is universally accepted by all people attending the lecture, it is more than likely that some (who might not want to adhere to the protocol) might be required to leave the room (and consequently, have their input discarded on the subject being discussed).

Likewise, in communications, a certain set of rules needs to be adopted by vendors of all participating devices on the network. Referring to the problem of data encoding, which was discussed earlier in this chapter, two examples were provided. In one, the bipolar encoding scheme, data is recovered from the wire by interpretation of the voltage level, whereas in the case of NRZI, data is recoverable by interpretation of signal transitions. It is clear, therefore, that both methods define incompatible protocols for the recovery of data from the wire. The data encoding scheme presents only a simple example of the too many data communications protocols required for the reliable exchange of data. You might ask, is there a one-to-one mapping between a communications layer and a protocol? The answer is no! As you will see in subsequent chapters, some of the layers are implemented in more than one protocol. All protocols at the layer level in question cooperate for the purpose of delivering a reliable service to the layer above. Together, all protocols at a given layer implement the features of that layer and maintain standard interfaces into and out of the layer.

Protocol Peer-to-Peer Talk

You have seen how the data header information, which is included in the data frame, helps in resolving some of the concerns relevant to data communications. To summarize, it was shown that the receive/transmit routine relies on the preamble as an alerting sign of an impending transmission, on address fields to decide who the communicating parties are, on the length field to determine how many bytes are in the information field, and on FCS field to perform integrity checks on received data.

The header information, thus included, is an integral part of the definition of the protocol governing the transmit/receive process, and it is relevant to this process only. The exchange, and use, of control information in this fashion is what is known in data communications jargon as *protocol peer-to-peer talk,* or simply *peer talk.* And the process of adding header information to an upper layer of data is defined as *data encapsulation.*

Peer talk happens at every level in the communications architecture, with each process adding, exchanging, and interpreting header control information that is relevant to it and its peer (that is, like process) only. Figure 1.12 illustrates the concept as applied to the previous simplistic two-layer model. Notice how two headers are added to user data: one at the applications-oriented layer (the top layer) and another at the bottom layer.

The top layer header and user data appear to, and consequently are treated together by, the bottom layer as what is known as a *service data unit* (SDU). To a lower layer, an SDU is simply the data that should be provided with the layer's services, with no concern about the details that the SDU might be hiding. When a protocol adds its own header information to an SDU, it is said to have formed a *protocol data unit* (PDU). Figure 1.12 illustrates the relationship between an SDU and a PDU.

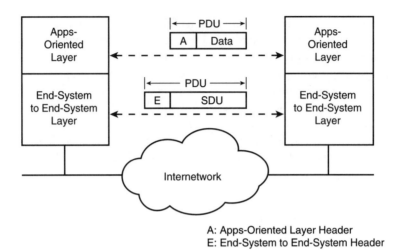

A: Apps-Oriented Layer Header
E: End-System to End-System Header

Figure 1.12. *Layers at the same level engage in peer talk, as headers provide the vehicle for the exchange of control information at each level.*

The Open System Interconnection Model

The OSI model of data communications was developed in 1984 by the International Standardization Organization (ISO). OSI specifies a seven-layer model (see Figure 1.13). In addition to forming the basis of ongoing development of OSI's own protocols, the model is being used by the industry as the frame of reference when describing protocol architectures and functional characteristics. This section briefly highlights the general model architecture and the concerns that are addressed at each layer.

Application
Presentation
Session
Transport
Network
Data Link
Physical

Figure 1.13. *The OSI model.*

The concept of layering in OSI is governed by two notions: the notion of the service provider and that of the service user. A layer in the OSI is a service provider to the layer above it, while it itself is a service user of the services provided by the layer below it. Taking the network layer (see Figure 1.13) as an example, it is service provider to the layer above it (that is, the transport layer) while it itself is a service user of the data link layer below it.

A service provider must provide its services while hiding the details on how it is doing it from the service user. In no way should the service user be concerned about how it is getting the service. OSI defines the services that each layer is required to provide to the layer above it. A protocol, or a set of protocols, at any layer is an implementation of those services. Next, you are provided with a brief description of the services handled at each layer.

The Physical Layer

This layer provides the physical transmission service. It accepts data from the data link layer in bit streams for the subsequent transmission over the physical medium. At this layer, the mechanical (for example, connector type), electrical (for example, voltage levels), functional (for example, ping assignments) and procedural (for example, the handshake) characteristics are defined. RS-232C/D is an example of a physical layer definition.

The Data Link Layer

This layer is responsible for the reliable transfer of data across the physical link. Its responsibilities include such functions as data flow control, data frame formatting, error detection, and link management, as discussed earlier in this chapter.

The Network Layer

The network layer is mainly responsible for providing routing services across the internetwork. It also shields the above layers from details about the underlying network (that is, the network topology and road map) and the routing technology that might have been deployed in order to connect different networks together.

The Transport Layer

This layer guarantees the orderly and reliable delivery of data between end systems. OSI defines five different protocols at this level with ranging levels of reliability. The transport layer also performs additional functions such as data multiplexing and demultiplexing.

The Session Layer

The session, presentation, and application layers are strictly application-oriented layers. They concern themselves with the services that are useful to applications. No attention is paid at these layers to any of the details governing the data exchange and routing service mechanisms that are well provided at the lower layers.

The session layer is responsible for establishing, maintaining, and arbitrating the dialogues between communicating applications. It is also responsible for the orderly recovery from failures by implementing appropriate checkpointing mechanisms (see the sections "Interprocess Dialogue" and "Session Recovery" in this chapter).

The Presentation Layer

The presentation layer is concerned with differences in the data syntax used by communicating applications. This layer is responsible for remedying those differences by resorting to mechanisms that undertake transforming the local syntax (that is, specific to the platform in question) to a common one for the purpose of data exchange. ASN.1, the Abstract Syntax Notation, is an example of such common syntax.

The Application Layer

The application layer provides the engines that drive user applications in an OSI environment. The reader should make the distinction clear in his mind between the application layer and end-user applications. To clearly see the distinction, consider the X.400 message handling system (MHS). X.400 defines the engine and protocols that govern message handling services. As such, X.400 is not the actual messaging application that end users use in order to deliver mail to the remote users. To do that, users need to install and use mail applications that are X.400 compliant, for only then will the application be able to employ OSI services for the subsequent handling of his mail.

Summary

Data communications is a very complex and sophisticated technology. The complexity stems from the too-many varied and distinct concerns that this technology had to address for the reliable exchange of data. Some of the main concerns were highlighted in this chapter, with the objective being to raise the reader's awareness of those concerns and to lead to the justification for the need of a layered approach to communications solutions. Finally, the OSI model was introduced, and the layers and services they provide were briefly described.

CHAPTER

♦

Overview of TCP/IP

Introduction

In Chapter 1, "Overview of Data Communications," elements of data communications and networking were discussed. The OSI model was presented with an emphasis on the importance and advantages of the layered approach to data communications. By introducing TCP/IP, this chapter serves as the platform to which principles learned in the preceding chapter are applied, as well as the foundation on which the remainder of the book relies. Following are the topics that will be covered in the next several sections:

- ♦ Historical overview
- ♦ TCP/IP protocol architecture
- ♦ The network access layer
- ♦ The internet layer
- ♦ The transport layer
- ♦ The application layer

Historical Overview

The TCP/IP protocol suite was developed by the Department of Defense (DOD) of the United States government. The effort was initiated in response to the need to have all DOD and government computing resources on a single internetwork. This setup would make all the necessary data managed by these resources available to authorized personnel, without respect to where they are on the network. This ambition was shared by researchers working mainly for universities and colleges across the United States. Researchers, in all aspects of science and engineering, wanted a network that would allow an easy and "instant" exchange of research papers and results and of electronic mail, as well as provide the capability to easily dip into a remote research body's computing resources.

Given the magnitude of diversity in the software and hardware computing platforms that the government and universities maintain, the DOD deemed it extremely expensive to have all of these platforms connected to one global network, without resorting to a vendor-independent solution of some kind. As a result, in 1969, the Defense Advanced Research Project Agency was given the mandate of looking at developing an experimental packet-switching network, in search of a solution that would meet the stated requirements. The network, called ARPANET, was built for use in the development and testing of technologies that would achieve the ultimate goal: that of reliable and vendor-independent connectivity that would allow any two platforms to talk to each other, regardless of their inherent differences.

While the effort was still in the experimental phase, participating parties used ARPANET for their actual daily needs, which made it all the more viable as a response to the needs and ambitions cited previously. In 1975, the ARPANET was declared an operational network, and its administration was delegated to the Defense Communications Agency (DCA). By then, TCP/IP had not been developed. ARPANET was based on a network of leased lines connected by special switching nodes, known at the time as Internet Message Processors (IMP). Conversion to TCP/IP began in 1983, after its formal adoption as a military standard (MIL STD). All networks connected to the ARPANET were required to conform to the new standard.

The term *Internet* was initially coined to imply ARPANET, which was later split by DCA into MILNET and a new, smaller ARPANET. MILNET was meant for military applications, whereas the ARPANET was meant for continued research. Over the years, however, ARPANET reached an unanticipated magnitude of popularity. Computing facilities all over North America, Europe, Japan, and, to a lesser extent, the remaining part of the world are currently connected to the Internet via their own subnetworks, constituting the world's largest network. In 1990, the ARPANET went out of existence, with Internet being declared as the formal global network.

With the rise of the Internet's popularity, the user community took interest in the TCP/IP protocol suite as a useful tool in building their own local networks, with the demonstrated capability to seamlessly integrate hybrid environments. As a consequence, most vendors jumped onto the TCP/IP bandwagon and implemented it on their platforms. Today, TCP/IP products include support for environments ranging from desktops to mainframes, with a wide range of operating systems running on them.

Request For Comments (RFCs)

TCP/IP-related standards are documented and made available to the public in what is commonly called Request for Comments. RFCs are assigned numbers that are used to identify a particular protocol or standard. As an example, IP (the Internet Protocol) is assigned number 791, and consequently the document is known as RFC 791. Numbers assigned to the RFCs reflect the chronological order in which they were published. When an RFC is revised, the later edition is always assigned a new, and higher, number. The reader is therefore advised to always seek the highest RFC number assigned to a specific standard in order to obtain the most current version.

Access to RFCs is made available to the public through the Internet using both electronic mail and FTP. You normally start by sending the following E-mail to rfc-info@ISI.EDU, using the following format:

```
To: rfc-info@ISI.EDU
Subject: getting rfcs

help: ways_to_get_rfcs
```

In response to this message, you get an E-mail detailing ways by which you can gain access to the RFCs.

TCP/IP Protocol Architecture

Figure 2.1 shows a four-layer model of the TCP/IP communications architecture. As shown in the diagram, the model consists of application, host-to-host, internet, and network access layers. This architecture is based on an understanding of data communications that involves three sets of interdependent processes: application representative processes, host representative processes, and network representative processes. Each set of processes takes care of the needs of entities it represents whenever an application engages in the exchange of data with its counterpart on the network.

An example of the needs that the application representative process might have to take care of is reconciling differences in the data syntax between the platforms on which the applications are running. Chapter 12, "Setting Up Network File System Services," illustrates how the External Data Representation (XDR) protocol is used to resolve such differences. The need for a host representative process is justified by the fact that applications can run on hosts that support multiuser/multitasking operating systems. As such, it becomes the responsibility of the host representative process to guarantee the integrity of the data being exchanged, without confusing the identities of the communicating applications. Finally, the network representative process takes care of the on-the-wire delivery of data to its destination host. If the destination host is attached to the same network, data is delivered directly to that host. Otherwise, if the destination belongs to some other network, the network representative process employs a routing process to help in the delivery.

In light of the preceding information, Figure 2.2 shows how the TCP/IP architecture maps to the OSI model. Note in particular how the application layer maps to the session, presentation, and application layers in OSI. Also note that the network access layer maps to the physical and data link layer.

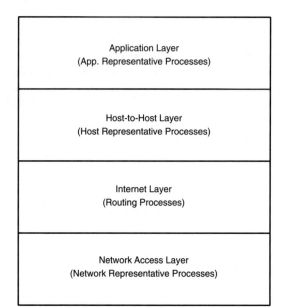

Figure 2.1. *TCP/IP communications architecture.*

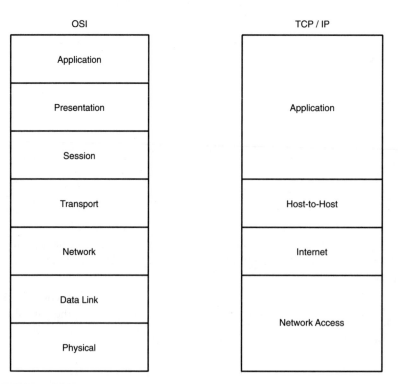

Figure 2.2. *TCP/IP and OSI.*

TCP/IP Data Encapsulation

In Chapter 1, "Overview of Data Communications," you saw how protocols communicate with their peers by encapsulating data as it is passed down across protocol boundaries. In a similar way, a TCP/IP protocol engages in peer talk with its counterpart across the Internet by adding header information to data before submitting it to the layer below. Figure 2.3 illustrates what happens as data is passed by the application layer in host A to the underlying protocols for delivery to host B. Notice how each layer adds header information (the shaded part) that is intended for its peer only.

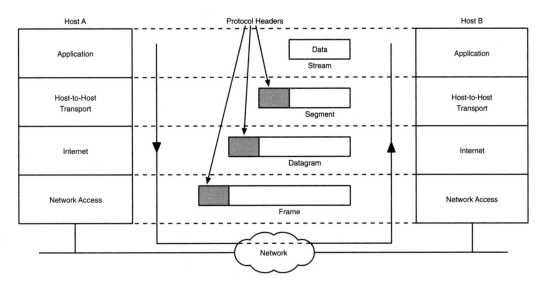

Figure 2.3. *Data encapsulation under TCP/IP.*

Following are examples of what each header can contain:

◆ At the transport layer, the header contents include destination and source port numbers. These are treated as process identification numbers, which help in the exchange of encapsulated data between designated processes, without confusing these processes with others that might be running simultaneously on the same involved hosts. The data and header at this layer form a data unit referred to as a *data segment.*

◆ At the internet layer, the header also contains the IP addresses (that is, complete addresses) of the ultimate communicating end systems. The data and header at this layer form a data unit commonly referred to as an *IP datagram.*

◆ At the network access layer, the header includes the media access control (MAC) addresses of source and destination devices communicating on the *same* physical network. The data unit formed at this layer is referred to as a *data frame.*

The Network Access Layer

As can be seen in Figure 2.2, the network access layer provides the same features as the physical and data link layers in the OSI model of data communications. Protocols implemented at this layer are responsible for the delivery of data to devices connected to the *same* physical network. The network access layer is the only layer that is aware of the details of the underlying network. Given that TCP/IP formalizes the exchange of data across protocol boundaries in the same host, you can see how a new network access technology can be introduced without affecting the rest of the protocol hierarchy. Ethernet and Token-ring are examples of underlying technologies that the network access layer relies on to receive data from, or deliver data to, the network; details on these and other media access technologies are included in Chapter 3, "The Network Access Layer."

The network access layer implementation includes the network interface card (that is, the communication hardware) that complies with the communication media, and the protocols that handle all the action (see Figure 2.4). An example of protocols implemented at this level is the Address Resolution Protocol (discussed in Chapter 4), which takes care of mapping the IP symbolic address to the corresponding hardware (MAC) address. It is worth noting, from the diagram, that not all data that the NIC card receives from the network is passed up the layer hierarchy. Some data might have to be passed by the MAC driver to adjacent protocols coexisting with the driver at the network access layer (for example, RARP and RARPD, which are discussed in Chapters 4 and 14, respectively). This feature is commonly known as *data multiplexing*. More details will be provided in this chapter, at both the internet and transport layers.

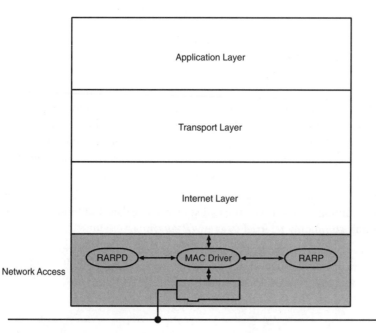

Figure 2.4. *The breakdown of network access layer constituent components.*

Among other functions, the network access layer encapsulates data (see Chapter 1), passed to it by the internet layer, into *frames* for subsequent delivery to the network. Keep in mind, however, that the frame format is a function of the media access technology in use. Refer to Chapter 3 for details on the differences between both Ethernet and Token-ring MAC frame formats.

The Internet Layer

The internet layer corresponds generally to the network layer in the OSI model. Two protocols are defined at this level: the Internet Control Message Protocol (ICMP, RFC 792) and the Internet Protocol (RFC 791). The purpose of the Internet Protocol (IP) is to handle routing of data around the internetwork (commonly known as the *Internet*), whereas that of ICMP is to handle routing error detection and recovery. IP is the cornerstone of the TCP/IP suite of protocols. All TCP/IP protocols communicate with their peers on the network by riding IP datagrams. Figure 2.5 shows the data structure of the IP datagram. IP's header fields are presented in the following text, in the context of a discussion of its functions. But first take a look at its two main characteristics.

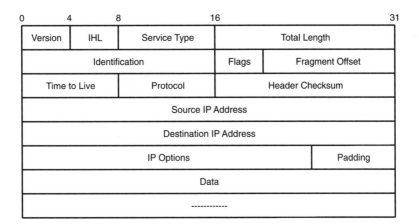

Figure 2.5. *IP datagram structure.*

Main Characteristics of IP

IP is a *connectionless* protocol. This means that IP does not attempt to establish a connection with its peer before sending data to it. A *connection-oriented* protocol undergoes some sort of a handshake with its peer in the remote system. The purpose of the handshake is twofold: it verifies the readiness of the remote peer to receive data before it is sent, and during the handshake, both ends of the connection try to reach a mutual agreement on some of the parameters that should govern the data exchange process. An example of a negotiated parameter is the maximum size of the data unit that can be exchanged during the connection.

In addition to being connectionless, IP delivers an *unreliable* service. The unreliability stems from the fact that IP does not provide error detection and recovery. All that IP cares about is the delivery of data to its designated destination. What happens to the datagram during shipment is a concern that is delegated, by design, to IP service users (that is, higher layer protocols). This is very similar to the postal service, which delivers mail on a best-effort basis while not caring about the quality of what is being shipped or received.

Functions of IP

IP functions include these:

◆ Data encapsulation and header formatting

◆ Data routing across the internetwork

◆ Passing data to other protocols

◆ Fragmentation and reassembly

Data Encapsulation

Data encapsulation involves accepting data from the transport layer and adding IP's header control information to it. As shown in Figure 2.5, the IP header is five or six 32-bit words in length; this is because the sixth word is optional, justifying the IHL field (that is, the Internet Header Length). The first field refers to the version of IP in use, with the current one being number 4. The third field is the type-of-service field (TOS). TOS can be set to specify a desired class of service, as requested by applications. Examples of classes of service supported by IP are minimum delay, which is requested by application protocols such as RLOGIN and TELNET, and maximum throughput, which is requested by applications such as FTP and SMTP. The total length field minus the IHL field indicates to IP the length of the data field. Both the identification and the fragmentation fields will be discussed in the section "Fragmentation and Reassembly." The time to live (TTL) field is initialized by IP to the upper limit on the number of routers that a datagram can cross before it ultimately reaches its destination. Assuming that TTL was set to 32, it is decremented by one by each router it crosses. As soon as TTL reaches zero, the datagram is removed by the next router to detect the anomaly. The underlying idea is that with TTL, a lost datagram can be stopped from endlessly looping around the network. The protocol number field will be discussed later in this section.

Although IP is an unreliable protocol, in the sense that it does not perform error detection and recovery, it still cares about the integrity of its own control information header. With the help of the *header checksum*, IP verifies the integrity of data in the header fields. If the integrity check fails, IP simply discards the datagram. IP does not communicate a notification of the failure, also called *negative acknowledgment*, to the sending host.

The source and destination addresses are 32 bits long. IP address classes and structure will be dealt with in more detail in Chapter 4, "The Internet Layer and Routing." Addresses included in the address fields describe the identities of the ultimate communicating hosts.

The final field is the options field, which can include other control information. An example of optional information is the route record, which includes the address of every router that the datagram traversed during its trip on the network.

IP Routing

IP routing is one of the simplest, yet most efficient, methods for the routing of data on a complex internetwork. IP distinguishes between *hosts* and *gateways*. A gateway in TCP/IP is actually a router that connects two or more networks for the purpose of providing forwarding services between them. Figure 2.6 shows a gateway forwarding a datagram between two networks. A host is the end system where user applications run. By default, routing on hosts is limited to the delivery of the datagram directly to the remote system, if both hosts are attached to the same network. If not, IP delivers the datagram to a *default* gateway (that is, router). The default gateway, defined on the host during TCP/IP configuration, is a router attached to the same network that the host should "trust" for assistance in deliveries made to other hosts on remote networks. Figure 2.7 illustrates the concept of default routers. Host X in the diagram is configured to gateway A as its default router. Accordingly, whenever X wants to send data to Y, it delivers the datagram to gateway A (its default router), not B. Upon examining the destination IP address, gateway A realizes that the address belongs to host Y, which is on a network to which gateway B is connected. Consequently, gateway A forwards the datagram to gateway B for the subsequent handling and delivery to host Y.

Routers and Gateways

Currently, the networking industry makes a distinction between a router and a gateway. Routers are said to provide routing services between like networks. Gateways, on the other hand, connect networks of dissimilar architectures (for example, TCP/IP to AppleTalk). Historically, however, the TCP/IP community used the term *gateway* to refer to routing devices. Throughout this book, the terms are used interchangeably to refer to routing.

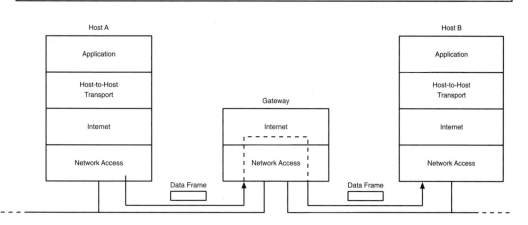

Figure 2.6. *A gateway providing routing services between two networks.*

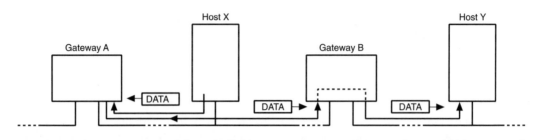

Figure 2.7. *A host on an IP network forwards all deliveries pertaining to remote networks to its default router. In the diagram, host X is configured to recognize gateway A as its default router, which makes host X forward data it wants to be delivered to host Y to gateway A, not B. Upon receiving the data frame, it becomes gateway A's responsibility to see that data is forwarded to gateway B, which is closer to host Y.*

Forwarding can optionally be enabled on hosts with more than one network interface card, attaching to different networks. A host that has more than one network interface card is known as a *multihomed host*. It provides forwarding services only if configured to do so. Otherwise, it behaves exactly the same as other hosts with a single interface card. The difference is that all hosts on networks to which it is attached can engage in the exchange of data with applications it supports.

One of the great benefits derived from using IP routers and multihomed hosts lies in their capability to connect dissimilar physical networks. Figure 2.8 depicts a scenario by which two Ethernet networks and one Token-ring network connect together using two gateways. This capability is attributable, once more, to the layered design of TCP/IP, which cleverly hides all details about the underlying network from IP.

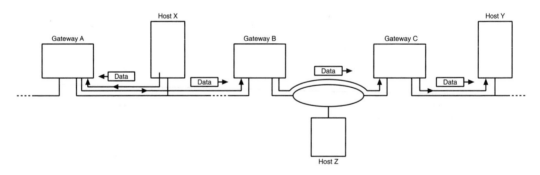

Figure 2.8. *IP routers are capable of connecting dissimilar networks.*

To summarize routing concepts covered so far, Figure 2.8 includes a depiction of the flow of a data frame that host X sent to Y:

1. Assuming that X's default router is gateway A, the data frame is first delivered to gateway A.

2. Using its routing table, Gateway A compares the destination IP address with destinations it knows about. An IP gateway maintains a routing table similar to the one

discussed in Chapter 1, "Overview of Data Communications." As was shown, the routing table includes information describing each destination the router is aware of, distance (how many hops, or equivalently routers) separating it from the destination in question, the next router to which to send the data, and the interface card to which delivery can be delegated. According to Figure 2.8, gateway A sends the datagram to gateway B, *trusting* that it is closer to the designated network where host Y is attached. The word *trusting* is italicized here to signify the fact that as far as gateway A can tell, B is the closest gateway to host X of all other gateways that it recognizes. How and where gateway B is going to deliver the datagram is none of gateway A's concern.

3. When gateway B recovers the datagram from the wire, it consults its routing table and forwards the datagram on the Token-ring network to gateway C.

4. Finally, gateway C, again based on its routing table, delivers the datagram to host Y. At Y, IP delivers data embedded in the datagram to the protocol described in the protocol number field in IP's header, which is discussed next.

Passing Data to Other Protocols

It was mentioned at the beginning of this section that all TCP/IP protocols send their data in IP datagrams. Hence, to assist IP in submitting a datagram it receives from the wire to the intended protocol, a *protocol* field is included in IP's header. By TCP/IP standards, each protocol that uses IP routing services is assigned a protocol identification number. Setting the protocol field to 6, for example, designates the TCP protocol, whereas 1 designates the ICMP protocol. A protocol number of 0, however, designates the IP protocol, in which case encapsulated data is processed by IP itself. Figure 2.9 illustrates how the protocol field is used to sort datagrams for subsequent delivery to their destined protocols.

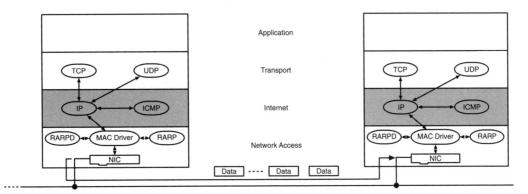

Figure 2.9. *When IP receives a datagram from the wire, it internally routes the datagram to one of the shown protocols based on identification information contained in IP's header protocol field.*

Fragmentation and Reassembly

As shown in Figure 2.5, the total length field in the IP header is 16 bits wide, which means that the largest datagram IP is allowed to handle is 64K (65,535 bytes). However, some underlying networks (that is, media access technologies) do not tolerate as much data in a single frame. An Ethernet frame, for example, cannot exceed 1,514 bytes. In cases like these, IP resorts to what is known as data *fragmentation*. Fragmentation takes place whenever data units in sizes exceeding the frame capacity are passed to IP by another protocol, for subsequent handling on the network.

Although all data fragments are normally delivered using the same route, there is always a possibility that a few of them will traverse alternative routes. This might happen due to rising congestion on paths followed by earlier fragments, or to link failure. Whatever the case, fragments following different routes stand the chance of reaching their destination out of the order in which they were sent. To allow for the recovery from such an eventuality, IP makes use of the *fragmentation offset* field in its header. The fragmentation offset field includes sequencing information that the remote IP peer uses to reorder data fragments it receives from the network, and to detect missing packets. Data is not passed to the protocol described in the protocol field unless all related fragments are duly received and reordered. This process of fragment recovery and resequencing is known as data *reassembly*.

How does IP deal with situations in which it is required to fragment two or more large datagrams at the same time? What if all data is being sent to the same remote host? How can the receiving host distinguish between fragments belonging to different datagrams? The answer to these questions lies in the *identification* field. Fragments belonging to the same datagram are uniquely associated by including the same value in the identification field. The receiving end uses this value to recover the IP fragments to their respective datagrams.

Finally, you might be asking yourself these questions: How can a receiving IP tell whether data is fragmented? How does it know when all fragments are being sent? Answers to both questions lie in the header *flags* field. Among other bits, the flags field includes a "*more fragments*" bit, which is set "on" in all fragments belonging to a datagram, except for the final fragment.

The Internet Control Message Protocol

The Internet Control Message Protocol (ICMP) forms an integral part of the IP protocol. It is the "messenger" that couriers messages between hosts. ICMP messages carry control, informational, and error recovery data. Following is a description of some of those messages:

Source quench: This is a flow control message that a receiving host sends to the source, requesting that it stop sending data. This normally happens as the receiving host's communications buffers are close to full.

Route redirect: This is an informational message that a gateway sends to the host seeking its routing services. A gateway sends this message to inform the sending host about another gateway on the network, which it trusts to be closer to the destination.

Host unreachable: A gateway, or a system encountering a problem in the delivery of a datagram (for example, link failure, link congestion, or failing host), sends a *host unreachable* error message. Normally, the ICMP packet includes information describing the reason the host can't be reached.

Echo request/echo reply: UNIX users commonly use the ping command to test for host reachability. When entered, ping invokes both ICMP messages: echo request and echo reply. Echo request is sent from the host on which ping was invoked to the remote system described on the command line. If the remote system is up and operational, it responds with an echo reply, which should be interpreted as proof of reachability.

The Host-to-Host Transport Layer

The host-to-host layer, also known as the transport layer, is the only layer that is aware of the identity of the ultimate user representative processes at the application level. As such, the transport layer represents the embodiment of what data communications is about: the transport layer delivers information from an application on one computer to an application on another computer.

At the transport layer, application layer protocols are assigned *port numbers*. Port numbers are used in the source and destination port fields included in the transport protocol header. Transport layer protocols use them in much the same way as IP uses the protocol field: for distinguishing between application layer protocols utilizing their services. Figure 2.10 illustrates this concept. In the figure, you are shown application protocols (that is, SMTP, FTP, DNS, and SNMP) that are engaged in the exchange of data with their respective counterparts on remote host B. Unless the transport protocol at both ends uses port numbers, it will be extremely confusing, if not impossible, for it to deliver the data to the appropriate application protocol.

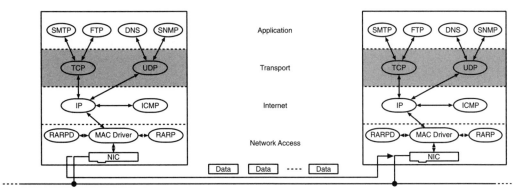

Figure 2.10. *While IP relies on the protocol field in its header to internally route data to one of TCP, UDP, or ICMP, the transport layer protocol (that is, UDP or TCP) relies on port numbers when routing data to the higher user protocols.*

The host-to-host layer is mainly supported by two protocols: User Datagram Protocol (UDP) and Transmission Control Protocol (TCP). UDP is a connectionless and unreliable protocol, in contrast to TCP, which is a connection-oriented and fully reliable protocol. UDP is normally used by applications that have the built-in capability of providing the required reliability. Should UDP fail to deliver an error-free datagram to its destination, the application will eventually detect such failure and attempt to rectify it by resending the datagram.

User Datagram Protocol

As stated previously, the User Datagram Protocol (UDP) offers a connectionless, unreliable (although optionally acknowledged) service to the application protocols. Being connectionless means that UDP does not undergo any handshaking mechanism, nor does it negotiate any control parameters with its peer before the exchange of application protocol data. Hence, UDP provides no means for controlling the exchange of data between application protocols, including flow control, datagram resequencing, and error control. It is left to the application to perform these functions.

UDP uses IP services to send and receive data from the network. Figure 2.11 shows the data structure of the UDP datagram; Figure 2.12 shows the relationship between the IP and UDP datagrams. Notice in particular how the UDP datagram becomes the occupant of IP's data field.

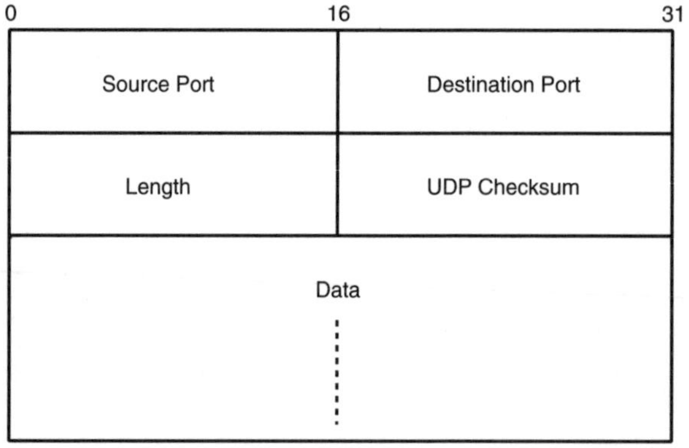

0	16	31
Source Port	Destination Port	
Length	UDP Checksum	
Data		

Figure 2.11. Format of the UDP datagram.

As can be seen from Figure 2.11, the UDP datagram is composed of two parts: the UDP header, which is structured to include fields pertaining to the exchange process, and the data field, where application data belongs. The header field is made up of four 16-bit fields. The source and destination port numbers designate the application protocols on whose behalf data is being exchanged on the network. The length field describes the total length of the datagram, including data and header information. The UDP checksum is optionally used to check for the integrity of transmitted data. Application programmers have the option of turning acknowledgment on, if they choose not to delegate error detection and recovery to their applications.

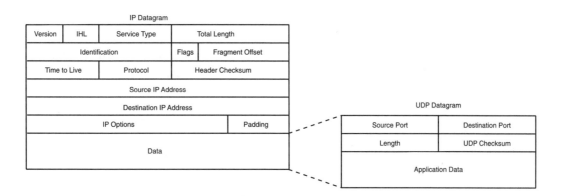

Figure 2.12. *Relationship between UDP and IP datagrams.*

The Transmission Control Protocol

At the internet and network access layers, unreliable data routing and transmission services are provided. Depending on the reliability of the physical media, and its immediate environment, data can be damaged or lost on the wire. Damages can be attributed to poor cabling, electromagnetic interference, or simply rising congestion on the link.

To applications that are designed to handle error detection and recovery, this poses no serious threats, and UDP becomes a viable service to use. Some applications, however, are not designed to handle error detection and recovery, in which case they might be subject to erratic behavior dictated by conditions arising on the wire. Those applications cannot afford to rely on UDP and the underlying network for the delivery of their data. What they need is a service that takes over error and data exchange control, and that guarantees the integrity of data as it is being exchanged. The service must also ensure the orderly delivery of the related data units without loss or duplication. This is the kind of service that TCP provides.

TCP Main Features

TCP is characterized as a fully reliable, connection-oriented, acknowledged, and data stream-oriented service. Like IP, TCP supports fragmentation and reassembly of data. It also supports data multiplexing/demultiplexing using source and destination port numbers as explained in the discussion of UDP.

Connection Orientation

An application requesting connection-oriented service at the transport layer cannot start sending data until TCP has established a connection with its peer at the remote end. Before the request is honored, both sides have to agree on certain parameters that will be used to govern the data exchange process, to ensure its reliability. They must also verify that applications on whose behalf the connection is attempted are available and ready to get "talking." After a connection request is accepted, TCP is said to have established a virtual circuit between applications, over which data can be exchanged. Figure 2.13 illustrates the concept of a virtual circuit. The dotted part in the diagram represents the applications' (FTP in the diagram) perception of what is going on for the duration of the connection. Communicating applications perceive the dialog as a direct one not involving any intermediate agents (lower layer processes) or overheads (protocol headers). This is due to the design of the TCP protocol, which cleverly hides the details of the underlying mechanisms of the data delivery system from user applications.

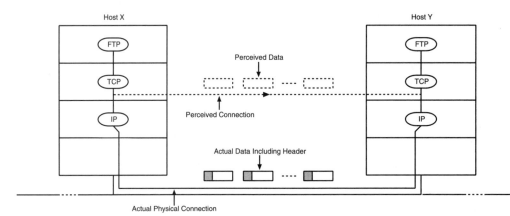

Figure 2.13. *TCP establishes a virtual circuit on behalf of application protocols. Dotted lines in the diagram represent what applications perceive to be real, versus what is actually happening on the wire.*

This is similar to making a phone call. When you dial a number, you are said to be placing a call (that is, requesting a connection). The underlying telephone network attempts the connection on your behalf. If the called number is not busy, a ringing tone is sent to both ends, after which you can start talking if someone picks up the line. At that time, a virtual circuit is said to connect you with the called party. For the duration of the conversation, you normally maintain the perception of talking directly to the other person. You do not, and should not, think of the underlying details, not even the simplest of them (such as that you are talking to the mouthpiece, and the mouthpiece converts your acoustic energy to electrical energy, and so on). It's funny, however, how the caller's perception changes when he encounters a difficulty in communications!

Reliability and Acknowledgment

TCP is said to provide a reliable service in the delivery of data. Being reliable means that TCP *guarantees* the delivery of corruption-free data between end systems, without loss or duplication. Developers benefit from TCP's reliability by not having to incorporate the necessary mechanisms into their applications, as opposed to those that rely on UDP.

TCP achieves reliability by employing what is known as the *positive acknowledgment with retransmission* technique. Figure 2.14 illustrates the technique. In the figure, you are shown a *laddergram* of the events taking place between two end systems, A and B. Arrows represent transmitted data and/or acknowledgments (that is, the events), and time is represented by the vertical distance down the ladder. According to the positive acknowledgment with retransmission protocol, TCP at each end is required to maintain state tables that help in tracking the status of both sent and received data. When TCP sends a data segment, it requires an acknowledgment from the receiving end, and it updates the state table accordingly. An acknowledgment can be positive or negative. A positive acknowledgment is good news, because it means two things: (1) data reached the destined host and (2) data passed the integrity check (that is, was not corrupted by noise or electromagnetic interference). A negative acknowledgment, on the other hand, can indicate that the data segment was found to be corrupt by the receiving end. In this case, the sender is required to retransmit the data segment in question.

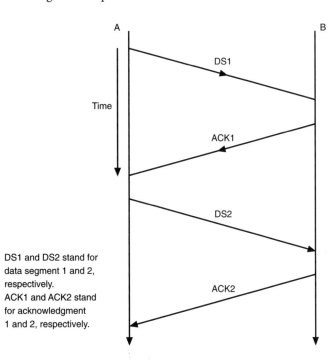

Figure 2.14. *Positive acknowledgment with retransmission technique is illustrated. In exchange for data segments it sends to the remote system, TCP on the sending host requires that an acknowledgment be sent by the remote system.*

What happens if a data segment is lost on its way to the remote host? The laddergram in Figure 2.15 illustrates the case. When A sends data, it starts a countdown timer. If the timer expires without receiving an acknowledgment, A assumes that the data segment was lost and therefore transmits a duplicate of it. At this point, it is worth noting that TCP always keeps a backup copy of the data segment that it transmits until a positive acknowledgment is received. As such, applications will not be asked to resubmit a copy of the data, should a requirement arise at TCP's level. This is a consequence of using the layered approach to communications problem solving.

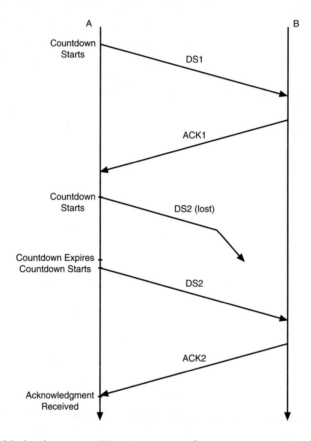

Figure 2.15. *The case of the lost data segment. Host A starts a countdown timer every time it transmits a data segment. Whenever a host times out waiting for an acknowledgment to a data segment it transmitted, the sending host retransmits that data segment (for example, DS2 in the diagram).*

Data Stream Orientation

TCP accepts data passed to it by applications as *unstructured streams* of bits, aligned around boundaries of 8-bit bytes. This means that TCP does not recognize any form of data structures (that is, does not recognize such things as records and fields). As such, TCP does not care about the actual nature of the application using its transport service, nor does it care about how the data may be delineated. It is left to applications to decide on how they would structure the data they exchange.

TCP Data Segment Format

Figure 2.16 shows the format of the TCP data segment. As can be seen from the diagram, it includes fields for the source and destination port numbers. These are used to identify user applications across the virtual connection discussed previously. Next are the sequence number and acknowledgment number fields, which are used to ensure the reliability of data transfer as discussed earlier in the "Reliability and Acknowledgment" section. No further details will be provided at this point about those fields (that is, sequence number and acknowledgment) and the remaining ones. Refer to Chapter 5, "The Host-to-Host Transport Layer," for further discussions on the TCP control information header.

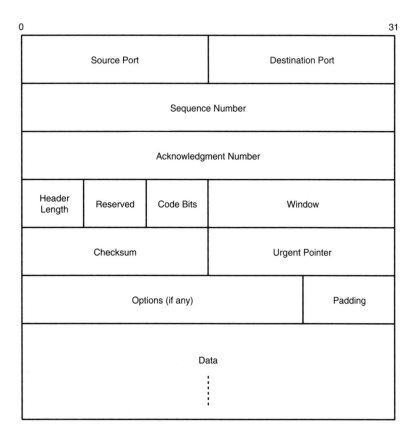

Figure 2.16. *The format of the TCP data segment.*

The Application or Process Layer

It is at this layer that user application protocols are deployed. Figure 2.17 shows a more detailed, though incomplete, breakdown of the TCP/IP layers into their constituent protocol sets.

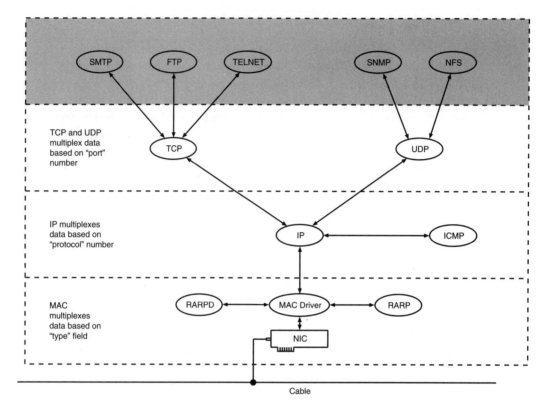

Figure 2.17. *Breakdown of various protocols to different layers in the TCP/IP architecture.*

Application protocols, shown at the top layer, provide the user-oriented functionality and features that lower layers neglect. At this layer, for example, a user will be able to use the ftp application protocol to transfer files across the network. Involved platforms need not be identical or similar, because ftp is designed to circumvent any differences that might exist between the communicating platforms. Following is a listing, including a brief description, of some of the application protocols operating at this layer. The interested reader might want to jump to Chapter 7, "TCP/IP Applications Overview," for further details.

◆ *File Transfer Protocol (FTP):* FTP (RFC 959) is, as noted previously, a file transfer protocol that handles file transfers between like or dissimilar systems across the TCP/IP network. Users on a DOS machine, for example, will be using the DOS implementation of TCP/IP to transfer files to and from a UNIX host. The user command to invoke FTP services is ftp. After it's invoked, users are required to use ftp commands to handle the session appropriately. Examples of commonly used commands are get (to transfer a file from the remote host) and put (to send a file to the remote host).

◆ *TELNET:* TELNET (RFC 854) provides users with terminal emulation and login services. Using telnet, a user can establish a connection with the remote host and use its resources. However, telnet is one of those user-unfriendly applications, because it requires users to be familiar with the commands on the target operating system. `telnet` is the command that users commonly use to invoke TELNET services. By entering

```
$ telnet jade
```

the user is requesting a connection to host `jade` and subsequently establishing a login and virtual terminal session at the host. The telnetting user will be required to enter his username and password before access is granted to the system.

◆ *Simple Mail Transfer Protocol (SMTP):* SMTP (RFC 821) is the Internet's workhorse for electronic mail applications. It is important not to confuse smtp, the engine, with the mail applications that interface directly with it. Users use *mailx,* or other programs providing a front-end interface, to format and deliver messages to SMTP on their behalf.

All the previous application protocols provide some services that the end user can see. TCP/IP, however, provides other services that the user might not notice. Examples of those services are the network file system (NFS) and simple network management protocol (SNMP). Following is a brief description of those protocols:

◆ *Network File System (NFS):* Specified by RFC 1094, NFS provides file sharing services on various hosts in the network. A host with NFS running in the background allows users on other hosts to have access to its file system resources, by connecting those resources to their local file systems. A user will be able to treat the remote file system as though it were local to his machine.

◆ *Simple Network Management Protocol (SNMP):* SNMP provides network managers and administrators with the capability to gather and analyze performance statistics pertaining to computers on their network. It also allows for the troubleshooting and reconfiguration of remote hosts and routers on the network from the network manager's desktop. Chapter 16, "Network Management Using SNMP," provides a detailed discussion on SNMP as both a network management tool and a tool for troubleshooting problems on the network.

An observation to make upon looking at Figure 2.17 is that whereas some application protocols employ TCP, others employ UDP for the delivery of their data to the remote host. This should not imply that whereas some applications care about having their data reliably delivered, others do not! As you will see in Chapter 7, not all applications share the same perspective of reliability. To cite an example, which will be explained later, NFS a is better behaved (and hence more reliable) service over UDP than TCP!

Summary

TCP/IP is a nonproprietary protocol architecture developed by the Department of Defense of the United States. TCP/IP was created to allow networks and systems to exchange and share data, regardless of differences in the hardware and software platforms they are using. TCP/IP is divided into four layers, with each layer defining a protocol set (see Figure 2.17) that takes care of concerns not addressed at any of the other layers. The layers are the network access layer, the internet layer, the transport (or host-to-host) layer, and the application (or process) layer.

The concern at the network access layer is the delivery of data frames to nodes sharing the *same* physical network. To do that, the network access layer is delegated the responsibility for the seizure and control of the data link for the duration of data transmission. It is also the responsibility of the network access layer to encapsulate the data passed to it by the internet layer, and to include in its control header the MAC addresses (that is, hardwired addresses on the network interface card) of the source and destination hosts. Because the network access layer cannot deliver data to systems belonging to networks other than its own, a layer was deemed necessary for performing the routing service. This is the internet layer (see Figure 2.17). IP, at the internet layer, is responsible for routing datagrams around the network. IP is an unreliable connectionless protocol supporting data segmentation and reassembly. As shown in Figure 2.17, IP accepts data from the network on behalf of too many protocols. To distinguish between them, IP relies on the *protocol number* that is included in IP's control header. Each protocol is assigned a unique number.

Moving up the architectural hierarchy is the transport, or host-to-host, layer. At this layer, two transport protocols are supported: (1) UDP, user datagram protocol, which provides a connectionless unreliable service, and (2) TCP, which provides a fully reliable connection-oriented service. The transport layer is the only layer that is aware of the identity of the user processes at the application layer, by virtue of having them assigned *port numbers*. Port numbers allow multiple user processes, in a multitasking host, to simultaneously exchange data with their counterparts on remote hosts, a feature known as data multiplexing/demultiplexing (see Figure 2.17). Finally, at the top is the application layer. In this chapter, application protocols were briefly introduced, leaving the details to Chapter 7, "TCP/IP Applications Overview," among other chapters in the book.

Starting with the next chapter up to and including Chapter 7, all the layers and their supported protocols will be revisited and exposed in greater depth and detail.

CHAPTER 3

The Network Access Layer

Introduction

The network access layer (see Figure 2.2) maps to the data link and physical layers in the OSI model of data communications. As defined by the TCP/IP protocol suite, it is responsible for the exchange of IP datagrams between devices connected to the same physical network. The devices can be hosts, routers, network printers, or any other shared resource.

To effectively exchange datagrams, the TCP/IP network access layer is made to broadly consist of two sets of protocols. The first set is closely related to, and therefore specific to, the media access control (MAC) technology (and therefore hardware) being used on the network.

Examples of MAC technologies are Ethernet and Token-ring. The second set, however, consists of protocols such as ARP (address resolution protocol), which incorporate functionalities that are required at this layer, independent of the MAC technology in use. The latter set is discussed in Chapter 4, "The Internet Layer and Routing," because it makes more sense to discuss it only after having introduced IP addresses and the need for ARP and some other protocols.

TCP/IP protocols support many different MAC technologies at the data link layer, including Ethernet and Token-ring. They also support wide area networking technologies. Of particular interest are the SLIP (serial line internet protocol) and PPP (point-to-point protocol) protocols, which handle the exchange of datagrams over asynchronous or synchronous links.

This chapter discusses some of the main features characterizing each of the mentioned data link layer technologies. The discussion is not intended to offer a comprehensive treatment of these technologies, which would easily require a full book. Enough details are presented, however, to help the reader develop an appreciation (and user-level insight) for the common issues that are addressed at this layer, and how different technologies address these issues.

Ethernet Technology

Originally, Ethernet data link technology was developed by Xerox in the early 1970s. In a joint standardization effort, three companies—Xerox Corporation, Intel Corporation, and Digital Corporation—helped set a standard for Ethernet in 1978. A few years later, the IEEE (Institute of Electrical and Electronic Engineers) formed the 802 committee, with the objective of introducing and establishing universally accepted networking technology standards. IEEE 802 reached an agreement on many data link technologies including the 802.3, which can be considered an adaptation, with slight differences, of the Ethernet technology.

In this section, both IEEE 802 and 802.3 standards will be discussed. Throughout the discussion, the term Ethernet is used to refer to both technologies, with differences between them highlighted.

Ethernet Physical Layer

Over the years, the IEEE 802 committee has introduced many supplements of the IEEE 802.3 standard. These supplements mainly affected the physical layer. Table 3.1 summarizes some of these supplements. At the physical layer, Ethernet defines the cable type, the connector type on the network interface card, the link speed, and the on-the-wire data encoding protocol, among many more electrical and mechanical definitions.

Table 3.1. Summary of different IEEE 802.3 standard supplements.

	10BASE-5	10BASE-2	10BASE-T	10BROAD-36
Physical Medium	Coaxial cable (50 ohm)	Coaxial cable (50 ohm)	Unshielded twisted pair	Coaxial cable (75 ohm)
Data Rate (Mbps)	10	10	10	10
Signaling	Baseband	Baseband	Baseband	Broadband
Max. Segment Length	500 m	185 m	100 m	1800 m

	10BASE-5	10BASE-2	10BASE-T	10BROAD-36
Network Span	2500 m	925 m	500 m	3600 m
Max. Nodes/Segment	100	30	N/A	N/A

As can be seen from the table, Ethernet supports various cable types such as the 50-ohm coax (10BASE-2), 75-ohm coax (10BROAD-36), and unshielded twisted pair (10BASE-T). Only the features and characteristics of 10BASE-T will be presented in the following discussion. This is because of the dominance of this wiring technology on Ethernet networks today.

10BASE-T, like its predecessors (10BASE-2 and 10BASE-5), defines baseband transmission (one station can send data at any given time) at the fixed rate of 10 megabits per second. The character T stands for the wiring specification to imply twisted pair cable type. 10BASE-T provides one of the least expensive, and most common, types of wiring networks, without compromising network performance.

According to 10BASE-T, workstations connect to wiring hubs (also known as wiring concentrators, or media attachment units) using four 22 to 26 AWG unshielded wires. These wires are attached to pins 1, 2, 3, and 6 of an RJ-45 jack (see Figure 3.1). Wires 1 and 2 are used for transmission, whereas 3 and 6 are used for reception. The maximum distance between nodes is 100 meters.

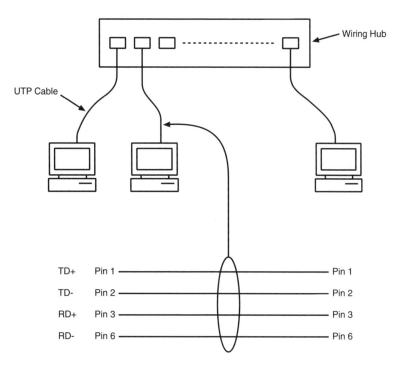

Figure 3.1. *10BASE-T wiring technology components.*

From the workstations' perspective, the wiring hub is treated as just another medium over which they will be contending for control, and subsequent transmission. The hub, however, is an active device that serves additional functions to that of relaying transmitted data from one device to another. These functions include the rejection of signals that are severely deformed, and the refreshing of signals with renewed levels of energy before they are retransmitted on the network. Wiring hubs can also be connected together to allow for network expansion. Figure 3.2 shows an example of this wiring arrangement.

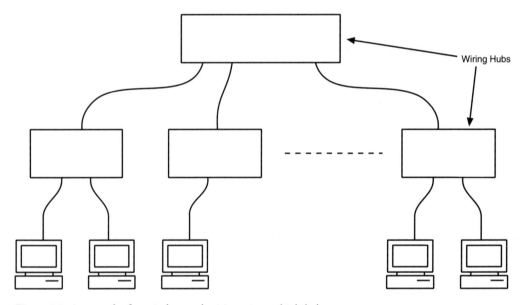

Figure 3.2. *An example of a typical network wiring using multiple hubs.*

Ethernet Link Access Arbitration and Control

Baseband Ethernet dictates that only one workstation can send data on the transmission medium at any given time. This being the case, there arises the need for some sort of a mechanism by which link access is *arbitrated* between devices sharing the medium. CSMA/CD is the link access arbitration and control mechanism defined for Ethernet. CSMA/CD stands for *carrier sense multiple access/collision detection.*

CSMA/CD can be described as a *random access,* or *contention*-based, method for link access and control. These descriptions stem from the fact that, under CSMA/CD, there is no central arbitration authority, nor a coordinating mechanism that schedules times, or priorities, at which stations can attempt transmission. It is left to the individual station to determine when is the appropriate time to transmit. While doing so, the station is not required, nor does it have the means, to coordinate its attempt with those of other stations that might be doing the same thing at the same time. As you can see, stations must contend among themselves for link seizure, and subsequent control and data transmission.

Figure 3.3 shows a simplified flowchart of the CSMA/CD *send* algorithm. Data passed from IP to Ethernet for transmission is first encapsulated (more on encapsulation later in this chapter) and made available to CSMA/CD. Before starting transmission, CSMA/CD requires that the workstation listen to the wire. If no carrier is sensed, it can be concluded that the medium is idle and that the workstation can start transmitting data one bit at a time.

Because CSMA/CD does not provide for the coordination of link access among workstations, it is likely that another workstation is doing just the same thing (that is, making an attempt to transmit data) at the same time. In this case, data transmitted by both workstations might collide on the wire, giving rise to data corruption. Should this happen, there is no sense in having a colliding workstation continuing transmission. For this reason, the workstation is required, while transmitting, to keep listening to the wire and determine whether a collision took place (see Figure 3.3). In case of collision, the workstation is supposed to reattempt transmission later. Before doing so, however, the station sends out a jamming signal (thus contributing to further collision!), the purpose of which is to alert other workstations of the collision and force them to cease transmission.

Before a workstation can renew its attempt to transmit, it is required to wait for a randomly calculated period, known as the *backoff period*. The station is also required to keep track of the number of attempts it has made. If collisions are deemed to be excessive, the attempt to transmit is aborted and an error is reported.

Ethernet and IEEE 802.3 Data Encapsulation

As explained in the first two chapters, user data is encapsulated before transmission. Each layer adds its own header to the data before passing it to the layer below. Headers contain control information, which peer protocols across the network use for the orderly and reliable exchange of data. In TCP/IP, by the time data is passed to the network access layer, it will have at least two headers added to it—the transport header pertaining to either TCP or UDP, and the IP header—to become an IP datagram (see Figure 3.4).

> **Note:** You are reminded that each layer adds its own header to the data undergoing transmission. The header serves in conveying protocol-specific information that the peer protocol at the receiving end needs in order to process the packet (that is, perform an integrity check, submit the information to the proper upper layer, and so on). After a header is interpreted, it is stripped before the information is submitted to the upper layer.

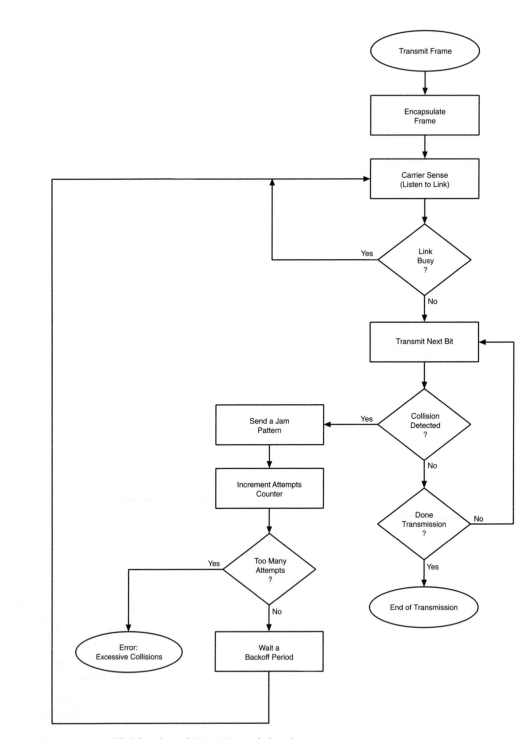

Figure 3.3. *Simplified flowchart of CSMA/CD send algorithm.*

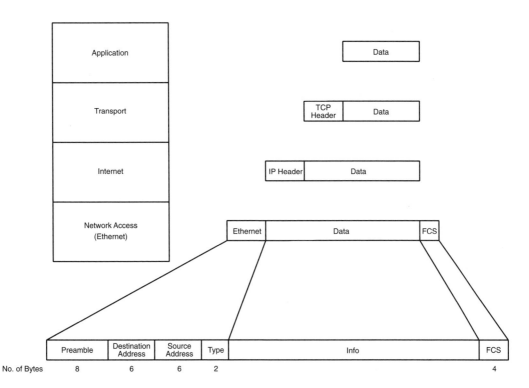

Figure 3.4. *Ethernet data encapsulation.*

At the network access layer, Ethernet encapsulates the IP datagram including a header and a trailer as shown in Figure 3.4.

The frame format you are looking at in Figure 3.4 is used by Ethernet, as standardized by Xerox, Intel, and Digital corporations. The first 8-byte field is the preamble (that is, the attention-getting signal that alerts workstations on the network about the impending transmission). Next are two 6-byte fields corresponding to the destination and source addresses of workstations belonging to the same physical network. The type field, 2 bytes long, is used to designate the service user (that is, the protocol to which data in the information field should be delivered). For example, a type field of 0x0800 designates IP, whereas 0x0806 designates ARP. Next to the type field is the information field, which Ethernet does not access, because it represents the data load to ship on the network. The information field, which is 46 to 1,500 bytes, can be an IP datagram, an ARP request (more on this in Chapter 4), or some other data. Finally, Ethernet adds a trailing 4-byte frame check sequence, which the receiving end uses to verify the integrity of the transmission.

IEEE 802.3 Data Encapsulation

The IEEE 802.3 frame format is based on an architecture that further divides the data link layer to two sublayers: the medium access control (MAC) sublayer, and the logical link control (LLC) layer (see Figure 3.5). While at the MAC sublayer concerns native to the underlying technology are addressed, the LLC sublayer addresses concerns that are deemed common to all MAC technologies.

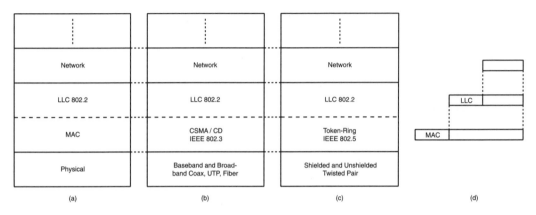

Figure 3.5. *The IEEE 802 architecture of the data link layer.*

With the introduction of sublayering at the data link layer, an additional level of data encapsulation was introduced. As can be concluded from Figure 3.5, an outgoing network layer packet is first passed to the LLC 802.2 sublayer, which encapsulates it with an LLC header. It then is passed to the MAC sublayer to undergo further encapsulation before being submitted to the physical layer (that is, network interface card transmit/receive circuit) for actual transmission.

Figure 3.6 compares the header format of the MAC sublayer IEEE 802.3 with Ethernet's. Notice that the 802.3 MAC header and trailer are similar to Ethernet's except for one field. The third field in the 802.3 MAC header designates the length of the information field, whereas in Ethernet it is treated as the type field, which identifies the protocol to which data will be delivered.

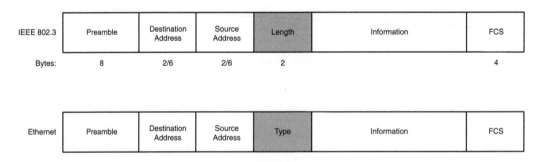

Figure 3.6. *Comparison between IEEE 802.3 and Ethernet headers.*

At the LLC sublayer, IEEE defined, over time, two header formats: so-called LLC 802.2 and LLC 802.2 SNAP (subnetwork access protocol) headers. Both formats are shown in Figure 3.7. The latter protocol header is the one used by TCP/IP implementations that are compliant with IEEE standards.

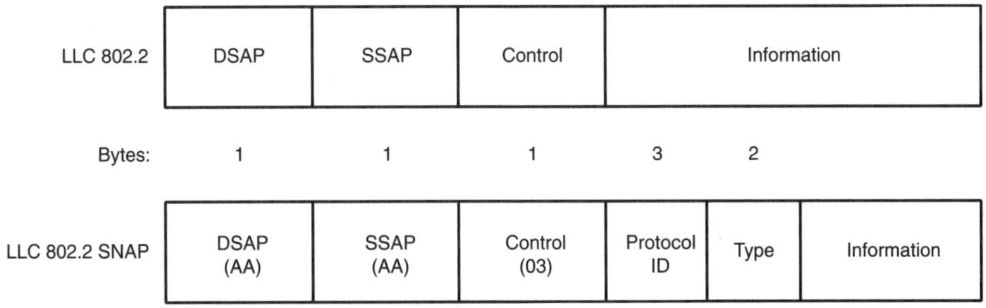

Figure 3.7. *Header formats of both LLC 802.2 and LLC 802.2 SNAP protocols.*

IEEE 802.2 Header Format

Because Ethernet's type field was changed to a *length* field in the IEEE 802.3 frame format, it is impossible for the data link layer to route data received from the network to appropriate upper layer protocols. This is especially true whenever more than one protocol exists at the network layer. To meet this internal routing requirement, the LLC 802.2 header includes two fields, the DSAP and the SSAP (the destination and source *service access points*, respectively), which designate communicating protocols at the higher layer (see the top portion of Figure 3.7). Following the DSAP and SSAP fields is the CTRL (control) field, which is used by the LLC layer for link control and management, including error detection and recovery. The information field contains the upper layer service data unit (for example, the routing data packet).

IEEE 802.2 SNAP Header

The header described previously was the first defined by the IEEE defined for the LLC sublayer. Afterward, it was realized that the one-byte DSAP and SSAP fields were too small to accommodate all the protocols that might require identification. To circumvent this problem, IEEE introduced changes to the original LLC 802.2 header, which became known as the LLC 802.2 SNAP.

The bottom portion of Figure 3.7 shows the LLC 802.2 SNAP header. Notice that for the LLC protocol to differentiate the LLC 802.2 SNAP from its predecessor, both DSAP and SSAP are fixed to the hexadecimal value AA, and the identification of the protocol type is delegated to the new *protocol information* field. The protocol information field is two parts. The first part is composed of three bytes describing the protocol family (for example, in the case of TCP/IP, the family ID is 0). The second part is composed of the remaining two bytes describing the upper layer protocol to which to route the data field (for example, 0x800 for IP, and 0x806 for ARP).

To summarize, Figure 3.8 shows the complete data link layer frame formats discussed thus far. The shaded area of each format represents the field used to identify the incoming protocol.

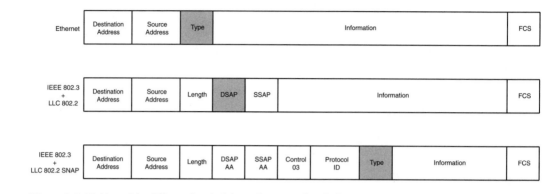

Figure 3.8. *Fields used by different data link layer frames to identify the incoming protocol. The SNAP frame format describes field values pertaining to TCP/IP.*

Token-ring Technology

Token-ring data link technology is IBM's most popular contribution to the networking industry. Like Ethernet, Token-ring was submitted to the IEEE committee for standardization, which resulted in the IEEE 802.5 medium access control standard at the MAC sublayer. Token-ring specifications include the physical layer, link access and arbitration rules, and frame format definitions.

Physical Layer

At the physical layer, Token-ring supports 4- and 16-megabits-per-second transmission speeds. Workstations and other devices are connected to a physical ring as shown in Figure 3.9. Data on the wire travels in one direction only. This is due to the fact that cable segments forming the ring connect the output (that is, transmit) circuit of one workstation to the input (that is, receive) circuit of the adjacent workstation down the data stream. Data originating on the network will be copied from one cable segment to the other by all workstations, making them behave as signal repeaters on the wire.

Because, by Token-ring rules, each originating station is responsible for the removal of data frames it puts on the wire, the repeating process continues past the destined station. As the destined station copies the frame to its output port, it recovers the intelligence embedded in the electrical activity and sets certain bits, carried by the frame, to indicate whether it recognized its own address, and whether the data was read reliably.

In addition to the physical ring depicted in Figure 3.9, workstations can use multistation access units (known as MAU) to connect to the ring. The MAU (see Figure 3.10) is internally wired to maintain a ring as workstations are connected or disconnected. This is achieved by employing a relay circuit, at each port, which is energized to open as a workstation connected to the port is powered up. This process is commonly referred to as *ring insertion.* A workstation is isolated (dropped out) from the ring upon relay closure, which can happen in one of two ways: the workstation fails to participate in ring activity, or it is powered down. The wiring topology thus formed is known as star-wired topology.

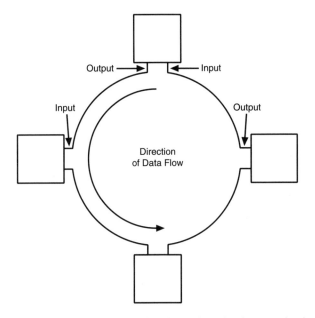

Figure 3.9. *Token-ring network. Notice how the output of one host is chained to the input of its downstream neighbor until the ring closes.*

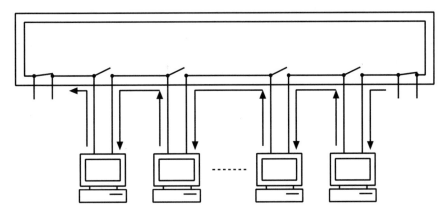

Figure 3.10. *Using a multistation access unit (MAU) in Token-ring wiring.*

MAUs can be connected as shown in Figure 3.11 to form a bigger ring. Each MAU comes with two ports marked as RI (ring-in) and RO (ring-out). As shown in the diagram, a bigger ring is formed by connecting the RO of one MAU to the RI of the adjacent MAU until the ring closes. This setup connects all workstations and all MAUs on a single ring. In this case, data originating on the network will have to pass by all participating workstations on the larger ring.

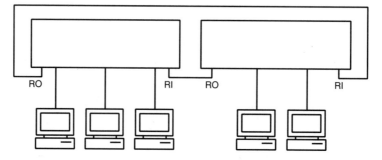

Figure 3.11. *Multiple MAUs can be connected to form a larger ring by connecting the ring output (RO) of one MAU to the ring input (RI) of the adjacent MAU.*

Token-ring Link Access and Arbitration

You have seen how Ethernet employs a contention-based, random-access technology for link access and arbitration, as implemented in the CSMA/CD protocol. This means that there is no central link arbitration authority to schedule and coordinate transmission times or priorities. Devices on an Ethernet network make independent attempts at grabbing the link to transmit their data loads. In Token-ring, link access arbitration takes the opposite approach, in which devices on the ring maintain the collective responsibility for coordinating link access, maintenance, and recovery from failure.

The right to transmit on the ring is governed by a *token*, which circulates around the ring as it is passed from one station to another (see Figure 3.12). The token has a special data format that is recognized by all workstations as an indication of an idle ring, or *free token*. A workstation wanting to transmit data can't do so until it captures the token. Data carrying frames sent down the ring include a special field to accommodate the token, in which case it is flagged as a *busy* token (that is, a busy network). Each workstation examines the destination address described in the MAC header to determine whether it is the intended party. In either case, it *repeats* the data frame onto the next cable segment, thus sending it to the nearest downstream station. The repeating process continues until the data frame comes back to the originating station, where it is removed from the ring. At this point, the workstation can continue to transmit (subject to time limitations) or release a free token to circulate on the ring.

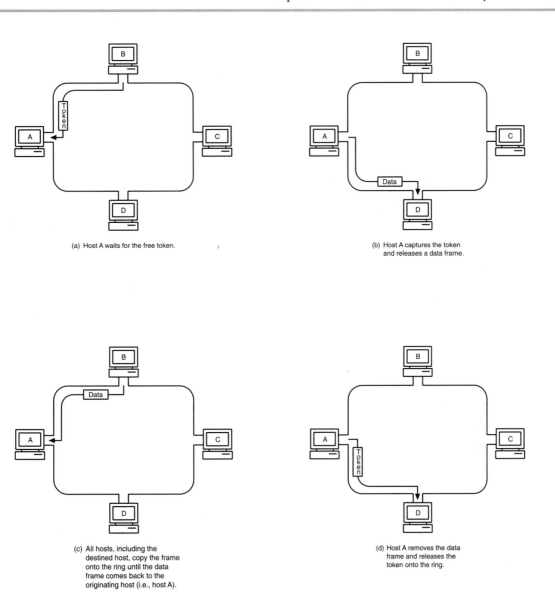

(a) Host A waits for the free token.

(b) Host A captures the token and releases a data frame.

(c) All hosts, including the destined host, copy the frame onto the ring until the data frame comes back to the originating host (i.e., host A).

(d) Host A removes the data frame and releases the token onto the ring.

Figure 3.12. *Token-passing protocol for link access arbitration on Token-ring networks.*

When a workstation recognizes itself as the party described in the MAC address, it reads the data as it copies the frame to the next cable segment, and it modifies the Frame Status field (see Figure 3.13) in the frame header to indicate the following:

◆ *Address recognized:* This setting implies that the intended workstation recognized the address as its own. It confirms to the sending workstation that the intended party is on the network.

♦ *Frame copied:* If set by the receiving station, frame copied implies that the data frame passed the integrity check and was routed to the appropriate upper layer protocol.

Upon recovery of the data frame from the ring, the originating workstation checks the Frame Status field to verify whether the data reached its destination reliably.

Token-ring Frame Format

Token-ring architecture conforms with the IEEE architecture of the data link layer, as depicted in Figure 3.5. By IEEE standards, Token-ring corresponds to the IEEE 802.5 MAC sublayer. Token-ring protocols also conform to both LLC 802.2 and LLC 802.2 SNAP specifications. TCP/IP is currently supported by the IEEE 802.5 and LLC 802.2 SNAP at the MAC and LLC sublayers, respectively. It should be emphasized that SNAP is SNAP; its properties and characteristics do not change, regardless of the underlying MAC sublayer that is responsible for sending or receiving data on the network. Hence, only the Token-ring (or equivalently, IEEE 802.5) frame format will be described.

Figure 3.13 shows the Token-ring frame format, including the LLC 802.2 SNAP header information. Following the figure is a brief description of what function each field serves.

Start Delimiter	Access Control	Frame Control	Dest. Address	Source Address	Information	FCS	End Delimiter	Frame Status

Figure 3.13. *Token-ring frame format.*

Start-of-frame delimiter: This one-byte attention-getting signal pattern alerts stations on the ring of an impending transmission.

Access control field: This one-byte field is formatted as *PPPMTRRR.* The Token-ring supports a prioritization scheme, according to which workstations can be assigned priorities reflecting the criticality of the applications they are running. *PPP* and *RRR* bits are used by Token-ring to manage prioritization and allocate the bandwidth accordingly. The *M* bit, known as the monitor bit, is used to prevent a data frame from continuing to circu-late on the ring, if the originating station should fail to remove it. This is achieved by virtue of assigning one station as an active monitor. Among the active monitor responsibilities is generating a new token in case the current one is lost or deformed, and setting the *M* bit the first time it repeats a data frame onto the ring. This way, the active monitor station will be able to identify, and therefore remove, the data frame if it passes the monitor a second time. The *T* bit, known as the token bit, is used to distinguish between a free token and a data frame.

Frame control: This one-byte field describes whether the frame carries an LLC frame or just a MAC frame. In the latter case, the information field carries link control data, and as such is destined to the MAC sublayer itself.

Destination and source addresses: These can be two- or six-byte fields describing the destin-ation and source addresses. The length of the address must be uniform through-out the network.

Information field: This field ranges from 0 to 4K or 18K, depending on whether the ring is respectively 4 Mbps or 16 Mbps. The information field can include the LLC control header.

Frame check sequence (FCS): This four-byte field is used for verifying the integrity of transmitted data.

End delimiter: This one-byte field signals the end of the data frame. It also carries the *I* and *E* bits. The *I* bit, also known as the intermediate bit, indicates that the current frame is an intermediate frame in a series of frames to follow. Setting it to zero implies that it is the last frame in a multiframe transmission. The *E* bit, also known as the error bit, is set to indicate that an error is detected. This bit can be set by any station that detects the error on the ring.

Frame status: This one-byte field contains the address-recognized and frame-copied bits discussed earlier in this section.

MAC Addresses

The IEEE 802 standardization committee has adopted an address format that is identical for all the MAC standards it defined (that is, 802.3, 802.4, 802.5,...). The address field can be either two or six bytes long. IEEE supports three types of addresses:

Individual addresses: These addresses are used to identify individual stations on the network.

Broadcast address: A broadcast address has all address bits set to 1 and is used for all active devices on the network.

Multicast address: This type of address is assigned to a logical group of workstations.

According to IEEE, 48-bit individual addresses can be either locally or universally administered. Locally administered addresses are set up by the LAN user, in which case it becomes the user's responsibility to ensure the uniqueness of each of the addresses he assigns. Universally adminis-tered addresses are assigned and maintained by the IEEE committee itself. A universally assigned MAC address is unique worldwide. This in turn implies that a workstation with a universal address can be connected to any network with addresses similarly assigned without any need to have the workstation reconfigured to a different address.

Figure 3.14 shows the format of the individual universal address. The two leftmost bits are always 0. Following these bits is a 22-bit unique organizational identifier that is assigned by the IEEE to communication vendors. The remaining 24 bits are organizationally assigned and should be guaranteed to be unique to the network interfaces that the vendor manufactures. Put together, the unique organizational identifier assigned by IEEE, and the uniquely assigned 24-bit address, result in a universally unique MAC address for the workstation. If you buy an Ethernet board from 3Com, a unique MAC address is assigned to that board out of the box (you don't need to do anything to assign it as a user). The 22-bit unique organizational ID is the same for all 3Com boards. The 24-bit address is unique among all 3Com boards. Together they form a universally unique MAC address for your board.

0	0	22-Bit Unique Organizational ID	24-Bit Organizationally Assigned Address

Figure 3.14. *Format of the IEEE universally administered address.*

TCP/IP Over WAN Links

In addition to the local network media, such as Ethernet and Token-ring, TCP/IP supports many kinds of serial links allowing multiple sites to connect over wide area networks (WANs). The serial links range in speed from 1200 bps to speeds reaching those of T1/T3 links (that is, 1.544/2.048 Mbps).

Among the reasons for the exploding popularity of serial link protocols are the increased affordability of home computers and the relatively recent availability of high-speed modems. These two factors have led many computer professionals and enthusiasts to set up their own computers at home, and to think about having these computers connected to their office networks, or the Internet.

Unfortunately, at that time, TCP/IP standards did not include any definition for the data link and physical layers over wide area serial links. This situation led to the chaotic development of uninteroperable vendor-specific IP WAN routers, which in turn put the Internet community under sustained pressure to standardize the WAN access technology.

Two serial link protocols are currently supported by TCP/IP: Serial Line Internet Protocol (SLIP) and the Point-to-Point Protocol (PPP).

SLIP

SLIP is specified by RFC 1055. It supports both synchronous and asynchronous dialup services, and it is used mainly to connect home computers to the Internet or other TCP/IP networks. SLIP employs a simple mechanism for delivering IP datagrams across the serial link. It calls for transmitting the datagram one byte at a time. For the receiving end to group a related set of bytes into one IP datagram, SLIP defines two special characters:

◆ *The SLIP END character (0xc0):* This character is used to mark the end of the current IP datagram. When the ESC character is encountered by the remote host, it knows that this byte is the last in the series of bytes that make the IP datagram that can now be routed up to IP.

◆ *The SLIP ESC character (0xdb):* This character is used to circumvent the possibility of encountering the SLIP END character in the middle of the datagram. There is always a risk of encountering the byte equivalent of the END character in the datagram. To prevent the remote host from interpreting it as the signal marking the end of the datagram, the sending SLIP replaces such an encounter with the two-character sequence 0xdb and 0xdc. The first is called the SLIP ESC character, whose value is different from the ASCII ESC character.

SLIP is a very simple protocol, yet it has some built-in deficiencies that prevent it from being suitable to some applications. These are the deficiencies:

◆ Systems communicating over the SLIP link are required to know their remote partner's IP address. There is no mechanism by which SLIP can inform the opposite end of its IP identity.

◆ SLIP does not support a link negotiation and establishment mechanism. Hence, there is no way for both ends of the connection to agree on a common set of link parameters. Both ends must have been configured exactly the same way before an attempt is made to establish a connection.

◆ SLIP does not include a type field similar to the type field in Ethernet. Consequently, SLIP has no means of supporting multiprotocol communications. Only IP datagrams can be exchanged across the link.

◆ SLIP does not perform any error detection and correction functions. This, however, is not a critical drawback because most new modems can handle these functions on the wire.

Despite those deficiencies, SLIP is still the preferred serial protocol that many users and organizations choose. Its popularity is attributable to its simple design and modest hardware requirements (only an RS-232C/D interface is required, which is commonly available on almost every computer, such as the COM1 and COM2 ports on PCs). Given the choice, however, you should look more seriously at the PPP protocol as an alternative to using SLIP. PPP corrects all the previously cited deficiencies and adds superior capabilities to IP serial communications.

Point-to-Point Protocol

Point-to-Point Protocol (PPP) is a standard developed by the Internet Engineering Task Force (IETF) PPP workgroup. It is specified in RFC 1331, and it defines services and functions corresponding to those performed at the data link and partly the network layers of the OSI model (see Figure 3.15). Although PPP is a TCP/IP standard, it is equipped to route multiple protocols across the same link, which makes it a viable choice for environments supporting more than just the IP protocol.

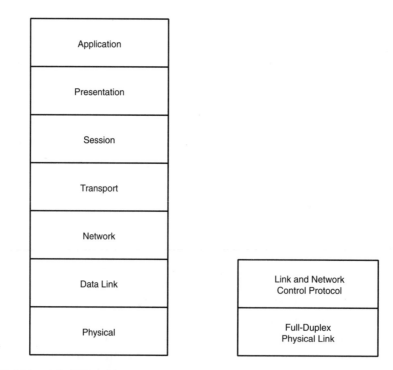

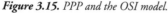

Figure 3.15. PPP and the OSI model.

At the physical layer, PPP is a media-independent protocol that supports both bit-oriented synchronous transmission and byte-oriented asynchronous transmission, at speeds ranging from 1200 bps to T1/T3 speeds. In addition, PPP connects over copper, fiber optics, microwave, or satellite links. Supported physical interfaces include RS-232C/D, RS-422, and V.35. These features offer users the flexibility of connecting multiple sites and home computers using the PPP link that they deem most suitable to the nature of the application they will be running across the link, and that meets their budgetary constraints.

Figure 3.16 depicts a scenario in which an organization implemented PPP, with varying physical characteristics, to connect three of its sites across WAN links. In one case, dial-up is deemed satisfactory, which may apply to sites needing to exchange E-mail only. The utilization of PPP over a full T1 link may be required for the frequent exchange of voluminous data files.

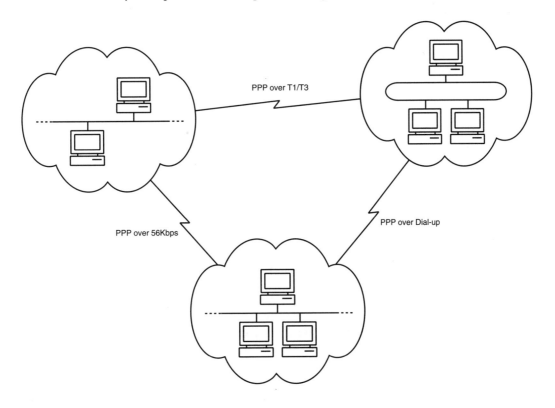

Figure 3.16. *PPP can be used over various link speeds and media.*

Another feature that can be inferred from Figure 3.16 is that PPP can be used to connect dissimilar networks such as Ethernet, Token-ring, and FDDI.

At the data link layer, PPP defines two protocols:

- ◆ *Link Control Protocol (LCP):* LCP is a connection-oriented protocol. As such, LCP is responsible for the negotiation, establishment, maintenance, and termination of a logical data link over a physical point-to-point connection.

◆ *Network Control Protocol (NCP):* PPP defines one NCP per supported network layer protocol, in which each NCP is responsible for negotiating, establishing, and terminating the connection between peer protocols it represents. For example, to multiplex data pertaining to multiple protocols, such as IP, IPX, and AppleTalk, three NCP connections need to be established on behalf of each of these protocols, over the already established logical LCP data link.

Data Frame Format

The PPP data frame format is an adaptation of HDLC (High-level Data Link Control) protocol format, which is characterized by both reduced overhead and high throughput. As shown in Figure 3.17, each data frame starts, and ends, with a one-byte *flag* set to 0x7e. A one-byte *address* field follows the start flag, and it is always set to all ones (that is, 0xff). Following the address field is a one-byte control field that is set to 0x03.

Flag 7E	Address FF	Control 03	Protocol Info	Information	FCS	Flag 7E

Figure 3.17. PPP frame format.

A two-byte *protocol* field comes next, which contains a universally assigned protocol identification number. The protocol identification number describes the nature of the data contained in the *information* field and allows for multiplexing multiprotocol data over the same logical link. If, for example, the protocol field contains 0x0021, then the information field is an IP datagram, whereas 0x002b implies an IPX packet.

In addition to carrying network layer datagrams or packets, PPP can use the information field to allow for the exchange of control data and negotiable options between peer LCPs or peer NCPs across the link. A value of 0xc021, for example, means that the information field contains LCP data, whereas 0x8021 implies IP NCP data, more commonly known as IPCP data.

The *frame check sequence* (FCS) field is used to verify the integrity of the transmission. All but the flag fields are included in the FCS check.

Frame Compression

To reduce bandwidth consumption due to overhead incurred by header information over slow data links, PPP can be configured to negotiate header compression with its peer across the link. Header compression involves the elimination of both the address and the control fields, in addition to the reduction of the protocol field from two bytes to one byte.

Header compression is particularly suitable to interactive applications, where in many cases a single character is all that needs to be sent in response to a prompt, or to select a menu option. This results in a sizable reduction of overhead and improved response time.

To summarize, TCP/IP supports both SLIP and PPP protocols for serial WAN communications. For historical reasons, SLIP has been the preferred choice for serial communications—in particular, for connecting home computers to IP networks. PPP was developed by the IETF to overcome some of the deficiencies inherent in SLIP, specifically in the areas of error detection, multiprotocol support, and link negotiation. Network designers and implementors installing new WAN links should seriously consider PPP as the governing link protocol. There are two good reasons for doing that:

◆ With PPP, users are guaranteed support for multiprotocol environments. Even if you presently do not belong to such an environment, given the ease with which multiplat-forms can be integrated on the wire nowadays, and the benefits derived from such an integration, it is more than likely that your environment will become multiprotocol in the future. Thus, with PPP, you'll be able to make a painless transition to supporting the involved protocols.

◆ Multivendor device interoperability is another reason to go with PPP. Compliant routers and bridges can talk together regardless of the manufacturer. This leaves the door open to better quality, cheaper cost, and ease of both device administration and operation.

Bridges

You've seen how workstations can be added to the network using 10BASE-T concentrators for Ethernet and MAUs for Token-ring. Most LAN technologies, however, put an upper limit on the number of workstations that can be connected using concentrators. 10BASE-T, for example, specifies a maximum of 1,024 workstations. In practice, however, will approaching that limit negatively affect network performance?

To answer this question, remember that on Ethernet networks, workstations might undergo collision on the wire as more than one workstation attempts transmission at the same time, and that colliding workstations must back off from transmitting data before making a new attempt. Hence, having more workstations on the same physical network increases collision rates, which in turn results in further backoffs and, therefore, reduced data throughput. Figure 3.18 shows a graph depicting data throughput as a function of actively transmitting devices on the network.

To remedy this situation, network users employ *bridges* to extend their network. As shown in Figure 3.19, a bridge is an intermediate device that connects multiple physical network segments. It operates at the data link layer (see Figure 3.20) and is used to increase data transmission throughput by filtering frames between the connected segments based on MAC addresses.

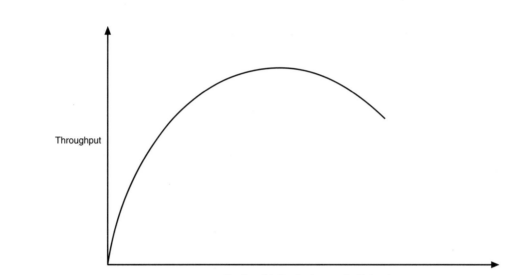

Figure 3.18. Throughput versus the number of active devices on the network.

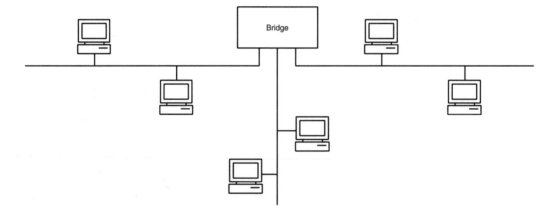

Figure 3.19. A bridge connecting multiple network segments

The IEEE 802.1D protocol is the most commonly adopted bridging protocol. Bridges built to IEEE 802.1D specifications are also called *transparent* or *learning* bridges. Transparency stems from the fact that a bridge is perceived by workstations on different segments as a pass-through connector rather than an active device. For example, when workstation A wants to send a data frame across the bridge to workstation B, it includes B's MAC address in the data frame (that is, as though B belonged to the same segment), *not* that of the bridge (see Figure 3.21).

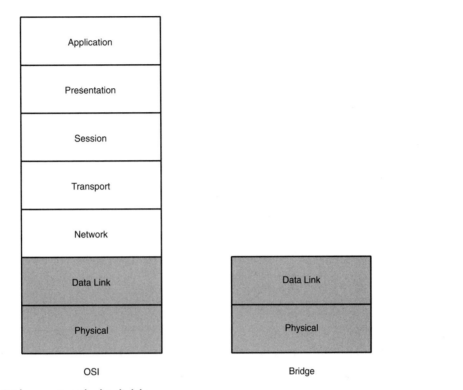

Figure 3.20. *Bridges operate at the data link layer*

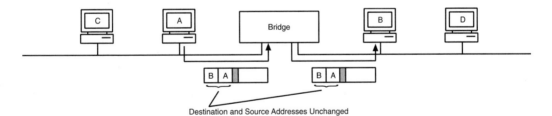

Figure 3.21. *Workstations perceive a bridge as a pass-through connector.*

Learning is attributable to the mechanism by which a bridge builds a database of MAC addresses it recognizes to exist on the network. This database is vital to the decision-making process used for frame filtering and forwarding. The database, as shown in Figure 3.22, is organized by the segment number; MAC addresses belonging to the same segment are entered under the corresponding column.

How does the bridge learn its neighborhood? The answer to this question is straightforward: by capturing every data frame emerging on all segments, and reading the MAC source address included in the header. In Figure 3.22, the bridge captures a packet transmitted by workstation X on segment 1, examines the MAC source address, and updates its filtering database.

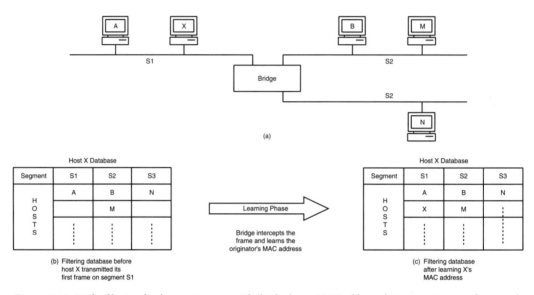

(a)

(b) Filtering database before host X transmitted its first frame on segment S1

(c) Filtering database after learning X's MAC address

Figure 3.22. *Bridge filtering database maintenance. The bridge learns MAC addresses by intercepting every frame on the network and reading the address of its originator.*

A bridge decides whether to forward a frame after it compares the frame MAC destination address with the filtering database. If the destination address is found to belong to the segment on which it originated, the frame is ignored (not forwarded). Otherwise, it is forwarded to the segment where the destination workstation is attached. When the destination is not yet described anywhere in the database (for example, in the case of a newly powered station on the network), the bridge forwards the frame to all segments except the originating one.

Thus, as can be seen from the previous discussion, the bridge effectively localizes traffic to segments to which they belong. This should be contrasted with how a repeater (that is, wiring hubs) deals with network traffic.

A repeater, as shown in Figure 3.23a, replicates all traffic onto connected segments, regardless of the destination address. This implies that when workstation A on segment S1 acquires the link to send data to workstation B on the same segment, stations on both segments S2 and S3 will not be able to communicate among themselves. A bridge instead allows workstations C and D to talk to each other or to X and Y on segment S3 in isolation of the ongoing traffic on segment S1 (see Figure 3.23b), thus resulting in a significant improvement in total data throughput on the wire (see Figure 3.24).

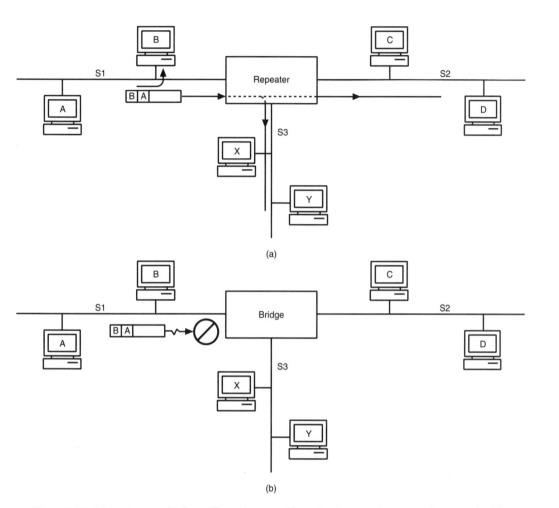

Figure 3.23. *(a) A repeater multiplies traffic on the network by replicating every frame onto all connected cable segments. (b) A bridge localizes traffic, thus allowing workstations on unaffected segments to talk to each other.*

Another advantage of a bridge over a repeater is that it regenerates the frame before it is forwarded, whereas the repeater simply replicates the signal on the wire. For the frame to be regenerated, it must pass the integrity check at the MAC sublayer. In this process, all forms of errors arising from collision on the wire (noise or electromagnetic interference) will remain local to the originating segment, thus relieving all other segments from the burden of dealing with the results of those errors.

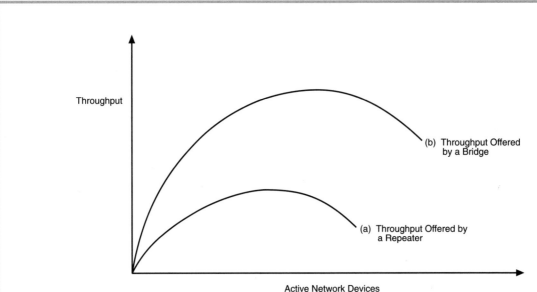

Figure 3.24. A bridge offers an improved throughput over that offered by a repeater.

Summary

At the network access layer, functions pertaining to the delivery of data to devices attached to the same physical network are defined. Ethernet and Token-ring are two of the most dominant medium access control technologies. They were both standardized by the IEEE 802 standards committee. IEEE standards split the data link layer to two sublayers, the MAC sublayer and the LLC 802.2 sublayer, with the latter being the common denominator (sublayer) among all MAC definitions. At the network access layer, WAN access methods are also well defined. Most notable of the WAN protocols are SLIP and PPP. PPP is the most recent serial link protocol standard, defining connectivity over synchronous, asynchronous, leased, or dial-up wires. PPP also provides multiprotocol support, which is suitable to multiplatform environments.

Repeaters and bridges are connectivity devices, at the physical and data link layers, that are used to extend the physical network. Bridges offer better data throughput, error recovery, and intelligent routing of traffic.

CHAPTER 4

The Internet Layer
and Routing

Introduction

To create an internetwork, connecting physical networks of different types so that they appear as one logical network requires a scheme for routing information across those physical networks. Basic to this goal is a unique set of addresses that identifies each network on the internetwork. This address, called the *network address*, then becomes part of the address identifying each host on that network.

In TCP/IP, routing is handled at the internet layer, which maps roughly to the network layer of the OSI reference model (see Figure 4.1). Chapter 2, "Overview of TCP/IP," conceptually describes IP routing and explains the IP protocol, including the IP datagram data structure. Of the fields defined by the IP header, two were described briefly. Those fields are the IP destination and source addresses (see Figure 2.5), which will dominate the discussions included in this chapter.

This chapter introduces you to the intricate details of IP routing. Because a good understanding of IP routing cannot be achieved without a solid background in the IP addressing structure, the first part focuses on establishing all the concepts underlying IP addresses. After that, IP routing-related protocols are examined, and different routing scenarios are presented, as well as the associated configuration and flow of events arising from these scenarios.

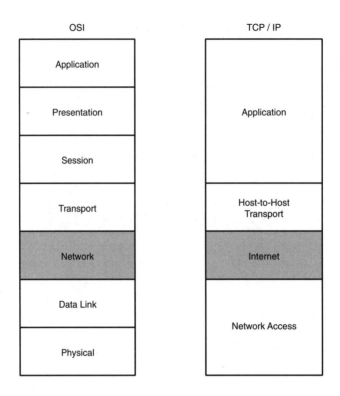

Figure 4.1. *The internet layer maps to the network layer in the OSI model.*

Among the protocols discussed in this chapter is the address resolution protocol (ARP), which, as many readers might already know, belongs to the network access layer (one layer below the internet layer). The relevance of this protocol to the way IP addresses work has dictated that this chapter is the natural place for discussing it.

IP Address Structure

In TCP/IP, every device on the network derives its unique *complete network* address by virtue of an address assignment to which the device is configured (more on configuration in Chapter 9). The assigned address, known as a *symbolic IP address*, is made of two parts: (1) the network address, which is common to all hosts and devices on the same physical network, and (2) the node address, which is unique to the host on that network.

As you will see, neither part has anything to do with the actual hardwired MAC address on the network address card. As a matter of fact, a network administrator has the freedom to change the node part of the address (with some restrictions), and to a lesser degree the network address, while paying no attention to the MAC address. For this reason, the IP address is described as symbolic.

Confusing as it might initially sound, the IP protocol uses these symbolic addresses to route data on the network. In other words, when a user requests that a telnet session be established with another host, TCP/IP uses the administrator-assigned 32-bit IP addresses to connect and establish the telnet session between both the requesting and the target hosts. The details of this process will be tackled later in the chapter. First, take a look at how IP addresses are made and the classes to which they belong.

The IP address is 32 bits (or four bytes) long, including both the network and the node addresses. It occupies the IP source and destination address fields of the IP header. How many bits of the address belong to the network part, versus the number of bits that belong to the node part, is dependent on the IP address class into which the address falls. IP defines three main classes: A, B, and C. There is a class D, which is lesser in significance than the other ones; it will be touched on briefly.

Figure 4.2 shows the different address formats corresponding to each of the three main classes that IP supports. Each IP address class is distinguishable by the first few bits of the network portion. Following the figure is a listing of the different IP classes and the rules by which they are governed.

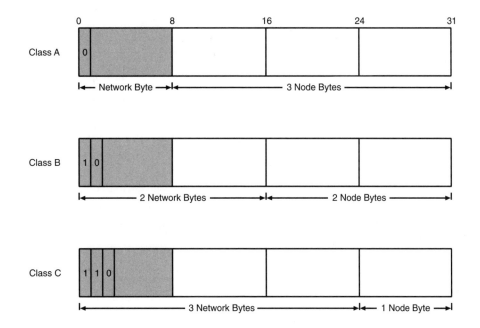

Figure 4.2. *IP address classes and their corresponding structures.*

◆ *Class A address:* The first bit is fixed to 0, and the first byte, called the network ID, identifies the network. The remaining three bytes are used to identify the host on the network; they constitute the host ID. You can calculate that there is a maximum of 127 class A networks, each capable of accommodating millions of hosts.

◆ *Class B address:* The first two bits are fixed to 10, the first and second bytes are used to identify the network, and the last two bytes are used to identify the host. There can be thousands of class B networks, capable of accommodating thousands of hosts.

◆ *Class C address:* The first three bits are fixed to 110; the first, second, and third bytes are used to identify the network; and the last byte is used to identify the host. Class C networks are the smallest of all classes; each can accommodate a maximum of 254 hosts (not 256, because 0x0 and 0xFF are reserved for other purposes, described later). With three bytes reserved to identify the network, millions of class C networks can be defined.

◆ *Class D address:* The first four bits are fixed to 1110. A class D address is a multicast address, identifying a group of computers that can be running a distributed application on the network. As such, class D does not describe a network of hosts on the wire.

To make address administration relatively easy, TCP/IP network administrators can configure hosts, and routers, with addresses by using what is commonly known as dotted decimal notation. Dotted decimal notation treats the 32-bit address as four separate, yet contiguous, bytes. Each byte is represented by its decimal equivalent that lies between 0 and 255 (that is, the decimal range equivalent to an 8-bit binary pattern). Figure 4.3 shows an example of a class A address in both binary and dotted decimal (that is, 65.18.11.135) notation.

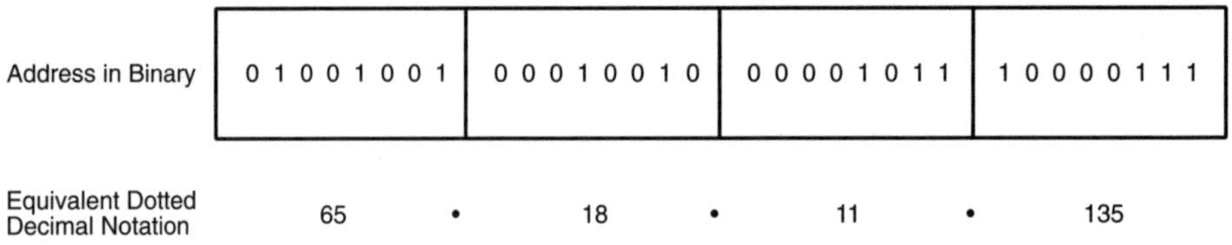

Address in Binary	0 1 0 0 1 0 0 1	0 0 0 1 0 0 1 0	0 0 0 0 1 0 1 1	1 0 0 0 0 1 1 1
Equivalent Dotted Decimal Notation	65 •	18 •	11 •	135

Figure 4.3. *An IP address in binary and the equivalent dotted decimal notation.*

Given that an 8-bit binary pattern can assume any decimal equivalent in the range of 0 to 255, and given the initial bits of a certain class, you should be able to tell from the first byte the class of the network. Table 4.1 depicts the range of values for the first byte of each IP address that classes can assume.

Table 4.1. IP address classes and the range of values their first byte can assume.

Address Class	*Decimal Range*
A	0–127
B	128–191
C	192–223

Consider the address 148.29.4.121. By applying the rules learned previously, you can determine that this is a class B address, because the first byte lies in the 128-to-191 range of values. And because a class B address has the first two bytes for a network address, you can derive that the network address is 148.29 and the host address is 4.121 on that network. To generalize, given an IP address, you can recognize its class by interpreting the first byte. Consequently, you can derive the network portion of the address from the remaining bytes.

Netmasks

Class A and Class B networks allow millions or thousands of hosts to share the same network ID. As explained later, IP routing defines what is known as *subnet masks* (or simply *netmasks*) as a means of allowing such hosts to reside on different physical networks while still maintaining the same network identity, hence resulting in optimal data throughput.

Figure 4.4a shows an example of a class B network. Notice how all the hosts have the 148.29 network address in common. A host misconfigured (for example, host X in Figure 4.4b) to any other network address will not be able to talk to other hosts on the network.

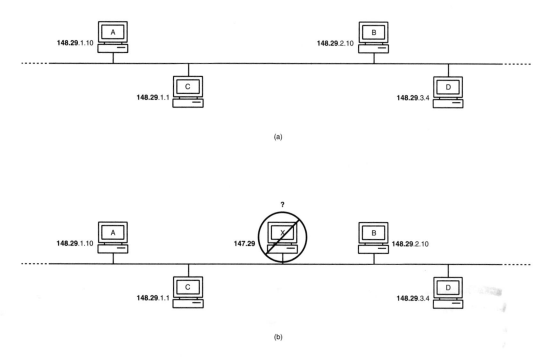

Figure 4.4. *(a) A properly configured network has all the hosts belonging to it assigned the same network address. (b) Host X is configured to a network address that is inconsistent with that of the other hosts. This makes it impossible to transmit data between host X and other hosts on the network.*

128.100 (handwritten)

When a host or any other network device is assigned an IP address, IP derives its network class and network address from that assignment (148.29). Later, when it is required to deliver a datagram to a host, it compares the network address of the destination address submitted by the transport protocol (TCP or UDP) to that of its own. If the addresses match, IP then refrains from routing the datagram. (In other words, the datagram won't be sent to a router for assistance in delivery. See Chapter 2, "Overview of TCP/IP," for a refresher on IP routing.) Instead, IP assumes that the host is on the same network and therefore attempts a direct delivery to the designated node address.

Assume that you are on host X and you want to establish a file transfer session with host A on the network. You can enter the following command:

```
ftp 148.29.1.10
```

> **Note:** It will be shown later how to specify a host by using a name rather than the IP address as shown previously.

TCP picks up the address and passes it to IP, at the internet layer, along with a TCP segment that it wants delivered to host A. IP, on host X, compares its own network address (147.29) with that of host A (148.29). Because they are not the same, IP concludes that host A must belong to a remote network, and therefore direct delivery is not possible. For simplicity, assume that the network in Figure 4.4b is the only one in its environment, in which case there can be no routers on the wire. IP won't be able to forward the packet any further and will report a failure to deliver to the upper layer or application.

In Figure 4.5, you are shown two networks, a class B Ethernet network and a Token-ring class A network. A router is also shown connecting the two networks together. An important observation to make is that the router is configured to two addresses, 148.29.15.1 and 198.53.2.8.

The question that normally arises is which of the two is *the* address? Well, as a matter of fact, an address you assign to the host is assigned to, or associated with, the network interface card that attaches the host to the network. Hence, in the case of a router and multihomed host, an address is required for every NIC card supported. Depending on which network the NIC attaches the host to, it must be assigned an IP address with a network part consistent with the network address assigned to the rest of the host's community. Hosts on the Token-ring network use 198.53.2.8 to address the router, whereas those on Ethernet use 148.29.15.1.

You saw earlier that all-0s (0x0) and all-1s (0xff) node addresses are reserved for special purposes and therefore cannot be used to designate a node on the network. This is because an all-0s node address refers to all nodes on the network. For example, in the routing table of the router in Figure 4.5, a destination address of 198.53.2.0 refers to all hosts on the Token-ring network, whereas an all-1s node address is normally used to broadcast a message to all hosts on that network. Therefore, a host transmitting a broadcast message to 198.53.2.255 will have the message picked up by all active hosts on the Token-ring network only. Similarly, a broadcast to 148.29.255.255 will be picked up by all hosts on the Ethernet.

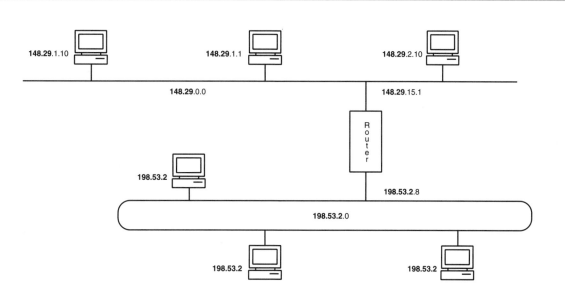

Figure 4.5. *Routers are assigned as many addresses as network interface cards supported.*

In addition to the reservations made on the node addresses described previously, there are two class A network addresses that bear a special significance and that cannot be used to designate a network. They are network addresses 0 and 127. Network 0 is used to designate the *default route,* and 127 is used to designate *this host* or the *loopback address.*

As you will see later in this chapter, the default route refers to a router configuration that makes the routing of packets to destinations unknown to the router possible. The loopback address is used to designate the *local host* and is used to send the interface an IP datagram in exactly the same way other interfaces on the network are addressed.

Conventionally, 127.0.0.1 is the address used to designate the local host. You can, however, use any other class A 127 address for the same purpose. For example, 127.45.44.89 is valid for designating the local host, as is 127.0.0.1. This is because a datagram sent to the loopback interface must not, in any case, be transmitted on the wire.

Subnetting the Network

Given that class A and B addresses can be large (with the former capable of accommodating millions of nodes, and the latter accommodating thousands of nodes), it is not practical to put all the nodes on the same physical network. Here are some considerations:

◆ *Network traffic:* You saw in Chapter 3 (see Figure 3.18) how throughput degrades on the network as the number of workstations attached to the network exceeds a certain limit. The limiting number of workstations is a function of the overall traffic offered on the wire.

◆ *Type of application:* Some applications are better behaved on a Token-ring type of network than Ethernet, and vice versa. Some other applications (for example, real-time multimedia and imaging applications) might even require nothing less than a high-speed fiber network such as FDDI. Hence it would be unwise, and potentially counterproductive, to try to enforce a single network on a large organization.

◆ *Organizational mergers:* It is not uncommon to find that merging organizations end up having to accommodate the dissimilar networks used to support them before the merger took place. This situation consumes valuable resources and causes "political unrest" if one network type is neglected in favor of the other.

◆ *Geographical proximity:* Many organizations have offices in more than one location. The computing resources of all site offices might be networked, and made available to the entire user community, using WAN routers. This setup requires that a unique network address be assigned to networks to which the router connects. Having multiple class B addresses assigned (more on assignment authorities later in this chapter) to an organization to accommodate this need might prove unachievable, in the light of wasted address space this approach causes.

For these reasons, you might find yourself having to break your network into smaller networks, with each *subnet* accommodating a certain number of users or type of application. To do this using a single network address, TCP/IP allows for the modification of the IP address structure, to extend the network address portion beyond its default boundary.

For example, in a class B address, only the first two bytes designate the network. Using a *subnet mask*, you will be able to include the third byte in the network address, leaving only the fourth byte to describe nodes on the subnet.

Upon configuring the network interface card on a host, using the `ifconfig` command, you will be required to specify the IP address and optionally the subnet mask. Failing to specify the subnet mask causes the address to revert to the structure for that particular class. Otherwise, the subnet mask you specify is applied against the IP address. As a rule, you are required to assign a value of 1 to those bits in the mask that correspond in position to the bits that you want IP to treat as a network address. As such, the default subnet masks corresponding to classes A, B, and C are `255.0.0.0`, `255.255.0.0`, and `255.255.255.0`, respectively.

There is no absolute requirement that you use an entire byte from the node address for the extension of the network address. In fact, you can set the mask to any number of bits, contiguous or not, to subnet your network. It is recommended, however, that you stick to a contiguous bit set because it is simpler to administer IP address assignment this way. The number of extra bits you need in order to extend the network address beyond the default is determined by the number of subnets you are planning to accommodate. If you are planning on a maximum of four subnets, you need to borrow only two extra bits from the node ID.

To develop a better feel for how subnet masking works, consider the case of extending a class B address by two bits. Figure 4.6a shows the default subnet mask (255.255.0.0), in case you don't want to break the network into smaller ones. Figure 4.6b, however, shows both the value of the applicable subnet mask (255.255.192.0) you have to pass to ifconfig when configuring the network interface card, and the new applicable address structure. As you can see, only 14 bits are left in this case for node identification on the subnets. If, instead, you decide to borrow the first three contiguous bits of the third byte of the node address for subnetting, the subnet mask becomes 255.255.224.0, in which case the network can be broken into eight subnets.

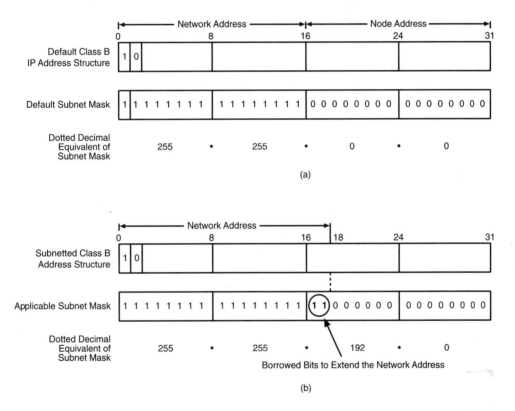

Figure 4.6. *Default subnet mask and two-bit extended subnet mask of a class B network.*

Figure 4.7 shows the effect of the subnet mask on the interpretation of the class B IP address of 148.29.179.27. In Figure 4.7a, because the subnet mask is left at the default value of 255.255.0.0, the IP address is interpreted following the standard (that is, 148.29 designates the network, and 179.27 designates a host on that network).

A subnet mask of 255.255.192.0, however, changes the perspective a bit. As you can see in Figure 4.7b, bits 0 through 17 now designate the network (or more precisely, the subnetwork), whereas bits 18 through 31 designate the host on the subnetwork.

Thus, in our example, all workstations that are on the same subnetwork as hosts 148.29.179.27 must have the 16th and 17th bits set to 1 and 0 respectively (a 192 network mask), in addition to having the binary equivalent of 148.29 in common. Some users apply the dotted decimal notation to interpret the address in Figure 4.7b as node 51.27 on subnet 148.29.2.

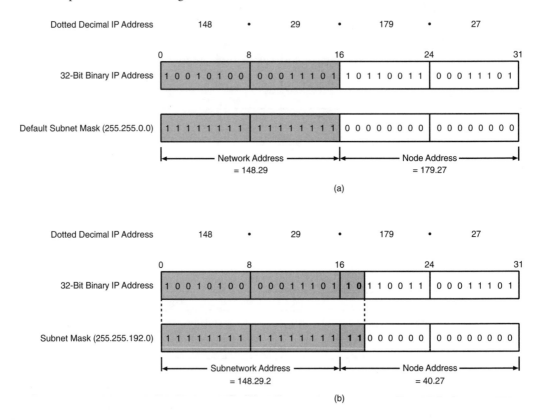

Figure 4.7. *Effect of the subnet mask on the interpretation of the same IP address.*

One last thing worth mentioning before leaving the topic on subnetting is that it is an internal matter, not recognized by the other networks to which the subnetted network might be connected.

Figure 4.8 illustrates what has just been said. In the figure, you are shown a two-subnetwork class B network connected via a router to a class C network. The class C network is left at the default mask, but the class B network subnet mask is set to 255.255.192.0. Although the latter mask allows for a maximum of four subnets, only two are being implemented. Now, as far as the hosts on the class C network are concerned, hosts on both subnets are *perceived* to belong to a class B network. Note that all network interfaces in hosts on both subnets must be configured to the same subnet mask (255.255.192.0). Failure to do so might produce undesirable results.

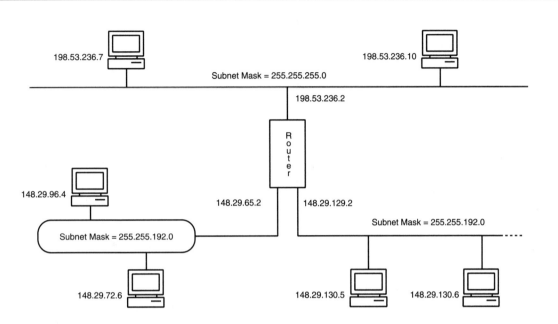

Figure 4.8. *A subnetted class B network appeals as one logical network to the class C network.*

Address Assignment Authority

You can see the need for assigning a unique IP address to each interface on the network. You can also see the need for a central address assignment authority whose main, if not sole, mandate is to ensure that no two interfaces share an IP address. This is particularly applicable to the global network of networks known as the Internet.

The Internet Network Information Center (InterNIC) is the central address assignment authority for the Internet. Organizations desiring connection are required to obtain a unique IP network address, which they can use on their own networks and on the Internet. The InterNIC authority assigns only the network portion of the IP address, leaving to organizations the freedom to assign the host addresses as they see fit.

Class C Address Assignment

As a matter of fact, you can get class C network numbers from Internet connection providers without applying directly to NIC. Internet connection providers are often delegated the authority to manage class C addresses, thus freeing up NIC to deal with larger organizations.

Section Summary

In the TCP/IP world, every host and device on the network is assigned a 32-bit symbolic IP address. IP addresses fall into three classes: class A, class B, and class C. When the full address uniquely identifies the host on the entire network, it is divided into two parts, one identifying the network, called the network address, and the second, called the host address.

The number of bytes identifying the network address versus those identifying the host address varies with the address class in use. IP networks can be reduced to multiple subnets by using the subnet mask feature. Subnet masks effectively allow for the extension of the network address, beyond its bit share of the IP address, by borrowing as many bits as needed from the host's share of the IP address.

Address Resolution Protocol (ARP)

The IP address you assign to a host is independent of the MAC address that is hardwired on the network interface card in that host. As such, every host (network interface) ends up maintaining two addresses: the IP address, which is significant to the TCP/IP protocols only, and the MAC address, which is significant to the network access layer only.

Data frames exchanged on the wire, however, rely on the MAC address, which indicates that there must be some sort of binding relation between these two forms of addresses. This section unravels this relationship. In particular, it shows how, given the IP address of a target host, the network access layer finds the corresponding MAC address, used later by the MAC protocol (for example, Ethernet) to communicate data frames with that host.

Figure 4.9 includes a depiction of the events that take place between two hosts when they try to communicate. In the diagram, both the IP address and the MAC layer addresses are shown for both hosts. It is assumed that a user on host jade wants to establish a telnet session with host orbit.

The following sequence shows what happens in this situation:

1. As a result of the user entering the command telnet jade, the application (that is, telnet in this case) resolves the name jade to its corresponding IP address. See the note that follows for an introductory description of name resolution under TCP/IP (more details are provided in Chapter 6). By the end of this stage, telnet will have determined that host jade's address is 148.27.34.1.

2. Next, telnet passes the address (148.27.34.1) to TCP/IP and requests connection to the target host. Subsequently, TCP packages the request in a TCP header and passes it with the address to the IP protocol, requesting delivery to the corresponding host.

3. At this point, IP compares jade's address with other destination addresses included in its routing database. Because both the source and the target host have the same network ID (148.27.0.0), IP decides to make a direct delivery to jade. Subsequently, IP encapsulates

the request passed to it by TCP in an IP datagram, including the destination (148.27.34.1) and source (148.27.2.5) IP addresses. Then it submits the datagram, with jade's IP address, to the network access layer for delivery on the physical network.

4. This is where ARP comes in to handle the resolution of the IP address, which is useless from Ethernet's point of view (assuming Ethernet at the MAC layer), to a MAC address that Ethernet understands. Put differently, ARP translates the symbolic address, assigned by the administrator, to the corresponding physical address that the host uses to identify itself at the physical and data link levels.

ARP handles address resolution by sending out of the MAC interface (for example, Ethernet) a broadcast message known as an *ARP request*, which simply says, "I, host 147.27.2.5, physically addressable at 0x0000c015ad18, want to know the physical address of host 147.27.34.1." Of all the hosts that receive the broadcast, only jade responds, using a directed ARP response packet, which says, "I am 147.27.34.1, and my physical address is 0x00001b3b21b2."

5. At this point, both hosts become aware of the other's physical identity. The network access layer (on host orbit) then proceeds to the actual phase of data exchange by encapsulating the IP datagram, which it kept on hold until the ARP query was favorably answered, in a data frame and sending it to host jade.

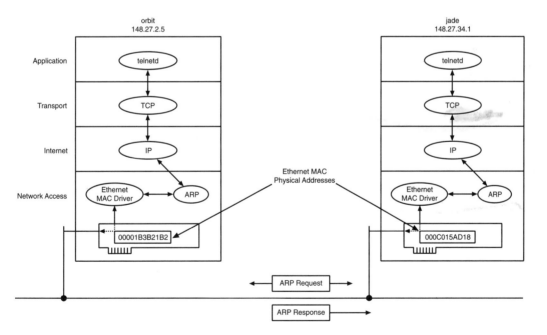

Figure 4.9. *IP address to physical MAC address resolution using ARP protocol.*

> **Note:** TCP/IP protocol suites define what is known as name services. Name services relieve users from the tedious and inconvenient task of entering target host IP addresses, simply by allowing them to specify a name designating that host. The *simplest* method of mapping the host name to its actual IP address involves the use of a hosts file, which is normally maintained in the /etc directory of every host. The hosts file is an ASCII file with two columns—the IP address column and the host name column—similar to the following one:
>
> ```
> #IP address       host name
>
> ...               ...
>
> 148.27.34.1       jade
>
> 148.27.2.5        orbit
>
> ...               ...
> ```
>
> When a user enters telnet jade, one way for telnet to find the corresponding IP address is by consulting the /etc/hosts database.

ARP Cache

When an IP address is resolved to its equivalent MAC address, ARP maintains the mapping in its own special ARP cache memory, improving transmission efficiency and the response time to user requests. Another benefit of ARP caching is the bandwidth saving realized by not requiring that a host send an ARP request broadcast every time it has data to send to the same target host.

ARP cache can be checked using the arp command as shown here:

```
$ arp -a
jade <100.0.0.10> at 0:0:1b:3b:21:b2
```

How long ARP maintains an entry in its cache table is a function of how often the host communicates with a specific host, and vendor implementation.

Proxy ARP

Proxy ARP is an implementation of ARP at the router that is designed to handle ARP queries on behalf of hosts on remote networks. Take a look at Figure 4.10. With proxy ARP on the router, whenever jade sends out an ARP query requesting the MAC address corresponding to IP address 129.34.2.6, the following events take place:

1. The ARP request broadcast is picked up by the router.

2. If the router recognizes the address as one belonging to a network it can reach, it responds to the "ARPing" host with its own MAC address. Otherwise, it discards the request silently.

3. From here, data destined to host emerald is delivered directly to the router, which in turn routes the data to emerald. (How? Remember that routers route data based on the IP address embedded in the IP header, which in this case will be emerald's.)

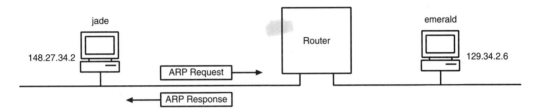

Figure 4.10. *Proxy ARP on the router handles ARP queries on behalf of remote hosts on the network. Proxy ARP captures an ARP request broadcast, which host* jade *sent out inquiring about the MAC address pertaining to host* emerald. *It responds to host* jade *using an ARP response containing the router MAC address.*

Internals of IP Routing

Chapter 2, "Overview of TCP/IP," introduced IP protocol features and functions. That chapter touched on routing concepts without going into much detail about the governing internal mechanisms that enforce IP's routing configuration and decisions. Given what has been learned in this chapter, it's time to present those details. Following are the relevant IP topics that will be covered in this section:

◆ Routing algorithm

◆ Routing information table

◆ Maintenance of routing information table

Routing Algorithm

Figure 4.11 shows the algorithm depicting the IP routing mechanism. When IP is given a datagram to route, it first matches the network address with that of its own. If the addresses match, the host belongs to the same network, and IP delivers the datagram directly to the designated host. If not, IP searches its routing database, known as the routing information table (RIT), attempting find the address of the next router, which it *trusts* to be closer to the designated destination. If one is found, the datagram is forwarded to that router.

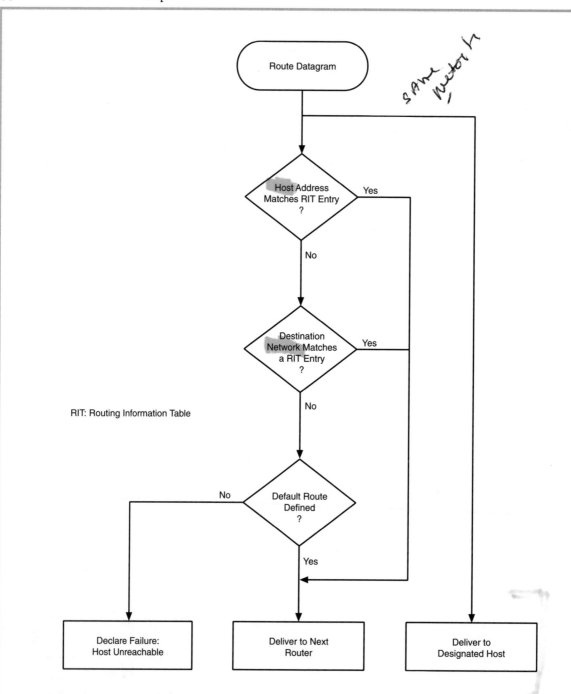

Figure 4.11. Depiction of IP routing algorithm.

IP searches the RIT table in the following order:

1. It first searches RIT for a specific route to the designated host. It does this by matching the complete host address (that is, including both network and host address) with the complete host addresses included in RIT.

2. Should the specific route search fail, an attempt is made to find a matching network address (the host address is ignored in the search). In this attempt, IP tries to find a router that is closer than the network to which the host is attached. For example, if the designated host is 145.34.23.1, and assuming a subnet mask of 255.255.0.0, only 145.34.0.0 is compared, rather than trying to match the entire address.

3. If matching the network address fails, IP looks through the RIT database for a default route entry. The default route includes the address of a default router, to which IP datagrams should be forwarded should both of the preceding searches fail. This should not imply that the default router is closer to the designated network. As a matter of fact, it might not even know how to handle routing to that network. The default router is just a last resort if everything else fails. What happens if the default router is not capable of forwarding the datagram any further depends on how that router is configured.

Routing Information Table (RIT)

A generic routing table is presented in Chapter 1, "Overview of Data Communications." The table includes information concerning the reachability of each route that the routing protocol in the host or router is aware of. The table includes the following information (see Figure 1.10) on each destination:

◆ *Distance:* Serves as an indication of how far the destination is from the host or router. Normally, it is equal to the number of intervening routers the datagram has to go through to reach its ultimate destination.

◆ *Next Router:* Includes the address of the router that is trusted to be closer to the destination, and therefore the one a datagram should be forwarded to in the delivery.

◆ *Output Port:* Specifies which of the interfaces in the host (if multihomed) or router is attached to the same network as the next router. The datagram should then be forwarded to that router.

IP's routing table is very similar to the generic table just discussed, as demonstrated using the UNIX netstat command. netstat is a feature-rich command that enables you, in addition to looking up the routing table of IP, to gather meaningful statistics that can be used in troubleshooting the network (more on this in Chapter 4). For the time being, netstat is used only to display routing information maintained by the UNIX kernel. To do this, enter netstat -rn, in which r stands for routing tables and n displays the next router's IP address, not its symbolic name:

```
$netstat -rn
Routing tables
```

```
Destination      Gateway          Flags    Refs    Use    Interface
127.0.0.1        127.0.0.1        UH       1       0      lo0
87.45.3.4        198.53.237.20    UGH      0       0      e3B0
100              100.0.0.2        U        4       51     wdn0
221.78.39        198.53.237.20    UG       0       0      e3B0
default          198.53.237.5     UG       0       0      e3B0
198.53.237       198.53.237.1     U        3       624    e3B0
```

Here is how to interpret the preceding information:

◆ The Destination column includes both specific destination addresses (that is, full host addresses), as shown in the first and second entries, and network addresses (that is, with host address bits set to 0), as shown in the remaining lines.

◆ The Gateway column includes the address of the next router. In line 2, for example, if IP is requested to deliver a datagram to host 87.45.3.4, it would have to forward it to the gateway (router) at 198.53.237.20.

◆ The Flags column describes the status of the route. Table 4.2 summarizes the flags and their meanings.

Table 4.2. Flags supported by IP routing table as reported by the UNIX kernel.

Flag	Meaning
U	The route is up.
H	If set, the route leads to a specific host (that is, the destination is a complete host address). Otherwise, the destination address pertains to a network. This flag is normally set on PPP-configured interfaces.
G	If set, the route is indirectly accessible via other routers. Otherwise, the route is direct (that is, the router has one of its interfaces directly attached to the destination).
D	If set, it implies that the route was created by an ICMP protocol route redirect message.
M	If set, it implies that the route was modified by an ICMP protocol route redirect message.

◆ The Refs column shows the number of active connections over that route. Every ftp and telnet session (both use TCP) established over that route increments this field by 1.

◆ The Use column contains the number of packets (datagrams) that have used this route since TCP/IP was started.

◆ The Interface column gives the name of the local interface. The interface name (or label) is assigned by UNIX upon configuring the network interface card. For example, e3B0 and wdn0, reported by the netstat command shown previously, refer to 3C503 and WD8003E network interface cards, respectively. The interface designated in the routing table is the one from which the datagram should be forwarded to the next router.

The previously shown example routing table pertains to host jade in Figure 4.12. The first line refers to the localhost or loopback interface. Datagrams addressed to the localhost do not show on the wire.

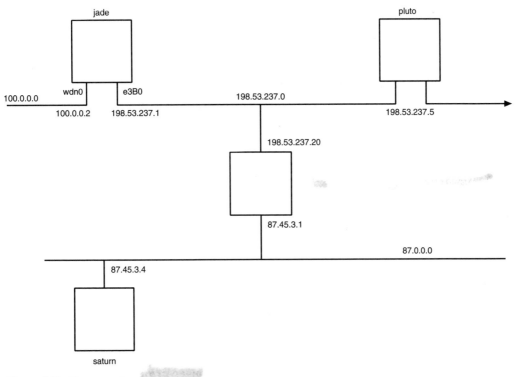

Figure 4.12. *IP-connected network.*

The second entry pertains to a host address (87.45.3.4), which explains the H flag. The G flag, however, implies that saturn (the host's symbolic name) is indirectly accessible. The next router to which to forward the datagram is at 198.53.237.20. The datagram is deliverable by interface e3B0.

The third entry, in contrast to the second one, refers to a network address (and hence the H flag is not set). With G not set, it can be concluded that the destination network is directly accessible out of host jade's interface wdn0. The IP address of the next router in this case is that of the wdn0 interface itself, *not* that of any other router.

In light of what has been said so far, it should be easy for you to interpret the fourth and sixth entries. The fifth entry is, however, worth discussing. This entry simply refers to all other routes (that is, routes not explicitly included in the routing table). Whenever jade wants a datagram delivered to a route that is not explicitly included in the routing table, it forwards the datagram to the default router, which in this case is 198.53.237.5 (host saturn).

Routing Table Maintenance

IP supports both static and dynamic means of maintaining the routing table. Although static configuration is partially handled when the network interface drivers are initialized, the network administrator has the option of suppressing dynamic configuration for reasons that will be mentioned later.

Static Route Maintenance

A network interface can be configured using one of two commands: `ifconfig` and `configure`. Of the configuration parameters, the network administrator has to specify both the associated IP address and the applicable subnet mask if subnetting the network. To configure the `wdn0` interface card using `ifconfig`, you would enter

```
$ ifconfig wdn0 100.0.0.2  255.0.0.0
```

in which `100.0.0.2` is the IP address you want to assign to the interface, and `255.0.0.0` is the subnet mask (the default mask, in this example). This command also updates the routing table with a static and direct route to destination `100.0.0.0` (setting no other flag but the `U` flag), in which the address of the next router is that of the interface itself (see the output of the `netstat -rn` command shown previously).

---

ifconfig

As explained in Chapter 9, "Installing and Configuring TCP/IP," `ifconfig` makes temporary changes to the network interface. Rebooting the system reconfigures the interface to old settings. For a permanent effect, you should use the `netconfig` command.

Hence, at a minimum, you should expect to see as many statically configured routes included in your routing table as there are configured network interfaces plus one (that of the loopback interface). Looking back at the output of the `netstat -rn` command, routes pertaining to addresses `100` and `198.53.237` are similarly entered.

In addition to the interface configuration commands, UNIX allows for the manual addition of static routes using the `route add` command. The command uses the syntax

```
route add destination_address next_router metric
```

in which

> *destination_address* is the route you want to add to the routing table,
>
> *next_router* is the address of the next router to forward datagrams to, and

metric is a measure of distance to the destination, normally expressed in number of intervening routers.

The following example shows how route add can be used to add a new destination to the routing table:

```
$ route add 87.45.3.4  198.53.237.20  1
```

The following route add command adds the default route entry to the routing table:

```
$ route add 0.0.0.0 198.53.237.5
```

Dynamic Route Maintenance

Aside from using tools such as ifconfig and route add to update the routing table, IP routers, on the internetwork, are equipped with the capability to dynamically update their routing tables. This is achieved by employing special protocols for the purpose of collecting and exchanging information about the reachability of other destinations. The exchange of *network reachability* information takes the form of regular updates, which each router sends down the wire to other routers.

Over time, TCP/IP defined several protocol sets for the exchange of routing information. Each set pertains to a different historic phase in the evolution of the Internet routing architecture.

Initially, the Internet defined a hierarchical architecture that was primarily based on a centralized view of routing. ARPANET served as the *core* backbone of the Internet, which served as the central medium that remote regional networks utilized for the exchange of data among themselves (see Figure 4.13). Special routers, with special routing protocol capabilities, were defined for use on the core backbone. Those routers, known as core gateways, are governed by mechanisms defined by the *Gateway-to-Gateway Protocol (GGP)*. GGP routers are responsible for the central collection and processing of routing information that the core network receives from the regional networks connected to it.

Member networks on the Internet are grouped into what is known as *autonomous systems* (AS). An autonomous system is a group of networks and gateways with its own mechanism and rules for the collection and distribution of network reachability information. The defined mechanisms and rules are implemented in what are known as *Interior Gateway Protocols* (IGP) and *Exterior Gateway Protocols* (EGP).

Whereas an IGP router is responsible for the collection and flow of information within the autonomous system itself, EGP routers are responsible for the flow of information to the core network. Information received by the core is centrally processed and distributed to core routers by the GGP protocol.

The Internet grew from this hierarchical architecture into something that is more of a *peer* architecture. This growth was motivated by the exponential increase in demand on the processing resources of the core network due to the tremendous increase in the size of the routing information that core routers had to handle centrally.

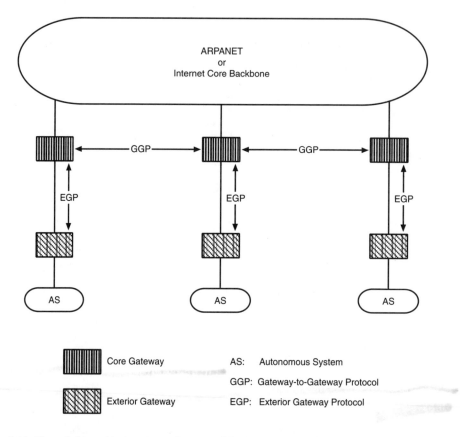

Figure 4.13. *The early hierarchical routing architecture of the Internet.*

Under peer architecture, all autonomous systems are regarded as peer *routing domains*, sharing equal responsibility in the collection and distribution of network reachability information within their individual domains and across domain boundaries (see Figure 4.14). A new protocol, the Border Gateway Protocol (BGP), was defined for the interdomain exchange of routing information and was intended to replace EGP. Domains implemented in this fashion reduced the processing burden on the core network as processing routing information became an individual responsibility of each domain.

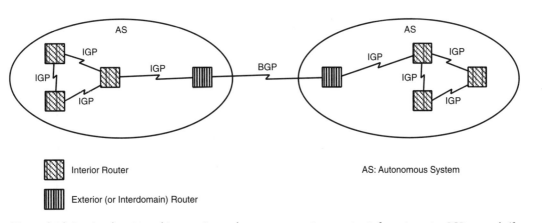

Figure 4.14. *Routing domains architecture. Internal routers communicate routing information using IGP protocols (for example, RIP, OSPF, and HELLO), whereas interdomain routing is handled by routers supporting BGP protocols.*

Routing Daemons

UNIX currently supports two routing daemons. These are routed and gated. routed is the most commonly run daemon, and it supports only the *Routing Information Protocol* (RIP), the most popular of all IGPs.

gated, on the other hand, is the more recent daemon, and it supports both IGP and EGP protocols. In addition to RIP, gated supports protocols such as *Open Shortest Path First* (OSPF) and *HELLO*.

The choice of which daemon to run is largely a matter of network size, and whether your network belongs to an autonomous system connecting to other networks on the Internet. In most cases, routed is sufficient. It makes more sense, however, to employ gated on large networks, or networks that are autonomously administered. The savings realized in processing power, and the gain in speed at which network convergence occurs (more on network convergence later in this chapter), are significant.

Routing Information Protocol

RIP protocol (RFC 1058) operates at the application layer of the TCP/IP architecture. It relies on UDP, at the transport layer, for the exchange of routing information among routers. Figure 4.15 shows the relationship between the RIP message, the UDP header, and the IP header.

A router uses RIP messages to request routing information or to propagate (that is, advertise) its own routing table. RIP allows the advertisement of a maximum of 25 routes per message. Among the information included in the route advertisement are the network *IP address* and the *metric* (see Figure 4.16).

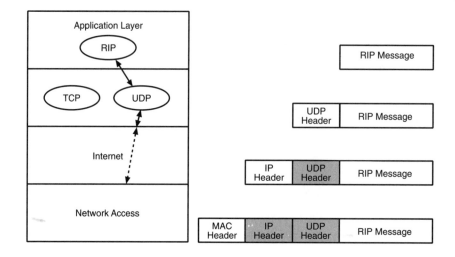

Figure 4.15. *RIP in relation to lower layer protocols.*

The metric (also referred to as the hop count) provides an indication as to how far the destination is from the advertising router. It is normally expressed in number of intervening routers. Of the other fields in the RIP message, the *command* field can be set to one of six defined commands. Of these commands, only two will be mentioned: a command of 1 to imply a *RIP request,* and 2 to imply a *RIP response.*

The *version* field refers to the version of RIP in use (currently, RIP is at version level 2). The *address family* specifies the protocol address family being advertised, which is currently IP only, and correspondingly, the address family field is always set to 2.

The following discussion explains how RIP works and is based on Figure 4.17. Shown in the diagram are two routers, R1 and R2, connected to three networks—two Ethernets and a Token-ring network. As previously discussed, when you initially bring up a router, it initializes its routing information table to directly connected routes. Figure 4.17a illustrates this, by including two entries per router only. In most cases, a directly connected route is assigned metric one.

After initialization, the router sends out a RIP request message, in which it advertises its routing table. This informs other neighboring routers of routes it can reach, while requesting that they send their own routing tables. So if in the diagram it is assumed that R1 was powered up last, R1 will send its limited routing table in the first RIP request it propagates. R2 receives the RIP request and examines the propagated table to discover that it can reach a new route (100.0.0.0) with R1's help. R2 consequently updates its own routing table (see Figure 4.17b), including the address (25.10.1.1) of R1 on the common network. One important observation to make is that R2 incremented the metric, assigned to the new route, by 1 to become 2. This means that the route is now 2 hops (or routers) away.

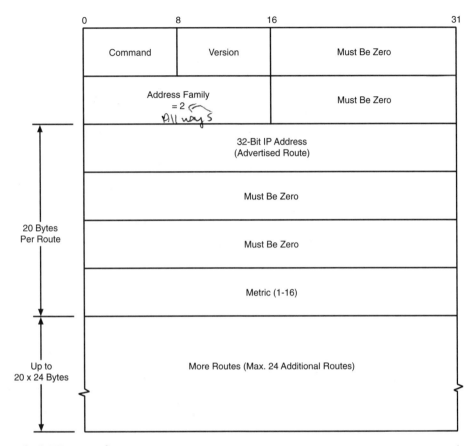

Figure 4.16. RIP message format.

In response to R1's RIP request, R2 responds with its own routing table. Now, R1 discovers a new route (130.25.0.0), which it can reach with R2's help. R1 updates its routing table with the new route it just discovered.

On a larger network, both routers would have received many more replies that could have brought about a significant increase in the size of the routing table. It is possible, however, that two or more routers advertise the same route. That is when the route-associated metric becomes important. A router always sticks to the path with the lowest metric, for it means a lower number of intervening routers, qualifying the path as being the *shortest* one.

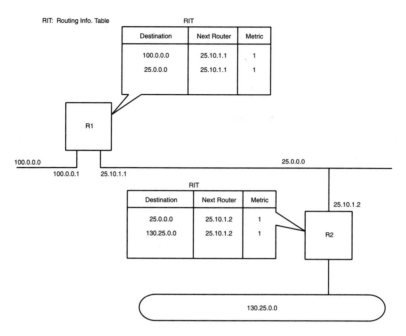

(a) Before RIP Exchange

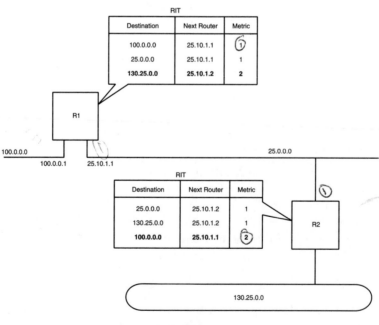

(b) After RIP Exchange

Figure 4.17. *RIP messages help a router discover new routes that other routers are aware of. Shown are the routing information tables of both routers (a) before and (b) after the exchange of RIP messages.*

Two more things to mention about metrics:

◆ The maximum value that a metric can reach is 16, which implies that the destination is infinitely far, and therefore unreachable. On an internetwork, no more than 15 routers should be intervening between any two networks, imposing a limit on the size an internetwork can reach. By default, packets that try to make more than 16 hops are discarded.

◆ When adding a route using the `route add` command, you have the option of incurring any metric you want up to a maximum of 16. One reason for doing that is to discourage other network devices from using this route as long as other alternatives are available.

Other Dynamic Routing Options

RIP belongs to the *distance-vector* family of routing protocols. The distance-vector connotation is derived from the nature of the information that RIP and other family members collect and compile in their routing tables (that is, route is the vector, and metric is the distance).

Distance-vector routing protocols, including RIP, have the advantage of being robust and easy to implement. They were also among the first to arrive in the routing industry. These features made them popular, in both the user and the vendor communities.

RIP has three serious shortcomings, however:

◆ The RIP message format does not leave any room for including a subnet mask as part of the advertised route. This makes it confusing, for routers, to differentiate between subnet IP addresses and host names.

◆ Because the maximum a metric value can reach is 16, RIP is more suitable for small to medium networks.

◆ Being a member of the distance-vector family of routing protocols, RIP suffers from slow *convergence*. Convergence is the time it takes a network to stabilize after a route update is reported. The longer it takes the update to spread across the network, the higher is the risk of having datagrams misrouted and lost. Slow convergence is attributable to what is known as the *count-to-infinity* problem.

In Figure 4.18, under stable conditions, routers R2 and R3 calculate the hop count to network A, based on information propagated by R1 when it initialized. Initially, the R1, R2, and R3 routing tables show that they are respectively one, two, and three hops away from network A. Should R3 fail, R2 does not detect the failure. Instead, it times out on the current route information it maintained about network A, ending up using reachability information propagated by R3 as part of its routine route advertisement.

Because R3 is advertising a hop count of 3 from network A, R2 updates its metric to become 4 hops (that is, 3+1). Afterward, R2 reports the change to its neighboring routers (only R3 in this case), informing them that it discovered a four-hop route to A. Because, under stable conditions,

R3 is described as the next router to network A in R2's routing table, the latter is forced to update its metric to 5 hops (that is, 4+1). This cycle of vicious updates keeps bouncing back and forth between R2 and R3 until the metric reaches infinity (that is, 16), at which time it is detected that the network is unreachable.

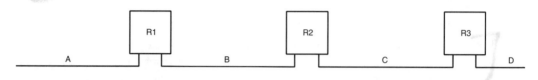

Figure 4.18. *The count-to-infinity problem.*

Several other protocols were developed to solve some or all of the previously mentioned problems. A new revision of RIP (version 2) was introduced (RFC 1388) that takes care of the subnet mask, among other improvements, making it a recognizable part of the RIP message. However, the most significant improvement on routing mechanisms came along with a new family of routing protocols known as *link-state* protocols. In TCP/IP, Open Shortest Path First (OSPF) (specified in RFC 1247) represents this new generation of protocols.

Open Shortest Path First

The count-to-infinity problem with distance-vector routing protocols, including RIP, stems from the way they collect and process reachability information, and the nature of this information (that is, hop counts). As discussed earlier, RIP routers rely on secondhand information to calculate and build their routing table.

In Figure 4.18, router R3 derived its information about route A from information propagated by R2, not R1. R3 *trusts* R2 for whatever it advertises as reachable and draws conclusions accordingly (simply by incrementing the metric by one, with no regard paid to actual validity of the information received). This left the system of route information interchange vulnerable to corruption as link conditions change or routers break down.

Instead of exchanging distance-vector information, OSPF routers exchange information about the status of links to which they directly attach. An OSPF router reports the status of each of its direct links to the neighboring routers sharing those links with it. Reported data includes link status and a metric (that is, hop count). The packet exchanged is known as a *Link State Protocol* (LSP) packet. Routers receiving the LSP packet copy it to their system, and in turn forward the packet, unmodified, down the network to their respective neighbor routers. This way, every router on the network will have an exact copy of the original LSP packet put on the wire by its peers. A router uses these LSP packets gathered to build a complete routing table.

A big plus of OSPF is rapid convergence. Because all routers use firsthand information in building their route tables, when a link or a router breaks down, routers know about it quickly. This happens either by virtue of timing out on the updates that the failing router was supposed to routinely propagate, or by virtue of an update sent from the router connected to the failing link to its neighbors.

Some features OSPF supports are subnet masks, multiple routes to the same destination, load balancing, *dimensionless metrics*, and *unnumbered networks*.

OSPF is capable of calculating, and supporting, multiple routes leading to the same destination. Each route might also be supporting a different type of service. OSPF uses two or more routes, with the same metric, for load balancing purposes by trying to split data traffic equally among them. This yields an improved overall throughput.

Dimensionless metrics, which OSPF supports, include such factors as link speed, reliability, and link congestion. A router connected to a noisy or 56 Kbps link can assign it a higher metrix than a less noisy Ethernet 10 Mbps link. In doing so, an OSPF router is effectively trying to discourage other routers from forwarding packets to it for delivery on the poor link, should there be other alternatives.

Finally, unnumbered networks refer to a feature by which direct point-to-point links (that is, dial-up and leased links) need not be assigned IP addresses at both ends. Figure 4.19 illustrates this feature.

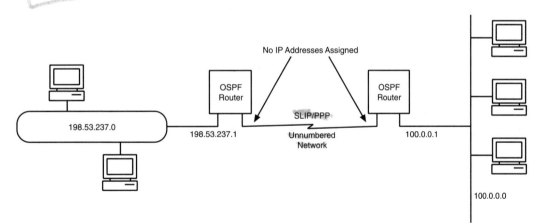

Figure 4.19. *OSPF routers support unnumbered networks. As shown previously, an unnumbered network refers to a point-to-point link with no IP addresses assigned at either end of the link.*

Internet Control Message Protocol (ICMP)

ICMP (introduced in Chapter 2, "Overview of TCP/IP") is another means for configuring the routing table. You know from Chapter 2 that ICMP sends out messages that influence IP's behavior and routing on the network. Of particular interest are the following messages:

◆ *Host or network unreachable error message:* A router sends this message whenever it detects an anomaly that prevents it from delivering, or forwarding, a datagram to its destination.

◆ *Host and network route redirect message:* A router sends this message to the source host or router when the datagram should have been forwarded to another router. Route redirects are normally sent whenever the router detects that the outgoing interface it is going to use to forward the datagram is the one that received it. This implies that the sending host, the receiving router, and the router to which the host was redirected all belong to the same network. When a host or a router receives a route redirect message, they modify their routing table to accommodate the suggested route. The change is applied to the routing table only after the host, or router, verifies that the new router is connected to the same network.

In addition to these messages, some UNIX systems (Solaris 2.*x*) support ICMP router discovery messages. This new set of ICMP messages allows a host, or a router, to send ICMP router solicitation messages requesting that routers send their routing tables.

Participating routers can respond with router advertisement messages. Soliciting hosts and routers use the advertisement messages to initialize their routing tables. A host that supports these messages uses solicitation messages at boot time to initialize its routing table. Whenever it receives the first router advertisement, it stops soliciting. Routers behave differently in that, after power up, they keep advertising at a random rate, whether solicited to do so or not.

Summary

The IP routing protocol is the cornerstone of TCP/IP networks. All data exchange is carried by IP datagrams. For IP to deliver datagrams to their designated hosts without any confusion, IP requires that each host, router, or other device participating on the network be assigned a 32-bit IP address.

IP network addresses belong to three main classes: class A, class B, and class C. TCP/IP defines the address structure pertaining to each class such that a certain number of bits is reserved to designate the network, and the remaining ones are used to designate individual hosts on *that* network. The number of reserved bits for the network address is a function of the network class.

For many different reasons, having to do with the size, geography, or organization, a network might have to be broken into smaller subnets. IP achieves this task by allowing the network administrator the freedom to borrow as many bits from the node bits as are needed.

The IP protocol relies on a routing information table to function properly. The routing information table can be influenced either by commands the administrator enters on the UNIX host or by protocols such as RIP and OSPF.

Both RIP, a distance-vector type of protocol, and OSPF, which is a link-state protocol, are known as routing information protocols. They are given the responsibility of route discovery, and updating the routing information table according to what they discover. OSPF, the newer protocol, is aimed at overcoming many of RIP's pitfalls, most notable of which is the slow convergence inherent to the design of RIP (that is, the count-to-infinity problem). Among other means of modifying the routing table, TCP/IP supports a set of ICMP messages, of which route redirect and destination unreachable are most common.

Routing protocols are run by special UNIX daemons. These are routed and gated. routed is the older and the most common. It supports only RIP. The gated daemon, on the other hand, supports both RIP and OSPF. Depending on your routing requirements, you will have to run one or the other. Chapter 9, "Installing and Configuring TCP/IP," provides the guidelines that can help you make the decision.

Exercises

Because IP routing is such a difficult concept to master, a supplementary Exercise section is included here to help you determine your level of understanding.

4.1. If the subnet mask is set to 255.255.192.0, which of the following IP addresses correspond to hosts belonging to the same subnetwork:

```
148.29.179.40
148.29.157.81
148.29.92.64
148.29.147.22
```

4.2. Using the ping command, network administrators can check on the reachability of hosts on the same or a remote network. Study the syntax of ping on your system, and use it to test reachability of hosts you are aware of.

4.3. In Figure 4.20, host B can reach both interfaces of router R2 but cannot talk to any of the hosts other than those on its own network. Host A, on the other hand, can talk to multihomed host R2 at address 35.0.0.1 but not via the other interface (for example, an ftp session with target address 45.0.0.1 consistently fails), and neither can it reach any host on 45.0.0.0 network. Also, host A can talk across R1 to any host on the Token-ring network 25.0.0.0.

What do you think is causing the problem? It is required that all hosts should be able to talk to each other regardless of where they belong. No security fire walls are in place. What command would you use to troubleshoot the problem?

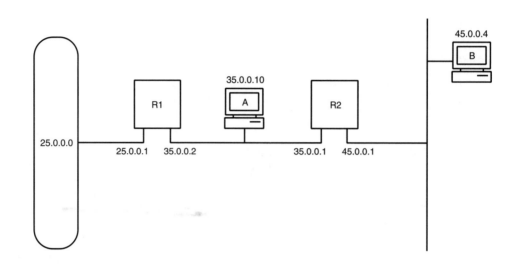

Figure 4.20. *A hypothetical network, relevant to Exercise 4.3.*

4.4. Identify, in the /etc/conf/cf.d/stune, two network configurable parameters.

4.5. Check the syntax of the ripquery command, and discuss its usefulness to the trouble-shooting exercise presented in Exercise 4.3.

4.6. In Figure 4.21, host A has just been powered up with R1 as the default router. The user enters the command

    $ ftp 45.0.0.4

to establish a file transfer session with host B.

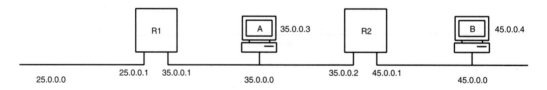

Figure 4.21. *A hypothetical network, relevant to Exercise 4.6.*

If you had the chance to enter netstat -rn before and after the user issued the preceding ftp command, what do you think you will see that's different?

CHAPTER 5

♦

The Host-to-Host Transport Layer

Introduction

The host-to-host transport layer is similar to the transport layer of the OSI model (see Figure 5.1). TCP/IP defines two transport protocols, the User Datagram Protocol (UDP) and the Transmission Control Protocol (TCP). Chapter 2, "Overview of TCP/IP," provided an overview of these protocols. In this chapter, a more detailed discussion will be presented about TCP/IP.

In particular, you will be looking at how TCP/IP implements the sliding window mechanism for improved transmission efficiency and flow control, as well as connection establishment and orderly connection termination mechanisms. The concept of data multiplexing and demultiplexing will be also revisited.

Before discussing the more intricate details of the TCP protocol, the chapter opens with a brief summary of both the UDP and the TCP transport protocols.

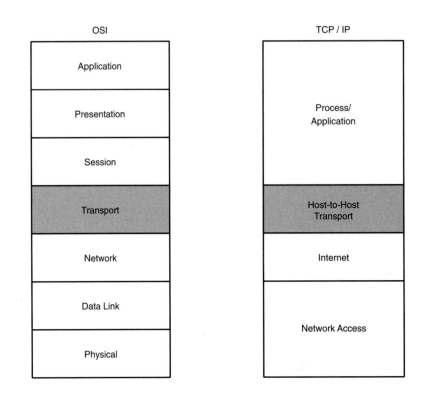

Figure 5.1. *The host-to-host transport layer and OSI.*

User Datagram Protocol

UDP is a connectionless, unreliable transport protocol. Being connectionless means that UDP does not undergo any handshaking mechanism, nor does it negotiate any control parameters with the destined peer before sending data to the remote end. Applications relying on UDP have to provide the means for error control, packet resequencing, and flow control.

Figure 5.2 shows the UDP datagram structure. It includes two 16-bit source and address destination port numbers (more details on this later), a 16-bit UDP length field, and a 16-bit checksum field.

The 16-bit checksum field is optionally used to check the integrity of the transmitted data, including the data field and the UDP header. If all checksum bits are set to 0, the receiving end assumes that integrity check on transmitted data is turned off. Otherwise, integrity check is turned on, and the receiving end is required to carry out the check. If its checksum of the received datagram matches what is being transmitted in the 16-bit checksum field, the data is assumed to be valid. Otherwise, UDP discards it as being erroneous.

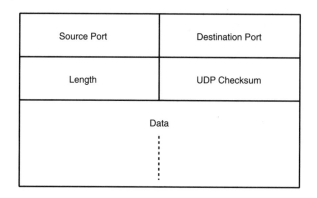

Source Port	Destination Port
Length	UDP Checksum
Data	

Figure 5.2. *UDP header.*

What if the checksum calculation yields a zero? In that case, the sending end sends an all-1s 16-bit checksum (that is, the ones-complement equivalent of zero). Hence, the rule is clear: An all-0s implies that the checksum field is disabled; otherwise, it is enabled. An all-1s field must be interpreted as a valid checksum of zero.

As you can see from the datagram field structure, UDP does not support data segmentation (also known as fragmentation and reassembly). This is another concern for applications to deal with. Applications that want this type of service on top of UDP might have to have this feature built into them.

Transmission Control Protocol (TCP)

TCP is a fully reliable connection-oriented protocol. Its header format is re-included here for your convenience (see Figure 5.3).

TCP safeguards data against loss, duplication, and damage arising from noise or physical failures on the wire. Following is a brief reminder of the main TCP features, some of which were discussed in Chapter 2, "Overview of TCP/IP." Other features will be introduced in this chapter.

◆ *Connection orientation:* TCP is a connection-oriented protocol. Before any user data is exchanged by applications, TCP has to undergo a handshake process, during which connection control parameters are negotiated and a *virtual circuit* connecting user applications is established. You'll find more on connection establishment and negotiable parameters later in this chapter.

◆ *Fragmentation and reassembly:* TCP is capable of breaking a large chunk of data into smaller segments that can be better accommodated on the underlying network.

◆ *Reliable transfer:* TCP achieves reliable data transfer by using sequence numbers, integrity checksums, acknowledgments, and retransmissions. Retransmissions are decided on by the value in the sequence number, acknowledgment number, and checksum fields.

◆ *Data stream orientation:* TCP transmits user data as unstructured streams of bits, aligned around boundaries of 8-bit bytes. TCP does not recognize any form of data structure such as records and fields, and its services are application independent. It is left to applications to decide how to structure the data they exchange.

◆ *Sliding-window technique:* TCP uses this technique for data transmission. This feature improves on the transmission efficiency by cutting the amount of time a connection is left idling. The sliding window technique, as implemented in TCP, also allows for the effective control of data flow.

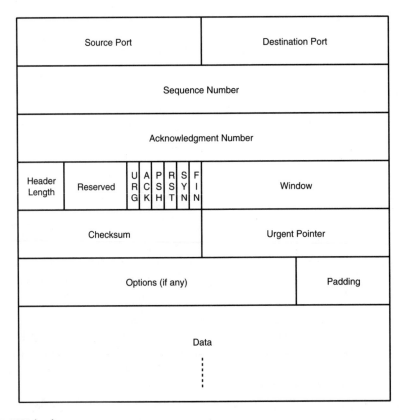

Figure 5.3. *TCP header.*

Data Ports Revisited

Source and destination port numbers (see Figures 5.2 and 5.3) are used at the transport layer to identify the upper layer applications from which data is received, and to which it should be submitted. The port number fields allow the transport layer to multiplex data pertaining to more than one application and to have it transmitted over the same physical connection.

How are the port numbers assigned? For two applications to exchange data, they clearly need to know the port number to use when addressing each other. Taking the telnet application as an example, a user only issues the host name on the command line to log in to a remote host. To establish the login session on behalf of the user, telnet must do two things:

1. First, it has to map the remote host name to the IP address assigned to that host. Name-to-address mapping is discussed in the next chapter.

2. Next, telnet has to determine the port number that accurately identifies its counterpart on the remote host.

TCP/IP approaches the solution to the second problem with a hybrid of two solutions. The first solution relies on a central authority that assigns fixed port numbers as needed and makes them publicly available so that other application developers avoid using them. Port numbers assigned this way are called *well-known port numbers*. They are reserved and are used to identify the applications to which they are assigned. Table 5.1 provides some examples of well-known port numbers. You can find more information about port assignments by looking at the /etc/services file on your system.

Table 5.1. Examples of well-known port numbers. Both UDP and TCP use them to reach services on remote hosts.

Port Number	Application	Description
11	users	Active users (recognized as systat)
13	daytime	Daytime
23	telnet	For remote login
25	smtp	E-mail protocol
53	nameserver	Named daemon (see next chapter)

In the example, therefore, the application (telnet) must have been built to recognize the fixed or well-known assignment (23) and should know how to use it to establish a login session.

The second approach to port assignment employs what is known as *dynamic binding*. Instead of assigning a fixed port number to an application, dynamic binding assigns it a number from a pool of numbers that are freely available for this purpose. Whenever an application protocol is brought up, it requests a number at which it can be reached. For a user on other hosts to reach this application, his host must send a probing packet to the target host, requesting that the application identify itself using the dynamically bound port number. After getting the response, the requesting host can proceed to the next phase of communicating with the target application.

The client application initiating a contact is almost always dynamically assigned a port number. This is because it is always possible for the client to identify itself when it initiates the contact. In the telnet example, the telnet client is assigned a dynamic number, normally drawn from the upper range of numbers. This port number might change the next time telnet is invoked. The telnet client, however, should consistently contact the telnet server on the target host using the same port number of 23 (see Table 5.1).

Connections and Endpoints

In addition to using the port number to identify the application, TCP pairs it with the host IP address to identify an endpoint of the connection over which data is being exchanged. It is possible to have more than one host simultaneously establish a connection with the same application on the same host. This possibility leaves identifying both endpoints of the connection using the source and destination port numbers somewhat unreliable. The pair (host IP, port number) leaves no ambiguity about the identity of either endpoint of the connection. Together, both endpoints identify the connection itself.

Here's an example: A user on a host with IP address 100.0.0.3 engages in a telnet session with another host whose IP address is 129.40.3.7. Assuming that the telnet client on 100.0.0.3 is assigned the port 1031, the connection endpoints become (100.0.0.3, 1031) and (129.40.3.7, 23), with the latter being that of the telnet server. Should another host with an IP address 178.45.6.4 start another connection to 129.40.3.7, a new connection will be created with (178.45.6.4, 1043) and (129.40.3.7, 23) serving as its endpoints. In both cases, at one end of the connection (the server end), the port number is fixed to 23, whereas the port number of the client end is 1031 in the former case and 1043 in the latter one.

Why do you need to know about connections and endpoints? Because TCP associates incoming data with the connection, not with the port, to deliver reliable service in situations in which more than one remote host is communicating data through the same port. As you will see later (in Chapter 15, "Network Troubleshooting and Performance Tuning"), you will be better able to troubleshoot TCP-dependent services if you have this knowledge.

Sliding Window Technique

TCP achieves its reliability by employing the *positive acknowledgment with retransmission* technique for the exchange of data (as discussed in Chapter 2, "Overview of TCP/IP"). If implemented in its simplest form, this technique might result in sizable loss of bandwidth. This is the result of idle times, during which a sending end has to wait for a positive acknowledgment for every data segment it sends before it can send the next one. This process is illustrated in Figure 5.4. This method of data transmission qualifies as a half-duplex scheme because only one end of the connection can transmit at a time. Bandwidth wasted on half-duplex transmission protocols can reach substantial levels, especially if data exchange is taking place over wide area and satellite links.

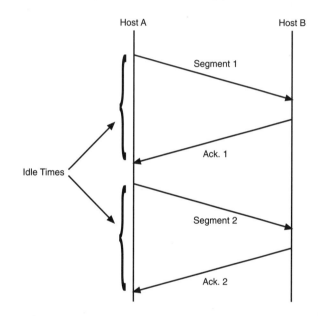

Figure 5.4. *Simple positive acknowledgment with retransmission technique. Notice how host A idles until an acknowledgment is received from host B.*

For better efficiency, an alternative technique known as the *sliding window* technique is being deployed by TCP/IP. This technique is not peculiar to TCP. Many other networking technologies have the sliding window capability built into their transport systems. This discussion will first present the generic concepts governing this technique. Afterward, it will highlight TCP-specific characteristics.

The sliding window technique improves performance by allowing a sending end to transmit multiple data segments before an acknowledgment is received. As shown in Figure 5.5, host A did not have to wait to get its first transmitted segment acknowledged before it sent the next two. Also notice how host B is sending the acknowledgment while host A is transmitting. This utilizes the link in full-duplex mode.

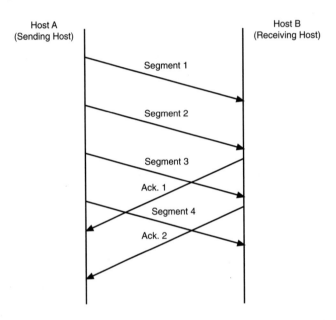

Figure 5.5. *The sliding window technique allows for the simultaneous transmission of data and acknowledgments.*

There is an upper limit on the number of segments that can be transmitted without acknowledgments. This limit is known as the sliding window size. Enforcing this limit helps in detecting transmission abnormalities early in the process. An unusual delay in receiving acknowledgments puts the sending host in a suspecting state, during which it stops transmission until the link is recovered (that is, until acknowledgments are received). Should the sending end fail to receive an acknowledgment within a predefined period, it reattempts transmission of all the unacknowledged segments.

To understand how the sliding window technique works, look at Figure 5.6. Assuming that the window size is set to five, the sender can transmit up to five segments without receiving any acknowledgment. Upon receiving acknowledgments, the sender slides its window by the number of acknowledged segments. The diagrams illustrate the state of transmitted segments at different phases of the process.

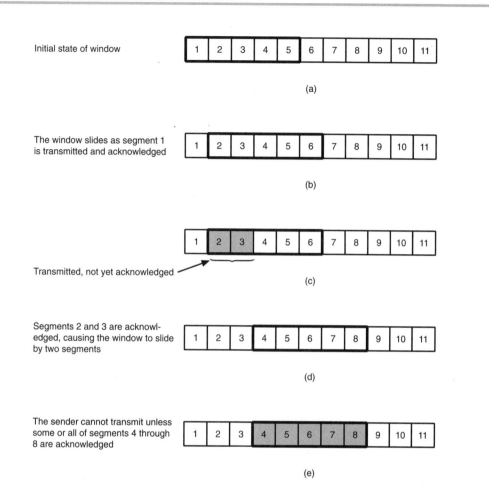

Figure 5.6. *Depiction of events governing the sliding window technique. The window size assumed in this depiction is five.*

To help illustrate the concept of the sliding window technique, a window is shown to enclose the number of segments equivalent to its size (five in this example). The shaded area represents packets that were transmitted and not yet acknowledged. Figure 5.6a reflects the initial state of the window before sending any data. Figure 5.6b indicates that the sender transmitted the first segment (and the only one so far) and had it acknowledged by the receiver. This made the sender *slide* its window to include segments two through six (that is, a total of five).

Figure 5.6c shows that the sender transmitted segments two and three and that they have not been acknowledged. Consequently, the sender can transmit only segments four through six before it stops sending, unless it receives an acknowledgment for some of the segments by the time the sixth is sent. According to Figure 5.6d, both segments two and three are acknowledged, which explains why the window slid to include segments four through eight. Finally, Figure 5.6e illustrates what happens should the sender transmit all data segments without receiving any acknowledgment. The window closes and the sender is bound to stop sending until some or all of the sent segments contained in the sliding window are acknowledged.

The window size is normally negotiated at connection startup time between peer protocols. The agreed on size should be carefully selected. A small size might increase network idleness. A window size of one, for example, reverts transmission to half-duplex mode. Too large a window size, on the other hand, might oversaturate the network and produce congestion and a subsequent rise in the error rate.

What if one data segment is received in a corrupt form? Some implementations of the sliding window technique allow for the selective rejection of the deformed segment, and the receiver asks the sender to retransmit only that segment. Other implementations, including the TCP protocol, require the sending end to retransmit all segments starting with the corrupted one, regardless of whether subsequent segments were transmitted reliably. The larger the window size, the worse this problem can become.

TCP's Sliding Window Technique

TCP's implementation of the sliding window technique is different from the generic one in two main aspects:

◆ Data transmission and reception operate at the byte level. The window size is expressed in the number of bytes, rather than data segments. With a window size of 40K, the sender can transmit only that many bytes before an acknowledgment is due, regardless of the number of segments it takes to reach the 40K limit.

◆ Under TCP, the window size is used to control the flow of data. This is achievable by allowing the window size to vary during the connection. As shown in Figure 5.3, the window size is piggybacked in the data segment itself, in the *window* field. As the receiver's communication buffers become full, it can send a smaller window size to the sending host. A window size of zero signals the sender to stop sending, after which transmission can be resumed only if the sender receives a nonzero window size.

Because TCP is a full-duplex protocol, it allows two hosts to exchange user data simultaneously. This implies that each host must maintain its own set of pointers. These are used for the maintenance of its own sliding window, and they keep track of outgoing traffic. Each host must also keep track of the incoming traffic it is receiving from the other host.

TCP Header Format Revisited

Now that you understand how data transmission is handled by TCP, the more complex fields of the TCP header can be discussed. Relevant to the discussion are the *sequence number*, the *acknowledgment number*, and the *SYN* and *ACK* code bits.

The sequence number is a cumulative field, used by the sender to inform the receiver of the total number of bytes that the receiver should have received including data carried by *this* segment. Assuming that a host initially sends 400 bytes in the first segment, the accompanying sequence number would be set to 400. If the second segment contains 800 bytes in the data field, the sender updates the sequence number to 1200 (400+800), and so on.

The acknowledgment number is also a cumulative field, used by the receiver to acknowledge all data received thus far. The number in this field should be set to the total received data bytes, plus one. In the example given in the preceding paragraph, should the receiver choose to acknowledge the first and second transmissions individually, the acknowledgment numbers would be set to 401 and 801.

Acknowledgments need not be sent separately from user data. A data segment can contain both a sequence number and an acknowledgment number. The former identifies the number of bytes that the *destination* host should have received so far; the latter acknowledges the data that the *source* host has received.

If set, the *SYN* code bit indicates that the sequence number is valid. Otherwise, the receiving end should ignore its contents. The SYN bit is set only in segments carrying data. Similarly, the *ACK* bit is set only when an acknowledgment is sent.

The *URG* code bit signals the receiving TCP that the data field includes urgent data and that the associated application protocol should be immediately notified of the event. If the URG bit is set, the *urgent pointer* is said to be valid. It specifies the position in the window where the urgent data ends.

The *PUSH* code bit was used to notify the receiving TCP of the need to push the data carried by the segment to the application protocol without delay. Most current implementations of TCP ignore this bit.

The *FIN* code bit is used to terminate a connection, and the *RST* bit is used to reset the connection.

TCP Scenarios

The use of TCP header information is illustrated in the following pages. You will be presented with three typical scenarios, depicting connection establishment, data exchange, and connection termination.

Connection Establishment

To establish a connection with its remote peer, TCP resorts to a *three-way handshake* routine. Figure 5.7 shows the proceedings of this phase. TCP in host A is the initiator of the connection. During the connection initiation phase, each host must randomly choose an initial sequence number that it will use to identify the data bytes it is sending (that is, the initial sequence number does not necessarily have to be set to one).

As shown in the diagram, host A (the connection initiator) begins by sending a segment with the SYN bit set and a sequence number, randomly chosen to be 100. This implies that if both ends succeed in establishing the connection, and if A sends its first data segment containing 50 bytes of user data, the accompanying sequence number will be updated to 150. In response to the initiation segment, host B transmits a segment in which it acknowledges host A's initial sequence number by setting its acknowledgment number to 101. Host B also includes in its response the initial sequence number (200 in this example) it chose for identifying its data. Finally, host A concludes the initiation phase by acknowledging host B's sequence number sending it a segment in which the acknowledgment number is set to 201. Only now can the hosts proceed to the data exchange phase.

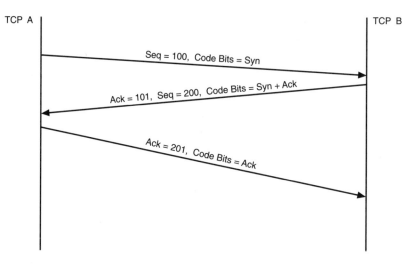

Figure 5.7. *TCP connection establishment phase.*

Data Exchange Phase

Figure 5.8 illustrates the events involved in the data exchange phase. The diagram *continues* the scenario depicted in Figure 5.7. The first segment indicates that host A is sending 50 bytes (obtained by subtracting seq = 100 in Figure 5.7 from seq = 150 in Figure 5.8). Notice how the acknowledgment number is set to 201. This implies that A has received no data. The second segment from host B is the one in which it acknowledges the data it received from A. As can be concluded from the sequence number, 100 user data bytes are being carried in this segment.

The third segment indicates that A received the data that B just sent (acknowledgment number = 301). It also indicates that A is now sending 70 bytes (obtained by subtracting the sequence numbers of the last two segments sent by A). Both the sequence and the acknowledgment numbers are cumulative, and TCP always increases these fields by the number of bytes received and transmitted, respectively. By calculating the difference between the sequence numbers corresponding to the preceding and the current segments, you can tell how much data is carried by the current one.

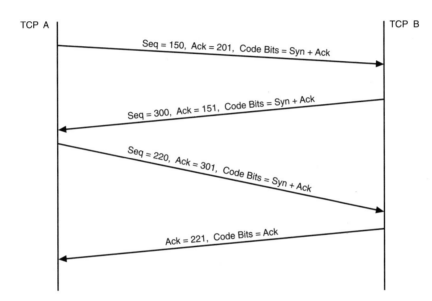

Figure 5.8. *TCP data exchange phase.*

The last segment is typical of an acknowledgment-only segment (that is, no data included). B uses it to acknowledge the receipt of the 70 bytes it received from A. No sequence number is included.

Connection Termination Phase

Whenever an application protocol has no more data to send, it asks TCP to terminate the connection on its behalf. Because TCP connections are full-duplex and data flows in both directions, the requested TCP can terminate only its own side of the connection (called half-connection). To do that, it sends a segment with the FIN bit to its counterpart in the remote host. The half-connection is terminated only after it is acknowledged by the receiver. More data can continue to flow in the opposite direction until the sending host decides to close its half of the connection. Figure 5.9 depicts this scenario.

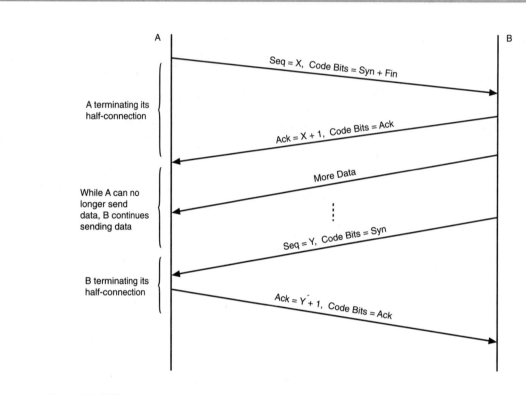

A

B

Seq = X, Code Bits = Syn + Fin

A terminating its
half-connection

Ack = X + 1, Code Bits = Ack

More Data

While A can no
longer send
data, B continues
sending data

Seq = Y, Code Bits = Syn

B terminating its
half-connection

Ack = Y + 1, Code Bits = Ack

Figure 5.9. *TCP connection termination.*

TCP Versus UDP

Why use UDP at all if TCP is as reliable and efficient as has already been described? There are several good reasons to use UDP, including the following two:

◆ Some software developers build into their applications reliability and integrity-check mechanisms that render reliance on TCP an unnecessary duplication of those mechanisms.

◆ Transactional services involving small amounts of data behave more efficiently using UDP services than TCP services. This is especially applicable to transactions in which all the data can be accommodated in one datagram. Should a datagram be lost or deformed, retransmitting that datagram incurs less overhead than is involved in establishing a TCP connection and releasing it later.

Some applications rely on both transport protocols. The Domain Name System (see Chapter 6 for more on DNS), for example, relies on both TCP and UDP using port 53 in both cases. DNS uses UDP for name queries in which small amounts of data are being exchanged. In a zone transfer, however, large amounts of data are being transmitted, in which case DNS relies on TCP.

Summary

The host-to-host transport layer maps to the transport layer in the OSI model of data communications. Two transport protocols are defined at this layer: an unreliable and connectionless User Datagram Protocol (UDP) and a fully reliable and connection-oriented Transmission Control Protocol (TCP).

TCP implements the sliding window technique for improved throughput and data flow control. Improved throughput is achieved by allowing the sender to transmit multiple data segments before an acknowledgment is due. Data flow control is achieved by allowing the window size (that is, the number of frames that can be transmitted simultaneously) to vary.

Before any exchange of data, TCP establishes a connection with its peer in the remote host. The technique being used is the three-way handshake technique, in which three data segments are exchanged. After the connection is established, data can flow in both directions simultaneously. Connection termination proceeds in two phases, with each phase terminating half of the connection.

CHAPTER 6

Name Services

Introduction

Each device (host, router, and so on) on the Internet is assigned an IP address that uniquely identifies it on the network. Routing protocols rely on this address for the delivery of data to the designated destination.

One way to reach a host is to specify its IP address on the command line. For example, to establish a file transfer session with a specific host on your network or on the Internet, you would enter ftp 78.23.1.5. The least that can be said about this method is that it does not appeal to the end user. Users prefer addressing network resources, including hosts, by names rather than by numbers. This is especially true if the names are conveniently chosen so that they are easy to remember and use.

This chapter covers three different, though related, means of assigning and administering names to hosts and the accompanying mechanisms responsible for resolving user-supplied names to machine-usable IP addresses.

This chapter takes off by discussing the simplest of all naming methods, in which a system administrator maintains a flat database describing names. Next, the domain name system (DNS) will be discussed. In particular, you will be shown how the DNS system provides for name resolution services that accommodate hosts and resources outside the boundaries of your network. This capability enables you to reach as far as any host on the Internet, regardless of its geographical proximity. Finally, a method for the management and dissemination of administrative databases, including name service databases, will be described. This method, known as Network Information Service (NIS), was developed by SUN Microsystems.

On a final note, this chapter, like all the preceding chapters, deals with governing concepts. Actual implementation and configuration issues will be dealt with in Chapters 10 and 11. Readers who are interested in applying the concepts as they learn them can jump to those chapters for the associated details.

Host Name and the *hosts* Table

The simplest method of resolving host names to IP addresses involves the maintenance of a host table on every UNIX system. This table is normally maintained in the /etc/hosts file. It is composed of a simple flat database in which each entry describes the IP address of a host and its associated (or assigned) name. Shown here are the contents of a sample hosts file as it existed on one of the author's hosts:

```
#
# Database of IP addresses and host names (including aliases) the format of
# this file is as follows:
# IP address    Hostname              aliases
#
127.0.0.1       localhost
100.0.0.1       netrix.unicom.com     netrix
100.0.0.2       jade.ott.unicom.com   jade
150.1.0.1       orbit.ott.unicom.com  orbit
198.53.237.1    pixel.ny.unicom.com   pixel
198.53.237.20   emerald.ny.unicom.com emerald
```

As shown, text lines preceded by the number-sign character are comments. The fourth commented line explains the format of the file entries. Each entry is composed of the host IP address, its fully qualified domain name (more on this later), and optional aliases to simplify referencing a host on the command line. For a user to establish a telnet session with jade, he has the choice now of entering

$ **telnet jade**

or

$ **telnet jade.ott.unico.com**

How does the name translate into the associated IP address (that is, 100.0.0.2)? All TCP/IP applications, such as telnet and ftp, have a built-in name resolution mechanism that looks at the hosts table and returns the corresponding IP address to the invoked process. With this in mind, have a look at entries in the example hosts table.

The first entry pertains to the class A address 127.0.0.1 and the associated host name localhost. You will recall from Chapter 4, "The Internet Layer and Routing," that this address refers to the *loopback* interface on the network interface card. Together, the 127.0.0.1 address and the localhost name simplify networking software as they allow the host to address itself the same way as it addresses other hosts on the network. There is one difference: datagrams sent to 127.0.0.1

are looped back and prevented from contributing to network traffic. It is important that each host includes an identical entry in its hosts file for the proper operation of TCP/IP.

By looking at all the IP addresses in the table shown previously, you can conclude that the hosts file includes entries pertaining to hosts that belong to different networks. If you are connected to the Internet, you can even include host name and IP address associations pertaining to systems on the Internet.

Looking at the third entry, you see that jade.ott.unicom.com is the host name assigned to the system with IP address 100.0.0.2. Also, the system is assigned jade as an alias name. A host can be assigned more than one alias. The host name and all aliases resolve into the IP address. When invoking any of the TCP/IP application sessions with another host on the network, you have the choice of using the host name or any of its aliases (you can even use the IP address itself, if that's what you prefer!).

When should you rely on the host table for the resolution of names to addresses? Host table-based resolution is convenient for small networks with few entries to include in the hosts file, provided that these networks are not connected to the Internet and have no need to run DNS services. Even if your network won't be part of the Internet, the fact that the hosts file has to be on every host on the network, and that changes made to one must be consistently applied to all others, makes this approach an administrative nightmare as the network increases in size.

Even if you will be running DNS (discussed next), having a limited version of a hosts file, including only key hosts on the network, would not be a bad idea. It allows users access to services that those hosts support should the DNS system accidentally fail.

Domain Name System

The origin of the /etc/hosts table approach dates back to an early evolutionary phase of the Internet, when it was composed of relatively few hosts, making name to address resolution a trivial task. The National Information Center used to centrally maintain a single flat database file called HOSTS.TXT, which contained information (including machine names and their IP addresses) pertinent to those hosts. To connect another host to the Internet, the host had to be assigned a name that did not conflict with already existing ones. The name, the IP address, and some other host information were then included in the flat database. Names assigned in this manner were flat in structure because no further hierarchy was followed.

Each connected system on the Internet, in its turn, had to maintain derivatives of the HOSTS.TXT file called /etc/hosts and /etc/networks. Using special commands, network administrators would routinely process a copy of a recent version of HOSTS.TXT that yielded the /etc/hosts and /etc/networks files. Whereas the former file contained the IP-address-to-name associations, the latter file contained IP-address-to-network name associations. As the Internet grew in size, this scheme revealed the following weaknesses:

◆ *Name collision:* With a flat name space, the likelihood of name collision increases with the number of connected hosts. This made assigning new host names more difficult.

◆ *Name administration:* Because every new name was subject to the approval of the central authority at NIC, the name administration task became very demanding. The flat name space scheme did not have the flexibility to allow for the partitioning of the name space and the subsequent delegation of administering different partitions to other organizations.

◆ *Ensured consistency:* As the number of connected sites grew in size, it became more costly and difficult to ensure the consistency of copies of the hosts table at each site.

◆ *Increased network traffic:* As both the HOSTS.TXT database and the number of sites grew, traffic generated on the Internet from requests for updated versions of the database became unreasonably high.

To remedy these failings, a new system of name resolution was required. The system would need to support a name space that would allow for the decentralization of its administration. This objective could be achieved if the proposed name space followed a hierarchy that allows for the partitioning of the name space into smaller partitions, or *domains*. Their management could subsequently be delegated to member organizations on the Internet.

To help you understand the need for hierarchical name space, just imagine life with the UNIX file system as a flat structure (that is, without any capability to organize directories and subdirectories). Imagine how difficult it would be to create new files, with unique filenames, as the number of files increased. Also, imagine how difficult your users' lives would be without each having a separate home directory on the system.

The hierarchical file-system name space alleviates these problems by allowing the division of the name space into directories and subdirectories. Under name space hierarchy, the system administrator can create and assign to users their own separate user or home directories. These directories are usually delegated to the users for management. Users are then left to create their own subdirectories and files (that is, to manage their area of the name space) further down the file system tree regardless of how the remaining part of the file system looks. A direct consequence of name space partitioning is the reduction of name collisions at the subdirectory level, where it becomes the owner's rather than the system administrator's concern.

The Domain Name System (RFC 1035) defines a similarly hierarchical, yet distributed, database of information pertaining to hosts on the network. The hierarchy allows for the subdivision of the name space into independently manageable partitions called *domains* (or *subdomains*). Its distributed nature allows for the relocation of the subdomain (that is, database partition) onto name servers belonging to the site to which subdomain management is being delegated. Such servers are called *authoritative* name servers.

With DNS services up and running, applications such as ftp and telnet are able to have target host names resolved into their corresponding IP addresses without necessarily maintaining a large /etc/ hosts file on each host in the network. Under DNS, all host information is included in database files, which are maintained on a few hosts.

Hosts maintaining database files run *server processes* that handle name-to-IP-address resolution in addition to providing some other pertinent host information. Hosts doing this job are called DNS servers. Figure 6.1 shows how a DNS server handles name resolution.

All TCP/IP applications have the DNS client component, known as the *name resolver*, built into them. In other words, no special UNIX daemon is required to support name queries on behalf of applications. So when a user enters `ftp jade.ott.unicom.com` to start a file transfer session, resolver routines package the name in a DNS query and send it to a DNS server that the resolver knows about. The DNS server looks up the requested information (in this case, the IP address) and sends a reply to the requesting host.

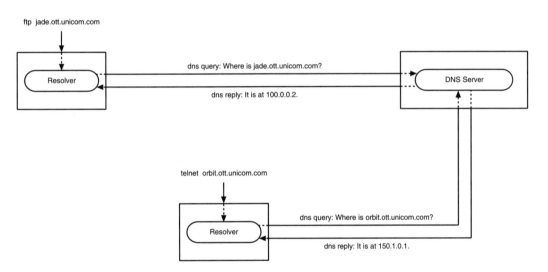

Figure 6.1. *Name resolution and name servers.*

DNS servers can be located anywhere on the network. Users can have access to DNS services running on hosts belonging to geographically distant locations on their internet. There is no absolute requirement that each site of a large network must have its own domain name servers. If your network is connected to the Internet, you will be using its DNS servers any time you connect to a host on the Internet, without having any idea about their actual locations.

In DNS, you need not have all host information maintained by a single server. Depending on the size of your network, you might have more than one name server to deal with performance and redundancy issues. On large networks, name services degrade in performance if the burden of responding to all name queries is put on one server. For this reason, you might want to take advantage of the distributed nature of the DNS service to share the service load over multiple name servers. Each server is delegated the responsibility of maintaining host information pertinent to a certain part of the network. But what if a host queries the wrong name server? All name servers, as you will see, are provided with information in the form of pointers to other servers. A server that cannot resolve a name query will send out queries to other servers to find the answer.

Logical Organization of DNS

When setting up DNS services, regardless of whether your network is connected to the Internet, you should follow certain rules in organizing your domain. Understanding those rules is as important to the proper implementation of DNS as understanding the rules that govern file system organization for the effective administration of your UNIX system.

The Internet's DNS organization is used throughout the chapter to illustrate DNS concepts. Also, a fictitious subdomain (unicom.com) will be introduced to illustrate some of the associated concepts at this level. It is important that you keep in mind that your situation might dictate a different organization from the Internet's. The rules and concepts, however, are still the same.

DNS is a hierarchical database of host information. Its structure resembles, to a great extent, that of computer file systems. Figure 6.2 draws an analogy between the organization of DNS and that of the UNIX file system. In both cases, the organization follows that of an inverted tree with the root at the top of the structure. Whereas the root of the file system is written as a slash (/), that of DNS is written as a dot (.) representing the null ( ) character. Below the root level, the uppermost domain is defined and can be subdivided into domains, which can then be further divided into subdomains—similar to dividing the UNIX file system into subdivisions called directories and subdirectories. Each subdomain is assigned a name (or a label). The name can be up to 63 characters long and can be divided further into subdomains. DNS allows nesting of up to 127 domains in one tree.

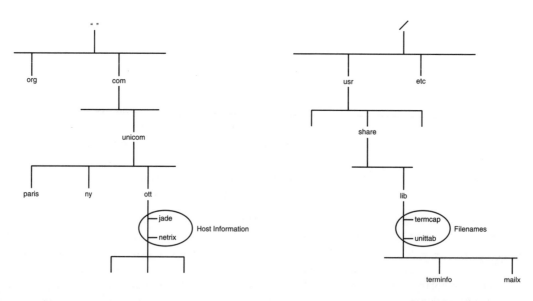

(a) Domain Name Space Organization   (b) File System Name Space Organization

Figure 6.2. *Analogy between DNS domain and UNIX file system organization.*

Each domain (or subdomain) represents a partition of the database that can contain information about hosts in that domain or information about lower domains (using the file system analogy, a directory or subdirectory represents a partition of the file system where information about both files and lower subdirectories is kept).

A directory, or file under the UNIX file system, can be referred to using relative paths or an absolute path specified relative to the root. The lib directory in Figure 6.2b can be referenced relative to its parent share directory, or relative to the root (/) to become /usr/share/lib. Similarly, a domain under DNS can be referred to relative to its parent domain using its name only, or relative to the root domain.

A domain name specification relative to the root is known as a *fully qualified domain name* (FQDN). As Figure 6.3 illustrates, an absolute file or directory name is written as a sequence of relative names from the root to the target directory, or filename. Under DNS, a fully qualified domain name is written as a sequence of labels, starting with the target domain name and ending at the root domain. For example, ott.unicom.com is the fully qualified domain name of the subdomain ott.

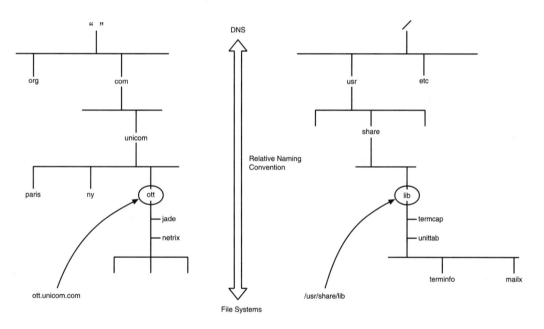

Figure 6.3. *Absolute domain naming convention compared with UNIX file system naming convention.*

To translate domain naming concepts into real terms, you are presented with a partial portrait of the organization of the top level of the Internet's domain. The Internet authorities have divided the root-level domain into top-level domains, of which only the org and com domains are shown in the diagrams. Whereas the root-level domain is served by a group of root servers, top-level domains are served in their turn by their own servers, with each maintaining a partition of the global database.

The unicom domain, created under the com domain, represents further subdivision of the database. This implies that the company Unicom (a fictitious communications solutions provider, with branches in Ottawa, New York, and Paris) undertook the responsibility of maintaining and administering its own name space by setting up its own *authoritative* server for its domain.

As shown in Figure 6.4, files represent the leaf nodes of the file system, below which no further subdivision of the name space is possible. Hosts (for example, jade and netrix) represent the leaf nodes in the domain system and, therefore, the actual resource. The type of information the leaf node might represent is quite general. For example, a leaf node might represent the IP address of the associated host, a *mail exchanger* (that is, mail router), or some domain structural information.

How does a DNS server know which type of information is being queried? Each *resource record* stored in the database is assigned a *type*. When a client sends a query to a name server, it must specify which type of information is requested. To be able to telnet to a host, for example, the client must request that the name be resolved into an IP address of a host. However, a mail application may request that the name be resolved into the IP address of a mail exchanger.

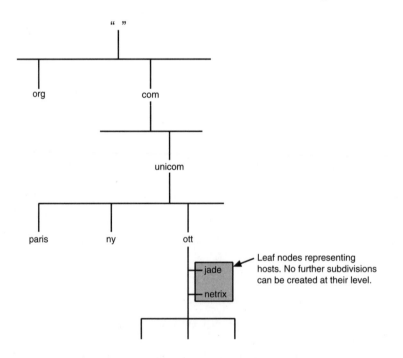

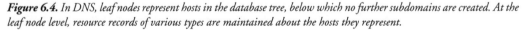

Figure 6.4. *In DNS, leaf nodes represent hosts in the database tree, below which no further subdomains are created. At the leaf node level, resource records of various types are maintained about the hosts they represent.*

One last rule to point out: the hierarchical structure of DNS allows two or more hosts to have the same name as long as they do not belong to the same subdomain. Similarly, two files can have the same filename as long as they belong to different subdirectories.

Delegation of Authority

One of the driving forces underlying the introduction of DNS services was the desire to decentralize the administration of the name space so that member organizations on the Internet, or any large network, would carry their fair share of the responsibility in administering it. The DNS hierarchical organization allowed for the breakup of this responsibility into smaller manageable parts, pertaining to the administration of smaller domains of the name space. Delegation in DNS is similar to the delegation of responsibilities in a large organization. At the top level, a large organization is broken up into divisions, below which smaller subdivisions or departments are set up, and so on.

When an organization joins the Internet, it is normally delegated the responsibility of administering its own domain name space. In Figure 6.5, the responsibility of the unicom.com domain is delegated to Unicom.

After authority for a domain has been delegated, the authority of that domain has the freedom to set up and make changes to subdomains with its own domain. An authority can even delegate partitions of its domain to other departments or member organizations. Referring to the unicom.com domain, Unicom set up lower-level domains reflecting their geographical organization. Instead of centralizing the administration of the entire domain in the headquarters at Ottawa, the MIS department might choose to delegate the responsibility for each subdomain to local authorities at each site.

The preceding discussion brings up two interesting, yet important points to keep in mind:

◆ Partitioning the DNS domain might have nothing to do with the details of the physical network to which member hosts of a certain domain belong. The Internet's com top-level domain, for example, includes subdomains pertaining to commercial and business organizations from all over North America, each maintaining its own underlying physical networking infrastructure. Unicom, for example, might have a hybrid of Token-ring, Ethernet, and some FDDI rings all over the place. A domain might be structured along geographical lines, as in Unicom's case, in which each site has its own domain. It might also be structured along organizational lines, in which case each department at each site sets up its own domain.

Unicom's New York office might have two lower subdomains, one for consulting, called con, and the other for marketing, called mark (see Figure 6.6). Hosts on both the con and the mark domains might belong to the same or dissimilar types of networks. Domain name administrators should not have anything to do with the way the network is physically set up. Therefore, when planning your domain, you should partition it in such a way that the delegation of, and the *autonomous* control of, name assignment is guaranteed. To summarize this point, a domain represents a set of *logically related* hosts. The logical relation might be geographical, common interest, or organizational.

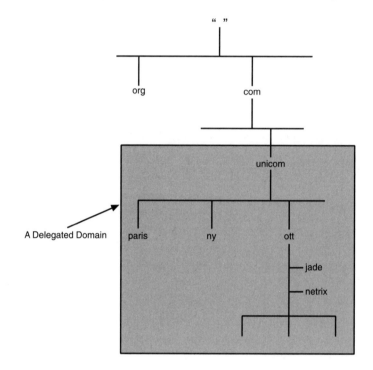

Figure 6.5. *Domain name space delegation.*

◆ Not every subdomain included in your design should necessarily be delegated. In certain cases, a subdomain is too small in size to justify delegating its autonomy to the site's authority. Or, for many different reasons, the site itself might not want to carry the burden of this responsibility (for example, the personnel might not have the required experience). In such cases, the authority over the subdomain might have to be made part of that of the parent domain.

Taking Unicom as an example, whereas both the Ottawa and the New York City offices are delegated the authority over their ott and ny subdomains, respectively, the head office might, while still maintaining a separate paris subdomain, decide to keep the authority to the paris subdomain to itself.

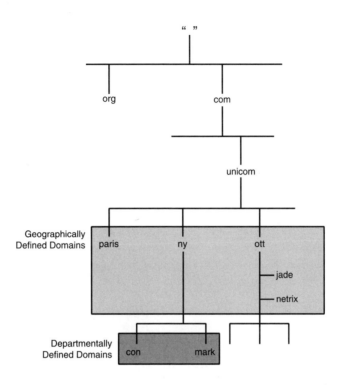

Figure 6.6. The domain unicom.com and its lower subdomains, con.unicom.com and mark.unicom.com.

The Distributed Nature of DNS

The delegation of parts of your domain to member organizations or departments translates in practical terms to the relocation of parts of your DNS database pertaining to those subdomains to other name servers. Hence, as Figure 6.7 illustrates, instead of maintaining all the information about subdomains you have delegated, your domain servers maintain pointers to subdomain servers. This way, when queried for information about hosts in the delegated subdomains, a domain server knows where to send the query for an answer.

Following is a summary of the advantages of distributing the database:

◆ *Distribution of workload:* By sharing the burden of responding to name queries, pressure on upper and top-level domain servers is reduced considerably.

◆ *Improved response time:* The sharing of the query load results in improved response time.

◆ *Improved bandwidth utilization:* Distribution of the database places servers closer to the local authority. This routes the traffic from name queries onto the local backbone.

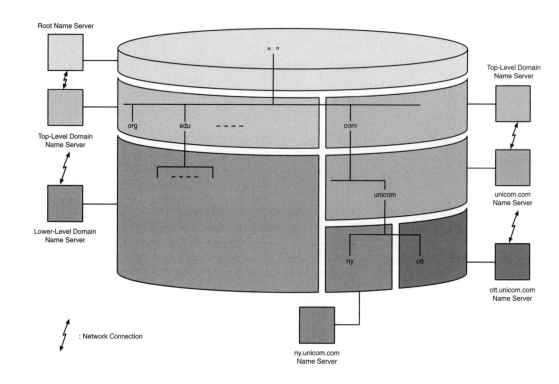

Figure 6.7. *DNS distributed database. Parts of the database belonging to delegated subdomains are maintained by different name servers.*

Resource Record Data Types

DNS defines several types of *resource records* where information about domain names are kept. Record types are divided into classes. The IN (internet) class is the most common and the only one you need to be concerned about.

The IN class defines several types of resource records (or RR), each taking care of a particular type of information. Corresponding to each record type, DNS defines a syntax that all records of the same type must adhere to. Following are a few examples of the resource record types that can be included in the database files:

◆ *Address record:* Known as an A record, this type is used by name servers to resolve a host domain name to its IP address mapping. An example A record is shown here:

```
jade.ott.unicom.com.    IN    A    100.0.0.2
```

jade.ott.unicom.com is the host domain name, IN corresponds to the Internet class, A identifies the record type as address resource record, and 100.0.0.2 is the IP address. If you specify the domain name when telnetting to a host, the resolver requesting name resolution specifies A as being the type of resource it wants. This makes the name server search through only the A records for the corresponding IP address.

◆ *Name server record:* Known as an NS record, this type is used to specify a host that will be authoritative for the specified domain. According to the following example, saturn.unicom.com is an authoritative name server for the unicom.com domain:

```
unicom.com.   IN   NS    saturn.unicom.com.
```

◆ *Pointer record:* Known as a PTR record, this type serves the opposite purpose of the A record. Using PTR records, a name server reverse-resolves an IP address into its corresponding domain name. This kind of resolution, as you will see later, is handled in a special way. The following example PTR record helps in resolving the 100.0.0.2 IP address into the domain name jade.ott.unicom.com:

```
2.0.0.100.in-addr.arpa    IN    PTR    jade.ott.unicom.com
```

Notice how the IP address is written in *reverse* order and how it is suffixed using the in-addr.arpa domain label. More details on reverse resolution will be presented later in this chapter.

These examples are meant to give you an idea of the type of information contained in DNS database files while leaving to Chapter 10, "Setting Up the Domain Name System," a more detailed and comprehensive treatment of those files and the associated resource records.

The Internet Top-Level Domains

Many readers might have already encountered domain labels in the form of rs.internic.net, or E-mail addresses in the form of NADEEM@unicom.com. This section will familiarize you with the organization of the Internet from which those labels are derived. This kind of familiarity is particularly important if your network is currently connected to the Internet, or if you are planning to make this connection some time in the future.

The Internet DNS name space is hierarchical in organization, and it follows the same rules depicted earlier. Figure 6.8 shows this hierarchical organization.

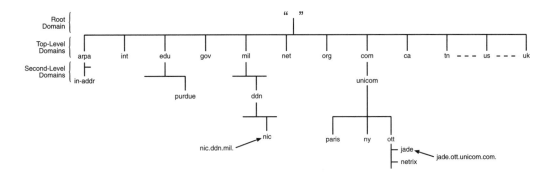

Figure 6.8. *The hierarchical organization of the Internet DNS domain name space.*

As depicted in the diagram, upper levels of the Internet domain adhere to certain traditions. At the top level, the Internet started by introducing domain labels that designate organization associations. Table 6.1 provides a list of those domains and the associated affiliations.

Table 6.1. Traditional top-level domains.

Top-Level Domain	Associated Affiliation
com	Commercial organizations
edu	Educational organizations
gov	U.S. government organizations
mil	Military organizations
net	Networking organizations
org	Noncommercial organizations
int	International organizations
arpa	Special domain, for reverse resolution

An example of an educational organization is Purdue University, which on the Internet is known as purdue.edu. Another example is ibm.com, which represents IBM's commercial domain.

Most of the organizations joining the top-level domains are located in the United States. This is because the Internet started as an experiment led by a U.S. agency (ARPA), in which only U.S. organizations participated. As the Internet success and popularity crossed U.S. national boundaries to become an international data highway, the top-level domains were reorganized to include domain labels corresponding to individual countries.

Country domain labels followed the existing ISO 3166 standard, which establishes an official, two-letter code for every country in the world. In Figure 6.8, labels such as ca and tn designate Canada and Tunisia. The United States also has its country domain label (us), which organizations can choose to belong to rather than a traditional domain.

The arpa domain (see Table 6.1) is a special domain used by DNS name servers to reverse-resolve IP addresses into their corresponding domain names.

Rules and traditions followed in organizing second-level domains vary with the organizations or countries that they represent. Whereas the us domain forks to 50 third-level subdomains corresponding to the 50 U.S. states, the uk and other country domains are organized by organizational affiliations, similar to the original organization of the Internet domain at the top level.

Domains and Zones

The earlier section "Delegation of Authority" pointed out that breaking down your domain into subdomains should not necessarily lead to delegating every subdomain's autonomy to other member departments in your organization. So although a domain is partitioned into many lower-level domains, authority over the domain can be aligned along *zone* boundaries, in which a zone contains a subset of the domains that the parent domain contains.

Figure 6.9 illustrates the difference between a domain and a zone. As shown in the figure, the unicom domain contains the ott, ny, and paris subdomains. Yet only two zones of authority are established: the unicom zone, which includes the ott and paris subdomains, and the ny zone, including the ny domain. When setting up name servers, you will be assigning zones of authority—you will be configuring them to maintain complete information about the zone for which they are said to have authority. You can, if you want, make a name server authoritative for more than one zone.

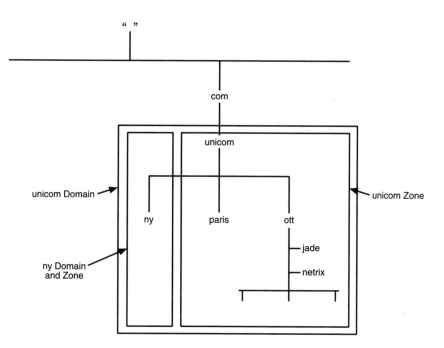

Figure 6.9. Domains and zones. Authority for the unicom domain is reduced to two zones: the unicom zone, which contains information about the ott and paris subdomains, and the ny zone, which contains information about the ny domain only.

Name Servers

After an organization is delegated authority for a zone, it becomes the responsibility of the organization to create a *set* of authoritative name servers for that zone. The setup must provide for one primary server and one or more secondary servers.

A primary name server is the server you will deal with most of the time. Any changes to the DNS database must be administered on the primary name server. For example, to add a new host to the network, you have to assign it both a name and an IP address, and you must enter those assignments in the DNS database contained on the primary server.

The secondary name server is different from the primary in that the primary loads its information on startup from disk files, and the secondary gets its information from the primary in what is known as *zone transfer*.

Any time a secondary server is restarted, it contacts the authoritative primary server for the zone for which they both are responsible, requesting all zone information that the primary server is maintaining. Then the secondary server polls the primary server regularly for any *updates* that might have been made to the database. This way, you don't have to worry about making copies of the database files on the primary server to copy over to the secondary servers.

> **Note:** A DNS secondary name server can be configured to back up zone data after transfer to disk files. The advantage of this is that the next time it is restarted, it reloads its data from the backup files, reducing bandwidth consumption arising from zone transfers. To ensure that its data stays current, the secondary server contacts the primary server and requests updates, if any. See Chapter 10, "Setting Up the Domain Name System," for more details.

Installing multiple name servers to support your own domain has the following two advantages:

◆ *Redundancy:* Any server is capable of responding to name queries. So, independent of whether the failing server is primary or secondary, the operational server can be queried for the same service.

◆ *Distribution of workload:* Because both types of servers are equally capable of responding to client queries, you can have the workload shared by all name servers. You can achieve this objective by ensuring that all name hosts have a name server in their neighborhood.

The number of secondary servers you need is dependent on the size of your organization, its geographical spread, and the level of redundancy you want to achieve.

Name Service Resolution Process

The name server's responsibility when responding to name resolution queries extends beyond its zonal limit. That is to say, whenever a resolver sends a query to a name server, it is the name server's responsibility to respond with the applicable answer. Should the server fail to respond from its database, it forwards the query to other name servers on the network for a response. To query other name servers on behalf of the client, every name server must maintain pointers (that is, the IP addresses) to the root servers. Root servers in turn must maintain data about all top-level domain servers, and so on.

Figure 6.10 illustrates how a name query can be resolved. In the diagram, a client sends a name query to its local domain name server, inquiring about the IP address of the host may.ny.unicom.com. Assuming that the queried server does not know the answer, it forwards the query to a root name server for help. Instead of responding to the query, the root server refers the local server to the com domain name server, which in turn refers it to unicom.com, where it is finally referred to the ny.unicom.com name server. The final name server is authoritative for the domain where the host belongs. Consequently, ny.unicom.com responds to the query with the address of may.ny.unicom.com.

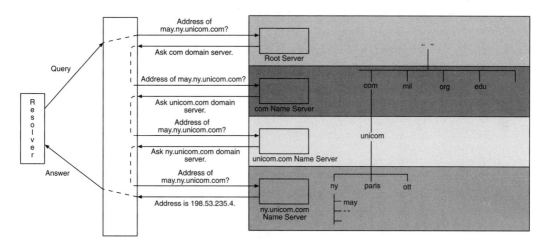

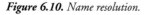

Figure 6.10. *Name resolution.*

The DNS resolution process dictates that whenever a name server is queried for information, it must respond with either the requested information or an error message. If the server does not find the requested data in its database, it forwards the request to a root server, which triggers a sequence of iterative referrals to lower domain name servers. This process continues until the requesting server ultimately contacts an authoritative server for the domain that maintains the requested data in its DNS database.

Caching

Reflecting on the resolution process described in the preceding section might lead you to think that it is a time-consuming and exhaustive process. Time-consuming because of the number of referrals that might be required before a name query is answered, and exhaustive because of the processing workload some of the root servers might have to sustain, in addition to the wasted bandwidth arising from every issued name query. Actually, things are not that bad. DNS design incorporates a caching feature into name servers that helps improve performance greatly.

Caching, as defined by DNS, allows name servers, both primary and secondary, to store the data that it sought for future reference. In the example in Figure 6.10, the local name server stores the IP address and host name association of may.ny.unicom.com after it gets the information. After that, if queried for the same host, the name server will be able to respond much faster from its cache without involving other servers, including the root servers, in its quest for the necessary data. Cached information is temporarily stored and is lost every time the server is rebooted.

Better still, name servers cache all the data they discover during the referral process. Remember that every referral provides the requesting name server with a list of authoritative name servers corresponding to the domain it should be contacting next for an answer. A name server caches those lists, relieving it from having to recycle the referral process when searching for data pertaining to any of the discovered domains.

In Figure 6.10, by the time the local name server gets the desired information, it will have discovered, and cached, the names of the authoritative servers for the domains com, unicom, and ny.unicom.com. If the local server is queried after that for host information in the unicom.com domain, it will be able, using the information in its cache, to bypass the root servers by addressing a unicom.com authoritative name server directly for the requested information.

To avoid having a name server continue using cached data after it has expired (due to changes made to that data on authoritative name servers), DNS defines a *time-to-live* (TTL) configuration parameter for that data. After the expiration of the TTL time, the server must discard the data in its cache and request an update from authoritative name servers.

The configuration of TTL is a decision you have to make based on two conflicting factors: performance and reliability. Performance dictates large TTL values, because it will take the name server longer before discarding its data. The large values also reduce reliability because there is a long time between updates. If you do not intend to connect your network to the Internet, and you trust that your domain data will be fairly stable, a large TTL might do the trick for both performance and reliability.

Reverse Resolution or Pointer Queries

A very special domain that has not been discussed yet is the in-addr.arpa second-level domain used in the *reverse resolution* of a host IP address into its domain name. Why would you want to know the domain name of a host, given its IP address? Primarily for reasons relating to the security of your network.

As you will see in Chapter 7, "TCP/IP Applications Overview," you can configure some of your hosts to provide remote services, such as remote login (rlogin) and remote copy (rcp) to remotely copy files between hosts. A host configured for these services requires that users come in from *trusted* hosts whose domain names are included in its .rhosts or hosts.equiv files. By using reverse mapping, a host will be able to authenticate a remote service request by getting the domain name of the requesting host for subsequent verification of its eligibility to the service.

One inefficient and very time-consuming method for doing the reverse mapping requires that every domain be queried for the resolution, until the host corresponding to the IP address in question is found. However, with the current size of the Internet, it might take days to respond to such a query.

The in-addr.arpa domain provides a clever and very efficient way to render the reverse resolution service. As seen in Figure 6.11, the in-addr.arpa domain is just another domain that uses IP addresses rather than host domain names. At the third-level domain (that is, below the in-addr.arpa domain), up to 256 subdomains can be created, one corresponding to each possible value in the first byte in the IP address. Similarly, below each of those subdomains, another set of 256 fourth-level subdomains can be created corresponding to the second byte, and so on, until the entire address space is covered by the in-addr.arpa domain.

In addition to obtaining authority over part of the domain name space when you join the Internet, you will be granted authority over part of the in-addr.arpa domain corresponding to the IP addresses that were assigned to your network. For example, if Unicom is assigned the address 198.53.237.0, the reverse address resolution domain delegated to unicom.com becomes 237.53.198.in-addr.arpa. No, it is not a mistake of any kind! When referring to the reverse resolution domain, you are required to read, write, and enter the network address in reverse order. For example, if the IP address of pixel.ny.unicom.com is 198.53.237.20, its in-addr.arpa domain name becomes 20.237.53.198.in-addr.arpa, which conforms with the way fully qualified domain names should be referenced.

Assuming that a host receives a remote login request from host address 198.53.237.20, for the receiving host to authenticate the request, it sends out a *pointer query* (type *PTR*) to its local name server. The local name server then must find the domain name corresponding to the specified IP address by starting the search at the subdomain 198.in-addr.arpa level, continuing down the tree through the 53.198.in-addr.arpa domain and the 237.53.237.in-addr.arpa domain. This process continues until it finally reaches the domain label 20.237.53.198.in-addr.arpa, which can then be fetched for the corresponding host domain label (pixel.ny.unicom.com).

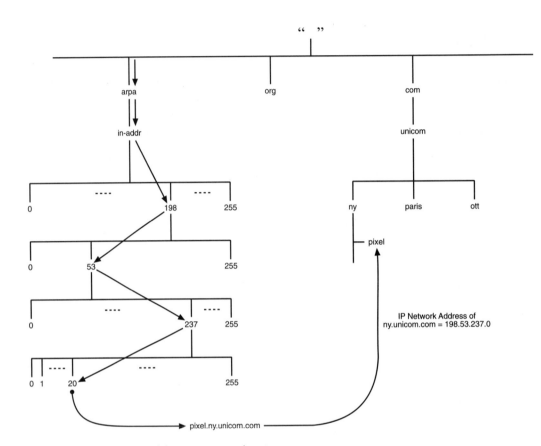

Figure 6.11. *Organization of the* in-addr.arpa *domain.*

Network Information Service (NIS)

Network Information Service, formerly known as Yellow Pages, is a distributed name service developed by Sun Microsystems to meet the administrative needs of large and evolving networks. It provides the mechanism for centrally administering and disseminating common databases, called NIS maps, across the network. NIS uses those maps to respond to queries regarding computing objects, and resources, independent of the underlying network layout and infrastructure.

NIS services are limited to the boundaries of the local area network. This means that NIS can be configured to replace DNS on isolated networks only. On networks connected to the Internet, you have the choice of running NIS in addition to DNS.

NIS Maps

NIS maps are non-ASCII administrative databases that are usually derived from equivalent UNIX ASCII files, traditionally located in the /etc directory. /etc/hosts, /etc/networks, and /etc/passwd are examples of the ASCII files from which NIS maps are derived. Each NIS map is assigned a map name that is used by programs to access it, and at least one NIS server is required per *domain* (not to be confused with DNS domains) to run the daemons required to administer the NIS maps.

NIS Domains

An NIS domain is a logical set of hosts using, and referencing, a common set of maps for information. Unlike DNS domains, NIS domains are not hierarchical in structure and therefore cannot be partitioned into subsets of autonomous subdomains.

Maps for NIS domains are maintained in the /var/yp/domainname directory of a central server that all clients on the network can reach. If an NIS domain is called sales, maps corresponding to this domain are located in the /var/yp/sales directory.

NIS Servers

An NIS server is a host that maintains copies of the domain maps and makes them available to all hosts on the network. NIS servers are two types, *master* and *slave* servers. Master servers resemble the DNS primary servers in functionality. A master server maintains master copies of the domain maps and is used to update them and have them propagated to slave servers on the network.

A slave server, as the name implies, maintains a copy of the set of maps as maintained by the master server. It is the master server's responsibility to maintain the consistency of all server copies of the databases by propagating any changes made to its map set to the slave servers. There is no requirement that you install slave servers. It would not be a bad idea, however, to have one or more slave servers installed on the network. Having multiple NIS servers allows for the even distribution of the load resulting from answering NIS queries.

All servers, both masters and slaves, can be queried by clients. The master is distinguished from the slave server only by virtue of maintaining the master map set. Only the master's set can be used to apply any updates.

Summary

Because users prefer that hosts are addressed using meaningful names as opposed to IP addresses, the TCP/IP protocol suite included domain name services that allow every host on the network to be assigned a name, known as the host domain name. DNS defines a hierarchical and distributed structure of the domain name space. The hierarchical organization allows for the partitioning of the name space and the delegation of its parts to member organizations or departments on the network. After a domain is delegated, the authority over that domain is free to partition it and make changes to it.

DNS defines two types of domain name servers, a primary server and a secondary server. Whereas the primary domain name server loads its data from files you directly administer, the secondary server loads data it transfers from the primary name server. Name servers cache their discovered data for a period of time, defined by a user-configurable parameter known as the time-to-live (TTL) parameter.

To accommodate authentication schemes that depend on machine names rather than IP addresses, DNS defines a reverse address resolution mapping. This mapping is taken care of by a special domain known as in-addr.arpa, containing the entire IP address space.

Name Information Service is yet another distributed name service. NIS allows for the management and administration of shared databases including host tables, /etc/passwd, and other information that DNS does not support. Unlike DNS, however, NIS cannot be implemented at the Internet level.

CHAPTER 7

TCP/IP Applications Overview

Introduction

Information exchange between applications is the goal of any networking architecture. Previous chapters addressed the architecture and concerns that are pertinent to the lower layers of the TCP/IP suite of protocols. Those concerns mainly dealt with transportation and exchange of user datagrams between two communicating partners.

Ultimately, the communicating partners are applications serving a specific purpose. This chapter examines those applications from a general architectural view and also examines the nature of the service they render on the network. Depending on their nature, some applications are covered to greater extent than others. Some of the briefly introduced applications will be addressed more thoroughly in later chapters.

The Client/Server Model

TCP/IP applications operate at the application/process layer (see Figure 7.1). They are dominantly protocol-driven, and they are based on an architectural view that splits an application into two components: the *server* and the *client*. The server component (also known as the *backend*) is a service provider that controls commonly shared resources pertaining to a particular application on the network. The server normally runs on a remote, high-powered machine to which authorized users have access. The client (also known as the *frontend*) is the service user. It is that piece of software that engages, on behalf of the user, with the server in a sequence of request-response datagrams fulfilling certain user-specified demands or requirements.

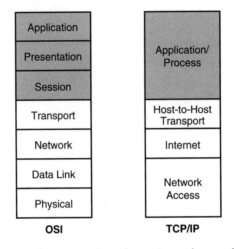

Figure 7.1. *TCP/IP application protocols operate at the application/process layer, and they map generally to the session, presentation, and application layers of the OSI model.*

In the database client/server technology, for example, the server acts as the central repository where all shared user data is maintained. In addition to this responsibility, as the database resource manager, the server is responsible for authenticating users for database access. This ensures that they get only what they wanted to get, in addition to securing the necessary file and record locks on already accessed resources. Accordingly, a user's request for data does not involve the transfer of the entire database to the user. Using scoping-and-filtering techniques, a client's request is normally satisfied by transferring only the needed records for subsequent processing.

Following are two advantages of the client/server architecture:

◆ Reduced processing requirement at the client's end of the connection. The client component has to deal with a smaller picture of the application, compared to the server. This, in turn, contributes to cheaper hardware to run the client (that is, minimal CPU power, memory, disk space, and so on). On the other hand, the server must be extremely powerful with whatever is necessary to make it respond quickly and to the user's satisfaction.

◆ Reduced loss of bandwidth from unnecessary data traffic, due to the exchange of data on an as-needed basis. In the case of an Ethernet LAN, this also contributes to reduced collisions and, therefore, better network availability.

Whereas the client component is a program that you would normally invoke in the foreground on your local machine, the server is usually a UNIX daemon that is made to run in the background at the remote site. Although in most cases there is one daemon per server, some services (for example, NFS) are supported by more than one daemon.

Not all daemons are started up when the UNIX operating system is being booting. Depending on how the system is configured, some of the daemons can be invoked and managed as the need for their services arises. As will be explained in Chapter 9, "Installing and Configuring TCP/IP," this functionality is achieved by delegating the responsibility of starting and managing those daemons to a superserver daemon called `inetd` (that is, the internet daemon).

In the following sections, the associated daemons and client programs will be discussed as application protocols are dealt with.

TELNET

TELNET (RFC 854) is a network terminal protocol that's intended to provide a remote login session and access to a computer connected to the network. A UNIX user invokes the `telnet` command (the client) to log in to the remote host, where telnet requests are handled by the `telnetd` daemon (the server). When invoked, `telnetd` provides its services using TCP for transport through the well-known port 23.

To start a telnet session with a host using `telnet`, use the following syntax:

```
$ telnet hostname
```

or

```
$ telnet IP_address
```

When invoked, the telnet client establishes a TCP connection with `telnetd`, the TELNET server, at the remote host. Then `telnetd` connects the telnet client to the login shell, using a pseudoterminal to which the user is accustomed. The pseudoterminal accepts only a specific set of characters as an input and generates a specific set of characters as output. A terminal emulation process is then set up to govern the interaction between the pseudoterminal and the user's terminal, specified by the `$TERM` environment variable in the `/$HOME/.profile` file.

All you need to do to terminate a telnet session is to issue the `exit` command as follows:

```
# exit
```

The connection is closed by a foreign host.

Optionally, you can start telnet without specifying the host name or IP address. If you do so, telnet enters the command mode and displays the telnet prompt, as shown here:

```
# telnet
telnet>
```

The command mode supports many telnet commands. To get minimal help, enter h on the command line:

```
telnet> h
```

Commands can be abbreviated:

close	Close current connection.
logout	Forcibly log out remote user and close the connection.
display	Display operating parameters.
mode	Try to enter binary or ASCII file transfer mode (mode ? for more). mode toggles the transfer mode. Optionally, the user can enter mode ascii or mode binary.
open	Connect to a site.
quit	Exit telnet.
send	Transmit special characters (send ? for more).
set	Set operating parameters (set ? for more).
unset	Unset operating parameters (unset ? for more).
status	Print status information.
toggle	Toggle operating parameters (toggle ? for more).
slc	Change state of special characters (slc ? for more).
z	Suspend telnet.
!	Invoke a subshell.
environ	Change environment variables (environ ? for more).
?	Print help information.

Of particular interest are the open command, which enables you to set up a telnet session with the target host specified on the command line, and close, which terminates the session.

Another way to temporarily enter the command mode, while a session is established, is by pressing the default escape character ^] (Ctrl+]). You might want to toggle back and forth between the telnet session and the telnet command mode to check on the status of the session using the status command. Status information shows whether you are connected to the remote host, the current option settings, and the current escape character.

Whenever telnet establishes a session, it negotiates a set of options or parameters with the remote host. The default options are generally acceptable to most situations and need not be tampered with. You can, however, make changes to telnet options by the entering the command mode, even while the connection is set up with the remote host.

Adapting a telnet session this way (on the fly) can be a confusing exercise to the ordinary user. For this reason, UNIX supports a special telnet user configuration file in which customized telnet startup options are maintained. The filename is .telnetrc, and the file must be saved in the user's home directory.

One way to go about configuring a user's session is to establish a session using the default, change the options on the fly, and test them while documenting the settings. If all goes well, you can create the user's $HOME/.telnetrc startup file, including the desirable options you arrived at during the live session. This should take care of future support to subsequent telnet sessions for this user. Refer to your vendor's documentation for more details on how to set telnet options.

If you are having difficulty setting the options, or you think they are not being processed properly, use the toggle options command to see the details of the options processing phase:

```
# telnet
telnet> toggle options
Will show option processing.
telnet> open jade
Trying 100.0.0.2...
Connected to jade.
Escape character is '^]'.
SENT DO SUPPRESS GO AHEAD
SENT WILL TERMINAL TYPE
SENT WILL NAWS
SENT WILL TSPEED
SENT WILL LFLOW
SENT WILL LINEMODE
SENT WILL ENVIRON
SENT DO STATUS
RCVD DO TERMINAL TYPE
RCVD DO TSPEED
RCVD DO XDISPLOC
SENT WONT XDISPLOC
RCVD DO ENVIRON
RCVD WILL SUPPRESS GO AHEAD
RCVD DO NAWS
RCVD DO LFLOW
RCVD DONT LINEMODE
RCVD WILL STATUS
RCVD IAC SB TERMINAL-SPEED SEND
SENT IAC SB TERMINAL-SPEED IS 38400,38400
RCVD IAC SB ENVIRON SEND
SENT IAC SB ENVIRON IS
RCVD IAC SB TERMINAL-TYPE SEND
SENT IAC SB TERMINAL-TYPE IS "VT220"
RCVD DO ECHO
SENT WONT ECHO
RCVD WILL ECHO
SENT DO ECHO


UNIX System V Release 3.2 (jade) (ttyp3)

RCVD IAC SB TOGGLE-FLOW-CONTROL ON
login: root
Password:
```

Very briefly, options processing and negotiation employ four simple verbs that the local and remote host use for the exchange of parametric values. The verbs are DO, DONT, WILL, and WONT. As you can easily infer, DO and DONT cause the communicating partners to exchange requests, whereas WILL and WONT are used to exchange offers. Preceding each verb statement is one of two keywords, RCVD and SENT, signifying the direction of the exchange. Refer to your manual for more details on telnet options.

Another very useful feature of the telnet command mode is that it enables you to go to the local shell to execute a single command or to invoke an interactive subshell. To execute a single command in a subshell on the local system, use !*command* while in the telnet command mode. The following example illustrates its use:

```
telnet>!ls
.profile
.rhosts
...
telnet>
```

To invoke an interactive subshell on the local system, enter just the ! character on telnet's command line. You can resume the telnet session with the remote host by entering exit.

File Transfer Protocol (FTP)

The File Transfer Protocol (RFC 959) is intended for the transfer of files between two hosts across the network. ftp is the client's program, whereas ftpd is the daemon that implements the server's end of the connection. Whenever invoked, ftpd establishes a TCP connection with the requesting client, using well-known port 21 as the command channel. User data exchange, however, takes place over another connection using well-known port 20.

FTP is widely available on platforms other than UNIX that implement TCP/IP. Under many circumstances, this makes it possible to transfer files conveniently across hybrid operating systems. Using a TCP/IP implementation for DOS, for example, a user can freely use ftp (subject to access rights restrictions) to transfer files between both UNIX and DOS platforms. ftp is very prevalent on the Internet. ftp sites are set up where anonymous users are expected to ftp in, move around, and then get and put files.

In its simplest form, ftp can be used to invoke a file transfer session with the target host:

```
# ftp targethost
```

targethost can be the IP address or the name of the remote host.

Being a secure service, ftp prompts for both your login name and your password. Unless you have a valid account on the remote server, ftp aborts requests to establish the file transfer session. In the following example, a user who is logged in to host jade uses ftp to establish a session with host netrix:

```
# ftp netrix
ftp>*** show prompts for login id and password.
# ftp netrix
Connection to netrix
220 netrix FTP server (Version 5.60 #1) ready.
Name (netrix:root) sam
331 Password required for sam
Password:
230 User sam logged in.
Remote system type is UNIX.
Using binary mode to transfer files.
ftp>
```

The ftp prompt, which in this case is displayed after the session is established, is the ftp command prompt. It is an indication that ftp is ready to execute any of the many commands you enter on the command line.

To find out what commands ftp supports, enter help at the prompt as shown here:

```
# ftp
ftp> help
```

Commands can be abbreviated. These are the available commands:

!	debug	mget	pwd	status
$	dir	mkdir	quit	struct
account	disconnect	mls	quote	system
append	form	mode	recv	sunique
ascii	get	modtime	reget	tenex
bell	glob	mput	rstatus	trace
binary	hash	newer	rhelp	type
bye	help	nmap	rename	user
case	idle	nlist	reset	umask
cd	image	ntrans	restart	verbose
cdup	lcd	open	rmdir	?
chmod	ls	prompt	runique	
close	macdef	proxy	send	
cr	mdelete	sendport	site	
delete	mdir	put	size	

Use get to transfer a file from the remote host to your station, and use put to send a file to the remote host. Using mget (multiple get) and mput (multiple put), you can transfer more than one file using wild characters. In the following example, a file called ftptest is being received from the remote host:

```
# ftp jade
Connected to jade.
220 Jade FTP server (Version 5.60 #1) ready.
Name (jade:root):
331 Password required for root.
```

```
Password:
230 User root logged in.
Remote system type is UNIX.
Using binary mode to transfer files.
ftp> get /usr/nadeem/ftptest
local: /usr/nadeem/ftptest remote: /usr/nadeem/ftptest
200 PORT command successful.
150 Opening BINARY mode data connection for /usr/nadeem/ftptest (1313 bytes).
226 Transfer complete.
1313 bytes received in 0.05 seconds (26 Kbytes/s)
ftp> quit
221 Goodbye.
#
```

One very useful ftp command to be kept in mind for use with multiple file operations, such as mget and mput, is glob. The glob command toggles filename expansion. If globbing is turned off, a filename including wild characters will be taken literally and won't be expanded. In the following example, globbing is turned on, and multiple files meeting the criteria set by the mget command arguments are transferred from the remote system:

```
ftp> glob
Globbing on.
ftp> mget t*
mget telnet.txt? y
200 PORT command successful.
150 Opening BINARY mode data connection for telnet.txt (474 bytes).
226 Transfer complete.
474 bytes received in 0.01 seconds (46 Kbytes/s)
mget trace? y
200 PORT command successful.
150 Opening BINARY mode data connection for trace (88 bytes).
226 Transfer complete.
88 bytes received in 0.01 seconds (8.6 Kbytes/s)
ftp> quit
221 Goodbye.
#
```

Whenever an ftp session is established, ftp sets the transfer *mode* to ASCII by default. This mode is suitable to text files only. To transfer binary files, or even text files, without conversion, a user must set the mode to binary before attempting file transfers. This can be done using the binary command. If desired, the mode can revert to ASCII upon issuing the ascii command. The following example illustrates setting the mode to binary, transferring a binary file, and resetting the mode to ASCII:

```
ftp> binary
200 Type set to I.
ftp> get binary.ftp
local: binary.ftp remote: binary.ftp
200 PORT command successful.
150 Opening BINARY mode data connection for binary.ftp (0 bytes).
226 Transfer complete.
ftp> ascii
200 Type set to A.
ftp> quit
221 Goodbye.
```

ftp supports many commands that help you navigate and manipulate the remote and local file systems. Commands such as del, cd, dir, and pwd enable you to delete files, change the directory, list the directory, and display the name of the current directory on the remote server, respectively.

As in telnet, in ftp a ! character can be used to conveniently invoke an interactive shell on the local host. To execute a single command and return to the ftp prompt, append the command, along with its arguments, to the ! character as shown in the following example:

```
ftp> !ping 100.0.0.2
PING 100.0.0.2 (100.0.0.2): 56 data bytes
64 bytes from 100.0.0.2: icmp_seq=0 ttl=255 time=10 ms
64 bytes from 100.0.0.2: icmp_seq=1 ttl=255 time=10 ms

--- 100.0.0.2 ping statistics ---
2 packets transmitted, 2 packets received, 0% packet loss
round-trip min/avg/max = 10/10/10 ms
ftp>
```

Status Check and Debug Mode

To check on the status of both the local and remote ends of the ftp session, use the status and rstatus commands, respectively.

```
# ftp jade
Connected to jade.
220 jade FTP server (Version 5.60 #1) ready.
Name (jade:root):
331 Password required for root.
Password:
230 User root logged in.
Remote system type is UNIX.
Using binary mode to transfer files.
ftp> status
Connected to jade.
No proxy connection.
Mode: stream; Type: binary; Form: non-print; Structure: file
Verbose: on; Bell: off; Prompting: on; Globbing: on
Store unique: off; Receive unique: off
Case: off; CR stripping: on
Ntrans: off
Nmap: off
Hash mark printing: off; Use of PORT cmds: on
ftp> rstatus
211-jade FTP server status:
     Version 5.60 #1
     Connected to 100.0.0.1
     Logged in as root
     TYPE: Image; STRUcture: File; transfer MODE: Stream
     No data connection
211 End of status
ftp> quit
221 Goodbye.
#
```

To follow up on the progress of an ftp session, use the debug command. debug toggles ftp debugging. Whenever debugging is enabled, debug displays session data indicating the direction of the exchange and the ftp messages being exchanged. As shown in the following example, ---> indicates that the local host is sending, whereas a three-digit code indicates that the remote host is sending:

```
ftp> debug
Debugging on (debug=1).
ftp> get trace
local: trace remote: trace
---> PORT 100,0,0,1,4,30
200 PORT command successful.
---> RETR trace
150 Opening BINARY mode data connection for trace (88 bytes).
226 Transfer complete.
88 bytes received in 0.01 seconds (8.6 Kbytes/s)
ftp> quit
---> QUIT
221 Goodbye.
#
```

The *.netrc* File

ftp's .netrc file is similar in functionality to telnet's .telnetrc. The .netrc file must be created in the user's home directory, and it should contain both login and ftp initialization parameters to be used by an auto-login procedure. Before you create the file, however, it is advisable that you test the desired settings on the command line first.

Multiple entries can be included in the .netrc file, one per remote host, specifying the auto-login authentication information and the pertinent initialization parameters. Following is a partial depiction of the syntax of the .netrc file entries:

```
machine hostname ¦ default  login login_id password password macdef macfilename
```

In this syntax,

machine *hostname*	Specifies the name or the IP address of the remote host you want to establish an ftp session with.
default	Matches any machine name not included in any of the .netrc entries. Only one default entry can be included, and it must show as the last entry in the file.
login *login_id*	Specifies the user's login ID on the remote host.
password *password*	Specifies the user's password. Note that, for security reasons, if this token is present, ftp requires that the file be protected from being read by anyone other than the user. The permissions on .netrc should, consequently, be set to 600. Failure to meet this condition aborts any attempt to auto-login to the remote host.

macdef *macfilename*   Specifies the name of a user-defined macro, defining all the initialization parameters. Refer to the manual for more information on this feature.

In the following two examples, the first entry auto-logs user tania in to host jade and establishes an ftp session on her behalf with that host. The second entry allows tania to log in to other servers with the specified default account specifications:

```
machine jade login tania password apassword
default login tania password jamsession
```

To establish a session with jade, Tania has to enter this:

```
$ ftp jade
Connected to jade.
220 jade FTP server (Version 5.60 #1) ready.
331 Password required for tania.
230 User tania logged in.
Remote system type is UNIX.
Using binary mode to transfer files.
ftp> quit
221 Goodbye.
$
```

To establish a session with any other host, tania must have an account maintained on all the servers she wants to log in to with the same login ID (tania) and password (jamsession).

Trivial File Transfer Protocol (TFTP)

TFTP, like FTP, is intended for the transfer of files between hosts across the network. The client's program is tftp, whereas the server's implementation is the tftpd daemon.

Unlike ftp, tftp does not rely on TCP for its services. Instead, tftp uses UDP's connectionless-oriented service with well-known port 69. Reliance on UDP means that tftp must resort to built-in capabilities to ensure the integrity of the file transfer process. To do that, tftp has to provide for timeout, retransmission, error handling, and acknowledgment mechanisms.

tftp does not log the user in to the target host before data is exchanged. As such, any user can transfer files to, and from, the target host subject to one restriction: that the permissions on the specified file enable anyone to read or write to the file. Hence, a potential hacker, for example, can extract any of the files flagged, or plant a virus on some of your hosts. Therefore, it becomes your responsibility to ensure that tftpd is secured against such attacks. One way to disable access to tftpd services is to go into the /etc/inet/inetd.conf file and comment out the entry that supports it. Following is a partial listing of this file, with the tftpd entry commented:

```
...
# Configuration file for inetd(8).  See inetd.conf(5).
#
# To re-configure the running inetd process, edit this file, then
# send the inetd process a SIGHUP.
#
```

```
#
# Internet services syntax:
#   <service_name> <socket_type> <proto> <flags> <user> <server_pathname> <args>
#
# Ftp and telnet are standard Internet services.
#
ftp     stream    tcp    nowait    root    /usr/sbin/in.ftpd      in.ftpd
telnet  stream    tcp    nowait    root    /usr/sbin/in.telnetd   in.telnetd
...
#
# Tftp service is provided primarily for booting.  Most sites run this
# only on machines acting as "boot servers."
#
#tftp   dgram     udp    wait      root    /usr/sbin/in.tftpd     in.tftpd -s /tftpboot
#
...
```

To start tftp, the user can simply enter

```
# tftp hostname
tftp>
```

Or the user can enter tftp without specifying the host name, then use the tftp connect command to specify the host with which the transfers are intended to take place. In the following example, the latter approach is illustrated, with the target host being jade:

```
# tftp
tftp> connect jade
```

Notice how the terms "session" and "connection" were avoided. This is because tftp is connectionless. In fact, the connect command is a misnomer—it shouldn't lead you to believe that, by entering it, tftp will attempt to establish a connection with the target host (which is jade in the preceding example). All that connect does is select the host name for subsequent transfers.

As in ftp, to transfer files between hosts using tftp, use the get and put commands. You can optionally include the host name of the destination if using put, or the source host if using get, in the destination or source file pathname. The pathname must then take the following format:

```
hostname:filename
```

Hence, to get the /usr/maya/tftptest file from host jade, you can enter this:

```
tftp> get jade:/usr/maya/tftptest
```

In tftp, you should set the transfer mode to either binary or ASCII using the binary and ascii mode setting commands. You can also use the status command to report on the current status of the tftp activity.

Other TCP/IP Application Protocols

In addition to the end-user application protocols discussed in the previous sections, TCP/IP includes applications that provide underlying services that are not specifically end-user utilities. Some of these protocols will be briefly introduced in the following pages, leaving details to upcoming chapters.

Simple Network Management Protocol (SNMP)

The Simple Network Management Protocol (RFC 1157) monitors and controls the performance of TCP/IP networks. Using SNMP, the network administrator will be able to gather network performance statistics pertaining to any SNMP-enabled host on the network from a single host. Statistics can include data pertaining to any of the TCP/IP protocols.

In particular, you can use SNMP management tools in troubleshooting situations to look up and change the routing tables of local and remote nodes. You can find out the number of ICMP route redirect messages, the number of active TCP connections, or the topology of the network, among many other useful features.

SNMP can also be used for proactively planning the growth and expansion of the network. SNMP statistics can be used to build a business case for adding bandwidth capacity before a bottleneck is reached on the network, or to redistribute network applications for better performance. Chapter 16, "Network Management Using SNMP," sheds more light on SNMP as both a network management tool and a troubleshooting tool.

Simple Mail Transfer Protocol (SMTP)

The Simple Mail Transfer Protocol (RFC 821) is intended for the transfer of user E-mail across the network. SMTP is not an E-mail application per se. Rather, it is the work engine that drives E-mail applications to provide the user with the necessary interfaces for the creation and formatting of their messages. SMTP runs on well-known port 25 and uses TCP for the reliable delivery of mail messages.

Unlike the other application protocols introduced so far, SMTP is implemented as part of other E-mail programs that provide user interface and mail routing capabilities. One such program is the very popular sendmail program. Users, however, normally use programs such as mailx to compose messages that are subsequently submitted by mailx to sendmail for mail routing and delivery.

This book does not include discussions on mail administration.

Network Time Services

UNIX supports two methods for the synchronization of timekeeping among hosts on the network. These are Berkeley Time Synchronization Protocol (TSP), supported by the timed daemon, and the Network Time Protocol, supported by the xntpd daemon. Only one of the services would normally be used.

HDName/Finger Protocol

The Name/Finger protocol (RFC 742), implemented in the fingerd daemon, provides information about the status of logged-in users at remote hosts. finger is the program that communicates your requests for status to the remote server. `fingerd` waits for connection requests on TCP well-known port 79 and terminates an established connection as soon as the service request is satisfied.

Included in the finger report are information items such as the user's login name and real name, the home directory and login shell, the last time the user logged in to the host, the last time mail was received or read, the name of the user's terminal, and how long it has been idling.

The following example illustrates the use of the `finger` command to determine who is currently logged in to the server `netrix`:

```
# finger
Login       Name          TTY        Idle     When        Where
georgia     Georgia       pts000     55d      Sat 09:59
joe         Joe           pts005              Sat 10:42   jade
```

The following example illustrates the use of finger for requesting information about user `alia` who is currently logged in to host `jade`:

```
# finger alia@jade
[jade]
Login name: alia      (messages off)  In real life: alia tawil
Directory: /usr/alia                  Shell: /bin/ksh
On since Feb  4 09:36:45 on ttyp0
```

One common usage of finger is to check for a user's activity before forcibly terminating his network connection.

Note: `fingerd` is normally disabled by default. This is due to known security holes in both the way it functions and the information that it makes available to outside intruders.

Network File System (NFS)

The Network File System protocol/daemon suite allows hosts across the network to transparently share file system resources among themselves. Moreover, NFS allows heterogeneous operating systems to become part of the NFS service. A DOS platform, for example, can "export" part or all of its file system so that it becomes part of the UNIX file system. Likewise, a UNIX host can export part or all of its file system to become part of another UNIX or DOS file system.

`nfsd`, `biod`, `lockd`, and `statd` are among the daemons that must be run to bring up NFS services. Chapter 12, "Setting Up Network File System Services," provides a comprehensive treatment of the actual operation and setup configuration of NFS on UNIX platforms.

Remote Services

Among the user remote services, a UNIX user can run rlogin (remote login), the server version of which is the `rlogind` daemon, and rcp (remote copy). Both of these services are discussed in Chapter 13, "Remote Access Utilities."

echo

`echo` service is internal to the `inetd` superserver daemon. It is available over both the UDP and the TCP transport protocols, using well-known port 7. As its name implies, `echo` simply echoes back to the administrator's screen whatever he enters at the command line. `echo` is particularly useful for checking transmission integrity, using any of the transport provider protocols.

The following example illustrates the use of the `echo` service:

```
# telnet jade 7
Trying 100.0.0.2...
Connected to jade.
Escape character is '^]'.
this is an echo
this is an echo
```

According to the listing, the user entered `this is an echo`; in response, `jade` echoed the same string, shown in the last line.

systat

The systat daemon is available over both UDP and TCP using well-known port 11. systat is started by `inetd` whenever a request for remote system status is received by this host. systat responds by starting a ps process on the server and reporting the ps's output to the requesting client.

netstat

The `netstat` server reports the network status pertaining to the server. It is available on TCP or UDP. `inetd` listens on well-known port 15 for `netstat` client requests. When a request is detected, the `netstat` server invokes a `netstat` command, querying this server for its network status. The command output is then packaged and shipped to the requesting client.

sprayd

`spray` and `sprayd` are the client and server components of, as the terms imply, an application that can be used to spray a host with a stream of packets. While using spray floods the host with the desired number of packets over a very short time interval, sprayd on the target host records the spray packets that have been received and reports related performance statistics to the requesting client. Statistics include packets received versus those lost, and the observed transmission rate.

Following is an example of the use of the spray service:

```
# spray netrix
sending 1162 packets of length 86 to netrix ...
        no packets dropped by netrix
        550 packets/sec, 47361 bytes/sec
#
```

Summary

TCP/IP supports many application protocols. Some of those protocols are immediately available to the user in terms of productivity tools, such as the file transfer protocol (ftp) and terminal emulation and login (telnet). Other protocols provide the engine driving certain applications such as SMTP, SNMP, and NFS. The protocols in the latter category are not immediately visible to the user. It's important to know about them, however, and to know how to administer them for better performance and potentially use them in troubleshooting situations.

In the next part of the book, you will be exposed to a more detailed and comprehensive treatment of most of what has been presented in this chapter.

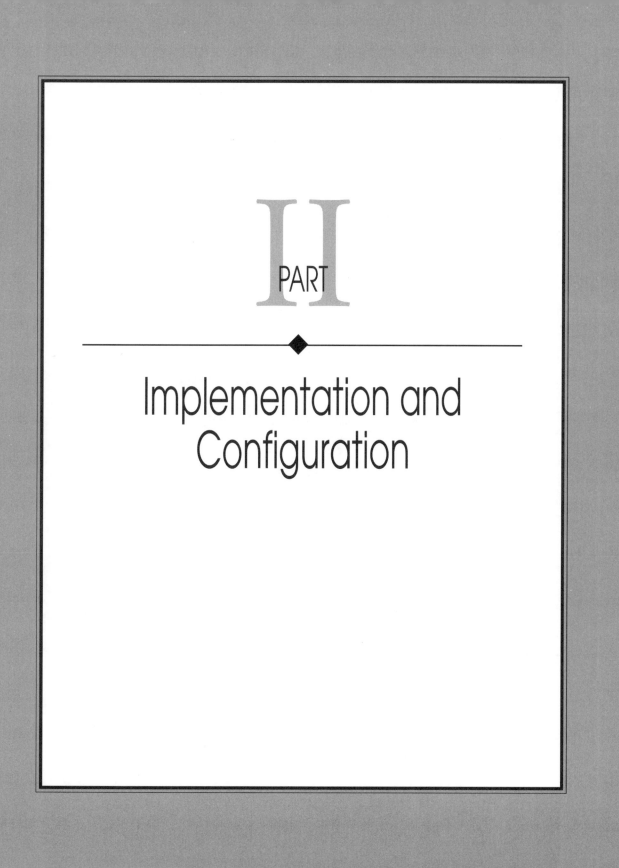

II
PART

Implementation and Configuration

CHAPTER

◆

Planning the Network

Introduction

Networking a UNIX environment, using TCP/IP, can become a challenging and time-consuming task. The overall complexity of a network is determined by its size, the nature of applications that will be running on the network, the geographical spread of the organization's premises, and budgetary and political constraints. Consequently, a network installation and configuration can range from a few days to a multiphase implementation lasting months.

To ease the challenge, ensure success, and, above all, avoid unnecessary expenditure and waste of productive time (which might affect your credibility), it is recommended that you spend some time planning the network. There is nothing as embarrassing as having to answer to your user community by trying to explain how, and why, you overlooked an aspect of the network design. Critical productivity factors can include inadequate response time, recurrent loss of network connections, or insufficient WAN bandwidth connecting to the outside world, to name a few.

Planning the network should be perceived as a challenge in its own right. For one thing, planning means direct dealings with the user community. You are trying to find out what requirements they have versus what is affordable. By consulting the user community, you will also be able to set the users' expectations at a reasonable level, which you should be able to deal with more comfortably.

The planning phase also enables you to see the big picture—its constituent components and the relationships that bind them all together. This helps you develop insight into the exact requirements necessary for successful post-implementation network operation. In addition to current requirements, proper planning helps in provisioning the network for future requirements as well.

In this chapter, planning a network implementation is discussed. The focus is on what needs to be done before any step toward network installation is attempted. Depending on the size and nature of your organization, as well as your ultimate goals, you might choose to adopt some or all of the elements discussed.

It is important to bear in mind that there is no right or wrong approach to planning. Do what you deem suitable to the situation you are dealing with. The material presented in this chapter only provides general guidelines, which the author hopes will assist you in achieving a job well done.

Identifying User Requirements

This task constitutes the first phase in the efficient planning of the proposed network. Following are the issues that should be considered as this phase is completed:

◆ Internet connectivity

◆ Nature of applications

◆ Print services

◆ E-mail services

◆ Multiplatform support

◆ Geographical requirements

◆ Security requirements

Internet Connectivity

Many networks survived, and to a large extent are still surviving, in isolation from the worldwide Internet. There is a growing realization, however, of the importance of the services the Internet is providing that organizations, big or small, cannot afford to live without for too long.

Independent of the motivation, the requirement to connect to the Internet drives many aspects of the network design process:

◆ *Unique IP address:* The organization must apply for a unique IP address that identifies it on the Internet. You cannot just pick any address you like. Applying for an IP address should take place as early in the process as possible so that it will be ready when network implementation starts.

> **Note:** Whenever an organization's application for an address is approved, NIC assigns it a unique network ID. The network ID represents a pool of addresses rather than only one address. Accordingly, it becomes the organization's responsibility to administer the address pool locally by assigning nodes on the network unique IP addresses from the address pool.

Depending on the class you are asking for, the process can be lengthy. It can involve convincing NIC that what you are asking for is justifiable. A Class C address is the least troublesome to obtain, and it shouldn't take too long to be granted. Given the current shortage of Class B IP addresses, most organizations stand little chance that their requests for Class B addresses will be honored.

◆ *Subnet mask:* Depending on whether you decide to subnet the network, you have to reach a decision on how you are going to structure the IP addresses and which subnet masks to use.

◆ *Internet point-of-presence (POP):* You have to shop around to find the means by which you are going to connect to the Internet.

◆ *Minimal WAN bandwidth requirements:* Depending on the nature of applications, you must reach a decision about the minimal sufficient bandwidth you are going to provision for Internet connection.

◆ *Unique domain name:* As with the IP address, you can't simply pick a domain name of your choice and starting using it on the Internet. To ensure uniqueness, you must apply to NIC for one. In your application, you can specify, in order of preference, a list of preferred names to register. Again, apply as early in the network design process as possible.

Nature of Applications

Determining the nature of applications that users will be running on the network is a key ingredient in the design process. The dominant nature of the applications dictates the selection criteria for many of the network components.

Applications that dominantly require character-based terminal emulation sessions put very little demand on network bandwidth. Terminal emulation sessions (using telnet or rlogin) reduce workstation-to-server traffic on the network to data arising from the exchange of keystrokes and screen updates. On the other hand, applications that are dominantly ftp or NFS-driven services introduce significantly more network traffic. This not only requires larger transmission bandwidth but might also require a different network topology, which aims at optimizing network traffic by restricting as much of the traffic as possible to its originating segment.

Graphical and imaging applications demand even larger amounts of bandwidth.

The nature of the applications does more than dictate the network topology and bandwidth requirements. It affects the hardware configurations of most server machines and, to a certain extent, the client machines. The CPU power, RAM memory, disk capacity and speed, and network interface card should be selected in light of the applications that are to be run on the server and acceptable response time.

Print Services

Obviously, print and E-mail services are among the prime functions expected from any network. All users on a network expect to be able to print and exchange E-mail, whether locally or with the outside world.

Provisioning for print services involves decisions affecting the number of printers, their respective types and capabilities, the printer locations on the network, and the servers to which the printers might be attached.

E-mail Services

Depending on the network topology and Internet connectivity, you should set up your E-mail services for both reliability and performance. Which hosts will act as mail servers and which as mail routers (or forwarders) are the main decisions you will need to make.

In a multiplatform environment, in which more than one network will exist on the wire, E-mail planning assumes an additional dimension. Consider, for example, an environment with both NetWare DOS users and UNIX users sharing the same backbone. Most likely (and naturally!), users from both environments need to exchange E-mail messages. Worse still, they want to do it transparently, without having to learn or use anything different from their current method. The answer to this dilemma is the E-mail gateway. This gateway, however, introduces additional design work, expenditure, and implementation time that should all be provisioned for before the final proposal is made.

Multiplatform Support

Users belonging to multiplatform environments might have more than the E-mail service in common. Depending on the network's mission and objectives, integrating network services can be extended to include the following items:

◆ *Integrated print services:* Due to budgetary constraints, an organization might decide to pool all, or some, of the high-quality printers. This action makes the printers available to all users, regardless of the environments from which they will be sending their print jobs.

Another possibility is allowing for unilateral printing. Expanding on the NetWare/ UNIX network example introduced earlier, unilateral printing can allow NetWare users access to UNIX printing resources while denying the reverse access.

◆ *Integrated file services:* There is more to file service integration than budgetary constraints. File service integration has to do with the sharing of production databases and, to a lesser extent, disk space. The advent of Network File System (NFS) made it all the more possible for users, regardless of their local operating system, to transparently access data files located on remote and "hostile" systems. Determining whether user applications require such access is your responsibility.

◆ *Application and database servers:* If you decide to include and support application or database servers on your network, you might as well consider implementations that accommodate more than one operating system-specific client (or frontend) interface. A database server supporting both DOS and UNIX client frontends enables all users of both operating systems to share the same engine and the organization's production data.

◆ *Multiprotocol support:* In most cases, multiplatform support implies support of multiple transport protocols. For both NetWare and UNIX users to share network resources, the network should be equipped mainly with routers that can handle both IPX and IP traffic. In certain cases, some hosts and client workstations also need to be configured for multiprotocol support. The comprehensiveness and sophistication of the required support vary with the network applications.

Geographical Requirements

A geographically dispersed network might have a requirement for WAN connectivity. Depending on the nature of traffic crossing the WAN, you have to consider different solutions to the connectivity puzzle. If anticipated WAN traffic is minimal (for example, due to E-mail only), a dial-up line might prove to be a cost-effective solution. Applications involving large file transfers might require the use of a high-speed leased WAN link. Examples of leased links include synchronous data links and T1 links ranging in bandwidth from 56 Kbps to 1.544 Mbps.

Security Requirements

Security requirements vary from one organization to another. They might involve more than simply deciding who has what access on the network. Certain security requirements might influence the choice of routers, the software, and definitely the associated implementation time. Security considerations might even influence the network topology and segmentation, which are hard and potentially very expensive to change after the network is installed. It is therefore worth your while (and your career) to spend the time it takes to sort out the security puzzle.

Network Design

During this phase, the details of the network layout, hardware and software requirements, and configuration issues are nailed down. Those details should be figured out in light of the identified user requirements. Network design should include details about all the following components:

- Naming conventions
- Servers' hardware configuration
- Workstations' hardware configuration
- Network topology and routing configuration
- Domain name service configuration
- NFS services configuration
- Security
- Other servers/services
- Disaster prevention and recovery

Naming Conventions

Rather than relying on random and arbitrary methods of naming services and hosts, you are strongly recommended to think out, possibly with the assistance of members of the user community, naming rules that should be adopted. The earlier the naming rules are adopted and enforced, the more conveniently you will be able to administer the network.

As you know by now, every host on the network has to be assigned an IP address and a domain name (or host name if no DNS services are planned). Consequently, if, for example, hosts and workstations are named after their users, which is not an uncommon habit in many organizations, can you imagine what will happen every time a person leaves the organization? Yes! You will have to assign the workstation a different name, edit the name servers' database files, and hope that you did not make an editing mistake.

The larger the network, the more important it is to adopt documented naming rules. This is particularly applicable to organizations adopting a decentralized approach to network administration and management. Consider a situation in which more than one administrator reigns over a part of the network, with each taking the freedom to adopt the by-the-moment naming standard. Imagine what would happen if you were delegated the responsibility of administering someone else's network segment while she is away on vacation. Without any degree of coherence or organization-wide naming standards, you might end up wasting considerable time figuring out what's what on the network.

It is recommended that naming rules be based on organizational and functional parameters. A host providing file services, for example, can be named after the *fs_department* convention, in which *fs* stands for file server, and *department* is the department to which the host belongs. A printer, on the other hand, can be assigned a name that makes it easier for users to locate it on the network, and a multihomed host serving as a router can be assigned a name that signals this functionality, and so on.

The naming rules should support short and simple names that users find convenient to use and easy to remember. Whenever possible, avoid elaborate and lengthy names, because they will defeat the purpose for which they were created.

Servers' Hardware Configuration

The server hardware that is required to support the UNIX services you want on the network is a function of two conflicting factors: required CPU bandwidth and budgetary constraints. As you go through the selection process, however, it is important to keep in mind that the server is the pivotal point of the network.

How you select the server's hardware is going to impact users' productivity for years to come. There is nothing as annoying as "unreasonably" slow response time, or frequent server crashes and extended downtime. Following are recommendations on how to select server hardware, based on the basic criteria of performance and availability:

◆ *CPU power:* Obviously, the more CPU power the better. The question might be, How much more? As much as the budget can afford. It is as simple as that, provided that the power you included in the server is not choked on the data channels by the selection of a low-performance bus architecture or a slow network interface card. Some UNIX flavors support multiple CPUs in the same server. You might consider this option when selecting the server.

Not all hardware platforms provide the architectural scalability that is compatible with such operating systems. Even if you do not have an immediate need for the power that multiple CPUs provide, having the option readily available makes it easier to pump up the server's CPU power when the need arises. Otherwise, the only choice you'll have left is to upgrade the entire machine whenever you need to. This might not be the cheaper alternative, considering the repercussions: the reinstallation costs and the downtime, coupled with the uncertainty about the server's stability and, hence, its future availability.

◆ *The bus architecture:* It is recommended that EISA or MCA bus architectures be considered for a minimum, because they provide an I/O bandwidth close to 40 Mbps, as opposed to the 2 Mbps that the ISA architecture provides. A slow bus can easily impact response time. Remember that a chain is only as strong as the weakest link. A server's response time, at least at the hardware level, is determined by the CPU, the bus architecture, and the network interface card. It does not make sense to invest in Pentium CPU power if either the bus or the network interface is unable to cope with the speed at which the data is delivered.

- ◆ *The network interface card:* Independent of the networking technology you decide to adopt (Ethernet, Token-ring, FDDI, and so on), it is recommended that you select a high-performance 32-bit network interface card for your server.

- ◆ *Hard disk:* Very-low-latency, fast-access-time disks are what you want, and the faster the better. Disk speed is, as well, a function of the SCSI disk controller to which the disks are connected. Some SCSI controllers outperform others. It is important, therefore, that you carefully study the SCSI specifications of any controller card you are considering before making any decisions. Most often you will find that proprietary superservers have the better SCSI interfaces.

A general note to make before leaving this section is that not every UNIX system supports every network card, SCSI adapter, or bus architecture. Before making any purchase, you should verify the compatibility of the hardware with the UNIX OS you intend to install. You might be able to obtain direct support from the hardware vendors themselves through vendor forums that are normally available on the Internet, CompuServe, or direct bulletin board systems (BBS's).

Workstations' Hardware Configuration

Depending on the nature of user applications, the type of hardware might vary considerably from one workstations to another. Power users, for example, might need top-of-the-line workstations including super quality graphical resolutions and huge internal disk space. Some others might simply need a modest machine to run their character-based applications.

Unless you decide to go with a proprietary technology, nothing less than a 486 CPU-powered machine is worth the money you will be investing in it. Although the 386 CPU might still serve quite a few applications, the decreasing price differential between the 386 and its 486 counterpart does not justify the compromise on the performance and longer life cycle.

The amount of memory to include is dependent on the applications that the workstation will be running. Fortunately, memory is scaleable on most systems; it can easily be increased to better sizes. The point here is this: do not over-provision memory at the cost of critical components. You can always add more should the need arise. It is not as easy or cost-effective to replace the network interface, for example.

A 16-bit high-performance network interface card is all you need at the workstation. Additionally, a remote boot PROM must be included in the interfaces designated for the diskless workstations.

Including a hard disk in the workstation is a controversial issue governed by conflicting factors such as cost, security, performance, and multiplatform support. With the declining prices of hard disks per megabyte of storage, you might be tempted to consider adding a local disk to every workstation. The point that you might be missing, however, is that decline is coupled with an ever-increasing demand on disk space per application. This is mainly due to the sophistication of applications that grew to satisfy user demands on quality, features, and ease of use.

Just compare the disk space a word processor requires today versus what its earlier versions required. In certain cases, the requirement is 20 times as much as it used to be! Hence, what was an acceptable minimum disk space a year ago might now be objectionable, if not counterproductive. The point is not that you shouldn't include hard drives in the desktop; the point instead is that cost should not be measured per megabytes as much as per your minimal requirements in the light of your budgetary constraints.

When deciding on disk space, consider the following factors:

◆ *Performance:* Hard disk-equipped workstations can be configured for better performance on the network. Swapping, for example, to the local hard disk relieves the network of the overhead associated with the exchange of swap data. Swapping also relieves the remote processor from the overhead of taking care of your swap data, the associated disk I/O, and disk space requirements at the server's end.

◆ *Backup management:* Backing up data distributed on workstations in addition to the server's data is not as conveniently manageable as backing up just the server's file systems. Many backup solutions are available that enable you to centrally back up all the user data on the local drives. Unless the user, however, keeps his station powered up while backups are performed, his data will not be taken care of, which consequently leaves the data unprotected and exposed to irrecoverable loss.

◆ *Disk controller:* IDE or low-end SCSI disk controllers might be sufficient for most desktop performance requirements. Consider investing in high-end controllers in a user's workstation only if the user is locally running disk I/O intensive applications.

◆ *Remote boot:* Diskless workstations incur additional administration time due to the lack of a local operating system to boot the machine. To remedy this problem, a boot server (discussed in Chapter 14, "Special Servers and Services") should be configured and brought up to allow diskless workstations to remotely boot using its boot service. Depending on many factors, remote boot configurations can vary with the system hardware configuration. Additionally, special remote boot PROM must be purchased and installed on each network interface. When brought up, the PROM uses hard-coded ftp to download a boot image file to the workstation's memory, which helps it boot properly.

◆ *Multiplatform support:* If the planned UNIX network will be part of a mixed operating system environment, local disk space might be required to bring up one operating system, while UNIX is taken care of by a remote server. A DOS and UNIX user, for example, can have her local disk configured for local DOS support. Using something like Novell's LAN WorkPlace for DOS, the user can load the TCP/IP stack and start a telnet session with the UNIX server whenever the need arises.

◆ *Security:* Depending on the level of security that is enforced in your environment, the size and availability of the local hard disk might be severely limited. Some organizations do not rule out support to local drives (floppy and hard disk) altogether to tightly support their security requirements.

Network Topology and Routing Configuration

Planning the network topology involves several factors, including these:

♦ Type of LAN

♦ Network segmentation

♦ Effective throughput and bandwidth

♦ Routing configuration

Type of LAN

Unlike in the earlier days of UNIX networking, currently many UNIX flavors support both Ethernet and Token-ring LANs. For historical reasons, TCP/IP on Ethernet is better supported than Token-ring. There are many more Ethernet-specific network administration and trouble-shooting tools on the Internet that you can freely download than there are for Token-ring.

Unless there is a very good reason for selecting Token-ring technology, it would be best for you to stick with Ethernet. It feels good to find the help you need whenever it is required.

Network Segmentation

Depending on the anticipated size of the network, dividing it into small segments separated by bridges and routers might take considerable effort before the final network layout is reached.

Mainly, motivational factors should be considered during this exercise:

♦ *Maximum number of nodes per segment:* Most networking technologies specify the maximum allowable number of nodes per segment. The maximum includes devices such as repeaters, bridges, routers, and network printers that are directly attached to the network.

♦ *Optimization of network traffic:* Depending on the anticipated traffic, the network might require segmentation using bridges or routers. The anticipated traffic is mainly depen-dent on the nature of the network applications; some applications saturate a network segment much faster than others. In those situations, you might have to set a lower upper limit of nodes per segment than the allowable maximum as defined by standards. Chapter 1, "Overview of Data Communications," explains the role of bridges and routers as traffic optimization devices.

♦ *Interconnecting hybrid networks:* Because routers operate at the network layer, they are capable of routing data between two dissimilar LAN technologies. For this reason, routers qualify as interconnectivity devices between hybrid networks.

♦ *Remote boot and RARP services:* Both remote boot and RARP services require that workstations and the supporting servers be on the same segment. Depending on the flavor of UNIX, you might be able to bring up remote boot relay agents on routers separating diskless workstations from their `bootpd` servers. Network segmentation must allow these requirements if diskless workstations are planned to be on the network.

◆ *Security:* Security requirements might dictate that a departmental segment be isolated from part of the network. Careful network planning should, therefore, avoid making this segment an intermediate transitory segment.

If you decide to deploy bridges on the internetwork, be careful not to assign different network IP addresses to hosts on either side of a bridge. Remember, from Chapter 1, that bridges are perceived by hosts as a pass-through connection. As such, hosts across a bridge must belong to the same network.

Take the time to plan for network segmentation. Having to redo a part of it can prove to be very expensive and time-consuming. Segmentation dictates how the IP addresses are going to be structured and assigned. Reconfiguring a host for a different IP address and domain name might incur several changes in both the affected host and the domain name servers—imagine reconfiguring entire segments!

Effective Throughput and Bandwidth

Not all traffic on the wire is user data. Partly, it is overhead due to protocol headers, and in the case of Ethernet, collisions incur additional overhead. This has the effect of reducing effective throughput to below the level necessary to guarantee a satisfactory response time. Although segmentation provides one way to improve the situation, the industry now offers other innovative alternatives that can be considered. One such alternative is the switched Ethernet technology.

Switched Ethernet technology is based on packet switching technology, in which a small segment is created between each active network device and a special device called a switched hub. The switched hub behaves much like a bridge in that it monitors data frames on every small segment, picks the frame, and examines its destination MAC address for subsequent delivery on the segment to which the designated host is connected. This has the effect of multiplying the available bandwidth to bring it up to double or more its actual level.

Another innovative technology is 100BASE-VG, which has been established as the 100 Mbps Ethernet standard. No rewiring of the premises is required if the current wiring is compliant with 10BASE-T grade 5 specifications.

Routing Configuration

After you decide on the network segmentation and layout, the next question is this: How should routing be configured on hosts and routers of each segment? Routing configuration involves two issues: which type of routing to use and which routing information protocols to use.

As you know from Chapter 4, "The Internet Layer and Routing," TCP/IP supports two types of routing configuration: static and dynamic. Under static configuration, the host's or router's routing table is initialized and updated by the network administrator. Consequently, static configuration is easily managed in a network with a limited number of routers.

Dynamic routing is a more suitable choice for large and complex networks. Dynamic routing configuration delegates the responsibility of maintaining the routing table to the routing information protocol. Large networks normally maintain multiple routes to the same destination.

It is therefore more convenient to rely on dynamic routing for the purpose of updating the routing tables as network conditions change. When a dynamically configured host and router detects changes, such as link failure and loss of a neighboring router, it attempts to recover from that failure by exchanging intelligent messages about network conditions with other routers.

Figure 8.1 shows the network layout of the fictitious company Unicom. The list following the figure depicts how hosts and routers, on each segment, could be configured.

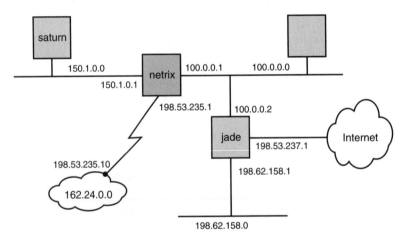

Figure 8.1. *Layout of Unicom's network.*

◆ Segment with network addresses 150.1.0.0: Because this segment's only window to the outside world is host netrix, which is acting as a router, it would be appropriate to configure all hosts to static routing. Further, every host on this network must have its default gateway set to 150.1.0.1 (see Chapters 4 and 9 for details on how to perform this task). Regardless of any changes external to this network that might be introduced whether due to failures or reconfiguration, the 150.1.0.0 network has only one way out to the rest of the world: host netrix.

◆ Segment with network address 100.0.0.0: It can be easily deduced from Figure 8.1 that all of Unicom's other networks use 100.0.0.0 to reach each other, and to reach the Internet. Routers on this network can still be configured for static routing, because there are two routers only. But if this network has not reached its maturity yet, and you are expecting to add more routers to it, it is more appropriate to configure for dynamic routing. This way, as changes to the network are implemented, you won't have to edit the routing tables manually, thus risking self-induced failures arising from errors made during the reconfiguration process.

◆ Segments with network addresses 162.24.0.0 and 198.62.158.0: Routing on both segments should be configured for static routing.

Hence, whenever you are configuring routing for a network segment connected to the outside world through one router, the choice is clear: static routing. If, however, the network is connected to other networks via multiple routers, then depending on the size and maturity of the network, routing can be configured for dynamic, static, or a combination of both routing configurations.

The advantages of dynamic routing should be weighed against the bandwidth wasted in the exchange of routing information, and security implications. In particular, wasted bandwidth might become an issue over WAN links with limited bandwidth. In such cases, it is more appropriate to configure for static routing. In terms of security implications, dynamic routing leaves the door open for potential hackers to break into your internetwork, or to advertise false routing information that might mess up the routing tables, leading to disruption in network services.

The Information You Need to Have

Depending on the adopted routing approach, some or all of the following information should be readily available before you attempt to configure for routing:

◆ *IP network addresses:* Depending on the topology of the internetwork, one or more IP network addresses might be required. If a network connection to the Internet is planned, the addresses must obtained from NIC or some local Internet service provider.

◆ *IP netmasks:* If the network is subnetted, all hosts and routers on the same subnet must have the same subnet mask.

◆ *Default router address:* Depending on the network topology, the IP address of a default router might be required.

◆ *Domain name servers:* If domain name services are planned for, addresses of at least one primary, and one secondary, name server are required to be in the /etc/resolv.conf file on each host.

◆ *Broadcast address:* The current default value is all ones in the host ID field of the IP address. Unless you are deviating from the default, you need not worry about it.

◆ *Routing protocols:* Based on your needs, the routers on the internetwork can be configured for one protocol or a combination of the following dynamic routing information protocols: RIP, EGP, and BGP. Your plan must clearly indicate which protocol combination is going to be deployed on which router, including all the required configuration information. Chapter 9, "Installing and Configuring TCP/IP," includes a detailed explanation of these options and the corresponding required information.

Domain Name Service Configuration

Following are the issues to consider if you are planning to install DNS services:

◆ *Domain name:* If the internetwork is going to be connected to the Internet, you must submit an application for a domain name. NIC won't allow two networks to share the same domain name. You will be able to pick a name as long as it is not used by any other member organization. Otherwise (that is, if it will not be connected to the Internet), take your pick, and name your domain whatever you want.

◆ *Subdomains and delegation of authority:* Depending on the network size and complexity, you should consider breaking the domain into smaller administrative domains. Delegation of authority of subdomains conveniently shifts the responsibility of maintaining those subdomains to the local authorities over which they are delegated. Should you decide to consider this option, you need to have decided on the subdomain names and how these are related to their parent domain levels. Chapter 10, "Setting Up the Domain Name System," provides the necessary details regarding DNS setup.

◆ *Number of name servers:* It is recommended that at least two DNS servers are set up per domain: a primary and a secondary name server. A secondary name server helps prevent a central point of failure on the network. Names and IP addresses of those servers should be available at the time of installation.

◆ *Location of DNS servers:* You should plan carefully for the placement of DNS servers. Your guideline is that a DNS server should be equally accessible by all hosts of a particular domain. Routers represent a perfect example of when a DNS server should be brought up. Hosts connecting to segments on which router interfaces are connected are symmetrically distanced from the DNS server brought up on that router.

Remember that a domain is a logical designation overlooking the underlying structure of the network. Accordingly, when planning your domain and subdomain breakdown, avoid focusing on the structure of the IP addresses, the subnets, and the LANs that make up the network. You will be much better off and will be able to achieve better results if your planning is based on a logical view of the network and the allocation of resources on departmental, geographical, and political grounds.

NFS Services Configuration

You should take the following considerations into account when planning for NFS services:

◆ Host names and addresses. Names and addresses of all NFS servers are required at the time of installation.

◆ A logical view of the virtual file system. A diagrammatic representation of the overall file system organization, supported by a depiction of what belongs to which host, can be used to facilitate the NFS configuration process, as well as for troubleshooting NFS services later.

◆ Names of exported paths per NFS server, and who the trusted clients are.

◆ Number of server and client daemons to support the anticipated workload per server and per client.

◆ Heterogeneous platform considerations. In a mixed environment (for example, UNIX and DOS), it might be required to integrate heterogeneous file systems under the NFS virtual file system. Should this be the case on your network, extra careful planning will be required to ensure the transparency of the service.

Security

Network security-related issues should be considered during all the phases of the planning cycle. Previous sections highlighted some of the security-related issues. This section addresses the implications of proper and improper security planning.

The most critical of all security issues is connectivity to outside networks. Depending on how the local network is connected to outside networks, including the Internet, local hosts can be left wide open to all forms of intrusion and vandalism, or they can be tightly restricted in terms of access and service.

Restricting access to the network from outside can be implemented using different methods. The most secure method is by creating *firewalls* at the boundaries of your network. A firewall is a properly configured UNIX host with multiple interfaces, one of them connecting the local network to the outside world. Using firewalls, you can restrict access to the network to certain IP addresses. Furthermore, a firewall can be configured to allow only certain application protocols (for example, E-mail and ftp only).

Equally applicable is planning for internal security. A decision should be made regarding who gets what on the network. A requirement might arise for internal firewalls to protect certain network segments from users on other parts of the network. You might even decide to disable some services or restrict others such as network printing and NFS.

It is your duty as a network administrator to plan network security in advance. Examine every network service you are planning to introduce, and weigh the risks versus the benefits of having it. If you have strong doubts about how secure a service is, seek help and advice before making a decision. After-thought planning, especially after the network is partially or fully installed, can prove to be a laborious exercise incurring additional cost. For one thing, different hosts and routers might need to be reconfigured differently.

Depending on the severity of the proposed changes, certain topological changes affecting the wiring and the structure of the internal network might require serious modifications. New network devices might even be required. As indicated in an earlier section, disabling tftp prevents diskless workstations from booting. To resolve this discrepancy, you either replace diskless workstations with others having enough disk space or invest in a UNIX host that you dedicate to tftp services for the sole purpose of supporting remote boot. All this can add up to additional costs that were not provisioned for in the budget, plus introduce delays for bringing up the network to a trusted state of maturity.

Other Servers/Services

Following are other services that should be planned:

♦ *ftp servers:* If the network is connected to outside networks, you might consider providing ftp access to data and information that the organization might want to make publicly available to its client base or to the world. Access to this server should be carefully controlled for obvious security reasons. Some organizations provide anonymous ftp access, in which a user logging in to the server does not have to have a valid login name and password. Chapter 14, "Special Servers and Services," provides details on setting up an anonymous ftp server. A suggested secure place to bring up an ftp server is outside the firewall, as shown in Figure 8.2. Alternatively, the ftp server can be brought up on the firewall host itself.

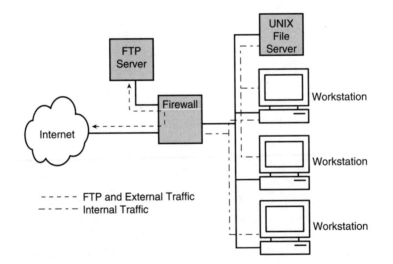

Figure 8.2. *Placing a public ftp server outside the firewall. This arrangement allows outside users access to information and data that the server contains while preventing them from breaking into the local environment.*

♦ *Remote boot (bootpd):* Remote boot servers are required if diskless workstations are to become part of the network. The actual location and particular capabilities of every bootpd service can critically affect the performance of the workstation's capability to boot remotely. Chapter 14 examines the issues involved and provides details on bringing up remote boot servers.

◆ *Reverse address resolution servers:* If you prefer to centrally manage the IP address assignment to workstations, you need RARP servers. How many you need depends on the size and complexity of the network layout (that is, the topology). Chapter 14 provides more details on RARP servers.

Summary

Network planning is a lengthy and exhaustive process during which you should seek user input to identify user requirements and define the objectives the network should meet. After the user survey is conducted, the network designer should systematically examine the different possible scenarios that can render the requested services. The three factors that should govern the design process are performance, security, and cost.

Proper network planning helps avoid after-install surprises. Major flaws in design can cause delayed implementation, suboptimal performance, and possibly extended downtime, and in certain situations might call for additional investment for equipment and outside help.

CHAPTER

Installing and Configuring TCP/IP

Introduction

Installing TCP/IP on a UNIX SVR4 host is a fairly simple and straightforward task. It helps a great deal, however, to have readily available all the necessary information and software packages required to complete the installation successfully. You also need to have one or more network interface cards already configured and inserted in the system before you proceed with installing the software.

Network Interface Card (NIC)

Despite the dominance of Ethernet physical media on TCP/IP networks, you have the option of running TCP/IP on Token-ring networks. Depending on your environment, you have to ensure that you have the right media-specific network interface card. Also, you have to verify that the NIC card you choose is supported by your UNIX operating system.

Before you fit the NIC card into the computer system, you have to configure its hardware settings so that it does not conflict with any of the existing hardware. In particular, you have to worry about the interrupt level, base input/output port address (base I/O), and memory address you assign to the NIC card.

To configure your card properly, however, you have to determine which of the hardware settings are already in use. Some UNIX systems enable you to figure it all out using a single command (for example, SCO's `hwconfig` or UnixWare's `/sbin/dcu` lists all the configured hardware on your system along with the actual settings). Other systems might require more tedious and time-consuming investigation. This highlights the need for a decent documentation of your system.

An Ethernet NIC card usually includes a transceiver that is used on 10BASE-2 (that is, thinnet coax) networks. The transceiver takes care of encoding computer data and transmitting it on the wire. Hosts connecting to 10BASE-5 (also known as thicknet) rely on an external transceiver and should consequently have the on-board transceiver disabled.

If you are connecting a host to a Token-ring network, then depending on the speed of the network, the interface card should be configured to 4 or 16 Mbps. Also, the NIC card should be configured to support the type of cable (that is, shielded twisted pair versus unshielded twisted pair) that attaches the host to the wiring multistation access unit.

IP Addresses and Domain Names

Every network interface card must be assigned an IP address that is not being used by another host on the network. A multihomed host (that is, a host with more than one network interface card) requires as many IP addresses as supported network interface cards.

If your network is broken into subnets, you must also have available the applicable subnet mask associated with each of the IP addresses you specify.

Each system must be assigned a host name. Typically, the host name is the name set during system installation. It is also known as the *network node name*. To determine the network node name of an existing host, enter

```
# uname -n
```

If you have domain name service installed on your network, you must decide where in the domain the host belongs and note the corresponding complete domain name of that host. For example, if a host called `jade` belongs to the subdomain `ny.unicom.com`, its full domain name becomes `jade.ny.unicom.com`.

Multihomed hosts require one domain name per interface. You cannot use the same name for all the network interfaces, or the smooth operation of name services will be jeopardized.

> **Note:** It is not an absolute requirement that you have the IP addresses and domain names ready before you install TCP/IP. You can temporarily use fictitious information and change it later. Reconfiguring for applicable information, however, is troublesome.

In addition, you need the broadcast address, the address of the default IP router (see Chapter 4), and the name server addresses (see Chapters 6 and 10).

Software Requirements

Under UNIX SVR4, operating system capabilities are packaged in independently installable software packages. In addition to the TCP/IP Internet package, you also need the packages on which TCP/IP depends. Those packages are

◆ The Network Support Utilities (NSU)
◆ The necessary software to drive your network interface card

To install a package, enter the command

pkgadd -d *device pkgset*

in which

device refers to the device alias from which the software will be installed, and *pkgset* refers to the package set name. For TCP/IP it is tcpset, for Network Support Utilities it is nsu, and for the Ethernet drivers it is eth.

For example, to install TCP/IP from diskettes, you enter

pkgadd -d diskette1 tcpset

It might be worth your while, however, to check whether any of the packages has previously been installed. You can do that by using the pkginfo -l command. For example, to find information about the NSU package, you enter this:

pkginfo -l nsu

```
    PKGINST:  nsu
    NAME:  Network Support Utilities
    CATEGORY:  system
    ARCH:  386
    VERSION:  1
    VENDOR:  UNIX System Laboratories
    PSTAMP:  SVR4.2 11/02/92
    INSTDATE:  Aug 21 1994 11:29 PM
    STATUS:  completely installed
    FILES:     182 installed pathnames
                45 shared pathnames
                 5 linked files
                55 directories
                48 executables
                21 setuid/setgid executables
              3135 blocks used (approx)
```

In particular, you must check the reported STATUS of the package set and make sure it reads completely installed.

During installation, you will be required to enter all the information described previously, and the last thing you want to do is abort the installation process because you had the wrong or incomplete piece of information. It wouldn't be a bad idea to use a planning sheet to collect all the required information before you proceed with the installation. In fact, you can also use this sheet to document the host's setup for future reference.

For the changes introduced in the TCP/IP installation process to take effect, you will be prompted to rebuild the operating system and reboot the host after completion.

TCP/IP Setup Files

At the end of the installation, several files will have been installed on your system. Also, changes will have been made to some of the files that existed before TCP/IP was installed. In the following pages, only the most pertinent of both file sets will be described. The intention here is to provide you with a quick summary of where to look for information to troubleshoot or modify the system setup. More details will be provided about the actual role that each file plays as the discussion evolves in the remaining sections.

/etc/hosts

The /etc/hosts file is where the host names to IP address associations are maintained. Following is an example of an /etc/hosts file as it is on host netrix (see Figure 9.1).

```
#
# Internet host table
#
# IP address  hostname      aliases
#
127.0.0.1     localhost
100.0.0.1     netrix        nfsserver
100.0.0.2     jade          ip_router
150.1.0.1     orbit         #netrix's second interface
150.1.0.10    saturn
134.12.3.1    samy
```

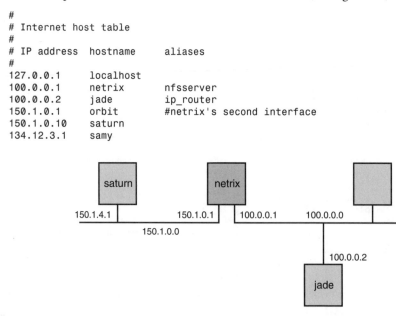

Figure 9.1. Host netrix acts as a router connecting both networks 100.0.0.0 and 150.1.0.0.

Text following the # character is ignored; this text is meant to include comments and documentation. As shown, every file entry consists of an IP address, the corresponding host name, and optional aliases. Three entries in this file pertain to host netrix:

◆ An entry that maps the 127.0.0.1 to localhost. This entry corresponds to the loopback interface (see Chapter 4 for more details). It is absolutely necessary that each system has an identical entry in its /etc/hosts file.

◆ An entry that maps 100.0.0.1 to the host's network node name netrix.

◆ An entry that maps IP address 150.1.0.1 to orbit, a host name assigned to another network interface card supported by TCP/IP in this host. As shown in Figure 9.1, netrix connects to two networks, 100.0.0.0 and 150.1.0.0.

Notice how netrix is also assigned an *alias*, nfsserver. An alias is just another name you can use to refer to the same host or interface. Because netrix supports NFS services for the rest of the network, it was conveniently aliased as nfsserver. Consequently, the network administrator and users will be able to reference the host by either its name or its alias.

/etc/hosts also includes IP address to name mappings pertaining to other hosts (for example, jade). If you do not have DNS installed on your network, the /etc/hosts file might have to be updated whenever a new host is set up on the network or an existing one is reconfigured to a different IP address.

/etc/networks

The /etc/networks file contains network names to network IP address associations. Optionally, aliases can be included. Names included in this file normally pertain to known networks that compose the Internet. Here is an example of an /etc/networks file:

```
# Name          Network Number

att             12
xerox-net       13
hp-internet     15
dec-internet    16
milnet          26
ucdla-net       31
loopback-net    127
```

/etc/services

As shown in Chapter 5, "The Host-to-Host Transport Layer," the /etc/services database contains the information that maps every recognized service protocol to a static port number, also known as a *well-known port number*. An application uses a uniquely assigned port number to identify itself to the transport provider (at the host-to-host layer) and to remote peers across the network.

Following is a list of well-recognized services as documented in RFC 1060. Every entry in this list consists of the service name and its associated port number/transport protocol provider. Some services run over both TCP and UDP (for example, `daytime` service). In such a case, the service is listed twice, once for TCP and once for UDP.

The `/etc/services` database file is created during TCP/IP installation. The only time you have to worry about it is when installing a new application or service. In this case, you will have to edit the file to include an entry as directed by the application vendor. You might find the file a useful reference while troubleshooting the network.

```
#
#       assigned numbers from rfc1060
#

#service        port/transport
tcpmux          1/tcp
echo            7/tcp
echo            7/udp
discard         9/tcp           sink null
discard         9/udp           sink null
systat          11/tcp          users
systat          11/udp          users
daytime         13/tcp
daytime         13/udp
netstat         15/tcp
netstat         15/udp
qotd            17/tcp          quote
qotd            17/udp          quote
ftp-data        20/tcp
ftp             21/tcp
telnet          23/tcp
smtp            25/tcp          ail
time            37/tcp          timserver
time            37/udp          timserver
name            42/tcp          nameserver
name            42/udp          nameserver
whois           43/tcp          nicname         # usually to sri-nic
whois           43/udp          nicname         # usually to sri-nic
nameserver      53/udp          domain
nameserver      53/tcp          domain
apts            57/tcp                          #any private terminal service
apfs            59/tcp                          #any private file service
bootps          67/udp          bootp
bootpc          68/udp
tftp            69/udp
rje             77/tcp          netrjs          #any private rje
finger          79/tcp
link            87/tcp          ttylink
supdup          95/tcp
hostnames       101/tcp         hostname        # usually to sri-nic
sunrpc          111/udp         rpcbind
sunrpc          111/tcp         rpcbind
auth            113/tcp         authentication
sftp            115/tcp
uucp-path       117/tcp
nntp            119/tcp         usenet readnews untp # Network News Transfer
eprc            121/udp
```

```
ntp          123/tcp                        # Network Time Protocol
ntp          123/udp                        # Network Time Protocol
NeWS         144/tcp        news            # Window System
iso-tp0      146/tcp
iso-ip       147/tcp
bftp         152/tcp
snmp         161/udp
snmp-trap    162/udp
cmip-manage  163/tcp
cmip-agent   164/tcp
print-srv    170/tcp
#
# UNIX specific services
#
# these are NOT officially assigned
#
exec         512/tcp
login        513/tcp
shell        514/tcp        cmd             # no passwords used
printer      515/tcp        spooler         # line printer spooler
timed        525/udp        timeserver
courier      530/tcp        rpc             # experimental
```

The /etc/services file is not used by UNIX to activate the services that the file includes. UNIX invokes only those services that are defined in the /etc/inet/inetd.conf file or those that are explicitly invoked using startup scripts. More details on both invocation methods are provided in this chapter as well as upcoming chapters.

/etc/protocols

Recall from Chapter 2, "Overview of TCP/IP," that the IP datagram includes a *protocol* field. This field contains a number that uniquely identifies the IP protocol service user. Similar in functionality to transport port numbers, protocol numbers help IP with internally routing data to their respective user protocols. /etc/protocols is created in your system during TCP/IP installation and should require no change. An example file listing follows:

```
#
# Internet (IP) protocols
#
ip       0    IP       # internet protocol, pseudo protocol number
icmp     1    ICMP     # internet control message protocol
ggp      3    GGP      # gateway-gateway protocol
tcp      6    TCP      # transmission control protocol
egp      8    EGP      # exterior gateway protocol
pup      12   PUP      # PARC universal packet protocol
udp      17   UDP      # user datagram protocol
hmp      20   HMP      # host monitoring protocol
xns-idp  22   XNS-IDP  # Xerox NS IDP
rdp      27   RDP      # "reliable datagram" protocol
```

/etc/ethers

Unlike the files discussed previously, /etc/ethers is not created by the system during TCP/IP installation. If you are planning to provide RARP or BOOTPD services (see Chapter 8), you need to create this file. RARP uses this file to map Ethernet addresses to IP addresses. An example of an /etc/ethers file follows:

```
#
# MAC to hostname mappings
#
# ether_mac_addr.    hostname        comments
#
00:00:c0:9e:41:26    saturn          #astronomy dep't
02:60:8c:15:ad:18    pluto
```

Rather than including IP addresses, the /etc/ethers file contains host names. Upon cross-referencing this file with /etc/hosts, any MAC address can easily be mapped to its IP address. This means that unless both /etc/hosts and /etc/ethers are consistently maintained, some users might end up having difficulties acquiring an IP address, and consequently connecting to the network at boot time.

/etc/netmasks

The /etc/netmasks file associates network IP addresses with network addresses. You need to create and maintain this file if you are planning to subnet your network. Here is a sample netmasks file:

```
#
#Network subnet masks
#
#Unless your network is subnetted, do not bother to maintain this file
#
#Network            subnet mask
134.54.0.0          255.255.255.0
167.12.0.0          255.255.192.0
```

/etc/hosts.equiv

/etc/hosts.equiv contains the names of *trusted* hosts. Users logging in to the system from a trusted host are not required to supply a password, provided that they already have a valid login ID in the /etc/passwd file on the target host. The following listing provides an example of /etc/hosts.equiv in its simplest form:

```
#
# Trusted hosts
#
jade
saturn
emerald
pluto
```

Users on jade, saturn, emerald and pluto can log in to the system on which the listed file is maintained without supplying a password, provided that they are in the /etc/passwd database of that system. This file and $HOME/.rhosts will be revisited in Chapter 13, "Remote Access Utilities."

$HOME/.rhosts

.rhosts must be created in the user's remote home directory. It allows or denies access to that specific user. In its simplest form, the $HOME/.rhosts file looks like the following one:

```
#
#$HOME/.rhosts file
#
jade
saturn
```

These entries mean that the user, in whose remote home directory .rhosts is created, can log in from jade and saturn without supplying a password, thus allowing for the transparent use of remote access services such as rcp and rsh. Refer to Chapter 13, "Remote Access Utilities," for more details on remote access services.

/etc/init.d/inetinit

Upon installation of TCP/IP, a startup script called /etc/init.d/inetinit is created. Also, a symbolic link is created between this script and a TCP/IP startup script in the /etc/rc2.d directory. On the author's system, the startup script is /etc/rc2.d/S69inet. This script is run whenever the system enters run level two (multiuser level) to start *some* of the TCP/IP services. More on this file later in the chapter.

/etc/inet Directory

This directory contains many TCP/IP setup files. Included in this directory are protocol configuration files such as gated.rip and ppphosts, which will be described later. Most important of all are the rc.inet and inetd.conf files.

rc.inet is the last script that the system executes when bringing up TCP/IP. It is responsible for spawning TCP/IP daemons such as gated, pppd, and named that provide basic TCP/IP services. inetd.conf, on the other hand, is a configuration file pertaining to the TCP/IP superserver daemon, inetd. The superserver daemon's responsibility is to invoke and control application protocol daemons whenever the need arises.

Some SVR4 systems maintain the hosts, protocols, and services databases, discussed earlier, in /etc/init, and they maintain symbolic links to /etc/hosts, /etc/protocols, and /etc/services.

/etc/confnet.d Directory

The /etc/confnet.d directory contains configuration files, tools, and scripts. Most relevant to this chapter are the following items:

◆ /etc/confnet.d/configure: A script that is normally used to further configure or update network interface drivers and enable routing.

◆ `/etc/confnet.d/inet/configure.boot.sh`: A script that executes at boot time. It is called from the `/etc/rc2.d/S69inet` startup script. One of this script's main responsibilities is to properly configure the network interface cards before the appropriate TCP/IP daemons are invoked by the `/etc/rc.inet` script introduced previously.

◆ `/etc/confnet.d/inet/interfaces`: A file containing the IP configuration parameters pertaining to each network interface card supported by the system. It is used by the `configure.boot.sh` script to configure those interfaces at startup time.

◆ `/etc/saf/_sactab`: A file that defines the port monitors that sac, the service access controller, should invoke whenever the system is booted or sac is restarted (refer to Appendix A for an overview of the Service Access Facility). When TCP/IP is installed, `/etc/saf/_sactab` is updated by the sacadm command to include two port monitors supporting TCP/IP. You can check the contents of _sactab by making the following entry:

```
# cat /etc/saf/sactab
# VERSION=1
tcp:listen::3:/usr/lib/saf/listen -m inet/tcp0 tcp 2>/dev/null #
inetd:inetd::0:/usr/sbin/inetd #internet daemon
```

Based on this, the two TCP/IP-related port monitors are defined. They are assigned port monitor tags `tcp` and `inetd`. Both port monitors listen on the network for user requests and spawn the daemons or processes to satisfy those requests.

TCP/IP Startup Process

TCP/IP is started at boot time when run level 2 (that is, multiuser run level) is entered by `/etc/init.d/inetinit`, which maintains a symbolic link to the `/etc/rc2.d/S69inet` file. This script sets out by configuring, linking, and loading various STREAMS modules and drivers that are required for the STREAMS TCP/IP protocol stack. If STREAMS is loaded successfully, `inetinit` executes the `/etc/confnet.d/inet/config.boot.sh` to configure all the supported network interfaces as defined in the `/etc/confnet.d/inet/interface` file.

`config.boot.sh` loops through all the interfaces, including the loopback interface, configuring each using `ifconfig` to the proper IP address, netmask, and broadcast address. It also uses the `slink` command to configure and load the protocol stack onto the Streams head for each interface device.

Note: Following is a listing of the supported interfaces on the author's system as defined in this file:

```
lo:0:localhost:/dev/loop::add_loop:
ne2k:0::/dev/ne2k_0:-trailers::
el3:0:orbit:/dev/el3_0:-trailers::
```

According to this listing, two network interfaces are supported. These are ne2k and el3, corresponding to the NE2000 and 3C509 network cards, respectively. The first entry (lo) pertains to the loopback interface. Each entry is made of colon-delimited fields. Entries in the interface file have the format

```
prefix:unit#:addr:device:ifconfig_opts:slink_opts:
```

in which

- *prefix* is used to identify the interface so that `ifconfig` or `netstat` commands can configure the interface or gather its statistics.
- *unit#* refers to the unit number (that is, instance number) of that interface.
- *addr* should contain either the IP address assigned to the interface, or an existing host name in the `/etc/hosts` file. If a null string is included instead, as in the second entry, then null will be expanded to `/usr/bin/uname -n`, and the interface will be configured to the IP address of the corresponding network node name of the local system.
- *device* refers to the node name of the transport provider. This field is used by the `slink` (that is, STREAMS link) command for the configuration and installation of the protocol stack onto the Stream head.
- *ifconfig_opts* normally contains options that are supported by the `ifconfig` command. One common option is the `-trailers` option (discussed later in the chapter).
- *slink_opts* is used by `slink` to initialize the device into the TCP/IP protocol stack. A null field allows for customization.

If the network interfaces are successfully configured and brought up, `/etc/init.d/inetinit` runs the `/etc/inet/rc.inet` script.

Note: `/etc/init.d/inetinit` is actually linked (or copied) to `/etc/rc2.d/S69inet`, which is run along with all the other scripts that begin with S in that directory when the user enters multiuser mode. Nothing is actually run from the `init.d` directory.

/etc/inet/rc.inet

The contents of the `rc.inet` script are shown in the following file listing. As can be seen from the listing, `rc.inet` starts TCP/IP daemons that have been verified as properly configured. Taking `gated`, the routing daemons, as an example, `rc.inet` checks in the `/etc/inet` directory for the corresponding configuration file (`gated.conf`). If `gated.conf` is found, the daemon is invoked.

Note: Some UNIX systems might use different startup scripts than the `/etc/inet/rc.inet` script described in this chapter. Consult your system's documentation for the applicable startup scripts.

```
#       @(#)rc.inet  1.5 STREAMWare TCP/IP SVR4.2  source
#       SCCS IDENTIFICATION
#ident "@(#)cmd-inet:common/cmd/cmd-inet/etc/inet/rc.inet    1.3.8.7"

# Inet startup script run from /etc/init.d/inetinit
LOG=/tmp/inet.start
PermLog=/var/adm/log/inet.start
export LOG PermLog
exitcode=0

# Label the error log
echo "The following commands were run from /etc/inet/rc.inet" > $LOG
#
# Add lines here to set up routes to gateways, start other daemons, etc.
#
#
# Run the ppp daemon if /etc/inet/ppphosts is present
#
if [ -f /etc/inet/ppphosts -a -x /usr/sbin/in.pppd ]
then
    /usr/sbin/in.pppd
fi
# This runs in.gated if its configuration file (/etc/inet/gated.conf) is
# present.  Otherwise, in.routed is run.
#
if [ -f /etc/inet/gated.conf -a -x /usr/sbin/in.gated ]
then
    /usr/sbin/in.gated
else
    #
    # if running, kill the route demon
    #
    kill 'ps -ef¦grep in[.]routed¦awk '{print $2}'' 2>/dev/null
    /usr/sbin/in.routed -q
fi
#
# /usr/sbin/route add default your_nearest_gateway hops_to_gateway
# if [ $? -ne 0 ]
# then
#    exitcode=1
# fi

#
#  Run the DNS server if a configuration file is present
#
if [ -f /etc/inet/named.boot -a -x /usr/sbin/in.named ]
then
    /usr/sbin/in.named
fi

#
#  Run the NTP server if a configuration file is present
#
if [ -f /etc/inet/ntp.conf -a -x /usr/sbin/in.xntpd ]
then
    /usr/sbin/in.xntpd
fi
#
# return status to /etc/init.d/inetinit
```

As will be shown in upcoming chapters, in some situations you have to make changes to this file. For example, to install static routes at boot time, you need to edit the rc.init file to include as many route add commands as might be required to support those routes, including support for the default gateway.

The *inetd* Superserver Daemon

The daemons invoked by the rc.inet script provide the basic TCP/IP services to UNIX. Of the TCP/IP suite of protocols, only the routing service, DNS name service, network time protocol, and PPP serial link service are individually invoked by the rc.inet script. As far as other services, such as telnet and ftp, are concerned, they are started on an as-needed basis. The daemon that starts them is inetd, known as the internet superserver or master internet daemon.

inetd is started at boot time by sac (the service access controller), which is in turn started by init whenever the system is brought to run level two. If you check the /etc/inittab file on your system, you should be able to find the following entry:

```
sc:234:respawn: /usr/lib/saf/sac -t 300
```

This entry guarantees that an invocation of the service access controller is attempted upon reboot. To check whether inetd is spawned by sac, you can use the ps command, or better still, you can use the sacadm command as shown here:

```
# sacadm -l
PMTAG   PMTYPE      FLGS RCNT STATUS   COMMAND
inetd   inetd       -    0    ENABLED  /usr/sbin/inetd #internet daemon
tcp     listen      -    3    ENABLED  /usr/lib/saf/listen -m inet/tcp0 tcp 2>/dev/null
```

According to the response shown, inetd is indeed started and is in an enabled state. This means that inetd is actively listening for network service requests and is capable of starting the appropriate daemon to handle a request.

When started, inetd fetches and reads the configuration file /etc/inet/inetd.conf. This file defines the service daemons on whose behalf inetd can listen for network service requests. Using any editor, you can add to, or delete from, the list of inetd-supported services. Following is a partial listing of this file as it existed on the author's system:

```
# Internet services syntax:
#  <service_name> <socket_type> <proto> <flags> <user> <server_pathname> <args>
#
# ftp and telnet are standard Internet services.
#
ftp     stream tcp   nowait root   /usr/sbin/in.ftpd    in.ftpd
telnet  stream tcp   nowait root   /usr/sbin/in.telnetd       in.telnetd
#
# Shell, login, exec, comsat and talk are BSD protocols.
#
shell   stream tcp   nowait root   /usr/sbin/in.rshd    in.rshd
login   stream tcp   nowait root   /usr/sbin/in.rlogind       in.rlogind
exec    stream tcp   nowait root   /usr/sbin/in.rexecd in.rexecd
comsat  dgram  udp   wait   root   /usr/sbin/in.comsat in.comsat
```

```
talk    dgram udp    wait    root    /usr/sbin/in.otalkd in.otalkd
ntalk dgram udp    wait    root    /usr/sbin/in.talkd in.talkd
#bootps         dgram udp    wait    root    /usr/sbin/in.bootpd in.bootpd
#
# Run as user "uucp" if you don't want uucpd's wtmp entries.
# Uncomment the following entry if the uucpd daemon is added to the system.
#
# uucp stream tcp    nowait uucp    /usr/sbin/in.uucpd  in.uucpd
#
# Tftp service is provided primarily for booting.  Most sites run this
# only on machines acting as "boot servers."
#
#tftp dgram udp    wait    root    /usr/sbin/in.tftpd  in.tftpd -s /tftpboot
#
# Finger, systat and netstat give out user information which may be
# valuable to potential "system crackers."  Many sites choose to disable
# some or all of these services to improve security.
#
#finger      stream      tcp    nowait    nobody /usr/sbin/in.fingerd   in.fingerd
#systat      stream      tcp    nowait    root    /usr/bin/ps           ps -ef
#netstat     stream      tcp    nowait    root    /usr/bin/netstat      netstat -f inet
#
# Time service is used for clock synchronization.
#
time    stream tcp    nowait root    internal
time    dgram udp    wait    root    internal
#
# Echo, discard, daytime, and chargen are used primarily for testing.
#
echo        stream tcp    nowait    root    internal
echo        dgram udp    wait    root    internal
discard     stream tcp    nowait    root    internal
discard     dgram udp    wait    root    internal
daytime     stream tcp    nowait    root    internal
daytime     dgram udp    wait    root    internal
chargen     stream tcp    nowait    root    internal
chargen     dgram udp    wait    root    internal
#
#
# RPC services syntax:
#   <rpc_prog>/<vers> <socket_type> rpc/<proto> <flags> <user> <pathname> <args>
#
# The mount server is usually started in /etc/rc.local only on machines that
# are NFS servers.  It can be run by inetd as well.
#
#mountd/1     dgram    rpc/udp    wait root /usr/lib/nfs/mountd     mountd
#
# ypupdated is run by sites that support YP updating.
#
#ypupdated/1 stream rpc/tcp    wait root /usr/lib/netsvc/yp/ypupdated    ypupdated
#
# The rusers service gives out user information.  Sites concerned
# with security may choose to disable it.
#
#rusersd/1-2 dgram    rpc/udp    wait root /usr/lib/netsvc/rusers/rpc.rusersd
➥   rpc.rusersd
#
# The spray server is used primarily for testing.
#
```

```
#sprayd/1 dgram   rpc/udp   wait root /usr/lib/netsvc/spray/rpc.sprayd    rpc.sprayd
#
# The rwall server lets anyone on the network bother everyone on your machine.
#
#walld/1  dgram   rpc/udp   wait root /usr/lib/netsvc/rwall/rpc.rwalld    rpc.rwalld
#
#
# TLI services syntax:
#   <service_name> tli <proto> <flags> <user> <server_pathname> <args>
#
# TCPMUX services syntax:
#   tcpmux/<service_name> stream tcp <flags> <user> <server_pathname> <args>
#
smtp   stream tcp  nowait root  /usr/lib/mail/surrcmd/in.smtpd  in.smtpd -H netrix -r
```

The second line in the listing depicts the syntax of the file entries. The syntax is repeated here along with a sample entry for convenience:

```
#  service_name socket_type proto flags user server_pathname args
```

service_name	Is an identifying label of the service as listed in the /etc/services file. For example, the first service entry in the file is labeled ftp, matching another one in the /etc/services file.
socket_type	Identifies the type of the data delivery service being used. Three types are most commonly recognized: (1) stream, which is a byte-oriented delivery service provided by TCP (see Chapters 2 and 5 for a detailed explanation); (2) dgram, which is a transactional-oriented service delivered by UDP; and (3) raw, which directly runs on IP. In ftp's case, the type specified is stream.
proto	Identifies the name of the transport protocol, which is normally either udp or tcp, and corresponds to the protocol name as specified in the /etc/protocols file. In ftp's case, the protocol type is tcp.
flags	Can be set to either wait or nowait. If it's set to wait, inetd must wait for the service protocol (or server) to release the socket connecting it to the network before inetd can resume listening for more requests on that socket. On the other hand, a nowait flag enables inetd to listen immediately for more requests on the socket. Upon examining the previous listing of the inetd.conf file, you can note that stream type servers mostly allow a nowait status, whereas the status is wait for the dgram type of servers.
user	Specifies the user (or uid) name under which the server is invoked. This is normally set to user root. user can, however, be set to any valid username.

`server_pathname`	Specifies the server's full pathname of the program that `inetd` must invoke in response to an associated service request. In ftp's case, the program's full path is `/usr/sbin/in.ftpd`.
	Upon examining the `inetd.conf` file, you will notice that some of the servers' paths are specified as `internal`. Examples of these servers include echo, discard, and daytime. These are typically small and nondemanding servers. So instead of being implemented individually in separate programs, they are implemented as part of the `inetd` server itself.
`args`	Includes command-line arguments that are supported by the program implementing the server. As can be seen from the listing, the argument list must always start with the `argv[0]` argument (that is, the program's name) followed by whichever arguments you deem suitable.

Here's the sample entry:

```
ftp     stream tcp    nowait root   /usr/sbin/in.ftpd    in.ftpd
```

There are a few occasions when you might have to make some changes to the `inetd.conf` file. You might want to enable a service, disable another one, or modify one already supported. Enabling or disabling a service is a matter of removing or inserting the # character in front of the service configuration entry. In diskless workstation support, for example, you need to enable the `bootpd` service (see Chapter 14, "Special Servers and Services"). One step is to use your favorite editor to scan the `inetd.conf` file and remove the # character in front of the `bootps` service name. If you want to disable remote command execution, you have to insert # in front of the entry starting with `exec`.

Modifying a supported service mainly involves changing the arguments passed to the program responsible for that service. Using the `-s` option with the `in.tftp` command, for example, enables you to specify a directory to which you can restrict file transfer applications. According to the supporting entry in the `inetd.conf` shown previously, the directory specified is `tftpboot` to allow for remote reboot. You can change this to any other directory name.

Configuration Tools

UNIX provides an impressive toolkit to help you deal with the various aspects of administering and managing TCP/IP networks. Included in this toolkit are commands to configure the network interfaces and gather statistical data about your network interfaces (how they're doing in terms of collision rates or error rates). This could prove extremely helpful in reconsidering your network layout, or when troubleshooting. In this section, however, only two commands will be discussed: `ifconfig` and `configure`, which are used to configure the network interface and check on its status. Other commands will be presented in upcoming sections.

ifconfig

The ifconfig command is commonly found in all the UNIX flavors and is used to configure, or to check the configuration values of, the network interface card. You can use ifconfig to assign the network interface an IP address, netmask, and broadcast address, or to change some of its parameters. ifconfig is always used at boot time by the TCP/IP startup scripts to set up those parameters as dictated by the /etc/confnet.d/inet/interface file for each of the interfaces supported by the system.

The general syntax of ifconfig is too comprehensive to be able to meaningfully explain with one example. Therefore, it will be presented piecemeal in the context of different situations in which ifconfig is used.

Setting the IP Address, Netmask, and Broadcast Address

In its simplest form, the syntax of the ifconfig command is as follows:

```
ifconfig interface IP_address netmask mask broadcast address
```

This syntax is used to set up the basic parameters of the network interface, in which

interface	Is the label identifying the network interface card. For example, the 3Com 3C509 is known as el30.
IP_address	Is the IP address assigned to the network interface. You can optionally use the host name, provided that the /etc/hosts file includes the corresponding name-to-IP address association.
netmask mask	Is the applicable subnetwork mask. You can ignore this parameter if the mask is left at its default (that is, the network is not segmented into subnets). All hosts on the same physical network must have their mask set to the same value.
broadcast address	Is the broadcast address for the network. The default broadcast address is such that all the host ID bits are set to one. Older systems used to have the bits set to zero. All hosts on the same physical network must have their broadcast address set to the same value. For example, the Class B 150.1.0.0 network address has 150.1.255.255 as a default broadcast address.

In the following example, ifconfig is used to set up the IP address, netmask, and broadcast address of a 3Com 3C509 network interface card:

```
# ifconfig el30 150.1.0.1 netmask 255.255.0.0 broadcast 150.1.255.255
```

Optionally, you can use the host name rather than the IP address to configure the interface as follows:

```
# ifconfig el30 orbit netmask 255.255.0.0 broadcast 150.1.255.255
```

orbit is the host name mapped to a valid IP address in the /etc/hosts file.

This example can be further simplified to become

```
# ifconfig el30 orbit
```

because both the netmask and the broadcast address are set to their default values.

Assume that host orbit is on a segmented network on which the seventh and eighth bits of the third byte of the IP address are being used to designate the subnetwork. The netmask then becomes 255.255.192.0. To configure the interface accordingly, you enter this:

```
# ifconfig el30 orbit netmask 255.255.192.0
```

> **Note:** A remark worth noting about using ifconfig to reconfigure the interface is that the changes it implements are temporary, good only until the system is rebooted. To make changes permanent, use the configure command, discussed later in the chapter.

Checking the Interface Using *ifconfig*

To check the configuration parameters of a supported interface, you must enter

```
# ifconfig interface
```

Hence, to check the configuration of the 3Com 3C509, enter

```
# ifconfig el30
el30: flags=23<UP,BROADCAST,NOTRAILERS>
    inet 150.1.0.1 netmask ffff0000 broadcast 150.1.255.255
```

The preceding response confirms that the 3Com interface is configured to IP network address 150.1.0.1, the netmask to ffff0000 (that is, the hex equivalent to dotted notation 255.255.0.0), and the broadcast address to 150.1.255.255.

The information included within the angle brackets of the response report make the following indications:

◆ UP   Indicates that the interface is enabled and actively participating on the network. If the interface was disabled, UP would have been substituted by the null character.

◆ BROADCAST   Indicates that the interface is configured to accept broadcasts.

◆ NOTRAILERS   Indicates that the interface does not support trailer encapsulation, a technique by which the fields of the Ethernet frame can be rearranged for better efficiency, should the host I/O architecture benefit from this arrangement. Because this technique is becoming less popular, it will not be discussed any further.

To check the configuration of all the interfaces supported by the system, use the -a option (for all interfaces) with the ifconfig command as shown in the following example:

```
# ifconfig -a
lo0: flags=49<UP,LOOPBACK,RUNNING>
     inet 127.0.0.1 netmask ff000000
ne2k0: flags=23<UP,BROADCAST,NOTRAILERS>
     inet 100.0.0.1 netmask ff000000 broadcast 100.255.255.255
el30: flags=23<UP,BROADCAST,NOTRAILERS>
     inet 150.1.0.1 netmask ffff0000 broadcast 150.1.255.255
```

The preceding response refers to three interfaces. The first one, the lo0 interface, refers to the loopback interface and is assigned the IP loopback address 127.0.0.1 and the default Class A netmask. The second (ne2k0) and the third (el30) interfaces refer to the NE2000 and 3C509 interfaces, respectively. All interfaces are enabled (that is, UP) for use.

Enabling/Disabling the Interface with *ifconfig*

The ifconfig command supports a few optional parameters, of which the up and down parameters can be used to enable or disable an interface. You normally disable an interface temporarily on a router whenever you are troubleshooting the network and want to isolate a suspect segment from the rest of the network. Also, on some systems, configuration changes made to an interface won't take effect unless the interface was disabled before using ifconfig to modify the interface's configuration. To use ifconfig to disable an interface, enter this:

```
# ifconfig interface down
```

As an example, to disable the 3C509 network interface, enter this:

```
# ifconfig el30 down
```

It is always a good idea to check that the interface was indeed disabled before trusting it. To do so, enter this:

```
# ifconfig el30
el30: flags=22<BROADCAST,NOTRAILERS>
     inet 150.1.0.1 netmask ffff0000 broadcast 150.1.255.255
```

Notice how the absence of the keyword UP from the information included in the angle brackets implies that the interface is down.

To bring it back up, simply enter this:

```
# ifconfig el30 up
```

Assigning a Metric to the Interface Using *ifconfig*

Whenever `ifconfig` is used to configure a network interface, it partially updates the routing table with a static and direct route to the network the interface is attached to. The metric, or cost, associated with that route defaults to one unless you specify otherwise using the keyword `metric`. In all of the examples, the metric was ignored, defaulting the cost to one. In the following example, the network interface is configured with a metric of three:

```
# ifconfig el30 150.1.0.1 metric 3
```

To verify the configuration, enter

```
# ifconfig el30
el30: flags=23<UP,BROADCAST,NOTRAILERS> metric 3
    inet 150.1.0.1 netmask ffff0000 broadcast 150.1.255.255
```

Recall from Chapter 4, "The Internet Layer and Routing," that RIP, the routing information protocol, on each host advertises the routing information table as maintained by that host. Among the parameters included in the routing table are the destination address, the next router (or gateway) to which data should be forwarded, and the metric (that is, the cost) applicable to that route. Hosts listening to RIP advertisements on the network use them to dynamically update their tables. Should more than one router advertise reachability to the same destination, hosts on the network decide which router's services to use, based on the lowest metric (that is, shortest path) associated with that destination.

The metric, as implemented in RIP, does not accommodate other factors on the network such as link speeds, prevailing congestion levels, and link reliability. Thus, a router advertising a metric of one to reach a certain destination might be considerably slower than another router advertising a higher metric. Over time, you should be able to assess the traffic patterns prevailing on your network and the factors influencing them. Using `ifconfig`, you can change interface metrics, wherever applicable, to alter those patterns to achieve better network performance.

configure

Configuration changes made to the network interfaces in the UNIX host, using the `ifconfig` command, are only temporary. The next time the host is rebooted, it reverts to the configuration that existed before those changes were made. This is because `ifconfig` does not update any of the configuration and TCP/IP startup files when using them. You can remedy this behavior by editing each of those files individually. By doing so, however, you run the risk of making mistakes that might introduce problems the next time TCP/IP is restarted.

The `configure` command, also known as the generic configure command, is similar to the `ifconfig` command in functionality with an added feature of updating the startup files. Hence, using `configure` to reconfigure the interfaces guarantees that the associated changes are implemented every time TCP/IP is restarted.

The `configure` command provides a user-friendly interface when invoked with the `-i` option. This option allows `configure` to execute in an interactive mode, walking you through the process of configuring the interface. The process starts by displaying all the interfaces that are supported by the system and then asking you to choose an interface to configure. The command proceeds by prompting you for all relevant information, including the IP address, netmask, and broadcast address. If you configure more than one interface, it asks you to confirm whether you want to enable routing. If routing is not enabled, `configure` exits without rebuilding the operating system.

Using *ifconfig* Versus *configure*

Which one to use, `ifconfig` or `configure`? For temporary changes, you should use `ifconfig`, because this command does not make any modification to any of the TCP/IP startup files. Even if the intended changes are to be made permanent, you should refrain from using `configure` until you are satisfied with the impact of the changes you made using `ifconfig`. This way, you do not risk losing your current *working* configuration until you are assured that the alternative one works properly.

Configuring the Serial Interface

In Chapter 3, "The Network Access Layer," both the SLIP and the PPP serial protocols were introduced. You can deploy either one to connect two UNIX hosts or two TCP/IP networks over serial links. SLIP is the more commonly used protocol, deriving its popularity from its simple design and ease of implementation. PPP, on the other hand, is the more modern (and preferred) means of connecting hosts over WAN links. It is more sophisticated in design and overcomes most of SLIP's shortcomings (see Chapter 3 for a detailed discussion of the advantages and disadvantages of each protocol).

In this section, configuring both SLIP and PPP serial interfaces will be discussed. It is assumed that the reader is familiar with the RS-232C/D serial interface, so it will not be discussed.

In the following discussions, always assume that hosts `jade` and `netrix` are being connected over a serial link.

Configuring SLIP Using *slattach*

Configuring the serial port for SLIP support is a fairly simple and straightforward task with UNIX SVR4. Whereas `ifconfig` is the command you would normally use to configure IP over Ethernet or Token-ring type of media, `slattach` is the command to use to configure IP over the serial port.

The following steps are required to bring up SLIP on both hosts `jade` and `netrix`:

1. Determine which serial port is available for use.

2. Verify that no port monitor or getty process is running on that port. Assuming that you want to configure COM2 for SLIP support, you can verify that no getty is controlling the port by entering this:

```
ps -ef ¦ grep tty01
```

If, in response to this command, you find that either getty or uugetty is running on that port, you should investigate further how this process is started. Checking /etc/inittab is a good starting point. Should you find an entry pertaining to the port in question, find out whether you can remove that entry and kill the corresponding getty or uugetty process before you go any further. If you cannot free up the port, consider another alternative.

To check whether there is a ttymon port monitor controlling the port, enter this:

```
# pmadm -l -p ttymon
```

Again, by going through the output of this command, you should be able to determine whether the port is being used by a ttymon port service.

3. Create the physical connection. slattach expects the physical connection to the remote system to exist before it is invoked. If you are connecting both systems using a null modem, you should verify that the null modem is wired correctly before you use it. Consult your hardware vendor documentation to obtain the exact wiring diagrams. Failure to do so might lead to long, frustrating hours of troubleshooting the SLIP connection.

If, instead, you are configuring for dialup with modems on both ends of the connection, you need to bring up the connection using the cu command before slattach is invoked.

4. Update the /etc/hosts file, on both hosts, to include the name to IP address mappings of both the local and the remote hosts. While doing that, remember to use a new host name for the SLIP interface. In the example, the host name associated with SLIP on jade is jadeslip, whereas that association on netrix is netrixslip.

The IP addresses, in the example, are 198.53.235.10 and 198.53.235.1, corresponding to jadeslip and netrixslip, respectively.

5. Now you are at the point of configuring SLIP using slattach. The syntax of slattach in its simplest form is

```
# slattach serialport local_IP_address dest_IP_address link_speed
```

in which

serialport   Represents the device special file corresponding to the serial port. The special file corresponding to COM2 would be /dev/tty01.

local_IP_address   Is the IP address assigned to the local SLIP interface. Remember that this address should not be in use anywhere on the network.

dest_IP_address   Is the destination address assigned to the remote SLIP interface. Make sure that both the local and the remote IP addresses have the same network address.

link_speed   Is the serial link speed in bits per second. Both ends of the SLIP
                                connection must be set to the same speed. In this scenario, SLIP
                                on both jade and netrix configured to 2400 bits per second.

Hence, to configure the SLIP interface on netrix, enter the following command:

```
# slattach tty01 198.53.235.1 198.53.235.10 2400&
```

And to configure SLIP on jade, enter this:

```
# slattach tty01 198.53.235.10 198.53.235.1 2400&
```

Notice how, in both cases, slattach is left to execute in the background.

If all goes well, you should be able to use either host to talk to the other one. Before doing so, however, it is best to check the configuration first. This can be done using ifconfig as shown here:

```
# ifconfig -a
lo0: flags=49<UP,LOOPBACK,RUNNING>
    inet 127.0.0.1 netmask ff000000
ne2k0: flags=23<UP,BROADCAST,NOTRAILERS>
    inet 100.0.0.1 netmask ff000000 broadcast 100.255.255.255
el30: flags=23<UP,BROADCAST,NOTRAILERS>
    inet 150.1.0.1 netmask ffff0000 broadcast 150.1.255.255
sl0: flags=11<UP,POINTOPOINT>
    inet 198.53.235.1 --> 198.53.235.10 netmask ffffff00
```

The last entry in the output of the ifconfig command corresponds to the SLIP interface that was just configured on the host netrix. According to this entry, the SLIP interface label is sl0. The interface is marked as up and as a point-to-point link. Notice how, unlike other interfaces, sl0's configuration information includes the destination IP address in addition to the local one.

slattach and the Routing Table

When slattach is invoked to configure SLIP, the host's routing table is automatically updated to include the new route to the remote host. You can check the host's routing table by entering the following netstat command:

```
# netstat -rn
Routing tables
Destination        Gateway        Flags  Refs  Use      Interface
127.0.0.1          127.0.0.1       UH     0     0          lo0
198.53.235.10      198.53.235.1    UH     0     172        sl0
150.1              150.1.0.1       U      0     0          el30
100                100.0.0.1       U      1     675        ne2k0
198.53.237         100.0.0.2       UG     0     0          ne2k0
```

This table pertains to host netrix. Notice how a route pertaining to IP address 198.53.235.10 (that is, that of host jade) is added, with the gateway address 198.53.235.1 being that of the local SLIP interface. For an interpretation of all the fields, refer to Chapter 4, "The Internet Layer and Routing," where the netstat command was first introduced.

Alternatively, you can enter netstat -in to obtain similar information. The following example illustrates the command:

```
# netstat -in
Name   Mtu   Network     Address           Ipkts  Ierrs  Opkts  Oerrs  Collis
lo0    8256  127         127.0.0.1           0      0      0      0      0
ne2k0  1500  100         100.0.0.1         498      0    543      0      0
el30   1500  150.1       150.1.0.1           9      0      9      0      0
sl0    296   198.53.235  198.53.235.1 153    0    138      0      0
```

On a few systems, you might have to enter the routing information manually using the route add command. Failure to do so might abort any attempt to communicate data over the SLIP link. Assuming that netrix is running a flavor of UNIX that requires manual intervention for updating the routing table, you would then enter

```
# route add 198.53.235.10 198.53.235.1 3
```

in which a metric of 3 is assumed to take into account the sluggish nature of the link compared with other links, such as Ethernet.

SLIP at Boot Time

Unfortunately, slattach does not update the TCP/IP startup files to bring up SLIP at boot time. To achieve that, you have to edit the /etc/inet/rc.inet file manually and include both the slattach command and possibly the accompanying route add command. Shown next are the contents of the /etc/inet/rc.inet file after being edited to include the slattach with the proper command parameters:

```
# Inet startup script run from /etc/init.d/inetinit
LOG=/tmp/inet.start
PermLog=/var/adm/log/inet.start
export LOG PermLog
exitcode=0

# Label the error log
echo "The following commands were run from /etc/inet/rc.inet" > $LOG

#
# Add lines here to set up routes to gateways, start other daemons, etc.
#
# The following is slip on COM2 configuration

/usr/sbin/slattach tty01 198.53.235.1   198.53.235.10 2400&

#
# Run the ppp daemon if /etc/inet/ppphosts is present
#
```

```
if [ -f /etc/inet/ppphosts -a -x /usr/sbin/in.pppd ]
then
    /usr/sbin/in.pppd
fi

# This runs in.gated if its configuration file (/etc/inet/gated.conf) is
# present.  Otherwise, in.routed is run.
#
if [ -f /etc/inet/gated.conf -a -x /usr/sbin/in.gated ]
then
    /usr/sbin/in.gated
else
    #
    # if running, kill the route demon
    #
    kill 'ps -ef¦grep in[.]routed¦awk '{print $2}'' 2>/dev/null
    /usr/sbin/in.routed -q
fi
#
# /usr/sbin/route add default your_nearest_gateway hops_to_gateway
/usr/sbin/route add default 100.0.1.2 1
# if [ $? -ne 0 ]
# then
# exitcode=1
# fi

#
#  Run the DNS server if a configuration file is present
#
if [ -f /etc/inet/named.boot -a -x /usr/sbin/in.named ]
then
    /usr/sbin/in.named
fi

#
#  Run the NTP server if a configuration file is present
#
if [ -f /etc/inet/ntp.conf -a -x /usr/sbin/in.xntpd ]
then
    /usr/sbin/in.xntpd
fi

#
# return status to /etc/init.d/inetinit
#
if [ $exitcode -eq 0 ]
then
#    rm -f $LOG $PermLog
    echo
else
    echo "\nTCP/IP startup was not entirely successful. Error messages in $LOG"
    cp $LOG $PermLog
fi
exit $exitcode
```

Other SLIP Options

The slattach command supports a few options that can be used to improve the performance of the SLIP link. Only the most commonly used options are examined in the following discussion.

Compressed SLIP Option

SLIP, as it was originally specified by RFC 1055, proved to be slow. Depending on the line speed, it was sometimes deemed unsuitable for interactive applications such as telnet and rlogin. Traffic generated by interactive applications tend to be dominantly made of small packets carrying a few bytes of user data. Any data-carrying packet, small or large, requires a fixed overhead of 40 bytes of IP and TCP header information. For small packets, this means that a SLIP link spends most of its time exchanging packet overheads rather than meaningful data.

To remedy this problem, a new version of SLIP was introduced (RFC 1144). Called [C]SLIP, this version reduces the amount of header information to three to five bytes by precluding those fields that are fairly static over the entire connection period. These smaller headers significantly improve the response time of interactive applications.

To turn on compression, the slattach command should include the +c option. The following example illustrates the enablement of compression on netrix using slattach:

```
# slattach +c tty01 198.53.235.1 198.53.235.10 2400&
```

Optionally, you can use the +e option to enable automatic compression detection on the SLIP interface. In doing so, SLIP turns on compression only if it determines that data packets it received from the remote end are indeed compressed. Consequently, you should not enable compression autodetection on both ends of the SLIP interface. If this happens, neither SLIP interface will take the initiative to compress SLIP packets.

Maximum Transfer Unit (MTU) Option

The maximum transfer unit sets a physical limit on the size of the data frame undergoing transmission. The MTU of Ethernet, for example, is 1500 bytes. User data sizes larger than the 1500 bytes force IP to resort to fragmenting the packet into multiple IP packets so that the MTU limit of the transmission media is never exceeded.

Unless otherwise specified, the default MTU size of SLIP is 296 bytes. For most applications, this limit provides reasonable performance. For a given MTU, performance is a function of both the nature of the applications running on SLIP and the link speed.

By using slattach with the +m option, you can modify the MTU of the SLIP interface to suit your needs.

The following example sets the MTU to 552 bytes:

```
# slattach +m 552 tty01 198.53.235.1 198.53.235.10 4800&
```

> **Note:** For performance reasons, it is always beneficial to set the MTU according to one of the following rules:
>
> ◆ If compression is disabled, set the MTU to 40 + 2n.
>
> ◆ If compression is enabled, set the MTU to 5 + 2n.
>
> In these calculations, n is a positive whole number.

Deciding on an optimal value takes some experimentation and compromise between non-interactive applications (such as ftp) and interactive applications (such as telnet). The former category of applications benefits more from large MTU sizes.

Configuring the Point-to-Point (PPP) Connection

UNIX supports up to four PPP connections, assigned interface names ppp0–ppp3. A PPP connection can be established over direct lines or dialup lines.

Configuring PPP involves editing up to five files, two of which pertain to uucp. These are the files:

◆ /etc/hosts: This file must be edited to include the remote PPP host name and IP address you intend to establish the connection with (refer to previous pages for a detailed description of /etc/hosts).

◆ /etc/inet/ppphosts: This file should be edited to include PPP configuration information for each host you intend to reach via PPP (details on this file will be provided later).

◆ /etc/confnet.d/inet/interface: This file must include all the interface configuration parameters that /etc/confnet.d/inet/config.boot.sh will be able to use to configure the PPP interface.

◆ /etc/uucp/Systems: This file should include an entry corresponding to every system defined in the /etc/inet/ppphosts file.

◆ /etc/uucp/Devices: This file should include an entry that compliments the one found in the Systems file to configure the communication port properly and determine which dialer to invoke to chat with the modem.

For the smooth and uninterruptable configuration of the PPP connection, you should have the following information available before you get started:

◆ The IP address and name of the remote PPP host. Remember, every IP interface must have a unique name. A host maintaining connections through three interfaces must have three names, each assigned a different IP address. Similarly, the PPP interface should be assigned both a name and an IP address.

◆ The IP address and name of the local PPP host. For convenience, the author normally calls the PPP interface *hostname*ppp. With the host node name jade, the PPP host name becomes jadeppp.

◆ The tty port over which the connection will be established.

◆ The dialer script compatible with the modem type connected to the port.

◆ tty port settings (that is, baud rate, parity settings, and so on).

◆ Any pppd-applicable configuration parameters.

◆ Login ID and password that the dial-out system can use to log in to the remote PPP host.

◆ Information from the modem manual as to how to set the S registers to the desired settings.

In the following two subsections, both hosts netrix and jade will be configured to establish a PPP connection. netrix will be configured for inbound (dial-in) PPP support; jade, for outbound (dial-out) PPP support.

Configuring an Inbound PPP Connection

To configure an inbound (dial-in) connection, you should configure a uucp connection. To do so for netrix, the /etc/uucp/Devices file is edited to include the following entry:

```
Direct tty01h - 2400 direct_modem
```

Refer to your manual for information on the Devices file and how to interpret its contents. Notice that the tty01h, rather than tty01, device special file was specified to allow for the use of hardware flow control.

In addition, a ttymon port monitor should be created and set to listen to connection and login requests on the tty01h port. The easier alternative is to run /etc/getty on the port. getty does the same job as the ttymon port monitor. It is enabled by the /etc/inittab file by including the following entry:

```
ppp:23:respawn:/etc/getty tty01h 2400
```

> **Note:** Some System V systems overwrite the /etc/inittab file when you rebuild the kernel. Therefore, all changes are lost if you edit the file directly. You can, however, edit the /etc/conf/init.d/kernel file, which is what's used to overwrite the inittab file.

Accordingly, getty will be spawned, by init, whenever the system enters run levels 2 or 3. Also, init restarts getty whenever getty terminates execution.

Next, the modem has to be configured such that the autoanswer mode is turned on. Also, the parity and speed of the modem must be set properly. Most important, however, is to turn on the quiet mode. The quiet mode is necessary to prevent the modem from echoing some of the login strings back to the port, leading to a vicious sequence of unsuccessful logins.

Modem settings can be effected by establishing a direct modem session, using the cu -l command, and entering a sequence of AT commands to write to some of the S registers. In the following sample session, netrix's modem was configured to support autoanswering mode (AT S0=1), proper parity (AT S15=130), and quiet mode:

```
# cu -l tty01h
AT S0=1
AT S15=130
ATQ1
ATQ2
AT&W
~.
```

Do not forget to save the modem settings using AT&W before terminating the session and exiting to the shell using the ~. command.

The preceding discussion concludes the necessary preliminary steps to configure the serial port in preparation for configuring the PPP connection. pppd is the daemon that runs in the background to look after the properly configured PPP connection. Configuring the daemon involves editing the /etc/hosts, /etc/inet/ppphosts, and /etc/confnet.d/inet/interface files.

Often, you don't have to do the editing yourself. Instead, UNIX provides configuration scripts to do the job for you. The author uses pppconf on his system (UnixWare 1.1). Check your manuals for the utility to use to do the same thing. pppconf is a user-friendly utility that walks through the process of setting up the link, whether for dial-in or dial-out.

Conversing with pppconf intelligently, however, involves providing it with the PPP-specific configuration parameters. Table 9.1 summarizes these parameters.

Table 9.1. The pppd configuration parameters. These options can be included in the /etc/inet/ppphosts configuration file.

Configuration Option	Default	Description
Timer Options:		
idle = *idle_time*	forever	Inactivity timeout.
tmout = *restart_time*	3 sec.	Seconds to wait for a response before a configure request or a terminate request is reattempted.
conf = *num*	10	Maximum reconfiguration requests before aborting the attempt.
term = *num*	2	Maximum termination requests before dropping the link.
nak = *num*	10	Maximum negative acknowledgments during the negotiation phase before assuming that negotiation is not converging.

continues

Table 9.1. continued

Configuration Option	Default	Description
		Link Options:
mru = *num*	296	Maximum size of datagram you want to receive. Increase the size over a reliable link for improved efficiency.
accm = *hex_num*	0x00000000	A hexadecimal number representing the asynchronous control character map. PPP can be configured to map ASCII control characters (hex 0 to hex 20) into a two-character sequence. Each bit in the *hex_num* enables the mapping of a corresponding control character. The least significant bit represents NULL (ASCII 0).
pap	Disable	Enable/disable password authentication.
nomgc	Enable	Enable/disable magic number generation. Magic number generation provides a way to test the link for quality.
protocomp	Disable	Turns on/off protocol field compression.
accomp	Disable	Turns on/off address-control field compression.
		IP Options:
ipaddr	Disable	Enable/Disable IP address negotiation. This is particularly useful if more than one host might dial in to the facility. Otherwise, turn it off.
rfc1172	Disable	Enable/disable old IP address negotiation (RFC 1172). Turn it on if any of the remote systems that will be dialing in still use old IP address negotiation.
vj	Disable	Enable/disable Van Jacobson TCP header compression.

In addition to all of these options, pppconf prompts you for the remote login ID, creates it in the /etc/passwd file, and prompts for the remote login password. pppconf also prompts for the IP addresses and interface names of both the local and the remote systems.

pppconf edits each of /etc/hosts, /etc/inet/ppphosts and /etc/confnet.d/inet/interface in the following manner:

◆ /etc/hosts is edited to include the IP addresses and host names pertaining to both the local and the remote host.

◆ `/etc/inet/ppphosts` is pppd's configuration file where all the parameters shown in Table 9.1 are specified. This file must contain one entry for each of the remote PPP hosts. Also, it must include a login entry per host. Following is the format of the file entries:

```
name  tty  system  [options]
```

In this format,

name	Specifies the name of the remote host, or the PPP login ID. A login ID must be prefixed with the * character.
tty	Specifies the tty port over which the PPP connection must be established. The - character is the default, corresponding to any port. If you're configuring for dial-in, leave it at the default.
system	Specifies the UUCP name of the remote host. The default is the - character. Leave it at the default if you're configuring for dial-in.
options	Specifies the parameters shown in Table 9.1. If a parameter is not specified, its default setting is assumed.

Following is netrix's `/etc/ppphosts` configuration file (comments are not included for the sake of brevity):

```
nppp - - accm=000a0000 accomp ipaddr rfc1172addr VJ old remote=198.53.235.10
```

According to the preceding entry, netrix is configured for dial-in, where the remote host's login ID is nppp. Notice how only the parameters deviating from their defaults are explicitly included. Also, the remote host IP address is included.

◆ `/etc/confnet.d/interface` is updated to include the ifconfig parameters that apply to the pppØ interface. Using cat, the following updated version of the file exists after PPP is configured:

```
pp:0:198.53.235.1:/dev/ppp:198.53.235.10:add_ppp:
el3:0:orbit:/dev/el3_0:-trailers::
ne2k:0::/dev/ne2k_0:-trailers::
```

Recall that at boot time, the `/etc/confnet.d/inet/config.boot.sh` script loops through all the interfaces defined in interface to configure them properly. As can be seen from the listing, pppØ is treated similarly.

Configuring an Outbound PPP Connection

Configuring an outbound (dial-out) PPP connection requires some additional UUCP administration. Otherwise, setting up PPP configuration parameters is pretty much the same as configuring for an inbound connection. This section describes what you need to add to the `/etc/uucp/Devices` and `/etc/uucp/Systems` files to dial out. The examples provided are based on the assumption that host jade (with PPP IP address 198.53.235.1) is being configured for dial-out PPP. netrix is assumed to be the remote host across the link and is configured as described in the preceding section.

Using your preferred editor, add the following two lines to the /etc/uucp/Devices file:

```
Direct ttyport - speed direct_modem
ACU   ttyport - Any dialer
```

The first entry allows for a direct modem connection using the cu command. *ttyport* and *speed* specify the serial port and baud rate of the connection. The second entry takes care of chatting with the modem on the user's behalf whenever a connection is requested. Consult your documentation for more on uucp.

Assuming that a 2400-bps Hayes-compatible modem is connected to COM2 of netrix, the preceding two entries become

```
Direct tty01h - 2400 direct_modem
ACU tty01h Any hayes
```

Next, edit the /etc/uucp/Systems file to add the following entry:

```
remotePPPhost Any ACU telephonenum "" \r\d "" \r\d in: —in: ppplogin word: password
```

In this format,

remotePPPhost	Specifies the remote host name (that is, the dial-system) as specified in this host's /etc/inet/ppphosts file.
telephonenum	Specifies the telephone number of the remote system.
ppplogin	Specifies the login ID that pppd will use on your behalf to establish connection with the remote system. The login ID you specify here must match the one specified in the /etc/passwd file of the remote dial-in system.
password	Specifies the login password to the remote host. The password specified here must match that specified in the /etc/passwd of the remote dial-in system.

Continuing on jade's example, its Systems file should include the following entry:

```
netrixppp Any ACU 2400 7369821   "" \r ogin: nppp word: cashewnuts
```

Next, use pppconf to configure the local PPP interface. Again, pppconf walks you through the configuration process. Be careful to pick the menu options corresponding to dial-out configuration as you do so. For example, configuring jade for dial-out PPP yields the following entry in its /etc/inet/ppphosts file:

```
netrixppp tty01h netrixppp  idle=5 tmout=3
```

According to this entry, the remote host name and its UUCP name are the same (netrixppp). Also, COM2 serial port is being configured to support PPP. Contrast this entry with that included in ppphosts of netrix, as configured in the preceding section.

Use cu to test the configuration of the UUCP files as shown here:

```
# cu -l tty01h
ATDT 7369821
```

If your system connects to the remote PPP host, you can proceed with testing the PPP connection. Otherwise, troubleshoot at the UUCP level. Refer to Chapter 15, "Network Troubleshooting and Performance Tuning," for discussions on troubleshooting the PPP link.

To test the PPP link, use rlogin or the ping command. Using ping, enter this:

```
# ping -s netrixppp
```

Be patient, because you have to wait before your host starts reporting ICMP ECHO_RESPONSES. By the time the remote host is dialed into and a PPP connection is established, your system will have lost a few ICMP ECHO_RESPONSES. Meanwhile, however, you should be able to follow the progress of the dialing activity, as reflected by the modem's status LEDs on the front panel.

Theory of Operation

As stated earlier, pppd is the daemon that takes care of PPP connections. Like many of the TCP/IP services, it is started from the /etc/inet/rc.inet startup file when the system enters run level two at boot time. The following pppd-relevant code is extracted from the rc.inet file:

```
# Run the ppp daemon if /etc/inet/ppphosts is present
#
if [ -f /etc/inet/ppphosts -a -x /usr/sbin/in.pppd ]
then
     /usr/sbin/in.pppd
fi
```

According to this listing, the operating system does not invoke the pppd daemon unless its corresponding configuration file, /etc/inet/ppphosts, exists. By this time, the config.boot.sh will have configured the interfaces, including the PPP interface. You can use the ifconfig command to check for ppp0 configuration. Checking netrix's interfaces yields this:

```
# ifconfig -a
ppp0: flags=31<UP,POINTOPOINT,NOTRAILERS>
     inet 198.53.235.10 --> 198.53.235.1 netmask ffffff00
el30: flags=23<UP,BROADCAST,NOTRAILERS>
     inet 150.1.0.1 netmask ffff0000 broadcast 150.1.255.255
ne2k0: flags=23<UP,BROADCAST,NOTRAILERS>
     inet 100.0.0.1 netmask ff000000 broadcast 100.255.255.255
```

According to the output, ppp0 is up and configured to IP address 198.53.235.10. Unlike other interfaces, ifconfig shows that the interface is configured to connect to 198.53.235.1 over a point-to-point link.

The following scenario depicts the flow of events from the time a user enters a command to access a remote system over PPP to the point when the link is established. It is assumed that a user logged in to jade is attempting to connect to netrix.

1. The user enters rlogin netrixppp. As a result, /etc/hosts is fetched for the corresponding IP address (198.53.235.10). The address is then submitted to IP for use in shipping the connection request.

2. IP determines that to reach the specified host, the user request must be delivered through the ppp0 interface. Hence, IP submits the datagram to pppd because this interface is controlled by pppd.

3. pppd fetches the /etc/inet/ppphosts file for information on how to make the call to the requested system (that is, which serial port, the UUCP system name, and the negotiable parameters).

4. The UUCP remote system name (the third field in the ppphosts file) is used to find a matching entry in the /etc/uucp/Systems file (the first field in Systems).

5. If a match is found in Step 4, the entry is buffered in memory, and the third field of the matching entry (that is, specifying ACU) is then matched with the first field of every record in the /etc/uucp/Devices file.

6. If a matching record is found in the /etc/uucp/Devices file, the modem is configured to the settings specified in the record. The line is dialed by the modem, using the specified dialer.

7. After the connection is established, the buffered chat script from Step 5 is run. Both ends of the connection exchange authentication information at this stage. jade will provide login ID nppp and password cashewnuts in order to login in to netrix. This is *not* user login, yet.

8. If all goes well, pppd drivers on both ends negotiate the connection parameters, as specified in their respective /etc/inet/ppphosts files.

9. Finally, the calling rlogind sends a request to the called inetd. inetd invokes rlogind on the remote system, which executes login on the port and prompts the user for login information.

Configuring Routing

In Chapter 4, "The Internet Layer and Routing," the Internet Protocol was introduced as the workhorse that makes things happen in the TCP/IP protocol suite. IP's main responsibility is to deliver user data submitted by upper-layer protocols to its prescribed destination.

IP interprets the IP address of the destined host, and based on a routing table, determines whether the packet (or datagram) belongs to a directly linked network or to a remote network linked via a router. In the former case, the datagram is delivered directly to the host. Otherwise, the datagram is sent to the router for forwarding.

IP relies on *reachability information* that is maintained in a special table known as the routing information table (RIT). Included in the table is one entry for each known route that contains information such as the destination network or host IP address, a metric (or hop count) describing how far the destination is (unless the destined host is attached to a directly connected network), which router to forward the datagram to, and the interface to make the delivery.

Routing table maintenance is not IP's responsibility. There are several other protocols that do the maintenance work, including the Internet Control Message Protocol (ICMP), and dynamic routing information protocols such as the Routing Information Protocol, Exterior Gateway Protocol (EGP), and Border Gateway Protocol (BGP).

UNIX relies on two daemons to support routing protocols: (1) `routed`, which supports RIP only, and (2) `gated`, which supports the other protocols in addition to RIP. Depending on the host's routing configuration, the RIT table might be statically maintained, or one or more of these protocols might be involved in gathering network reachability information that will be used to update the RIT table.

In the following sections, configuring for both static and dynamic routing will be discussed. The hypothetical internetwork shown in Figure 9.2 will be used to illustrate the configurations. As can be seen from the diagram, the internetwork connects geographically distributed networks belonging to different sites. Multihomed hosts including `netrix`, `jade`, and `fashion` are acting as routers supporting both local network segments and remote links. Assigned network addresses are shown in the diagram. No subnetting is assumed.

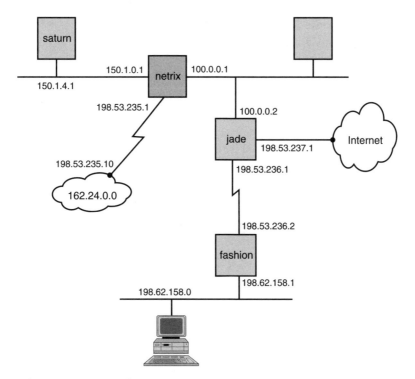

Figure 9.2. *The* `unicom.com` *network.*

Configuring the Kernel for Routing

For a host supporting more than one network interface to act as a router, its UNIX kernel must be reconfigured to enable its IP forwarding capability. Doing so is an easy three-step process:

1. Invoke /etc/confnet.d/configure -i, and when prompted as to whether you want the host to act as a gateway, respond with a y for yes.

2. Build a new operating system by entering /etc/conf/bin/idbuild at the command line.

3. Reboot the host for the new operating system, with enabled IP forwarding, to take effect.

Static Routing

Under static routing, the RIT table maintains its information without regard to network changes. As such, a static configuration is suitable to small networks on which routes are stable. Also, a static configuration is suitable to hosts belonging to a network that has only one route leading to the outside world. In Figure 9.2, for example, all hosts on the 150.1.0.0 network have netrix as their only way out to the other segments of the internetwork and to the Internet. In this case, it makes better sense to configure all hosts on the 151.1.0.0 network for static routing. This way, the bandwidth lost to background route information exchange activity is saved at no risk. Even in the worst-case scenario, if netrix goes down, there is no other route to adjust the RIT table to.

A static routing table can be maintained using two commands: ifconfig and route add. As shown earlier in the chapter, UNIX uses the ifconfig command to initialize the network interfaces with information including the assigned IP address, the subnet mask, and a metric. In particular, at boot time, ifconfig is invoked by /etc/confnet.d/inet/boot.config.sh to initialize all the defined interfaces in the /etc/confnet.d/inet/interface file. While doing so, UNIX uses the interface information to install static routes in the RIT table. These routes pertain to the networks connected directly to the supported interfaces.

With dynamic routing disabled on host netrix, and without any route add commands being included in the TCP/IP startup files, the RIT table includes only the static routes initialized by ifconfig. You can verify this by using the netstat -rn command (see Chapter 4 for command syntax) as shown here:

```
# netstat -rn
Routing tables
Destination         Gateway          Flags  Refs   Use  Interface
127.0.0.1           127.0.0.1        UH     0      0       lo0
198.53.235.10       198.53.235.1     UH     0      172     sl0
150.1               150.1.0.1        U      0      0       el30
100                 100.0.0.1        U      1      675     ne2k0
```

Using only this configuration has a very serious shortcoming: netrix is left without information about reachability to remote networks. This means hosts on the 150.1.0.0 network, for example, cannot communicate with those on network 198.53.237.0 or those across the WAN links. As it stands, this minimal configuration is suitable for the simple case in which all hosts belong to the same network or backbone, and there is absolutely no need for routers.

To add routes to the minimal configuration while keeping it static, use the route add command. Chapter 4 depicts the syntax of, and provides examples for, route add. The following example shows how route add can be used to add routes to hosts on networks 162.24.0.0, 198.53.237.0, and 198.62.158.0:

```
# route add 162.24.0.0 198.53.235.10 3
# route add 198.53.237.0 100.0.0.2 1
# route add 198.62.158.0 100.0.0.2 3
```

Entering netstat -rn verifies the additional routes:

```
# netstat -rn
Routing tables
Destination       Gateway           Flags  Refs  Use    Interface
127.0.0.1         127.0.0.1         UH     0     0         lo0
198.53.235.10     198.53.235.1      UH     0     172       sl0
162.24            198.53.235.10     UGH    0     0       ne2k0
150.1             150.1.0.1         U      0     0       e130
100               100.0.0.1         U      1     675     ne2k0
198.53.237        100.0.0.2         UG     0     0       ne2k0
```

This configuration allows netrix to go places on the network. But what if a connection to the Internet was installed on jade? How should netrix's routing table be updated so that hosts using its routing capabilities can communicate with the outside world? That is where the *default route* comes into the picture.

Recall from Chapter 4 that the default route applies to all routes that are not explicitly described in the RIT table. The Internet comprises hundreds of thousands of hosts scattered around the world, each of which has its own IP address. This makes it impossible to update the routing table with every conceivable route that your users might require to talk to their preferred target hosts. Using route add default, shown in the following example, allows netrix to forward to jade all datagrams destined for routes not described in netrix's RIT table, including foreign hosts on the Internet.

```
# route add default 100.0.0.2 1
add net default: gateway 100.0.0.2 flags 0x3
```

To verify the update, enter this:

```
# netstat -rn
Routing tables
Destination       Gateway           Flags  Refs  Use    Interface
127.0.0.1         127.0.0.1         UH     0     0         lo0
198.53.235.1      100.0.0.2         UGH    0     0       ne2k0
198.53.235.10     198.53.235.1      UH     0     0         sl0
default           100.0.0.2         UG     0     0       ne2k0
150.1             150.1.0.1         U      0     8       e130
100               100.0.0.1         U      1     61      ne2k0
198.53.237        100.0.0.2         UG     0     0       ne2k0
162.24            198.53.235.10     UGH    0     0       ne2k0
```

How can static routing on hosts such as saturn be configured to communicate with others on the private network, as well as those on the Internet? Aside from the ifconfig command and a RIT with the route to which the interface is connected, saturn requires only a single route add command. The purpose of using route add is to add netrix to RIT as the default router for data not addressed to the local network segment. Hence, saturn's routing table assumes the simplest form, as shown here:

```
# netstat -rn
Routing tables
Destination         Gateway        Flags  Refs   Use    Interface
127.0.0.1           127.0.0.1        UH     0      0          lo0
default             150.1.0.1        UG     0      0        ne2k0
150.1               150.1.4.1         U     0      8         el30
```

Testing for Reachability and ping

You might have wondered many times how to test your configuration for reachability to the desired networks. Although telnet and ftp can be used to do some testing, TCP/IP provides ping as a better, and more convenient, testing tool.

ping uses the ICMP's ECHO_REQUEST datagram to elicit a response (another ICMP datagram called ECHO_RESPONSE) from a target host or gateway. If the target host or gateway fails to respond, ping reports the failure with an explanation.

In its simplest form, ping is used as shown here:

```
# ping  hostname ¦ IP_address
```

The hostname or IP_address specifies the target host or gateway. If the target host responds with an ECHO_RESPONSE datagram, ping prints hostname is alive. In the following example, jade pings netrix:

```
# ping netrix
PING netrix is alive
```

You can use ping with the -s option to send the target host a continuous flow of ECHO_REQUEST datagrams, one per second. The following example illustrates this option:

```
# ping -s jade
PING jade: 56 data bytes
64 bytes from jade (100.0.0.2): icmp_seq=0. time=10. ms
64 bytes from jade (100.0.0.2): icmp_seq=1. time=0. ms
64 bytes from jade (100.0.0.2): icmp_seq=2. time=0. ms
64 bytes from jade (100.0.0.2): icmp_seq=3. time=0. ms
64 bytes from jade (100.0.0.2): icmp_seq=4. time=0. ms

----jade PING Statistics----
5 packets transmitted, 5 packets received, 0% packet loss
round-trip (ms)  min/avg/max = 0/2/10
```

In this example, ping was interrupted after the fifth datagram was sent. According to the output, all five datagrams were responded to successfully by jade. Also, ping provides statistical data that might prove helpful in assessing the quality of the transport service.

The first line of the statistics includes total packets sent, packets received (that is, responses), and percent packet loss. ping reported no loss (0%) in this example. The second line reports the minimum, average, and maximum round-trip times. Notice how individual responses are also reported, including the size of the datagram, the target address, and the round-trip time each datagram spent on the wire.

The following example illustrates the case of an unreachable network:

```
# ping -s 134.3.2.4
PING 134.3.2.4 (134.3.2.4): 56 data bytes
ping: sendto: Network is unreachable
ping: wrote 134.3.2.4 64 chars, ret=-1
ping: sendto: Network is unreachable
ping: wrote 134.3.2.4 64 chars, ret=-1
ping: sendto: Network is unreachable
ping: wrote 134.3.2.4 64 chars, ret=-1

--- 134.3.2.4 ping statistics ---
3 packets transmitted, 0 packets received, 100% packet loss
```

Boot Time Installation of Static Routing

Unless the /etc/inet/rc.inet startup file is properly edited, all the static routes you installed using route add will be lost when the host is rebooted. To make the static route configuration permanent, you must edit /etc/inet/rc.inet as follows:

1. Include the route add statements necessary to include all the desired routes.
2. Comment any statements that might run any routing protocol at startup.

Applying this to netrix, its /etc/inet/rc.inet file looks like the following listing. In this example, the lines in bold type include the updates made to this file.

```
#       @(#)rc.inet  1.5 STREAMWare TCP/IP SVR4.2  source
#       SCCS IDENTIFICATION
#ident "@(#)cmd-inet:common/cmd/cmd-inet/etc/inet/rc.inet    1.3.8.7"

# Inet startup script run from /etc/init.d/inetinit
LOG=/tmp/inet.start
PermLog=/var/adm/log/inet.start
export LOG PermLog
exitcode=0

# Label the error log
echo "The following commands were run from /etc/inet/rc.inet" > $LOG

#
#
# Add lines here to set up routes to gateways, start other daemons, etc.
#
route add 162.24.0.0 198.53.235.10 3
route add 198.53.237.0 100.0.0.2 1
```

```
route add 198.62.158.0 100.0.0.2 3
route add default 100.0.0.2 1

#
# Run the ppp daemon if /etc/inet/ppphosts is present
#
if [ -f /etc/inet/ppphosts -a -x /usr/sbin/in.pppd ]
then
     /usr/sbin/in.pppd
fi

# This runs in.gated if its configuration file (/etc/inet/gated.conf) is
# present.  Otherwise, in.routed is run.
#
#if [ -f /etc/inet/gated.conf -a -x /usr/sbin/in.gated ]
#then
#    /usr/sbin/in.gated
#else
#    #
#    # if running, kill the route demon
     #
     #kill 'ps -ef¦grep in[.]routed¦awk '{print $2}'' 2>/dev/null
     #/usr/sbin/in.routed -q
#fi
#
# /usr/sbin/route add default your_nearest_gateway hops_to_gateway
# if [ $? -ne 0 ]
# then
#    exitcode=1
# fi

#
#  Run the DNS server if a configuration file is present
#
if [ -f /etc/inet/named.boot -a -x /usr/sbin/in.named ]
then
     /usr/sbin/in.named
fi

#
#  Run the NTP server if a configuration file is present
#
if [ -f /etc/inet/ntp.conf -a -x /usr/sbin/in.xntpd ]
then
     /usr/sbin/in.xntpd
fi

#
# return status to /etc/init.d/inetinit
#
if [ $exitcode -eq 0 ]
then
```

```
#    rm -f $LOG $PermLog
     echo
else
     echo "\nTCP/IP startup was not entirely successful. Error messages in $LOG"
     cp $LOG $PermLog
fi
exit $exitcode
```

Notice that there are four `route add` statements, including one supporting a default route. Also, notice how all references to `in.routed` and `in.gated`, the routing daemons, are commented to prevent them from being run at boot time.

Keep in mind that this configuration is valid and consistently operational as long as the network topology does not change. Any changes made to this topology, as simple as adding a subnet or as complex as resegmenting the network, might require introducing significant changes to the routers' and hosts' startup files. This should be contrasted with dynamic routing, in which routers pick up most of the changes as they are made.

Dynamic Routing

In Chapter 4, "The Internet Layer and Routing," different dynamic routing options and protocols were introduced. In the following subsections, some of the most prevalent concepts are reviewed as a prelude to the upcoming sections on dynamic routing configuration.

Autonomous System

TCP/IP defines two categories of routing information protocols. These are the interior gateway protocols (IGPs) and the exterior gateway protocols (EGPs).

An IGP protocol is responsible for the collection and flow of information within what is known as an *autonomous system* (AS). An autonomous system is defined by the Network Information Center (NIC) (RFC 1163) as a set of routers under a single technical administration. Routers within an autonomous system use a common IGP protocol and common metrics to route packets among themselves.

When dealing with the outside world (that is, other autonomous systems), an AS resorts to an exterior gateway protocol for the exchange and processing of reachability information for remote networks. An AS does not have to agree with another AS on the IGP protocol it is using to handle its internal traffic. AS's must agree on using the same exterior protocol, or they won't be able to communicate. Figure 9.3 illustrates the concept.

Not every network connected to the Internet is, or needs to be, an autonomous system. A network can belong to a group of networks that together form an autonomous system. Exterior gateway protocols distinguish autonomous systems by virtue of a unique AS identification (AS ID) number that NIC assigns upon application to every autonomous system.

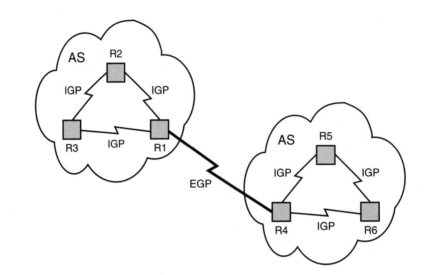

Figure 9.3. *Within an autonomous system, routers use IGP protocols for the collection and distribution of reachability information. For AS's to exchange routing information among themselves, an EGP protocol is used. In the diagram, routers R1 and R4 are EGP routers, belonging to different autonomous systems, exchanging routing information using EGP protocols.*

Interior Gateway Protocols

The administration authority of an AS has access to various IGP protocols. These protocols are Routing Information Protocol (RIP), Open Shortest Path First (OSPF), and HELLO. Of the three, RIP is the most commonly used. HELLO is the least popular protocol, and OSPF's popularity is expected to exceed that of RIP. The merits of both the RIP and the OSPF protocols were discussed at length in Chapter 4 and won't be discussed any further here.

Exterior Gateway Protocols

Exterior gateway protocols include the Border Gateway Protocol (BGP) and the Exterior Gateway Protocol (EGP). (Be sure to read the following cautionary remark.)

> **Caution:** The acronym EGP is used in this book, and probably many other books, to refer to the family of exterior gateway protocols (EGPs) in the generic sense. The same acronym is also used to refer to a well-defined exterior protocol, the Exterior Gateway Protocol. You should exercise caution when interpreting the acronym. Examination of the context in which it is used should be enough to convey the associated meaning.

It was noted in Chapter 4 that EGP is the older of the two protocols and was developed at a time when the Internet defined a hierarchical architecture, based primarily on a centralized view of routing. According to that view, ARPANET was made to serve as the core backbone of the Internet. Special routers supporting Gateway-to-Gateway Protocols (GGP) were made responsible for the central collection and processing of routing information, which the core network receives from the regional networks connected to it. EGP routers, on the other hand, were the point of contact between AS's and the core network. They were made responsible for collecting AS's routing information and passing it on to the GGP core routers for further processing.

Today, the Internet no longer favors this view. For one thing, the hierarchical system put the burden of processing all routing information on the central GGP routers. It also proved detrimental in terms of the link bandwidth lost to routing information traffic. To remedy the situation, a new view emphasizing decentralization of routing responsibilities was introduced, with a supporting infrastructure. At the heart of this view is a peer architecture in which the Border Gateway Protocol (BGP) (RFCs 1267 and 1268) plays a central role.

BGP Protocol

BGP-based routers are intended to replace EGP routers and share the processing burden introduced by the increasing size of the routing information exchanged among autonomous systems.

BGP characterizes traffic in an AS as either *local* to the AS or *transit* traffic. Local traffic is carried by IP datagrams originating from, or destined to, a host in the AS itself. Otherwise, traffic is considered transit in nature. To BGP, the Internet is viewed as an arbitrary interconnection of the following three categories of autonomous systems:

 ◆ *Stub AS:* An AS with one connection to one other AS. Because all traffic in a stub AS either originates from, or is destined to, hosts within this AS, its traffic is local to itself.

 ◆ *Multihomed AS:* An AS with more than one connection to more than one AS. Traffic carried within a multihomed AS is local in nature. No transit traffic is allowed within this category of AS's.

 ◆ *Transit AS:* Similar to the multihomed AS, except that it allows transit traffic (policy restrictions applying) on its internetwork.

Routing policies are determined by the AS administrator. They can be specified using special statements in the /etc/inet/gated.conf configuration file.

For BGP to exchange reachability information with a peer router, it establishes a TCP connection with that router. After it's up and running, BGP qualifies the status of the connection by regularly sending a BGP *keepalive* message to its peer. Should the peer persistently fail to respond to this message, the sending BGP disqualifies the route and deletes its corresponding entry from the routing table.

The *routed* Daemon

The `routed` daemon supports only the RIP protocol. If you do not need an exterior gateway protocol to run on the host, or router, then `routed` is all you need.

> **Note:** On some systems, such as UnixWare and Solaris, the routing daemon is called `in.routed` rather than `routed`.

`routed` is invoked at boot time from the `/etc/inet/rc.inet` file. When started, it determines which interfaces are supported by the system and are marked up. If multiple interfaces are found to be configured and up, it assumes that the host is acting as the router and is capable of forwarding packets between networks. `routed` then transmits a RIP request packet in which it asks other routers to send their updates. Afterward, `routed` listens on the network to RIP requests and responses and uses them to update its own routing table.

`routed` is an easily configured and activated daemon. All you need to do is check the `/etc/inet/rc.inet` startup file and make sure that references to `routed` are not commented. Depending on whether you want to run `routed` on a host or a router, you might consider the following options when running it:

◆ If you're running `routed` on a host and you want it to listen to RIP packets without contributing its information to other hosts and routers, add the `-q` option (quiet mode) to the `routed` command in the `/etc/inet/rc.inet` file. This saves some bandwidth, especially on a network with a large base of hosts sharing a single interface. The corresponding entry in the `/etc/inet/rc.inet` file becomes this:

```
if [ -f /etc/inet/gated.conf -a -x /usr/sbin/in.gated ]
then
    /usr/sbin/in.gated
else
    #
    # if running, kill the route demon
    #
    kill 'ps -ef¦grep in[.]routed¦awk '{print $2}'' 2>/dev/null
    /usr/sbin/in.routed -q
fi
```

◆ Otherwise, in a host acting as a router, you should remove the `-q` option and use the `-s` option instead. This setting forces `routed` to supply its routing information every 30 seconds to the rest of the network.

`routed` supports a few more options that are particularly useful in troubleshooting situations. Those options, among other techniques, will be explained in a later section.

Upon startup, `routed` checks an `/etc/gateways` file. This optional file contains routing information entries that `routed` includes in the initial routing table. Each entry must be in the following format:

```
net ¦ host name ¦ address gateway name ¦ address metric value passive ¦ active
```

In this format,

net ¦ host	Indicates whether the route pertains to a network or a specific host.
name ¦ address	Following the net or host keyword, it identifies the name or IP address of the reachable network or host. The name ¦ address after the keyword gateway identifies the name or IP address of the router associated with that route.
gateway	Indicates that the following name or IP address pertains to a router.
metric value	Fixes a metric indicating the hop count to the destination or network.
passive ¦ active	Routers not expected to exchange routing information should be marked as passive. Those expected to exchange routing information should be marked as active. A router marked active is removed from the RIT table should routed stop receiving updates from that router. Those marked passive, on the other hand, continue to exist in the routing table regardless of their actual status, and routed continues to include them in its RIP response updates.

Following is a sample entry that could have been included in /etc/gateways on host netrix in Figure 9.2:

```
net 198.53.237.0 gateway 100.0.0.2 metric 1 active
```

The entry simply says that the route to network 198.53.237 passes through the router at IP address 100.0.0.2 (that is, host jade). The applicable metric is 1 (that is, one hop away), and the entry is marked active. If netrix stops hearing from jade for a prolonged period, netrix's routed deletes the entry.

gated Daemon

The gated daemon supports interior as well as exterior gateway protocols. The supported interior protocols include RIP, OSPF, and HELLO. The exterior protocols it supports are EGP and BGP. Hence, gated allows a multihomed host to function as both an interior and an exterior gateway, as opposed to the routed daemon, which is intended for interior gateways only.

Before gated can be run, its configuration file, /etc/inet/gated.conf, must be created. gated.conf is supported by a comprehensive and feature-rich command language. Using this language, you can include configuration statements pertaining to more than one protocol.

In the following few pages, both `netrix` and `jade` will be configured as routers running `gated`. Also, an example of a host configuration will be presented, with the host being `saturn`. But before this can be done, an overview of `gated.conf` configuration statements and related concepts is in order.

gated.conf Statements

The `gated.conf` file consists of a sequence of statements, each terminated by a semicolon (;). The configuration statements fall into six categories:

♦ *Directives:* These provide directions to `gated` about INCLUDE files.

♦ *Trace:* These provide trace control options. This might prove helpful for troubleshooting a configuration.

♦ *Definition:* These provide `gated` with definition statements identifying the AS, interface options, and martian networks.

Martian Networks

Sometimes a misconfigured router advertises invalid destination addresses. Such destinations are commonly referred to as martian networks. As will be shown later, `gated` can be configured to discard routing information for martian networks.

♦ *Protocol:* These are used to enable and disable use of protocols. They also include associated control protocol control statements.

♦ *Static:* These are used to define static routes.

♦ *Control:* These define what routes are accepted from other routers, and what routes the gateway should propagate to those routers.

Except for the directives and trace options statements, the remaining four statements must appear in the `gated.conf` file in the order in which they are listed in the preceding text. The former two classes of statements can appear anywhere in the file.

Directive Statements

Directive statements provide information that `gated` uses to locate "include" files. An include file is one that is external to the `gated.conf` file and whose contents are accommodated in the configuration as though they were part of `gated.conf` itself. Unless your `gated.conf` is large, you should not need to create any include files. Maintaining all configuration statements in a single file makes it more convenient to administer `gated`.

There are two directive statements:

%directory *pathname:* Sets the directory to *pathname* where gated must look for include files.

%include *filename:* Specifies the filename to be included. The filename cannot start with a / character.

No more attention will be paid to these directives, because they are rarely used on small to medium-sized networks.

Trace Statements

gated supports a tracing feature that enables you to keep track of what is going on behind the scenes. This feature might prove extremely helpful when you're having gated or specific protocol-related routing problems. Using the proper trace statements, you can specify the output in which traces are to be recorded, as well as the events that can be traced. You have the option to enable tracing on all events, or the ones you see fit.

Following are the only two trace statements that gated supports.

tracefile filename *[replace]:*

This statement identifies the file in which traces must be recorded. Unless replace is used, output is appended to the specified file. Otherwise, the file is overwritten the next time gated is started. Following is an example of what a trace file can contain:

```
Dec  7 21:36:51
Dec  7 21:36:51 Tracing flags enabled: general internal external route bgp
Dec  7 21:36:51
Dec  7 21:36:51
Dec  7 21:36:51 parse: /etc/inet/gated.conf:5 Syntax error at 'end-of-statement'
Dec  7 21:36:51
Dec  7 21:36:51 bgp_init: getservbyname(bgp, tcp): Error 0 - using port 179
Dec  7 21:36:51 rip_init: Acting as RIP supplier to our direct nets
Dec  7 21:36:51 init_if: PointoPoint RIP supplier to: ppp0
Dec  7 21:36:51
Dec  7 21:36:51 if_rtinit: interior routes for direct interfaces:
ADD      150.1.0.0       gw 150.1.0.1        Direct    pref   0  metric 0  <Changed
➡Int>
KERNEL ADD    150.1.0.0       mask 255.255.0.0     gateway 150.1.0.1        flags <>
➡SIOCADDRT: File exists
ADD      100.0.0.0       gw 100.0.0.1        Direct    pref   0  metric 0  <Changed
➡Int>
KERNEL ADD    100.0.0.0       mask 255.0.0.0       gateway 100.0.0.1        flags <>
➡SIOCADDRT: File exists
Dec  7 21:36:51 rt_close: 2/4 routes proto IF table revision 2
Dec  7 21:36:51
Dec  7 21:36:51
Dec  7 21:36:51 ***Routes are being installed in kernel
```

```
Dec  7 21:36:51
Dec  7 21:36:52
Dec  7 21:36:52 main: commence routing updates
Dec  7 21:36:52
ADD      198.53.235.1    gw 100.0.0.2    RIP    pref 100  metric 2  <Changed Host>
ADD      198.53.235.10   gw 100.0.0.2    RIP    pref 100  metric 2  <Changed Host>
ADD      100.0.0.0       gw 100.0.0.2    RIP    pref 100  metric 2  <Changed Int>
ADD      198.53.237.0    gw 100.0.0.2    RIP    pref 100  metric 2  <Changed Int>
Dec  7 21:36:52 rt_close: 4/1 routes proto RIP from 100.0.0.2 table revision 3
Dec  7 21:36:52
Dec  7 21:38:07 timer_dispatch: interval timer interrupt 1 seconds late
Dec  7 21:40:08 timer_dispatch: interval timer interrupt 1 seconds late
CHANGE   0.0.0.0         gw 100.0.1.2    Kernel pref 255  metric 0  <Ext HoldDown>
CHANGE   150.1.0.0       gw 150.1.0.1    Direct pref   0  metric 0  <Int HoldDown>
CHANGE   198.53.235.1    gw 100.0.0.2    Kernel pref 255  metric 0  <Host HoldDown>
CHANGE   198.53.237.0    gw 100.0.0.2    Kernel pref 255  metric 0  <Ext HoldDown>
Dec  7 21:40:21 rt_close: 4/4 routes proto RT table revision 4
Dec  7 21:40:21
Dec  7 21:40:21 rt_time: above 0 routes deleted and 4 routes helddown
DELETE   0.0.0.0         gw 100.0.1.2    Kernel  pref 255  metric 0 <Ext HoldDown>
Dec  7 21:42:21 interface timeout - deleting route to 150.1.0.0
DELETE   150.1.0.0       gw 150.1.0.1    Direct pref   0  metric 0  <Int HoldDown>
DELETE   198.53.235.1    gw 100.0.0.2    Kernel pref 255  metric 0  <Host HoldDown>
DELETE   198.53.237.0    gw 100.0.0.2    Kernel pref 255  metric 0  <Ext HoldDown>
Dec  7 21:42:21 rt_close: 4/4 routes proto RT table revision 5
Dec  7 21:42:21
Dec  7 21:42:21 rt_time: above 4 routes deleted and 0 routes helddown
Dec  7 21:42:38 bgp_connect_complete: peer 150.1.23.6 state Connect Connection error:
Transport endpoint is not connected
Dec  7 21:43:39 timer_dispatch: interval timer interrupt 1 seconds late
Dec  7 21:43:39 bgp_connect_start: connect 150.1.23.6: I/O error
Dec  7 21:43:39
Dec  7 21:43:39 Abort in.gated[602] version @(#)2.0.1.14.development: I/O error
Dec  7 21:43:39
```

Traceoptions [traceoption [traceoption [...]]]:

traceoptions identifies the events for gated to trace. If no options are included, tracing is turned off. Table 9.2 summarizes the traceable events you can specify.

Table 9.2. Trace options that are supported by gated.

Option	Description
all	Enables tracing on all events.
general	Enables tracing on internal, external, and route-related events.
internal	Includes internal errors and informational messages.
external	Includes external errors.
nostamp	Does not timestamp all messages in the trace file (see the previous listing of the sample trace file).
mark	Forces gated to record an "I am alive" type of message to ensure sanity of the routing services.

Option	Description
timer	Implements timer scheduling.
parse	Parses recognized tokens in the gated.conf file.
config	Adds verbosity to the startup process by allowing gated to redisplay statements from the gated.conf file as they are parsed (helpful when trying the configuration for the first time).
route	Records updates applied to the gated routing table.
kernel	Records updates applied to the kernel's routing table.
bgp	Traces BGP packets that are sent and received.
epg	Traces EGP packets that are sent and received.
rip	Traces RIP packets that are sent and received.
hello	Traces HELLO packets that are sent and received.
icmp	Traces ICMP packets that are sent and received.
protocol	Provides traces of state transitions if used with BGP or EGP.
update	Traces the contents of protocol packets (can be used with BGP, EGP, RIP, HELLO, and ICMP).

Definition Statements

Definition statements are configuration statements that apply to all protocols enabled in the gated.conf file. Definition statements must precede all other statements. gated currently supports the following four definition statements:

```
options option_list
```

option_list can be one or both currently supported options. These are the options:

noinstall, which prevents gated from installing the routes in the kernel routing table. This is a useful feature to employ whenever gated.conf is being tested for potential errors before it is actually put to production.

gendefault, which causes the BGP and EGP peers to generate a default route when up. This route is not installed in the kernel's routing table, and it is used only if this host is advertised as a default router.

```
autonomoussystem as_id
```

as_id is the officially assigned AS ID by NIC. This statement, therefore, identifies the AS to the EGP and BGP protocols. Both protocols use this number whenever they communicate reachability information with their peers.

```
interface if_list options_list
```

This statement is similar in functionality (but not identical) to the `ifconfig` statement. It defines configuration options applicable to all interfaces included in *if_list*. *if_list* can include interface names such as `ne2k0` (for the NE2000 interface) or the IP address of that interface, or if you want to affect all interfaces, you can simply include the keyword `all`.

Configuration options are defined in the *options_list*. These are the supported options:

> `metric` *value* has the same significance as the `metric` option used with the `ifconfig` command. It applies only to the RIP and HELLO protocols.

> `preference` *pref* assigns a preference number for this interface. Based on this number, `gated` decides which route to choose from multiple routes to the same destination. See the following note for more details.

> `passive` prevents `gated` from deleting this interface from its routing table, even if the interface is marked down. To `gated`, an interface is down if it persistently fails to receive routing information through this interface.

`martians { ` *martian_list* ` }`

martian_list is a semicolon-separated list of symbolic addresses about which you want `gated` to discard all routing information received through the interfaces identified in the *if_list*.

---

gated Preference Number

Different routing information protocols use different metrics. For example, RIP's metric represents the hop count that can be any where between 0 and 16, with 16 indicating that a route is unreachable. HELLO's metric represents the round-trip delay in milliseconds, with 30,000 ms signifying unreachability. Other protocols have their own different representations of the metric. The only thing these different metrics have in common is that the lower the value, the closer the destination is.

`gated` has no problem advertising information originated by any of the protocols it is configured to support. It simply uses that protocol's metric when doing so. When advertising information via RIP, it uses RIP's metrics (that is, the hop count), and when advertising via HELLO it uses HELLO's metrics (that is, delay time).

Given that it is likely that more than one protocol would advertise the same destination, the `gated` designers were faced with the question, How can a receiving `gated` decide which route to take? Given the lack of equivalencies among the various adopted metrics, it was deemed impossible to let `gated` decide on the shortest path using any form of comparison based on those metrics. Instead, `gated` was designed to use its own metric value, which was called *preference.*

`gated` associates a preference value with each routing information protocol. The following table shows the default value assigned to each protocol:

Routing Protocol	Default Preference
Direct route	0
ICMP	20
Static route	50
HELLO	90
RIP	100
BGP	150
EGP	200

The range of preference values is 0–255, with 0 being the most preferred and 255 being unreachable.

gated uses these preference values to create its own unified routing table. When gated receives reachability information for the same route from two, or more, routing protocols, regardless of the advertised metric that each routing protocol is using, it looks up its preference list (shown previously). Then it considers the one with the lowest preference value as the shortest route. According to the preceding table, gated prefers routes learned through ICMP over other protocols. A direct route (that is, to which an interface is connected) is, expectedly so, the most preferred.

Different preference values can be associated with the same protocol over different interfaces. You can, for example, set a preference of 100 to RIP packets received on one interface while setting it to 125 for RIP packets received from another interface on the same host. Preference values are set in the /etc/inet/gated.conf file.

Protocol Statements

Protocol statements enable and disable the use of routing information protocols. Also, they are sophisticated enough to give you control over the way any particular protocol behaves in relation to its peers.

Each protocol is configured via a protocol-specific statement. The structure of the protocol statement is the same for all protocols. There is a great deal of similarity among many of the common clauses that different protocol statements support. For this reason, only RIP, BGP, and ICMP protocol statements will be discussed in this chapter.

A clause that is common to several protocol statements will be described only on the first encounter. With a good understanding of what is covered in the following pages, you should be able to resort to the vendor's documentation for details on other protocol statements.

All protocol-specific statements have two parameters in common: (1) preference (see previous note for explanation), which, if not specified, assumes the default value depicted in the table, and

(2) defaultmetric, which is the metric used in association with routes advertised by the supporting protocol. If not specified, defaultmetric is set to the highest value in its range, which normally implies unreachability.

Following is the syntax of the RIP-specific protocol statement:

```
rip yes ¦ no ¦ off ¦ quiet ¦ pointtopoint ¦ supplier [ {
    preference preference ;
    defaultmetric metric;
    interface interface_list [ noripin ] [ noripout ];
    ...
    trustedgateways gateway_list ;
    sourcegateways gateway_list ;
} ] ;
```

If rip yes (or rip on) is specified, RIP packets will be generated on a host with multiple interfaces. Otherwise (that is, in the case of a host with a single interface), RIP will assume the quiet mode, which prevents it from generating RIP packets. rip no disables RIP completely. supplier specifies that RIP will be generated, even with a single interface.

pointopoint and sourcegateways are used together. When specified, pointopoint restricts RIP to supplying routing information to routers listed in the sourcegateways only. Otherwise, RIP packets are broadcast to all routers.

The interface clause is used to enable or disable RIP packets on all interfaces identified in the interface_list. An interface can be specified using a symbolic name, the interface name as known by the operating system (for example, e130 for 3C509), or the IP address. The noripin option makes RIP discard any RIP packets received on those interfaces, whereas noripout disables sending RIP packets out of those interfaces.

The trustedgateways clause specifies the routers from which you will accept RIP packets. If it's not specified, packets received from any router are generated.

Here is an example of a RIP protocol-specific statement that can be included in saturn's gated.conf (refer to Figure 9.2):

```
#
#   saturn's gated.conf file
#
# Because saturn has only one interface connecting it to the
#   150.1.0.0 network, only rip is enabled. The interface is also marked passive so
#   that gated does not declare it dead if it stopped receiving RIP packets through
#   this interface.
#
#   The following is a definition statement:
#
interface 150.1.4.1 passive ;
#
#   In the following RIP protocol statement, RIP is enabled, and to prevent saturn
#   from accepting RIP packets from bogus routers, a trustedgateways clause is
```

```
#  included specifying that netrix is the only router from which routing information
#  should be considered
rip yes {
    interface el30 ;
    trustedgateways 150.1.0.1 ;
} ;
```

In fact, the preceding gated.conf file is all you need for saturn. It is self-documented and should require no further explanation.

Next, the BGP protocol statement is explored:

```
bgp yes ¦ no ¦ on ¦ off [ {
    preference preference ;
    defaultmetric metric ;
    peer host
        [ linktype [ up ¦ down ¦ horizontal ¦ internal ]]
        [ metricout metric ]
        [ asin as_id ]
        [ asout as_id ]
        [ nogendefault ]
        [ gateway gateway ]
        [ interface interface ]
            ;
    ...
} ] ;
```

The first three lines should be familiar to you by now. peer specifies the IP address of the BGP peer that the local BGP protocol should establish a connection with for the subsequent exchange of routing data. More than one peer can be specified. If the peer's autonomous system is the same as this host, linktype is set by default to internal; if not, it is set to horizontal.

asin specifies that BGP should accept routing data only from that peer with the as_id autonomous system number. If asin is not specified, the default is to accept BGP traffic from all autonomous systems.

asout specifies the autonomous system number to accompany all BGP packets sent out to that peer. If asout is not specified, the number specified in the autonomoussystem definition statement is sent instead.

Unless specified, nogendefault allows BGP to generate a default route upon receiving valid routing information from this peer. Depending on the network topology, a default route might contribute to excess ICMP route redirects.

gateway specifies the IP address of the next hop to use for the routes received from this peer. You do not have to specify a next hop if both this host and its peer BGP router share the same network. Otherwise, use gateway with the interface parameter to identify the gateway through which the learned routes are reachable, and the interface through which to reach the peer, respectively.

In Figure 9.4, both R1 and R3 are BGP peers. Because R2 is an intermediate router through which R1 and R3 communicate BGP routing data, it is meaningless for R1 to identify, in its routing table (see Chapter 4 for details), R3 as the next router for routes learned from R3. Using the gateway parameter, you will be able to specify R2's address instead.

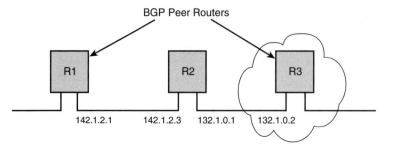

Figure 9.4. *Two BGP peers on two different networks. In this case, R1's* gated.conf *should include a BGP protocol statement setting the next hop to R2's address for all routes learned from R3.*

Assume that unicom.com maintains a connection to the Internet via host jade (see Figure 9.2). Also assume that unicom.com's AS ID is 519 and that jade uses BGP to exchange routing information with another router on the internet that has an IP address of 179.45.3.1. This router is part of another autonomous system with AS ID 820. jade's IP address is 198.53.237.1. Here is the BGP protocol statement that fits jade's gated.conf:

```
bgp yes {
 peer 179.45.3.1 linktype horizontal asin 820 gateway 198.53.237.5 interface
198.53.237.1 } ;
```

According to the preceding statement, jade's BGP peer is the host with IP address 179.45.3.1. Because both jade and its peer belong to different autonomous systems, the linktype horizontal was specified. Only BGP packets with AS ID 820 (asin 820) are accepted from this peer. Also notice that because both routers do not share the same network, a gateway parameter was used to specify the next hop for routes learned from that peer.

The final protocol statement that will be examined pertains to ICMP:

```
redirects yes ¦ no ¦ off [ {
    preference preference ;
    interface if_list [ noicmpin ] ;
    trustedgateways gateways_list ;
} ] ;
```

The ICMP redirects statement is used to allow, or prevent, ICMP route redirect updates from modifying the routing table. If it's disabled, gated has to clean up the kernel routing table as it is changed by the kernel, due to received redirects. This is due to ICMP being an integral part of the IP protocol. When an ICMP redirect is received, IP processes it and updates the routing table accordingly. gated has to ensure that such updates are deleted if ICMP redirects are disallowed.

Using interface *if_list*, ICMP redirects can be disabled on an interface-by-interface basis.

The trustedgateways parameters specify the gateways from which the host can accept ICMP redirects.

Static Statements

Static statements have a function similar to that of the route add command. They define static routes for gated. You can define as many static routes as you deem fit. The syntax of the static statement is as shown here:

```
static {
    destination gateway gateway [ preference preference ];
    ...
    destination interface interface [ preference preference ] ;
    ...
} ;
```

Both forms of the statement are self-explanatory. The first form (with the keyword gateway) is the one most commonly used. It simply specifies the route (*destination*) and the next hop (gateway *gateway*). Unless a preference is included, a default of 50 is assumed.

The second form of the statement is rarely used to assign an interface to more than one IP address. You would normally do this to allow two IP network numbers to share the same physical network. Another situation in which the author has seen it used was in allowing users enough time to reconfigure their stations to new addresses in conformance with recent changes made to the IP network. Each router interface was assigned dual addresses so that users were allowed a grace period during which they could have their configurations updated. Meanwhile, routers configured in this fashion could handle traffic from both the old and the newly configured environments. Also, they were able to route traffic between both environments sharing the same network.

It is worth noting that static routes are the next preferred routes to gated (provided that the default preferences are always adhered to). Only ICMP redirects can cause gated to override routes learned through static statements.

Here is an example of a static route statement:

```
static { 156.3.4.34 gateway 198.53.237.20 ;
    } ;
```

Control Statements

gated currently supports two control statements: (1) an accept statement that controls information flow from routing peers, and (2) a propagate statement that controls the outflow of routing information from the router.

There are two forms of each statement, one for interior protocols and another for exterior protocols. Following is the syntax of the accept statement to use with interior protocols:

```
accept proto rip ¦ hello ¦ icmp [ interface if_list ¦ gateway gateway_list ]
➥[ preference preference ]{
    acceptance_list } ;
```

Depending on the specified protocol after the keyword proto, accept configures gated to accept routing information from that protocol. Optionally, you can specify the only interfaces (using interface if_list) or routers (using gateway gateway_list) from which routing information can be accepted. The acceptance_list defines routes for which routing information can be accepted from the interface, or gateway, sources listed in the if_list or gateway_list, respectively. If no acceptance_list was specified, the default is to accept all routes from the listed sources.

The acceptance_list takes two forms:

◆ listen destination [preference preference]: This form is used to define an individual acceptable route. The route is specified by destination using its IP address, the keyword default, or the keyword all. If specified, default configures gated to accept a default route received from that source, whereas all allows gated to accept all routes received from that source.

◆ nolisten destination: This form configures gated to discard information about the specified destination. The destination can be specified as described in the previous form of the acceptance_list.

Following is an example of the accept statement:

```
accept proto rip interface el30 {
    listen 198.62.158.0 ;
    listen 150.1.0.0 ;
} ;
```

This example configures gated to accept, through interface el30, the RIP routing information pertaining to routes 198.62.158.0 and 150.1.0.0.

propagate is the second control statement. Its syntax will be discussed shortly.

The following form of the accept statement applies to exterior protocols:

```
accept proto bgp ¦ egp as as_id
    [ preference preference ] [ {
    acceptance_list
} ] ;
```

This exterior form of the accept statement is very similar to the one used for interior protocols. This form does not enable you, however, to specify routers or interfaces through which routes can be accepted. Instead, using the as parameter, you can specify the autonomous system ID (in the as_id) that is acting as the source of routing information for the protocol specified after the proto keyword. The acceptance_list can assume any of the forms discussed previously.

The propagation of routing information is controlled by the propagate statement. The propagate statement decides what routes can be advertised by a specific protocol. Like accept, propagate assumes two forms, one for interior protocols and another for use with exterior protocols.

The interior form of the statement is as shown here:

```
propagate proto rip ¦ hello
    [ interface if_list ¦ gateway gateway_list ]
    [ metric metric ] {
    propagation_list
} ;
```

The exterior form of the propagate statement is this:

```
propagate proto bgp ¦ egb as as_id
    [ metric metric ] {
    propagation_list
} ;
```

Except for the *propagation_list* and *metric*, all the parameters in both forms of the propagate statement have the same meaning and can assume any of the values defined in the accept statement.

The propagate statement configures gated to advertise routes using the protocol specified after the proto keyword. Whereas *if_list* and *gateway_list* are used by accept to define sources through which routes can be accepted, they are used by propagate to define the interfaces, or routers, through which gated can advertise routes.

One thing that might have drawn your attention is the use of metric values, rather than preference values, in the exterior form of the propagate statement. There is no contradiction between what is being said here and what was said several pages earlier (see the note titled "gated Preference Number").

As was pointed out, gated uses preference numbers to evaluate incoming routing information to select the "best" path to any specific route. When advertising routes via a certain protocol, gated uses the metrics defined by that protocol. It is therefore your responsibility to assign a valid metric (unless you want the applicable default to prevail) to routes advertised by that protocol.

There are two forms of the *propagation_list*. The first one applies to interior protocols:

```
proto rip ¦ hello ¦ direct ¦ static ¦ defualt
    [interface if_list ¦ gateway gateway_list ]
    [ metric metric ] [ {
    announce_list
} ] ;
```

The second one applies to exterior protocols:

```
proto bgp ¦ egp as as_id
    [ metric metric ] [ {
    announce_list
} ] ;
```

The *propagation_list* is to be interpreted in the following manner: The *announce_list* defines the routes that gated is to advertise. The proto keyword defines the source protocol through which the advertised routes were learned, *not* the protocol used to advertise the route that is defined after the proto keyword at the beginning of the propagate statement.

as, `interface`, and `gateway` define the source autonomous system, interface, or router from which announceable routes are learned.

Finally, the `announce_list` recognizes two forms:

◆ announce `destination` [metric `metric`]: This form defines destinations that gated is allowed to advertise. `destination` can be an IP address or the keyword `all`.

◆ noannounce `destination`: This form serves the opposite purpose of announce. noannounce prevents gated from advertising the route indicated in `destination`. You can include as many noannounce statements as you want, provided that you end the list with an announce `all` statement to allow for the advertisement of all other routes.

Following is an example of a propagate statement:

```
propagate proto rip gateway 100.0.0.1 {
    proto rip interface 198.53.235.10 {
        noannounce 162.24.1.0 ;
        announce all ;
    } ;
} ;
```

According to this statement, gated is to advertise all RIP routes out of interface 100.0.0.1. The propagation list specifies that all routes received from gateway address 198.53.235.10, except the 162.24.1.0 route, are announceable.

Sample *gated.conf* Configurations

Applying what has been explained about gated.conf to the hypothetical network unicom.com, take a look at the gated.conf files corresponding to both netrix and jade.

The following gated.conf is for host netrix:

```
#
# Because netrix connects to internal segments of the network, RIP is all that is
#   needed:
rip yes ;
#
#   Announce 150.1.0.0 to the rest of the network via 100.0.0.1 and 198.53.235.1
#
propagate proto rip interface 100.0.0.1; 198.53.235.1
{
    proto direct
    {
        announce 150.1.0.0 metric 0
    } ;
};
#
# Announce on 150.1.0.0 all routes learned through 100.0.0.1 and 198.53.235.1
# (i.e., declare 150.1.0.1 a default route for network 150.1.0.0)
#
propagate proto interface 150.1.0.1
```

```
{
    proto rip interface 100.0.0.1 ; 198.53.235.1
        {
            announce all ;
        } ;
} ;
#
# Also, declare 198.53.235.1 the route that the network across the link should use to
# get on to the Internet
#
propagate proto rip interface 198.53.235.1
{
    proto rip interface 100.0.0.1
        {
            announce all ;
        } ;
} ;
```

The following gated.conf applies to jade. Remember that jade is connected to the Internet and is part of autonomous system number 519, explaining the need for BGP in addition to RIP:

```
#
# jade's gated.conf
# This gated.conf starts with two definition statements
# The first enables tracing on some events, while the second sets the global AS ID
traceoptions internal external route bgp ;
autonomoussystem 519
#
# Now enable RIP out of 100.0.0.2 interface. Only trust netrix for RIP routing
# information
rip yes {
    interface 100.0.0.2 ;
    trustedgateways 100.0.0.1 ;
} ;
#
# Enable and configure BGP
# Because the BGP peer belongs to a different AS, linktype is set to horizontal.
# The peer and jade do not share the same network, hence the gateway parameter
#
bgp yes {
    peer 167.2.1.2 linktype horizontal asin 820 gateway 198.53.237.5 interface
➡198.53.237.1 ;
} ;
#
# Here come the propagate statements
# The following propagates all routes learned via RIP to the BGP peer. This way, the
# world can reach us. A metric has to be specified to avoid the default of 16
# (i.e., unreachable route(s)).
propagate proto bgp as 820 metric 5 {
    proto rip {
        announce all ;
    } ;
} ;
#
# Now, propagate routes learned from BGP to the internal network so that we can reach
# the world
```

```
propagate proto rip metric 2 {
    proto bgp as 519 {
        announce all ;
    } ;
} ;
```

Starting *gated*

When `gated` is properly configured, you have the option of starting it at the command line or by rebooting the machine. If you are starting it at the command line, you must ensure that `routed` is not running. Otherwise, kill `routed` first:

 # kill 'ps -ef ¦ grep in[.]routed ¦ awk '{print $2}''

Then you can start `gated` at the command line by entering `in.gated` followed by some options. Following is the general syntax of the `in.gated` command:

in.gated [-cn] [-t *trace options*] [-f *config file*]

In this syntax,

-c   Specifies that the configuration file be parsed for syntax errors after which `gated` exists. The results are dumped in the `/usr/tmp/gated` dump file. This is a useful option because it enables you to correct any syntax errors before the `gated.conf` file is trusted.

-n   Prevents `gated` from modifying the kernel's routing table. This is another useful option to use to test your `gated` configuration before it is trusted.

-t   Specifies the trace options. Those were discussed earlier in the chapter and will not be repeated here. If `-t` is specified, the name of a trace file must also be specified. The trace file is where all the event traces are dumped.

-f   Specifies an alternative configuration file. The default is `/etc/inet/gated.conf`.

Here's an example of an invocation of `gated` on the command line:

 # in.gated -c -f gated.test gated.traces

According to this command, `gated` checks the syntax and the configuration described in `gated.test`, a temporary file, and dumps any syntax errors and event traces in the `gated.traces` file. Later, the LAN administrator can check the `gated.traces` file to rectify errors reported by `gated` before `gated.test` is copied over to `/etc/inet/gated.conf`, and running `gated` at boot time is enabled.

Running *gated* at Boot Time

As can be anticipated, `/etc/inet/rc.inet` is the script that enables the invocation of `gated` at boot time. The following `gated`-related lines are extracted for the `rc.inet` file:

```
# This runs in.gated if its configuration file (/etc/inet/gated.conf) is
# present. Otherwise, in.routed is run.
#
if [ -f /etc/inet/gated.conf -a -x /usr/sbin/in.gated ]
then
    /usr/sbin/in.gated
else
    #
    # if running, kill the route demon
    #
    kill 'ps -ef¦grep in[.]routed¦awk '{print $2}'' 2>/dev/null
    /usr/sbin/in.routed
fi
```

As you can tell from this code, both the routed and the gated run commands are included. To decide which of the two routing daemons to invoke, UNIX checks whether the /etc/inet/gated.conf exists. If that is the case, gated is invoked via the /usr/sbin/in.gated command. Otherwise, routed is invoked.

Depending on how your system was originally installed, the previous lines might have been commented and therefore skipped during the startup process. It is important, therefore, that the first thing you do, after creating gated.conf, is to check the rc.inet file and verify that the previous code is enabled for execution.

Summary

Installing TCP/IP might involve additional packages, including Network Support Utilities, the TCP/IP Internet package, and hardware drivers. After its installation, the LAN administrator still has to configure the interfaces. UNIX provides several tools to assist in the installation and configuration process. Of the tools presented in this chapter, ifconfig and configure were used to configure the network interfaces, and ping and netstat were used to check on the success of the configuration.

Rebooting UNIX after installing and configuring TCP/IP involves the invocation of a startup file in the /etc/rc2.d directory when the system enters run level two. The startup file runs several daemons that are necessary for providing the basic services for other TCP/IP applications. inetd, an internet superserver, or a master daemon is also started at boot time by sac. inetd starts application daemons, upon request, as defined in the /etc/inet/inetd.conf configuration file.

TCP/IP provides for various routing options. Categorically, routing can be done using static configuration or dynamic configuration. Dynamic routing itself is configurable using one of two routing daemons: routed and gated. routed supports the RIP protocol only, whereas gated supports all flavors of internal and external routing protocols. gated is the more complex to configure. Unless there is a real requirement for gated's features and flexibility, you would be better off sticking with routed.

CHAPTER

10

◆

Setting Up the
Domain Name System

Introduction

This chapter takes the Domain Name System (DNS) theory, described in Chapter 6, and applies it to concrete procedures for configuring DNS. The treatment is based on practical examples, using a fictitious domain, hosts, and networks. In particular, you will be shown how to perform the following tasks:

◆ Set up and boot a primary DNS server

◆ Set up and boot a secondary DNS server

◆ Set up subdomains and authority delegation

◆ Simplify implementation after learning the hard way

While these skills are being introduced and explained, some DNS-specific commands such as nslookup and whois are introduced. The commands are described again in Chapter 15, "Network Troubleshooting and Performance Tuning," where they are illustrated as DNS troubleshooting tools.

Before this text embarks on these objectives, however, a refresher of the DNS governing concepts (explained in greater detail in Chapter 6) is due.

DNS Concepts Refresher

Domain Name System refers to a name service that provides for the central, or distributed, administration of a database where host-related information is maintained. At a minimum, the information that DNS database files maintain includes host name-to-IP address associations, resembling the /etc/hosts file in functionality.

DNS defines a hierarchical, yet distributed, database of information pertaining to hosts on the network. As explained in Chapter 6, "Name Services," hierarchy allows for the subdivision of the name space into independently manageable partitions called *domains* (or *subdomains*). Distributivity allows for the relocation of the subdomain (that is, database partition) onto name servers belonging to the site being delegated the management of the subdomain. Such servers are called *authoritative* name servers.

DNS is organized much like the UNIX file system is organized. The root of the DNS tree is represented by the null character. At the root, there are root name servers that maintain a database of hosts belonging to the root, and pointers (addresses) to name servers maintaining data about the lower, or second-level, domains. In their turn, second-level name servers maintain database files of hosts belonging to the domain (or subdomain), and pointers to name servers responsible for the lower domain, and so on.

Domains are assigned names that should be approved, and registered, by NIC. Chapter 6 included details about the names of the top-level domains, and how organizations are assigned a domain according to the nature of the organization's mandate. A business or commercial organization, for example, belongs to the COM domain. Hence, Unicom, the fictitious company on which the examples of this chapter are based, will have UNICOM.COM for a domain name.

Only registered domains can be connected to the Internet. The administration and management of a registered domain is the sole responsibility of the organization to which the domain belongs. The organization is given the freedom to break up its domain into smaller subdomains, each managed independently from the parent domain.

A domain can be supported by as many as three types of DNS servers: primary, secondary, and cache-only. The primary name server is the server authoritative for the domain (or subdomain) in question, and it is the server where the DNS database is originated. The secondary server, in contrast, is a backup server providing for better performance and robustness to the actual DNS setup.

With minimal configuration, a secondary name server obtains its data by initiating *zone transfers*. A zone transfer involves the transfer of the DNS database of a particular domain, or subdomain, from the primary server to the secondary server. Both servers are equally capable of responding to user queries, which normally are initiated by client applications.

Finally, for a workstation to have access to the database (that is, to name services), the workstation must have a client, called the *resolver*, properly configured. The resolver issues name queries, on behalf of communicating applications, to the name servers it is configured to communicate with. Refer to Chapter 6 for more details on the resolution process.

A Sample Scenario: *UNICOM.COM*

As stated earlier, setting up a DNS server will be illustrated using examples based on the fictitious UNICOM domain. Unicom is a commercial organization specializing in offering communications consulting services. It applied for domain name registration, to manage its own domain. Being a commercial company, Unicom was registered in the COM domain and was authorized to name its own domain after the company's domain. Hence, the company's domain becomes UNICOM.COM, which can also be written unicom.com (because DNS is case-insensitive, a lowercase representation is used in the rest of the chapter).

Figure 10.1 depicts the network layout of the unicom.com network. The network is composed of three Ethernet networks, joined together, with two multihomed hosts, netrix and jade, acting as routers. jade also connects the internetwork to the Internet via a network interface with the IP address 198.53.235.10. The internetwork is currently assigned three IP network addresses: a Class A address (100.0.0.0), a Class B address (150.1.0.0), and a Class C address (198.53.237.0). The company is initially planning to maintain a flat domain to which all hosts belong. Depending on future expansion and requirements, the domain might have to be split into subdomains, with the management of each delegated to the department to which the corresponding network resources belong.

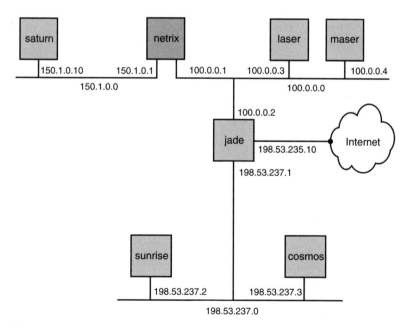

Figure 10.1. *The* unicom.com *network layout.*

Figure 10.2 depicts the resulting four domains (or subdomains) that the company should maintain. unicom.com maintains the host information, such as host name-to-IP address mappings.

The remaining three domains (100.in-addr.arpa, 1.150.in-addr.arpa, and 237.53.198.in-addr.arpa) are for the purpose of maintaining the inverse address mapping corresponding to hosts on the three networks in Figure 10.1. Refer to Chapter 6 for details on the inverse mappings and the in-addr.arpa domain.

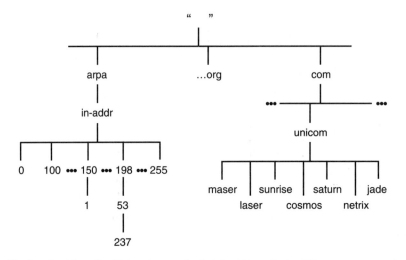

Figure 10.2. *The domains delegated to Unicom's network administration authority. Whereas* unicom.com *is where the host information, such as host name-to-IP address mappings, is maintained,* 100.in-addr.arpa, 1.150.in-addr.arpa, *and* 237.53.198.in-addr.arpa *are used to maintain the inverse mappings (that is, IP to host name) corresponding to each of the networks.*

Because both jade and netrix connect to more than one network, it would be a good idea to bring up DNS name services on both of them. This way, all hosts will have a DNS server directly attached to their network, resulting in a better response time. It was decided that netrix will be the primary domain name server, and jade will act as the secondary name server. Because unicom.com is the domain name, every host is assigned a domain name according to the following syntax:

hostname.unicom.com.

jade's and netrix's domain names, respectively, become jade.unicom.com. and netrix.unicom.com. In this chapter, the host name and the host domain name are used interchangeably.

Before explaining how to configure jade and netrix for DNS name services support, the following sections describe how to configure a DNS client, and they introduce the configuration files that are necessary to bring up a DNS server.

Configuring the DNS Client: The Resolver

The resolver is the client component that takes care of resolving host names to IP addresses. The resolver client is built into each of the TCP/IP applications and therefore does not run as an independent daemon on a UNIX host. For example, there is a resolver routine in ftp that takes care of determining the IP address of the host that the user wants to establish a file transfer session with.

Unless configured to contact a name server, the resolver normally checks the /etc/hosts file to get the IP address corresponding to the specified host name.

Configuring the resolver to recognize, and contact, name servers on the network is probably the simplest of all the tasks associated with setting up a DNS service. All you have to do is create and edit a small file called /etc/resolv.conf. Using this file, you can configure the resolver to recognize the domain to which the host belongs, and the addresses of the name servers to contact for name queries.

The resolver recognizes the domain to which the host belongs by virtue of the following entry:

```
domain domainname
```

The domain entry defines the default domain name. This is normally the name of the domain to which the host belongs. Whenever a user specifies the name of a host excluding the domain to which it belongs, the resolver appends the domainname to the host name before issuing a name query to a name server. Here's an example entry:

```
domain unicom.com
```

This should be included in the /etc/resolv.conf file on every host on the unicom.com network. Hence, if a user specifies only jade when invoking ftp, for example, the resolver appends the domain name unicom.com to become jade.unicom.com before submitting it to a name server for address resolution.

The resolver knows which servers to contact for name queries by virtue of the following entry:

```
nameserver nameserverIPaddress
```

There can be multiple nameserver entries specifying the IP addresses of the servers that the resolver can resort to for name queries. Name servers are queried, in the order in which they are listed, until either the query is answered or the list is exhausted. Following are the name server entries that /etc/resolv.conf should contain to ensure reliable service:

```
nameserver 100.0.0.1
nameserver 100.0.0.2
```

Note that the addresses of both netrix (the primary server) and jade (the secondary server) are included. Accordingly, netrix will always be addressed first by maser for name queries. Should maser fail to hear from netrix, it addresses jade next.

The complete /etc/resolv.conf file for host maser should then look like this:

```
domain unicom.com
nameserver 100.0.0.1
nameserver 100.0.0.2
```

> **Tip:** To achieve optimal performance, the name servers specified in the `/etc/resolv.conf` file should pertain to the servers closest to the host being configured. Furthermore, the addresses should be listed in ascending order of proximity (that is, the closest at the top, followed by the next closest, and so on). Also, note that it is advisable to have a name server on each subnet to circumvent the consequences of router failures.

DNS Database and Startup Files

Configuring a name server can involve the creation of many database and startup files. The number of files, as shown later, varies with the size of the organization, its internetwork structure, and the number of domains it has been delegated to administer. In the following discussion, four different file types are presented. Depending on the type of the name server (that is, primary, secondary, or cache) you might end up configuring different combinations of these file types. You might also end up configuring multiple files of the same type.

Following are the *generic* names and the basic definition (leaving the in-depth details for later) corresponding to each DNS database and startup file:

- ◆ `named.hosts`: This file defines the domain for which the name server is authoritative, and it mainly contains host name-to-IP address mappings.
- ◆ `named.rev`: This file defines the reverse `in-addr.arpa` domain for which the name server is authoritative. It also contains the IP address-to-host name reverse-mapping records.
- ◆ `named.local`: This file is minimal in contents. It is used to resolve the `127.0.0.1` loopback address to `localhost`.
- ◆ `named.ca`: This file contains the names and addresses of the Internet's root domain servers. Using the information maintained in this file, a name server will be able to contact root servers for name queries.
- ◆ `named.boot`: This file is the first file looked up by `named` (the DNS daemon) at startup. Using its contents, `named` determines the database filenames and their locations in the file system on this host, as well as remote hosts.

The filenames can be changed to anything that makes better sense to you. Later, these files will be explained in great detail, and you will be shown how different filenames can be accommodated in `named.boot` (that is, the DNS startup file).

Data is entered into these files in the form of resource records (RRs). Each record assumes a certain structure that must be adhered to for DNS to behave flawlessly. In the following few subsections, a group of resource records will be presented. The discussion will concentrate on the resource records immediately required to set up a *minimal* name service (that is, only for the purpose of the bidirectional mapping of host names and IP addresses). After that, the purpose and nature of the data that each of these files maintains will be presented.

DNS Resource Records (RR)

DNS resource records were introduced in Chapter 6, in the "Resource Record Data Types" section. If you skipped that text, you should go back to it. The section provides a general feel for the purpose and nature of some of the information that resource records can contain, making the following discussion easier to understand.

DNS RFC 1033 defines a multitude of resource records, of which only a few of the most relevant are described here. Readers interested in more information are referred to the noted RFC.

This is the general syntax of any RR:

```
[name] [ttl] class type data
```

In this syntax,

name	Is the name of the resource object being described by this resource record. *name* can be as specific as the name of a host or as general as the name of a domain. If it's left blank, the *name* of the preceding record is assumed. Two widely used special values for *name* are the single dot (.), which refers to the root domain, and the @ sign, which refers to the current origin, derived from the current domain name (more on this later).
ttl	Is the time-to-live value, in seconds. For better performance, a DNS client normally caches the information it receives from the name server. *ttl* defines the duration for which this entry can be trusted and therefore kept in cache. If it's not included, the default specified in the SOA applies.
class	Defines the class of the DNS record. DNS recognizes several classes of RR of which IN (Internet) is the only class relevant to this discussion. Some of the other classes are HS (Hessiod name server) and CH (Chaosnet information server).
type	Defines the type of information the RR record represents. The most commonly used record types are SOA, NS, A, and PTR. An A RR record, for example, contains the host name-to-IP address mapping and belongs to the named.hosts file. The PTR RR record does exactly the opposite (that is, it reverse-maps the address to the corresponding host name), and it belongs to the named.rev file. More on record types later in the section.
data	Is the actual data pertinent to the object specified in the *name* field. The nature of the contents of *data* varies with the RR record. *data* represents an IP address if RR is of type A, as opposed to *hostname* if RR is of type PTR.

Rather than bore you with an extensive treatment of all the resource record types that DNS supports, the following discussion includes only the most relevant ones. Information about other RR types is available in RFC 1033. The order in which the various types of RR records are depicted does not suggest the order in which they must be placed in the database files. As a matter of fact, the order is irrelevant. You are welcome to adopt whichever order is more convenient for you.

Start of Authority (SOA) Resource Records

The SOA record identifies the upper boundary of a partition (also known as a zone) of the global DNS database. Every configuration file must contain an SOA record identifying the beginning of the partition for which the server is authoritative. All RR records following the SOA record are part of the named zone. In reference to Figure 10.2, a primary name server for the `unicom.com` domain recognizes the partition boundaries by including an SOA record in its `named.hosts` configuration file.

This is the syntax of the SOA record:

```
[zone] [ttl] IN SOA origin contact (serial refresh retry expire minimum)
```

`zone`	Identifies the name of the zone.
`ttl`	Was described previously; is left blank in SOA records.
`IN`	Identifies the class.
`SOA`	Is the record type.

The remaining part is the data affecting the named zone.

As shown in the syntax, the data field itself is structured:

`origin`	Refers to the primary name server for this domain. In `unicom.com`'s case, this is `netrix.unicom.com`.
`contact`	Refers to the E-mail address of the person responsible for maintaining this domain. The root's E-mail address is commonly used. You can specify the E-mail address of any account you want. Assuming that login `root` on `netrix.unicom.com.` is responsible for the `unicom.com.` domain, `contact` would then be specified as `root.netrix.unicom.com`. Notice how the notation to specify the E-mail address uses the dot (.) rather than the @ character after `root`.
`serial`	Refers to the version number of this zone file. It is meant for interpretation and use by the secondary server, which transfers data from the primary server. Normally, the first version number is 1. The serial number must be incremented every time the file containing this resource record is modified. A secondary name server relies on this field to determine whether its database is in synchronization with the master replica maintained by the primary server. Before initiating any transfer, the secondary server compares its own version number with that of the primary's file. A larger primary version number flags an update. Failure to increment `serial` as changes are made to the file prevents the secondary server from transferring and including the updates in its tables. This can cause serious disruption in the way the DNS service behaves on the network.

refresh		Refers to how often, in seconds, a secondary server should poll the primary for changes. Only when a change in version number is detected is the database transferred.
retry		Refers to how long, in seconds, the secondary server should wait before reattempting zonal transfer if the primary server fails to respond to a zone refresh request.
expire		Defines the duration of time, in seconds, for which the secondary server can retain zonal data without requesting a zone refresh from the primary. The secondary server should discard all data upon expiration, even if the primary fails to respond to zone refresh requests.
minimum		Defines the default time-to-live (ttl) that applies to resource records whose ttl is not explicitly defined (see the description of the syntax of RR records).

As an example, the SOA record defining the upper boundary of the unicom.com domain should read as shown here:

```
unicom.com.   IN    SOA     netrix.unicom.com. root.netrix.unicom.com. (
                    2         ; Serial
                    14400     ; Refresh (4 hours)
                    3600      ; Retry (1hr)
                    604800    ; Expire ( 4 weeks )
                    86400 )   ; minimum TTL (time-to-live)
```

This record must be included in the named.hosts file. It makes the DNS server aware of where its authority (and responsibility) starts. Accordingly, named.hosts must contain all the *necessary data* for answering name queries pertaining to hosts belonging to unicom.com. The data can be in the form of resource records that explicitly include host name-to-IP address mappings, or pointers to other DNS servers for which authority over subdomains (if any) is delegated.

Address (A) Resource Records

The A address resource records belong to the named.hosts file. They are used to map the host name to its corresponding IP address, which is the most commonly used functionality of DNS. Following is the syntax of the A record:

[hostname] *[ttl]* IN A *address*

In this syntax,

hostname		Is the name of the host being affected. The host name can be specified relative to the current domain, or with a fully qualified domain name (that is, relative to the root domain).
ttl		Is the minimum time-to-live. This is normally left blank, implying the default as defined in the SOA record.

IN	Defines the class, which is almost always Internet class.
A	Defines the record type (an address record).
address	Is the IP address corresponding to the host name.

As an example, following is the A record pertaining to `netrix.unicom.com.`:

```
netrix.unicom.com.  IN  A  100.0.0.1
```

The host name is a fully qualified domain name (FQDN). For this reason, it is mandatory that it ends with a dot (.). Alternatively, it can be written like this:

```
netrix  IN  A  100.0.0.1
```

Because `netrix` belongs to `unicom.com.`, DNS has enough intelligence to qualify the name by appending the domain name to `netrix`, becoming `netrix.unicom.com.` More details on the *period rule* will be provided later.

Name Server (NS) Resource Records

Name server resource records are the glue that makes the DNS hierarchical structure stick. An NS record defines which name server is authoritative for which zone or subdomain. It is especially used to point a parent domain server to the servers for their subdomains.

As shown in Figure 10.3, a name server authoritative for the com domain must include an NS record identifying the server that is authoritative for the `unicom.com` domain (that is, `netrix.unicom.com.`).

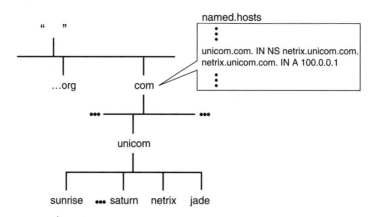

Figure 10.3. *A server authoritative for the* com *domain must include an NS record identifying the server that is authoritative for the* `unicom.com` *domain (that is,* `netrix.unicom.com.`).

The syntax of the NS record is as shown here:

```
[domain] [ttl] IN NS server
```

In this syntax,

domain	Is the name of the affected domain (that is, the domain for which *server* is an authoritative name server).
ttl	Is the time-to-live. If it's left blank, the default specified in the SOA record applies.
IN	Identifies the class as IN (Internet).
NS	Identifies the RR record type as NS (that is, a pointer to a name server).
server	Is the name of the host providing authoritative name service for the domain specified in *domain*.

Applying this to the unicom.com. situation, a server for the com domain should contain the following NS record in its named.hosts file:

```
unicom.com. IN NS netrix.unicom.com.
```

This NS record must also be included in the named.hosts file of netrix.unicom.com. When a server for the com domain is queried for the host IP address of jade.unicom.com., it checks its database to determine that netrix.unicom.com. is the server to which the query should be redirected. Hence, the com server must return the IP address of netrix, not its name, to the client station issuing the query. This means that it is not enough to include an NS record describing which server is authoritative for a given domain. The NS record should always be coupled with an A record specifying the address of the domain's server. Thus, the com server in question must include both of the following records in order to redirect queries pertaining to the unicom.com. domain to netrix:

```
unicom.com. IN NS netrix.unicom.com.
netrix.unicom.com. IN A 100.0.0.1
```

Canonical Name (CNAME) Records

A CNAME record defines an alias pointing to the host's official name. Following is the syntax of the CNAME record:

```
aliasname [ttl] IN CNAME [host]
```

In this syntax,

aliasname	Defines the alias for the host specified in *host*.
ttl	Defines the time-to-live. If it's left blank, the default specified in the SOA record applies.
IN	Is the IN class.
CNAME	Identifies the record type as CNAME.
host	Is the official name of the host.

Following is an example of a CNAME record:

```
fake.unicom.com. IN CNAME jade.unicom.com.
```

If a client issues a name query for host fake, the name server replaces fake with jade, using the preceding CNAME record, during its search for the queried information.

CNAME records are particularly useful whenever host name changes need to be made. In such a situation, you would change the official name, then maintain the old one as an alias for the new official name. You would allow a grace period until users are accustomed to the new name and applications affected by name changes are reconfigured.

Pointer (PTR) Records

PTR records are used to map IP addresses to names. Recall, from Chapter 6, "Name Services," that to reverse-resolve IP addresses into host names, the Internet included the in-addr.arpa top-level domain in its DNS tree. Below that domain, a subtree was created such that each network ID had a domain named after itself. For example, network ID 198.53.237.0 has 237.53.198.in-addr.arpa. for a reverse domain. Refer to the section "Reverse Resolution or Pointer Queries" in Chapter 6 to understand why the network ID is written in reverse order. Normally, when an organization like Unicom (the fictitious company) is delegated authority over its domain unicom.com, NIC delegates the organization the authority over the reverse domain corresponding to the network IDs belonging to that organization. In Unicom's case, the reverse domains are 100.in-addr.arpa, 1.151.in-addr.arpa, and 237.53.198.in-addr.arpa.

PTR records are maintained in the named.rev file and are meant to maintain the reverse domains.

Following is the syntax of the PTR record:

```
name [ttl] IN PTR host
```

In this syntax,

name	Specifies the reverse domain name of the host. The reverse domain name of a host has the following format:
	reverse_IP_address.in-addr.arpa
	Because jade's IP address is 198.53.237.1, its reverse_IP_address becomes 1.237.53.198. Hence, the reverse domain name of host jade becomes 1.237.53.198.in-addr.arpa.
[ttl]	Specifies time-to-live. If it's left blank, the default specified in the SOA record is assumed.
IN	Shows the record class as IN.
PTR	Signifies the record as being of type PTR.
host	Specifies the host name.

Referring to host jade, for example, a PTR record resolving its IP address to host name should read as shown here:

```
1.237.53.198.in-addr.arpa IN PTR jade
```

Confused? The following section will help you develop a clear picture. This section explains in detail, and in the context of configuring a primary name server, each of the configuration files by including a complete listing of the DNS setup pertaining to the unicom.com domain. You will be shown how all resource record types contribute to the setup, and where each type belongs.

Configuring a Primary Name Server

The following few subsections describe the contents of the database files required to bring up named as a primary name server on host netrix. Configuring a primary server is the most time-consuming, and sometimes confusing, process when compared to setting up secondary or cache servers. Why is the primary server's configuration presented first? Because the success of bringing up other server types is completely dependent on the primary. So read carefully.

named.hosts

named.hosts primarily maintains the host name-to-IP address mappings for all hosts in the designated zone. In unicom.com's case, because the domain is not partitioned, named.hosts must contain the name-to-IP address mappings for all hosts on this network. In addition to these mappings, named.hosts can contain other information such as names of hosts acting as mail exchanges (that is, mail routers), or CPU type, and well-known services supported by a host.

For the purpose of simplicity, a minimal service including name-to-address and address-to-name mappings will be described. The description will be based on the DNS setup files maintained on hosts netrix and jade in support of name services for the unicom.com domain.

Given what you have learned so far, and that netrix is the primary server for the unicom.com domain, this is what netrix's named.hosts file should look like:

```
;
; Section 1: The SOA record
;
unicom.com.    IN    SOA     netrix.unicom.com. root.netrix.unicom.com. (
                     2        ; Serial
                     14400    ; Refresh (4 hours)
                     3600     ; Retry (1hr)
                     604800   ; Expire ( 4 weeks )
                     86400 )  ; minimum TTL (time-to-live)


;
; Section 2: The following are the name servers for the unicom domain
;
```

```
unicom.com.    IN    NS     netrix.unicom.com.
unicom.com.    IN    NS     jade.unicom.com.

;
; Section 3: The following records map hosts' canonical names to their corresponding
; IP addresses
;
localhost.unicom.com.     IN A    127.0.0.1
saturn.unicom.com.        IN A    150.1.0.10
pluto.unicom.com.         IN A    150.1.0.11
laser.unicom.com.         IN A    100.0.0.3
maser.unicom.com.         IN A    100.0.0.4
sunrise.unicom.com.       IN A    198.53.237.2
cosmos.unicom.com.        IN A    198.53.237.3

;
; Section 4: Multihomed hosts
;
netrix.unicom.com.        IN A    150.1.0.10
netrix.unicom.com.        IN A    100.0.0.1
jade.unicom.com.          IN A    100.0.0.2
jade.unicom.com.          IN A    198.53.237.1
jade.unicom.com.          IN A    198.53.235.10
```

The file is conveniently broken down into sections, with each being titled by the section number and purpose of that section.

Section 1 contains the SOA record which declares netrix.unicom.com as being the DNS authoritative server for the unicom.com domain. A named.hosts file can contain only one SOA record, and it must be the first record in the file. The record also indicates that correspondence regarding this domain should be addressed to root@netrix.unicom.com (remember that the dot following the root should be replaced with the familiar @ character). Refer to the description of SOA records for details on the values enclosed in parentheses.

Section 2 includes two NS records declaring hosts netrix and jade as name servers for the unicom.com domain. You might be wondering how the name service daemon named knows which is a primary and which is a secondary server. The type of the name server is defined, as you will see later, in the named.boot file.

Section 3 includes all the A (address) records that map host names to IP addresses. When a client station queries a name server for the IP address of a given host, named scans the A records in its named.hosts for one matching the requirement and returns the corresponding IP address to the querying station.

What if named finds more than one record matching the subject of the query? According to the preceding listing, named.hosts includes two A records pertaining to netrix, and three pertaining to jade. In situations like these, named returns all the addresses it finds in its A records. To achieve optimal performance, named returns the address closest to the querying station first, followed by the other ones in order of proximity.

> **Caution:** All entries in the DNS database files must start on the first column of the file.

named.rev

`named.rev` serves the opposite purpose of `named.hosts`. It is used to maintain PTR records, which the `named` daemon uses to reverse-map IP addresses to host names. As in `named.hosts`, `named.rev` must include an SOA record marking the boundaries of the reverse domain for which the server is authoritative.

If an internetwork is assigned more than one network ID, multiple `named.rev` files must be created, one per reverse domain. Multiple reverse resolution database files with the same name (`named.rev`) can be implemented if the files are created in different directories. This approach, however, is less convenient and more confusing to manage. The other choice involves creating a file per reverse domain, with conveniently chosen filenames. The convention used in this book is

reversenetID`.rev`

in which *reversenetID* is the assigned network ID.

Applying this to the three reverse domains for which `netrix` is made authoritative, the three reverse domain files become `100.rev`, `1.150.rev`, and `237.53.198.rev`. Each of these files contains an SOA record defining its start-of-authority, and the PTR records pertaining to the reverse domain. You can choose your own conventions too. Later, you will read how, using `named.boot`, `named` can be flagged to read all of these, and other, files. Following are the complete listings of each of the reverse domain files as created on host `netrix`.

The following listing shows the contents of the `100.rev` reverse domain file as they should be on `netrix.unicom.com`:

```
100.in-addr.arpa.        IN SOA    netrix.unicom.com. root.netrix.unicom.com (
                         1         ; serial
                         14400     ; Refresh (4 hours)
                         3600      ; retry   ( 1 hour )
                         604800    ; expire  ( 1 week )
                         86400 )   ; TTL = 1 day
;
; name servers
;
100.in-addr.arpa.        IN NS     netrix.unicom.com.
100.in-addr.arpa.        IN NS     jade.unicom.com.
;
; Reverse address mappings
;
1.0.0.100.in-addr.arpa.  IN PTR    netrix.unicom.com.
2.0.0.100.in-addr.arpa.  IN PTR    jade.unicom.com.
3.0.0.100.in-addr.arpa.  IN PTR    laser.unicom.com.
4.0.0.100.in-addr.arpa.  IN PTR    maser.unicom.com.
```

The following listing shows the contents of the `1.150.rev` reverse domain file as they should be on `netrix.unicom.com`:

```
1.150.in-addr.arpa. IN   SOA    netrix.unicom.com. root.netrix.unicom.com. (
                         1      ; serial
                         14400  ; refresh ( 4 hr )
                         3600   ; retry ( 1 hr )
```

```
                              604800  ; expire ( 1 week )
                              86400 ) ; TTL = 1 day
;
; name servers
;
1.150.in-addr.arpa. IN      NS      netrix.unicom.com.
1.150.in-addr.arpa. IN      NS      jade.unicom.com.
;
; reverse address mappings
;
1.0.1.150.in-addr.arpa.     IN      PTR     netrix.unicom.com.
10.0.1.150.in-addr.arpa.    IN      PTR     saturn.unicom.com.
11.0.1.150.in-addr.arpa.    IN      PTR     pluto.unicom.com.
```

The following listing shows the contents of the 237.53.198.rev reverse domain file as they should be on netrix.unicom.com:

```
237.53.198.in-addr.arpa. IN SOA     netrix.unicom.com. root.netrix.unicom.com. (
                         1       ; serial
                         14400   ; refresh ( 4 hr )
                         3600    ; retry ( 1 hr )
                         604800  ; expire ( 1 week )
                         86400  ); TTL = 1 day
;
;
; name servers
;
237.53.198.in-addr.arpa.    IN      NS      netrix.unicom.com.
237.53.198.in-addr.arpa.    IN      NS      jade.unicom.com.
;
;
; Reverse address mappings
;
1.237.53.198.in-addr.arpa. IN       PTR     jade.unicom.com.
2.237.53.198.in-addr.arpa. IN       PTR     sunrise.unicom.com.
3.237.53.198.in-addr.arpa. IN       PTR     cosmos.unicom.com.
```

Notice how closely the organization of the first two parts of each file follows that of named.hosts. All files start with an appropriate SOA record marking the upper boundaries of the in-addr.arpa domain for which the server is authoritative. Next is a block of NS records, declaring the name servers that have authority for the domain. In all three files, both netrix and jade are declared as domain name servers.

The last part consists of PTR records. Each of these records contains the IP address-to-domain name associations that named uses for reverse address resolution.

named.local

If you reexamine the named.hosts file, you will find that it contains an entry corresponding to the special loopback host name localhost (refer to Chapter 4, "The Internet Layer and Routing," for the significance of the loopback interface). This entry maps localhost to the familiar IP address 127.0.0.1. Yet there is no PTR record in any of the reverse domain data files (listed previously) that takes care of the reverse mapping. None of those files is suitable for such a PTR record because the loopback address belongs to none of the in-addr.arpa domains that the files support.

To remedy the discrepancy, a new reverse domain file is required. This file is called, by default, `named.local`. Following are the file's contents:

```
0.0.127.in-addr.arpa. IN SOA       netrix.unicom.com. root.netrix.unicom.com. (
                       1           ; serial
                       14400       ; refresh ( 4 hours )
                       3600        ; retry ( 1 hour )
                       604800      ; expire ( 1 week )
                       86400 ) ; TTL = 1 day
;
; name servers
;
0.0.127.in-addr.arpa. IN   NS      netrix.unicom.com.
0.0.127.in-addr.arpa. IN   NS      jade.unicom.com.
;
; reverse address PTR mapping
;
1.0.0.127.in-addr.arpa. IN  PTR    localhost
```

Compare this file with any of the reverse domain files listed in the preceding section. You will find that its organization is identical to that of those files. As can be understood from the SOA record, this file identifies `netrix.unicom.com` as the server originating the `0.0.127.in-addr.arpa` domain. Again, there are two NS records identifying both `netrix` and `jade` as the name servers for this domain. Finally, there is only one PTR record to take care of the reverse address resolution of the loopback address (`127.0.0.1`) to the loopback host name `localhost`.

named.ca

Chapter 6, "Name Services," explained that to achieve optimal levels of performance, name servers are allowed to cache responses to queries they make to other servers on behalf of a requesting application. Furthermore, name servers cache all the data they discovered during the referral process that led to the desired response.

In caching referral data, name servers gradually learn and retain the necessary information about the neighborhoods that hosts on your network communicate with frequently. The learned information includes domain names and their corresponding name server IP addresses. Servers attempt to respond to a name query using information in their cache before looking elsewhere.

To expedite the caching process, and to further improve the performance of the name service, DNS defines a cache file called `named.ca`. In this file, the network administrator can include information about other neighboring and remote domains, their name servers, and the A records identifying their IP addresses. This information is used to initialize the cache buffers of the name server every time `named` is restarted.

For reliability, you should include only information you believe to be stable for prolonged periods. You also should periodically verify the validity and accuracy of the included data.

One of the most commonly included pieces of information in the `named.ca` file is information about the Internet root servers. This information is stable over long periods. It makes sense to initialize your server's cache with this information, given the likelihood that users on your networks will want to reach places on the Internet. A minimal `named.ca` file should, therefore, look as shown here:

```
;
;Servers for the root domain are listed below
;
.    99999999  IN  NS   TERP.UMD.EDU.
     99999999  IN  NS   AOS.BRL.MIL.
     99999999  IN  NS   C.NYSER.NET.
     99999999  IN  NS   NS.NASA.GOV.
     99999999  IN  NS   NS.NIC.DDN.MIL.
     99999999  IN  NS   NIC.NORDU.NET.
     99999999  IN  NS   NS1.ISI.EDU.
     99999999  IN  NS   NS.ISC.ORG.
     99999999  IN  NS   NS.INTERNIC.NET.
;
;Root servers by address
;
TERP.UMD.EDU.      99999999  IN  A   128.8.10.90
AOS.BRL.MIL.       99999999  IN  A   192.5.25.82
C.NYSER.NET.       99999999  IN  A   192.33.4.12
NS.NASA.GOV.       99999999  IN  A   192.52.195.10
NS.NIC.DDN.MIL.    99999999  IN  A   192.112.36.4
NIC.NORDU.NET.     99999999  IN  A   192.36.148.17
NS1.ISI.EDU.       99999999  IN  A   128.9.0.107
NS.INTERNIC.NET    99999999  IN  A   198.41.0.4
NS.ISC.ORG         99999999  IN  A   192.5.5.241
```

As can be seen, this `named.ca` file is composed of two blocks of entries. The first one contains NS records identifying the names of the root servers. There are two things you should have noticed in this file: the dot (.) in the first column at the beginning of the first NS record, and the lack of object names in the subsequent NS records (refer to the general syntax of RR records for details). Because the root domain is represented by a null character, the dot is the character used in DNS files. Also, whenever multiple contiguous records refer to the same object, the name field can be left blank in subsequent records following the first one. Hence, because all the NS records pertain to root servers, only the first record has to include the name of the object being affected (that is, the root domain).

The second block contains A records, providing the IP addresses corresponding to the servers identified in the first block. Whenever `named` is brought up, it reads `named.ca` and caches all the information contained in this file. This way, your name server is guaranteed a good starting point from which it can navigate the Internet when looking for servers having authority for other domains.

> **Tip:** A current list of root name servers is always available through anonymous ftp from `nic.ddn.mil` in the `/netinfo/root-servers.txt` file.

> **Note:** It is your responsibility to regularly verify the validity and accuracy of the information contained in `named.ca`, including information about root servers. Failure to do so might seriously disrupt name service on your network, leading to undesirable degradation in performance. NIC is responsible for the information on an as-is basis at the time of downloading the `root-server.txt` file cited previously.

Starting *named* and the *named.boot* File

The BIND daemon, `named`, is started at boot time by the `/etc/inet/rc.inet` script. Here is the code from the `/etc/inet/rc.inet` file that takes care of the startup process:

```
#
#  Run the DNS server if a configuration file is present
#
if [ -f /etc/inet/named.boot -a -x /usr/sbin/in.named ]
then
    /usr/sbin/in.named
fi
```

As shown, the command to start the `named` daemon is `/usr/sbin/in.named`. Before starting `named`, the system checks for the existence of `named.boot` in the `/etc/inet` directory. It is used by `named` to find where all the other files (that is, `named.rev`, `named.hosts`, and so on) are, and to determine whether the server being brought up is primary, secondary, or cache. If the `named.boot` file exists, the name server is started and configured as dictated by the file contents.

Following is the listing of the file `named.boot` as it should be on `netrix` to bring it up as a primary name server:

```
directory       /usr/lib/named

primary         unicom.com                  named.hosts
primary         100.in-addr.arpa            100.rev
primary         1.150.in-addr.arpa          150.1.rev
primary         237.53.198.in-addr.arpa     198.53.237.rev
primary         0.0.127.in-addr.arpa        127.localhost
cache           .                           named.ca
```

The first line starts with the keyword `directory`. This line defines the directory where `named` is supposed to look for the remaining configuration files.

The subsequent lines represent `primary` statements, each telling `named` that this server is the primary server for the domain described in the next column. The third column tells `named` the name of the file containing the corresponding domain information. The filename is expressed relative to the directory specified in the directory statement. The first `primary` statement, for example, tells `named` that this server is a primary server for the `unicom.com` domain. The third column instructs `named` to look for the domain data in `named.hosts`, which is kept in the file `/usr/lib/named`.

The third statement says that this server is the primary server for the reverse domain 100.in-addr.arpa, and it points named to 100.rev for the relevant domain information. Similarly, the fourth, fifth, and sixth statements take care of the remaining reverse domains, including the loopback domain (0.0.127.in-addr.arpa).

Finally, the last statement is a cache statement. This statement configures named to maintain a cache of responses to name queries. As discussed before, named caches information acquired through referrals during name resolution processes. The cache statement also initializes the server's cache with the data included in the named.ca file.

Starting *named*

Now that all the files, including named.boot, are created and contain all the information necessary to bring up a primary name server on netrix, you can proceed either by invoking named on the command line or by rebooting the host.

Enter the following command to invoke named on the command line:

```
# /usr/sbin/in.named
```

This syntax directs named to search for /etc/inet/named.boot. If, however, you want named to boot using another file, you can do so by using the -b option. To make named boot using named.test.boot, enter this:

```
# /usr/sbin/in.named -b /etc/inet/named.test.boot
```

The -b bootfile option is particularly useful for testing changes to the name service. Unless the change is trusted to work properly over a reasonable period, you should not overwrite the contents of the current configuration files using new configuration data.

To force named to adapt to changes made to the configuration files, send it the SIGHUP signal. The other signals you can send to named include SIGINIT, SIGUSR1, and SIGUSR2. Because those signals are typically used when troubleshooting DNS, they are explained in Chapter 15, "Network Troubleshooting and Performance Tuning."

Section Summary

To bring up a primary domain name server, you need to create several database files, one per domain, containing information resource records for which the server is authoritative. The files include named.ca containing the cache initialization data, the reverse loopback domain file (its generic name is named.local), and the named.boot file.

Each of these files can contain several types of resource records following well-defined formats. The most commonly used types are SOA, NS, A, and PTR. The named.boot file is named's startup file. It points to the actual path of each of the resource files pertinent to each of the domains for which the server is authoritative. `named.boot` also identifies the type of server being brought up. The server type is set on a per-domain basis. A server can be primary for one domain and secondary for another.

The next section explains the necessary preparations required to bring up a secondary name server.

Configuring a Secondary Name Server

Configuring a secondary server involves configuring three files, `named.boot`, `named.ca`, and `named.local`. To simplify your life, copy all three files from the primary server to the machine where you intend to bring up the secondary server. You can achieve this by using either rcp (explained in Chapter 13, "Remote Access Utilities") or ftp.

To bring up a secondary name server on `jade`, you would log in to it as `root` and start an ftp session with `netrix`. If name service is already started on `netrix`, you can configure `/etc/resolv.conf` to include the domain and the `nameserver` name of the network. Consequently, you can enter the command

```
# ftp netrix.unicom.com
```

to start the file transfer session. Alternatively, you can invoke the session by specifying the IP address of `netrix` as shown here:

```
# ftp 100.0.0.1
```

In either case, after completing the login process, the administrator can change to the directory where the files are and issue multiple `ftp get` commands to have the files transferred to `jade`.

> **Note:** The files being transferred in this case are `named.boot`, `127.localhost`, and `named.ca` (`127.localhost` corresponds to the generic file `named.local`).

The only file that requires a few changes is `named.boot`. The following listing shows how `named.boot` on `jade` should read:

```
directory   /usr/lib/named

secondary   unicom.com                  100.0.0.1
secondary   100.in-addr.arpa            100.0.0.1
secondary   1.150.in-addr.arpa          100.0.0.1
secondary   237.53.198.in-addr.arpa     100.0.0.1
primary     0.0.127.in-addr.arpa        127.localhost
cache       .                           named.ca
```

As can be seen from this, the configuration of `named.boot` includes mostly secondary, rather than primary, statements. The second entry, for example, configures `jade` as a secondary server for the `unicom.com` domain and tells it to obtain a copy of the pertinent domain database from the server at IP address `100.0.0.1` (that is, `netrix`). The third, fourth, and fifth entries, likewise configure `named`, on `jade`, as the secondary server for the reverse domains `100.in-addr.arpa`, `1.150.in-addr.arpa`, and `237.53.198.in-addr.arpa`, respectively. All secondary statements direct `named` to host IP address `100.0.0.1` for a copy of the pertinent database files.

The sixth and seventh entries are identical to their counter-entries in `named.boot` on `netrix`. They also point `named` to local filenames for information. Because both `127.localhost` and `named.ca` hardly change their contents, it makes sense to access the information they contain locally, thus saving bandwidth that could otherwise have been lost to file transfer operations.

Startup of the Secondary Server

A secondary server is started in the same way as the primary server. When the host enters run level two at boot time and executes the `/etc/inet/rc.inet` script, the `named.boot` file is checked for existence. If the file exists, `named` is brought up and configured according to the statements included in the file. Copies of database files pertinent to domains for which the server is authoritative are then obtained via the zone transfer process, from sources specified by the secondary statements.

The secondary server can also be started using the `/usr/sbin/in.named` command, including the use of any of the options described earlier.

Secondary but Robust!

The preceding configuration works fine as long as the primary server is up at the time the secondary server is restarted. But what if the primary server is down? The secondary server will not be able to come up, because there might not be another source for the required data. To circumvent this possibility, DNS enables you to do two things: specify up to 10 alternative IP addresses in the secondary statements from which the server can obtain zonal data, and configure the server to maintain disk copies of files it obtains via zonal transfers.

Alternative addresses can be added after the first IP address. They must pertain to hosts running primary name service. Following is an example of a secondary statement with two specified IP addresses:

```
secondary unicom.com 100.0.0.1 100.0.0.4
```

According to the statement, the secondary name server must seek data from `100.0.0.4` should `netrix` fail to respond to `jade`'s initial requests for zonal transfer of data.

Robustness can be improved by allowing the secondary name server to maintain backup copies of the transferred data files. This way, the secondary will always have a last resort from which it can obtain zonal data. The caveat, however, is that this data has an expiration date, as set in the SOA record. Upon expiration, the backup files are discarded. Hence, unless a primary server is found to respond to zonal transfer requests, the secondary server drops out of service.

All that is necessary to enable `named` to maintain a backup copy is specifying, in the last column of each secondary statement, the name of the file to which data should be copied. Following is a revised version of jade's `named.boot` file, including support for backup files:

```
directory       /usr/lib/named

secondary       unicom.com                  100.0.0.1      named.hosts
secondary       100.in-addr.arpa            100.0.0.1      100.rev
secondary       1.150.in-addr.arpa          100.0.0.1      150.1.rev
secondary       237.53.198.in-addr.arpa     100.0.0.1      198.53.237.rev
primary         0.0.127.in-addr.arpa        127.localhost
```

Notice that the filenames do not have to be the same as those on `netrix`. Instead, entirely different names could have been chosen. For convenience, they were left identical to those on `netrix`. When `named` is started, it contacts the specified servers for data to keep in specified files in the `/usr/lib/named` directory. If you examine any of the files, you will find some of the resource records written slightly differently. Here are the contents of `named.hosts`, as backed up by host jade:

```
$ORIGIN com.
unicom          IN      SOA     netrix.unicom.com. root.netrix.unicom.com. (
                2 14400 3600 604800 86400 )
                IN      NS      netrix.unicom.com.
$ORIGIN unicom.com.
netrix          IN      A       150.1.0.10
                IN      A       100.0.0.1
$ORIGIN com.
unicom          IN      NS      jade.unicom.com.
$ORIGIN unicom.com.
jade            IN      A       100.0.0.2
                IN      A       198.53.237.1
                IN      A       198.53.235.10
jadeppp         IN      A       198.53.235.10
netrix150       IN      A       150.1.0.1
saturn          IN      A       150.1.0.10
maser           IN      A       100.0.0.4
jadepixel       IN      A       198.53.237.1
netrix100       IN      A       100.0.0.1
pluto           IN      A       150.1.0.11
localhost       IN      A       127.0.0.1
jade            IN      A       100.0.0.2
                IN      A       198.53.237.1
                IN      A       198.53.235.10
laser           IN      A       100.0.0.3
cosmos          IN      A       198.53.237.3
sunrise         IN      A       198.53.237.2
netrix          IN      A       150.1.0.10
                IN      A       100.0.0.1
```

Differences between the syntax of resource records just shown and what you previously have been told to follow will be explained later, when shortcuts to minimize the tedium of entering information into the database files are presented.

Configuring a Cache-Only Server

A cache-only server is, as the name implies, a server that does not maintain any database files. Instead, it caches responses to queries requested from remote servers. Cached responses are used to resolve future queries for the same data.

A cache-only server is the simplest of all servers to configure. Following is the named.boot file of a hypothetical cache-only server connected to the unicom.com network:

```
;
; Cache-only server for the unicom.com domain
;
primary       0.0.127.in-addr.arpa      /usr/lib/named/127.localhost
cache         .                         /usr/lib/named/named.ca
;
```

As can be concluded from the listing, two more files, in addition to named.boot, are needed. These are named.ca and 127.localhost. The cache statement configures the server to cache responses, in addition to initializing its cache with the data maintained in named.ca. The primary statement has the same functionality described in earlier sections.

What makes this server cache-only is the *lack* of primary, or secondary, statements declaring it as being an authoritative server for a domain on the network. The cache statement has always been part of the previously examined named.boot files. As such, it is absolutely necessary for inclusion in the named.boot of a cache-only server, and it is equally necessary to avoid all forms of primary, or secondary, statements in the file, except for the one pertaining to the local loopback domain.

nslookup

nslookup is an interactive name service querying tool. Using nslookup, you can perform tasks such as verifying DNS server setup and troubleshooting. Chapter 15, "Network Troubleshooting and Performance Tuning," illustrates the use of nslookup as a troubleshooting tool. This section illustrates its usefulness as a tool for establishing the operational sanity of a new server before it is trusted to production environments. In particular, the following features are covered:

◆ Using nslookup on-line help
◆ Using nslookup to query the local server
◆ Using nslookup to query a remote server
◆ Using nslookup to download the DNS database

nslookup On-line Help

nslookup is a feature-rich command, which means that it can take a novice some time to fully utilize it. Using nslookup, as illustrated later, you can talk interactively to the local name server and query it for any information you need. You can use nslookup to query the name server for host-to-address mappings, reverse address mappings, well-known services, and other information that the database includes about hosts.

With nslookup, you can also find out who is on the system, and many other things. Better still, all the operations can be performed on remote name servers, so you don't have to be there to verify their setup when troubleshooting the service. You can download any domain's database to a local file, either to view it within the nslookup session or for use with any of the UNIX file lookup or editing tools.

You can refer to the UNIX manual pages for help on the nslookup command. You also can get help while in an nslookup session. To start nslookup, you enter the command name at the shell prompt:

```
# nslookup
Default Server: netrix.unicom.com
Address: 100.0.0.1

>
```

When invoked, nslookup targets, by default, the local server. In the preceding example, nslookup targeted the netrix name server, as indicated by the nslookup response. The response included the name of the target server and its address. This can be considered as a sign of partial success in configuring name service on netrix.

The angle bracket (>) is the nslookup prompt. At this prompt, you can start issuing name service queries, or setup commands, to configure nslookup to suit your upcoming queries. Among the things that nslookup can be asked to do is provide you with on-line help. To do that, enter help at the command prompt as shown here:

```
# nslookup
Default Server:  netrix.unicom.com
Address:  100.0.0.1

> help
#       @(#)nslookup.help        1.1 STREAMWare TCP/IP SVR4.2  source
#       SCCS IDENTIFICATION
#       @(#)nslookup.hlp 4.3 Lachman System V STREAMS TCP  source
Commands:        (identifiers are shown in uppercase, [] means optional)
NAME            - print info about the host/domain NAME using default server
NAME1 NAME2     - as above, but use NAME2 as server
help or ?       - print info on common commands; see nslookup(1) for details
set OPTION      set an option
    all         - print options, current server and host
    [no]debug   - print debugging information
    [no]d2      - print exhaustive debugging information
    [no]defname - append domain name to each query
    [no]recurs  - ask for recursive answer to query
    [no]vc      - always use a virtual circuit
    domain=NAME - set default domain name to NAME
    srchlist=N1[/N2/.../N6] - set domain to N1 and search list to N1,N2, etc.
    root=NAME - set root server to NAME
    retry=X     - set number of retries to X
    timeout=X - set initial time-out interval to X seconds
    querytype=X  - set query type, e.g., A,ANY,CNAME,HINFO,MX,NS,PTR,SOA,WKS
    type=X       - synonym for querytype
    class=X     - set query class to one of IN (Internet), CHAOS, HESIOD or ANY
```

```
server NAME   - set default server to NAME, using current default server
lserver NAME  - set default server to NAME, using initial server
finger [USER] - finger the optional NAME at the current default host
root   - set current default server to the root
ls [opt] DOMAIN [> FILE] - list addresses in DOMAIN (optional: output to FILE)
    -a -  list canonical names and aliases
    -h -  list HINFO (CPU type and operating system)
    -s -  list well-known services
    -d -  list all records
    -t TYPE   -  list records of the given type (e.g., A,CNAME,MX, etc.)
view FILE     - sort an 'ls' output file and view it with more
exit   - exit the program, ^D also exits
> exit
#
```

Rather than explaining all the different options, the following sections attempt to lay a solid foundation for understanding, and using, some of the most useful features of nslookup. It is left to your imagination and initiative to experiment and discover the usefulness of the other features.

Using *nslookup* to Query the Local Server

There are at least three situations in which you might have to use nslookup: to test a newly brought-up server, to verify changes made to the configuration of an existing server, or to troubleshoot the DNS service. Regardless of the reason you are using it, a good way to start an nslookup session is by querying the local server. Depending on the results, you can escalate by targeting other servers in your own domain or other remotely located domains on the Internet.

Now that netrix has been configured and brought up, it's time to start testing it to verify its operation. To do that, the network administrator logs in as root and issues the nslookup command. By default, nslookup responds to name queries (that is, name-to-address mappings). Following is a depiction of what happens when a host name (for example, saturn) is entered at the nslookup prompt:

```
# nslookup
Default Server: netrix.unicom.com
Address: 100.0.0.1

> saturn
Server: netrix.unicom.com
Address: 100.0.0.1

Name:   saturn.unicom.com
Address: 150.1.0.10
```

Notice how the response includes both the resolution and the name and address of the server that resolved the query. You should carry out a few more similar tests to verify the capability of the local server to resolve name-to-address queries flawlessly. Of particular interest are multihomed hosts, such as netrix and jade in the unicom.com domain. As said before, a name server should respond with all the addresses assigned to the interfaces attaching the host to the internetwork. In the following example, nslookup is used to resolve jade's name to its corresponding IP addresses:

```
# nslookup
Default Server:  netrix.unicom.com
Address:  100.0.0.1

> jade
Server:  netrix.unicom.com
Address:  100.0.0.1

Name:    jade.unicom.com
Addresses:  100.0.0.2, 198.53.237.1, 198.53.235.10
```

nslookup displays addresses in the order in which they were received (that is, 100.0.0.2 was received first, followed by 198.53.237.1 and 198.53.235.10). This order is not accidental. Whenever a query affects a multihomed host, the name server returns the address corresponding to the closest route first. Because both jade and netrix share the 100.0.0.0 network, 100.0.0.2 qualifies as the closest route.

Next, you should verify the server's capability to handle reverse resolution queries. Again, it is a simple matter of entering an IP address that exists on your network. Here is an example carried on netrix:

```
# nslookup
Default Server:  netrix.unicom.com
Address:  100.0.0.1

> 198.150.1.0.11
Server:  netrix.unicom.com
Address:  100.0.0.1
```

Try as many reverse queries as it takes to verify the reliability of the reverse resolution process. If all goes well, you can proceed to the next phase of testing other servers by using nslookup on the local server.

Using *nslookup* to Query a Remote Server

Using nslookup, you can query remote name servers on the network. You can use this feature to troubleshoot remote servers or to check the robustness of the overall DNS service you recently brought up on the network. In the following example, the unicom.com administrator invokes nslookup on netrix to query jade (that is, the secondary name server) for the IP address of saturn:

```
# nslookup
Default Server:  netrix.unicom.com
Address:  100.0.0.1

> saturn jade.unicom.com
Server:  jade.unicom.com
Addresses:  100.0.0.2, 198.53.237.1, 198.53.235.10

Name:    saturn.unicom.com
Address:  150.1.0.10
```

As shown, to force `nslookup` to send the query to `jade`, the remote server's name (`jade.unicom.com`) must be entered after the host name (`saturn`) on the command line. A better way of conversing interactively with the remote server is to use the `server` command, letting `nslookup` default to the remote server. The following example shows how to do this:

```
> server jade
Default Server:  jade.unicom.com
Addresses:  100.0.0.2, 198.53.237.1, 198.53.235.10

> saturn
Server:  jade.unicom.com
Addresses:  100.0.0.2, 198.53.237.1, 198.53.235.10

Name:     saturn.unicom.com
Address:  150.1.0.10
```

Using *nslookup* to Download the DNS Database

Using `ls`, an `nslookup` command, you can do zonal data transfers to the local host. By default, data is directed to the standard output, as shown in the following example:

```
# nslookup
Default Server: jade
Address:  0.0.0.0

> ls unicom.com
[jade]
 unicom.com.                server = jade.unicom.com
 jade                       100.0.0.2
 jade                       198.53.237.1
 jade                       198.53.235.10
 unicom.com.                server = netrix.unicom.com
 netrix                     150.1.0.10
 netrix                     100.0.0.1
 saturn                     150.1.0.10
 maser                      100.0.0.4
 pluto                      150.1.0.11
 localhost                  127.0.0.1
 unicom                     server = netrix.unicom.com
 netrix                     150.1.0.10
 netrix                     100.0.0.1
 jade                       100.0.0.2
 jade                       198.53.237.1
 jade                       198.53.235.10
 laser                      100.0.0.3
 sunrise                    198.53.237.2
 cosmos                     198.53.237.3
 netrix                     150.1.0.10
 netrix                     100.0.0.1
> exit
#
```

This listing is helpful in verifying that information about all hosts is indeed being included. You can use it to perform host counts or check for individual hosts. Also, notice how the listing conveniently points out the names and addresses of the servers in the domain in question.

Creating and Delegating Subdomains

The larger the domain becomes, the more demand is put on the services of DNS servers. This can, consequently, lead to degradation in performance. Part of your mandate as a network administrator is to monitor the growth of the organizational network, foresee potential bottlenecks, and plan proactively for circumventing them before they become real problems.

Creating subdomains and delegating the authority for them to other name servers is one way of accommodating growth. Growth (and related performance) is not the only reason for creating and delegating subdomains. There are nontechnical reasons such as politics or geographical distribution of the network.

Some organizations plan their domains to mirror their departmental structure. They might also delegate the responsibility of individual subdomains to the management of the departments to which the subdomains belong.

It is easier to delegate the management of remote sites to their local authorities than to have it all centralized in one site. Delegation is also less demanding on the WAN bandwidth, contributing to better DNS performance by ensuring relative independence in the event of WAN failures.

This section shows how to create subdomains and how to set up subdomain servers. As in previous sections, the fictitious unicom.com domain is used to illustrate the covered concepts.

The Primary Subdomain Server

Figure 10.4 shows both the physical layout of the unicom.com network and the layout of the domain's logical organization. The parent domain, unicom.com, has as its members all the hosts on both networks 100.0.0.0 and 150.1.0.0. The subdomain, pulse.unicom.com, has the router jade and hosts belonging to network 198.53.237.0 for members. Hosts netrix and jelly are elected to become the primary and secondary servers for unicom.com, whereas jade and wing are elected to serve as the primary and secondary servers for pulse.unicom.com.

Following are the contents of the named.hosts file, including A records for all hosts connected to the pulse.unicom.com subdomain. This file, among others, must exist on host jade to bring it up as the primary server for the pulse.unicom.com domain:

```
pulse.unicom.com. IN SOA jade.pulse.unicom.com. root.jade.pulse.unicom.com. (
        1         ; Serial
        14400     ; Refresh
        3600      ; Retry
        604800    ; Expire
        86400 )   ; TTL
;
; name servers for the pulse.unicom.com. domain;
```

```
;
pulse.unicom.com.     IN    NS      jade.pulse.unicom.com.
pulse.unicom.com.     IN    NS      wing.pulse.unicom.com.
;
; name servers for the parent domain unicom.com
;
unicom.com.    IN    NS     netrix.unicom.com.
unicom.com.    IN    NS     jelly.unicom.com.
;
; A records for the hosts in the pulse.unicom.com. domain
;
localhost.pulse.unicom.com.    IN   A     127.0.0.1
jade.pulse.unicom.com.         IN   A     198.53.237.1
jade.pulse.unicom.com.         IN   A     100.0.0.2
jade.pulse.unicom.com.         IN   A     198.53.235.10
sunrise.pulse.unicom.com.      IN   A     198.53.237.2
cosmos.pulse.unicom.com.       IN   A     198.53.237.3
wing.pulse.unicom.com.         IN   A     198.53.237.7
netrix.unicom.com.             IN   A     100.0.0.2
netrix.unicom.com.             IN   A     150.1.0.1
jelly.unicom.com               IN   A     100.0.0.35
```

Compare this `named.hosts` with that of `netrix` when it was configured as the primary server for `unicom.com`. Although the general structure is the same, there are observations that are worth comment:

◆ Host `jade`'s `named.hosts` includes two NS records pointing to the server of the parent domain. They identify both `netrix` and `jelly` as the authoritative servers for the parent domain `unicom.com`. These records tell server `jade` to send queries pertaining to hosts in the parent domain to `netrix` and `jelly`. The query is relegated to the parent domain server only if the response has not already been cached from an earlier query.

◆ Knowing the name of a server is not enough, however, to reach that server. As you know, hosts rely on IP addresses rather than names to get anywhere on the network. Reaching a name server is no exception. For this reason, two A records pertaining to both `netrix` and `jelly` are included in the `named.hosts` file. Using the name, `jade` knows which server to contact for name queries pertaining to the parent domain. The address helps `jade` get there.

What happens if these records are eliminated from the `named.hosts` file? Will server `jade` still be able to resolve queries pertaining to the parent domain? The answer is yes. Remember, it was explained that whenever a server fails at resolving a query by itself, it submits the query to a root server. This, in turn, triggers a cycle of referrals until the server authoritative for the domain in question is identified and contacted for resolution. Including these records short-circuits the referral cycle by making the necessary information readily available to hosts `jade` and `wing`.

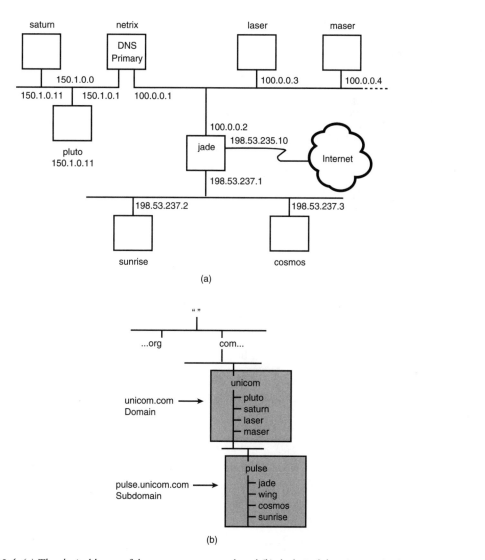

Figure 10.4. *(a) The physical layout of the* unicom.com *network and (b) the logical domain organization.*

Because network 198.53.237.0 belongs to the pulse.unicom.com domain, the reverse domain 237.53.198.in-addr.arpa should belong to the same authority. Following the convention depicted earlier, PTR (pointer) records are maintained in the 237.53.198.rev file. Here are the file contents:

```
237.53.198.in-addr.arpa. IN SOA jade.pulse.unicom.com. root.pulse.unicom.com. (
                1       ; Serial
                14400   ; Refresh
                3600    ; Retry
                604800  ; Expire
                86400 ) ; TTL
```

```
;
;name servers
;
237.53.198.in-addr.arpa. IN  NS    jade.pulse.unicom.com.
237.53.198.in-addr.arpa. IN  NS    wing.pulse.unicom.com.
;
; Pointer records
1.237.53.198.in-addr.arpa. IN PTR jade.pulse.unicom.com.
2.237.53.198.in-addr.arpa. IN PTR sunrise.pulse.unicom.com.
3.237.53.198.in-addr.arpa. IN PTR cosmos.pulse.unicom.com.
7.237.53.198.in-addr.arpa. IN PTR wing.pulse.unicom.com.
```

There is nothing special about this file. Just remember that it no longer belongs to server jade because jade is no longer authoritative for the 237.53.198.in-addr.arpa domain.

> **Note:** It is important to note that the reverse-domain delegation process has to pass through NIC authority. Although you can create and delegate subdomains without informing NIC of the changes, you cannot do the same thing with the reverse domains being assigned to you. You're required to contact NIC and submit an application for the redelegation of any of the reverse domains for which you have authority.

Because 127.localhost (generically known as named.local) and named.ca are identical for most configurations, you are referred to earlier sections for a refresher on them.

Here are the contents of named.boot, the configuration startup file of named:

```
directory      /usr/root/named.pulse

primary        pulse.unicom.com.          named.hosts
primary        237.53.198.in-addr.arpa    237.53.198.rev
primary        0.0.127.in-addr.arpa       127.localhost
cache          .                          named.ca
```

As you see, there is no difference between this file and any of the named.boot files that were examined earlier.

The Secondary Name Server of *pulse.unicom.com*

Creating the named database and configuration files for the secondary server (wing.pulse.unicom.com) is a simple two-step process:

1. Copy named.ca, 127.localhost, and named.boot from server jade to a directory in host wing, using either rcp or ftp.

2. Edit named.boot to look as shown here:

   ```
   directory   /usr/root/named.pulse

   secondary   pulse.unicom.com.          named.hosts
   secondary   237.53.198.in-addr.arpa    237.53.198.rev
   primary     0.0.127.in-addr.arpa       127.localhost
   cache       .                          named.ca
   ```

This completes all the steps necessary to bring up both host jade as the primary name server and host wing as the secondary server. Before bringing up and testing the servers, take a look at how the servers for the parent domain are configured.

The Primary *unicom.com* Domain Server

According to the scenario at the beginning of the chapter, host netrix was authoritative for the entire domain and all the reverse domains. In this scenario, however, netrix is responsible only for the hosts connecting to networks 150.1.0.0 and 100.0.0.0. This means its database files must include named.hosts, 100.rev, 1.150.rev, 127.localhost, and named.ca.

Notice that the netrix database does not include 237.53.198.rev pertaining to the 237.53.198.in-addr.arpa reverse domain. This reverse domain is now the responsibility of hosts jade and wing, and its corresponding file is now a property of jade.

Only the contents of named.hosts and named.boot on host netrix will be presented. For a refresher on the contents of the other files, refer to the earlier sections.

named.hosts should read as shown here:

```
unicom.com.    IN     SOA      netrix.unicom.com. root.netrix.unicom.com. (
                      3        ; Serial
                      14400    ; Refresh (4 hours)
                      3600     ; Retry (1hr)
                      604800   ; Expire ( 4 weeks )
                      86400 )  ;MinimumTTL (time-to-live)

;
; The following is the name server for the unicom.com domain
;
unicom.com.    IN     NS     netrix.unicom.com.
unicom.com.    IN     NS     jelly.unicom.com.
;
; The following are the name servers for the pulse.unicom.com domain
;
pulse.unicom.com.    IN     NS     jade.pulse.unicom.com.
pulse.unicom.com.    IN     NS     wing.pulse.unicom.com.
;
; The following records map hosts' canonical names to their corresponding
; IP addresses
;
localhost.unicom.com. IN    A     127.0.0.1
saturn.unicom.com.    IN    A     150.1.0.10
pluto.unicom.com.     IN    A     150.1.0.11
laser.unicom.com.     IN    A     100.0.0.3
maser.unicom.com.     IN    A     100.0.0.4
;
; Multihomed hosts
;
netrix.unicom.com.       IN    A     150.1.0.10
netrix.unicom.com.       IN    A     100.0.0.1
jade.pulse.unicom.com.   IN    A     100.0.0.2
jade.pulse.unicom.com.   IN    A     198.53.237.1
jade.pulse.unicom.com.   IN    A     198.53.235.10
wing.pulse.unicom.com.   IN    A     198.53.237.7
```

Notice how the file includes two NS records identifying both hosts jade and wing as the authoritative servers for the pulse.unicom.com domain. Also included are two A records that resolve the names to IP addresses. Accordingly, when named is brought up, it knows how to reach both servers for queries pertaining to the subdomain.

Next, here are the contents of the named.boot file on host netrix:

```
directory      /home/root/named.pulse

primary      unicom.com               named.hosts
primary      100.in-addr.arpa         100.rev
primary      1.150.in-addr.arpa       150.1.rev
primary      0.0.127.in-addr.arpa     127.localhost
cache        .                        named.ca
```

The only thing that is different about this file, compared with its predecessor (when there weren't any subdomains), is that 237.53.198.rev is missing because it now belongs to host jade.

Testing the DNS Service

Now that all the pieces are in place, the name servers can be brought up and tested. Following is a depiction of a series of tests, using nslookup, to verify that the servers can be reliably put to production.

First, the parent domain server netrix is tested. The following listing illustrates the outcome of an nslookup session that was invoked on netrix:

```
# nslookup
Default Server:  netrix.unicom.com
Address:  100.0.0.1

> unicom.com
[netrix.unicom.com]
 pulse.unicom.com.              server = jade.pulse.unicom.com
 jade                           100.0.0.2
 jade                           198.53.237.1
 jade                           198.53.235.10
 pulse.unicom.com.              server = wing.pulse.unicom.com
 wing                           198.53.237.7
 wing                           198.53.237.7
 jade                           100.0.0.2
 jade                           198.53.237.1
 jade                           198.53.235.10

> cosmos.pulse.unicom.com
Server:  netrix.unicom.com
Address:  100.0.0.1

Name:   cosmos.pulse.unicom.com
Address:  198.53.237.3
```

As shown, netrix.unicom.com responded to the first query for information about the unicom.com domain. The response confirms that server netrix recognizes the existence of subdomain pulse.unicom.com, and that servers jade and wing are authoritative for the subdomain. The next query (ls unicom.com) requests a listing of the information about all hosts in the unicom.com domain. Once again, included in the response are the names of both jade and wing as pulse.unicom.com servers. Finally, the last query positively verifies that server netrix can resolve names belonging to the pulse subdomain.

Next, jade is tested. Following is the output of the nslookup session that was invoked on jade for testing:

```
# nslookup
> netrix.unicom.com
Server:  jade
Address:  0.0.0.0

Non-authoritative answer:
Name:    netrix.unicom.com
Addresses:  100.0.0.1, 150.1.0.1

> saturn.unicom.com.
Server:  jade
Address:  0.0.0.0

Non-authoritative answer:
Name:    saturn.unicom.com
Address:  150.1.0.10
> set type=ns
> unicom.com.
Server:  jade
Address:  0.0.0.0

Non-authoritative answer:
unicom.com     nameserver = netrix.unicom.com

Authoritative answers can be found from:
unicom.com          nameserver = netrix.unicom.com
netrix.unicom.com   internet address = 100.0.0.1
netrix.unicom.com   internet address = 150.1.0.1
pulse.unicom.com.
Server:  jade
Address:  0.0.0.0

pulse.unicom.com          nameserver = jade.pulse.unicom.com
pulse.unicom.com          nameserver = wing.pulse.unicom.com
jade.pulse.unicom.com     internet address = 198.53.237.1
jade.pulse.unicom.com     internet address = 100.0.0.2
jade.pulse.unicom.com     internet address = 198.53.235.10
wing.pulse.unicom.com     internet address = 198.53.237.7
> exit
#
```

The first and second queries reveal that server jade can indeed resolve name queries pertaining to the parent domain. The last query requests information about all name servers in the unicom.com domain. Notice how server jade responds with the details pertaining to servers in both the unicom.com and the pulse.unicom.com domains. After all, pulse is a subdomain of unicom.com.

These tests might not be as exhaustive as they should be. The more testing you do before the servers are put into production, the less likely are unpleasant and potentially embarrassing surprises.

Making Life Simpler

Now that you are familiar with DNS concepts and capable of setting up your own name servers, it is time to show you two conventions that make editing the DNS database files a simpler task.

One of the things you might have wondered about is whether it was necessary to include the full domain label for every host to be included in the `named.hosts` database file. The answer is no, provided that you make a slight change to the SOA record of the affected files. If the domain name in the SOA record is the same as the domain name (called the *origin*) in the primary statement of the `named.boot` file, you can replace the domain name in SOA with the @ character. The @ character has the effect of telling `named` to append the domain level specified in the primary statement to every host name not ending with a dot. Taking server `netrix` as an example, following are the `named.boot` and the SOA record as shown in the chapter.

The contents of `named.boot`:

```
directory       /home/root/named

primary         unicom.com                  named.hosts
primary         100.in-addr.arpa            100.rev
primary         1.150.in-addr.arpa          150.1.rev
primary         237.53.198.in-addr.arpa     198.53.237.rev
primary         0.0.127.in-addr.arpa        127.localhost
```

The SOA record in `named.hosts`:

```
unicom.com.  IN  SOA netrix.unicom.com. root.netrix.unicom.com. (
                2          ; Serial
                14400      ; Refresh ( 4 hr )
                3600       ; Retry (1hr )
                604800     ; Expire ( 1 week )
                86400 )    ; Minimum TTL
```

Because the domain name in the SOA record is the same as the name specified in the first primary statement in the `named.boot` file, the SOA record can be rewritten with the @ character replacing the domain label `unicom.com`, as shown here:

```
@  IN  SOA netrix.unicom.com. root.netrix.unicom.com. (
        2          ; Serial
        14400      ; Refresh ( 4 hr )
        3600       ; Retry (1hr )
        604800     ; Expire ( 1 week )
        86400 ) ; Minimum TTL
```

Hence, instead of writing an A record, for example, as

```
saturn.unicom.com.  IN  A  150.1.0.10
```

you now can write it as

```
saturn  IN  A  150.1.0.10
```

The second convention has to do with multiple resource records pertaining to the same DNS object. If you group all resource records pertaining to the same object together, you only need to specify the object name in the first record of the set. Then you can neglect the object name in subsequent records, provided that each is indented by a space or a tab.

Instead of entering the two A records for `netrix` as

```
netrix  IN   A    100.0.0.1
netrix  IN   A    150.1.0.1
```

you could enter them as shown here:

```
netrix  IN  A  100.0.0.1
        IN  A  150.1.0.1
```

The previous examples assume that the @ notation is specified in the SOA record of `named.hosts`.

For the sake of completeness, this listing illustrates the effect of using the previous notations on `named.hosts`:

```
@   IN   SOA netrix.unicom.com. root.netrix.unicom.com. (
         2        ; Serial
         14400    ; Refresh ( 4 hr )
         3600     ; Retry (1hr )
         604800   ; Expire ( 1 week )
         86400 )  ; Minimum TTL
;
; The following are the name servers for the unicom.com. domain
; The domain name is omitted. That specified by @ is therefore assumed
;
         IN      NS      netrix.unicom.com.
         IN      NS      jade.unicom.com.
;
; The following are the A records
;
localhost      IN      A       127.0.0.1
saturn         IN      A       150.1.0.10
pluto          IN      A       150.1.0.11
laser          IN      A       100.0.0.3
maser          IN      A       100.0.0.4
sunrise        IN      A       198.53.237.2
cosmos         IN      A       198.53.237.3
;
; Multihomed hosts
;
netrix         IN      A       100.0.0.1
               IN      A       150.1.0.1
jade           IN      A       198.53.237.1
               IN      A       100.0.0.2
               IN      A       198.53.235.10
```

The Period Rule

If you compare the recent listing of `named.hosts` with the earlier versions, you will notice two different things about the way the host name is entered in the A records: (1) host names do not include domain labels, a difference that is taken care of by the preceding section, and (2) the trailing period (.) is missing.

In Chapter 6, "Name Services," an analogy was made between the UNIX file system and the DNS name space. The analogy helped in explaining the hierarchical nature of DNS and in illustrating how the name space can be searched for the desired piece of information. It was found that both name spaces require that a full path be specified to get the information. Under UNIX file systems, the full path is specified by starting at the top of the tree and proceeding all the way down to the resource that is the subject of the search. Using vi, to edit the file /etc/inet/inet/rc.inet, you would enter this:

```
# vi /etc/inet/rc.inet
```

But, as you know, this is not the only way you can specify a path. If, for example, your current directory is /etc/inet, you can equally enter this:

```
# vi rc.inet
```

Or, if the current directory is /etc, the following entry will also do:

```
# vi inet/rc.inet
```

What is different between the first example and the other two examples? In the first example, an absolute pathname was specified, whereas in the other two, relative pathnames were used. The leading forward slash (/) in the first example is the notation you must use to tell UNIX that the path specified is *absolute*. It includes the root of the file system and therefore must not be altered. In contrast, a missing leading forward slash, as in the second and third examples, qualifies the path as being *relative* to that of the user's current directory. To fully qualify it, UNIX prefixes it with the path to the current directory, before the search for the identified resource is triggered.

The only difference between specifying the search path in UNIX and the domain name in DNS is the order of the search items, listed with the period (.) replacing the forward slash (/). Here too (that is, in DNS) a search path can be either absolute or relative. Including a trailing period in the host's domain name tells named that the domain name being specified is absolute and must be used without any modifications. This was the case for all resource records included in the database files illustrated in all sections but the preceding one. For example, jade.unicom.com. specifies without ambiguity the full DNS search path for host jade.

In the preceding section, we wanted to be able to specify only the host name, leaving to named the mission of appending the full domain name specified in the SOA record—hence the requirement to preclude the trailing period from the host name.

What happens if the trailing period is accidentally included? It prevents named from appending the domain name, in SOA, to the host name. This means that name queries pertaining to that host will most likely fail. Names ending with a period are called fully qualified domain names (FQDNs) and are therefore treated as absolute names.

Summary

The complexity of configuring a name server depends on the type of server being installed. Primary name servers are the most complex to install because they require the manual updating of the database files. For each domain, a file must be created in which all the associated resource records must be included.

Resource records come in different types, of which the A, NS, PTR, CNAME, and SOA were mostly used. Depending on the nature of the information being described, the administrator must use the appropriate resource record type. For example, to map a host name into its IP address, the A record is required, whereas to do the reverse, a PTR record is required.

Name services are started by the named program in the /usr/sbin directory. When invoked, named checks in the /etc/inet directory for its own startup file, named.boot. This file includes statements that configure named to a primary, secondary, or cache-only server. It also includes information including the paths for the database files containing the domain data.

To assist in the troubleshooting and verification of the sanity of DNS services, UNIX provides the nslookup command. nslookup enables the network administrator to issue DNS queries to the local server and remote servers, including name queries, reverse queries, and the entire domain data, among other data types.

More information on troubleshooting the DNS name service is presented in Chapter 15, "Network Troubleshooting and Performance Tuning." If you're interested, you can skip directly to that chapter to learn more about nslookup and a few tricks that can be helpful in troubleshooting situations. Otherwise, you are invited to continue with the next chapter, dealing with setting up the Network Information Service—another name service.

CHAPTER

◆

Setting Up the Network Information Service

Introduction

Chapter 6, "Name Services," briefly introduced the Network Information Service (NIS). This chapter elaborates on NIS-related concepts with an emphasis on the details of setting up the NIS service. The chapter begins with a refresher of NIS, followed by sections presenting the following topics:

- ◆ NIS administration files
- ◆ Establishing the NIS domain
- ◆ Setting up a master NIS server
- ◆ Setting up a slave NIS server
- ◆ Setting up the NIS client
- ◆ Administration and management of NIS

Skills introduced throughout the chapter are based on the fictitious network depicted earlier in Chapter 10, "Setting Up the Domain Name System."

NIS Refresher

NIS service provides for the centralized management and distribution of network-wide administrative databases (called *maps*). Using NIS tools, the network administrator can aggregate all the traditional UNIX administration databases (see Table 11.1 for a list of the most commonly used files) in one host, called the *master* NIS server. In doing so, the administrator is relieved from the task of the individual administration of hosts on the network. Hosts, configured as NIS clients, will be able to draw on the databases maintained in the master server for network-wide resource identification and access.

Table 11.1. Some of the most commonly referenced administrative files. NIS allows for the central administration and dissemination of the contents of those files across the network.

File	Description
/etc/hosts	Host table containing IP address-to-host name associations
/etc/ethers	Ethernet MAC address-to-IP associations
/etc/passwd	User identification database containing user login name, uid, gid, password, and so on.
/etc/group	User group names and members
/etc/netmasks	IP network masks
/etc/protocols	Network protocol-to-number associations (see Chapter 2)
/etc/services	Port number-to-application protocol associations (see Chapters 3 and 5)
/etc/rpc	Remote procedure call program numbers

To reduce the load on the master server, improve the overall performance of NIS, and avoid single point of failure, NIS supports so-called slave servers. A slave server is similar in functionality to the DNS secondary server. A slave server must be configured to replicate NIS administrative data as maintained on the master server. Whenever the master server's NIS map is updated, it propagates the updates among the slave servers. From the client's perspective, there is no difference between master and slave servers. Both types of servers offer the same service in answering client NIS-related requests. Figure 11.1 illustrates the relationship among the servers and clients.

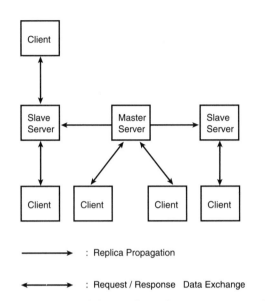

: Replica Propagation

: Request / Response   Data Exchange

Figure 11.1. *Relationship among NIS servers and clients. Whereas slave servers are routinely updated by the master server with changes as they occur, client hosts make no distinction between master and slave servers when making service requests.*

Hosts sharing and referencing a common set of maps for information are said to belong to the same administrative *domain.* NIS allows for the subdivision of a network into more than one administrative domain. Unlike DNS, however, NIS domains are not related by any hierarchical structure.

Sometimes it does not make sense to group all hosts and network resources in a single domain. For one thing, different departments might have different administrative and security needs on the network, and hence might require distinct policing guidelines and strategies. Also, on a very large network, having multiple domains allows for the decentralization of network administration by delegating the responsibility of administering individual domains to the departments to which they belong.

An organization might have, for example, one administrative domain for accounting, another for sales, and yet another for research, with each defining and maintaining its own administrative database. Hence, the map corresponding to the /etc/passwd file, for example, would be different for each domain. Unless a user has an account in domains other than the default one to which his host belongs, he will not be able to log in to hosts belonging to other domains.

The lines along which the network is subdivided into domains might have nothing to do with the underlying physical and topological layout of the network. As in DNS, an NIS domain is simply a logical grouping of hosts sharing a common set of configuration and administration data. Whereas in DNS a host can belong to one and only one domain, under NIS a host can belong to more than one. As such, a host can establish a binding with any domain on the network for the subsequent retrieval of desired information from one of its servers.

The NIS service is not meant to, and cannot, replace DNS if your network is connected to the Internet or any other network based on DNS services for name and address lookups. NIS is meant for the local centralization and dissemination of administration data. There are no national or international organizations, such as NIC in the case of DNS, that regulate and delegate authority for NIS domains. Again, it is purely a local matter, internal to your network.

NIS Administration Files

At the center of NIS administration is the master NIS server. The master server contains all the data files, called maps, that govern the configuration and administration affecting all hosts belonging to the served domain.

The master server derives its maps from the standard UNIX administration files depicted previously in Table 11.1. The relation between NIS maps and these files is not a one-to-one relationship. Take, for example, the /etc/hosts file. When the master server is initialized to generate its maps (more on this later), it generates two files corresponding to /etc/hosts: hosts.byname and hosts.byaddr. NIS uses hosts.byname to look up host data by name, whereas it uses hosts.byaddr to look up host information by address. Table 11.2 depicts the correspondence between the standard UNIX administration files and their counter maps.

Table 11.2. Correspondence between standard UNIX administrative files and NIS domain maps. The ypservers map is generated by ypinit during the server initialization process. All domain maps are maintained in /var/yp/domainname.

Filename	Corresponding Maps	Map Nickname
/etc/ethers	ethers.byname	ethers
	ethers.byaddr	
/etc/hosts	hosts.byname	
	hosts.byaddr	hosts
/etc/group	group.byname	group
	group.bygid	
/etc/passwd	passwd.byname	passwd
	passwd.byuid	
/etc/netmasks	netmasks.byaddr	
/etc/networks	networks.byname	
	networks.byaddr	networks
/etc/protocols	protocols.byname	
	protocols.bynumber	protocols

Filename	Corresponding Maps	Map Nickname
/etc/rpc	rpc.bynumber	
/etc/services	services.byname	services
	ypservers	ypservers

> **Note:** For convenience, NIS recognizes some of the maps by nicknames, as shown in Table 11.2. Consequently, instead of using the actual map names when making direct queries using NIS commands, you can use the nickname whenever available.

Information that is contained in all the previously listed files will be included in the NIS maps when the master server is generated. It is therefore of the utmost importance that you check each of those files for any data that might jeopardize the sanity of the NIS service and network security.

In particular, you should check the /etc/passwd file and clean up any of the obsolete user login records or loosely protected accounts. Just remember, when the maps are generated, they become globally available to network users and programs because they will replace, or add to, locally administered files on client hosts.

Local administrative files on slave servers bear no significance to the NIS database. When initialized as slave, the server completely ignores, and therefore bypasses, any references to its local files. A slave server derives all of its information from map replicas sent to it by the server that the slave is configured to recognize as the domain master server.

Taking advantage of local databases requires including their contents in the master's files in the /etc directory. For example, to include part or all of the slave's /etc/hosts file in the maps in the master server, you must append the file contents to the master's /etc/hosts file before the maps are generated. After the server is initialized as slave, no changes should be attempted to the server, because it must simply contain an exact replica of the master's set of domain maps.

A client host treats its local administrative files a bit differently from slave servers. Whereas most of the files are replaced, thus forcing the client to ignore their /etc counterparts completely, both the /etc/passwd and /etc/group files can still be referenced before the associated NIS maps are queried. When looking up a login ID, for example, an NIS-enabled client searches its local /etc/passwd file first. If no matching record is found in the local file, the client issues a query to an NIS server. The server being queried can be either a master or slave server because they both contain synchronized replicas of the domain maps.

One commonly asked question is whether NIS allows for the consolidation and central administration of files other than those depicted in Table 11.1. The answer is yes. NIS is a very flexible and versatile service that can be extended to accommodate other data files.

An example of files to which you might want to extend the NIS service are the NFS automounting maps (discussed in the next chapter). Those files and others can easily be taken care of, provided that certain modifications are applied to the NIS configuration files. These modifications won't, however, be explained in this book.

NIS Service Daemons

Depending on the host's function, one or both of the following daemons might be required to run on the host:

◆ ypserv: This is the server daemon, and it is run on both the master and slave servers. ypserv is responsible for answering client queries for lookups.

◆ ypbind: This is the client daemon (also known as the *binder* daemon), and it should be run on all client hosts. ypbind is responsible for establishing a contact with a domain server (master or slave) when it is brought up, and for remembering the information necessary for communicating with that server. This process is known as the *binding* process, because after the contact is established with a server, ypbind is *bound* to direct its lookup requests to that server.

For NIS servers to be able to use the NIS database information, they also run the ypbind daemon. In this case, unless implemented carefully, ypbind on the NIS server might end up contacting ypserv on hosts on the network other than the local ypserv process for information. This might introduce unnecessary network traffic and unduly long response times.

The Binding Process

Binding is the process by which the client daemon, ypbind, locates and contacts a name server. It also involves remembering the IP address and the port number at which the ypserv process is listening on the server for NIS request.

When invoked, ypbind transmits a broadcast message for any servers within its own domain. Although it is highly possible that more than one server might respond offering its services, ypbind commits to using the first server to respond to the broadcast. The server response includes both its IP address and the port on which ypserv is listening to requests. The client is then said to be bound to the server.

The association between the client and the server is retained by ypbind as long as the server responds without failure. If the server crashes or its performance degrades to unacceptably low levels, the binder unbinds itself from this server and retriggers another search cycle for a name server within the same domain.

To find out which server the client host is bound to, use the ypwhich command as shown here:

```
# ypwhich
netrix
```

Using message broadcasts to locate a name server might not fit certain network topologies. Because a broadcast address cannot cross routers, if the server is on a different network than the client, the server won't stand the chance of receiving the bind request and consequently won't respond to it. For this reason, it is recommended that in situations like these you bring up a server on the routing host (that is, multihomed host) to make it better available to clients on the IP networks to which the router is connected. But this is not the only remedy to this situation.

You can optionally force ypbind to send out a direct request for a bind to a server of your choosing, wherever the server is on the network. Later in the chapter, you will learn how to modify the behavior of ypbind. For now, just keep in mind that unless ypbind is specifically told to locate a particular server by name, it triggers a search for an NIS server on its local IP network only.

Establishing the NIS Domain

Establishing the NIS domain requires some planning. By the end of the planning phase, you should have answered the following questions:

◆ How many NIS domains are needed? In most cases, one NIS domain is sufficient. The needs of your organization might dictate more than one. Factors dictating more than one NIS domain include network size, geographical span of the network, and political considerations. Just keep in mind that the more domains you decide to set up, the more confusing the job of administering NIS service becomes. NIS was meant to conveniently centralize the administration of network-wide resources. If you must have more than one domain, try to keep the number to a minimum.

◆ What are you going to call the NIS domain? Choose a name that makes sense to the users who have their hosts defaulting to that domain. Do not make arbitrary name assignments, especially if there will be more than one domain. If the network is to be connected to the Internet, you might consider calling the NIS domain by the registered DNS domain name. Aside from this consideration, you might choose to name the NIS domain after the department, the organization, or a hybrid of organizational and locational names.

◆ Which hosts will be served by the NIS domain? Make a list of the hosts that will be served by the NIS domain in question. Mental notes do not last long enough! You will need this list to attend to every host it includes in order to configure the host to become a domain member so that it can receive NIS services.

◆ Which host should be the master server? Which hosts should be slave servers?

If you intend to integrate any of the slave servers' administration databases in the NIS map, have a listing of each of these databases ready. You will need those listings during the installation of the master server. In particular, you will use them to update the master's databases before the corresponding maps are generated.

After the answers to the preceding questions are ready, you can start establishing the NIS domain on all hosts: master servers, slave servers, and clients. There are three ways to establish a domain on any of the hosts:

◆ Log in as root or NIS administrator to every host, and enter the following `domainname` command:

```
# domainname name
```

`name` is the name assigned to the NIS domain. In Unicom's case, the administrator chose `unicom` as the domain name. Hence, the `domainname` command becomes this:

```
# domainname unicom
```

◆ The preceding method has a temporary effect. To have the domain established any time the hosts is rebooted, it is better to edit the `/etc/rc2.d/S75rpc` startup file (the `rpc` startup file might have a different name on your machine; check the vendor's documentation for the exact name) to include the `domainname` `name` command after the `start` line. This way, the domain name is assigned at boot time whenever the system enters run level two (multiuser level).

◆ Edit the `/etc/conf/pack.d/name/space.c` file to assign the name of the domain to the `SRPC_DOMAIN` parameter. `SRPC_DOMAIN` is originally assigned the null character. For the assignment to take effect, you must rebuild and reboot the operating system. Check your documentation for the command to use to rebuild the operating system.

Note: `SRPC_DOMAIN` is the constant name on the author's system (UnixWare 1.1.2). Check your documentation for the corresponding filename and parameter name to edit.

Of the three methods, the second method is the recommended one. The first method is obviously flaky because you have to remember to establish the domain manually whenever the system is rebooted. Although the third method takes care of permanently establishing the domain name, it requires the inconvenient rebuilding of the operating system. The second method, in contrast, achieves the same result without any major disruption and the associated downtime that rebuilding the operating system demands.

Setting Up the Master NIS Server

Setting up and starting the master server requires that you perform the following preparatory steps:

1. Clean up all the files from which the NIS maps will be generated on the host to become the master server. In particular, closely examine both `/etc/passwd` and `/etc/group` for loosely protected accounts and privileges. Also, remove obsolete records from all files.

2. Update the administration databases in the /etc directory with the data you ported from the to-be slave servers and that you wanted to include in the master's maps. Remember, failure to do so prevents clients from referencing such data. When brought up as slave servers, hosts lose the capability to look up their local databases, because they replicate data as it exists on the domain's master server.

3. Establish the domain name, if you did not do that yet, using any of the methods described in the preceding section.

Now you are ready to generate the NIS maps and start the master server. To generate the NIS maps, you have to log in to the server as root and invoke the ypinit command with the -m option as shown here:

```
# /usr/sbin/yinit -m
```

The -m option denotes the server as master. ypinit generates the domain map's database on the server. It can be used to set up a master server, a slave server, or an NIS client. The -m option specifies that the server being initialized is a master server. When invoked, ypinit creates the subdirectory /var/yp/domainname, in which domainname is the name of the domain being established. If the domain name is unicom, for example, ypinit creates the directory /var/yp/unicom. This directory is where all the maps are maintained.

Next, ypinit generates all the maps defined in a default makefile in the /var/yp directory. Unless you want ypinit to generate maps in addition to those defined in this file, you should have no reason to tamper with the contents of /var/yp. After the maps are created, you will be asked by ypinit for the names of all hosts that will be slave servers. ypinit saves the names of the servers in the ypservers map file in the /var/yp/domainname directory along with other domain maps.

Finally, the NIS server daemon, ypserv, should be started. You can do that either by invoking the daemon from the command line or by rebooting the host. For manual invocation, enter the following commands:

```
# /usr/lib/netsvc/yp/ypesrv
```

The ypserv daemon can be invoked only if the system is in the multiuser level. Otherwise, just bring the system up to multiuser state by entering the init 2 command. Consequently, ypserv will be invoked by init upon processing the /etc/rc2.d/S75rpc file. This file, which invokes other RPC services, must include the following code to start NIS:

```
if [ -f /usr/lib/netsvc/yp/ypserv -a -d /var/yp/'domainname' ]
then
        /usr/lib/netsvc/yp/ypserv
        (echo \c ' ypserv' ) > /dev/console
fi
```

Check the RPC startup file on your system, and make sure that the code is included, uncommented, in that file. This code checks for the /var/yp/domainname directory returned by the domainname command. Only if the directory exists is the ypserv daemon started.

To allow the master server to use information maintained in its maps, you need to start the client daemon, ypbind, on this server. To do that, make the following entry:

/usr/lib/netsvc/yp/ypbind

To ensure that ypbind runs at boot time, check your RPC startup file, and verify that the following code is included and uncommented:

```
if [ -d /var/yp ]; then
     /usr/lib/netsvc/yp/ypbind
     (echo \c ' ypbind') > /dev/console
fi
```

There are several tests you can use to verify that the server is running as it should. To start with, you can use the ypwhich command, as shown here, to determine whether the server is bound to itself:

```
# ypwhich
netrix
```

Here, netrix is the host name of the machine on which the server is brought up.

Another test you can perform is to query the NIS service for information. This can be done using the ypmatch command. Following is the syntax of ypmatch:

ypmatch *key mapname*

In this syntax, *key* is the subject of the search, and *mapname* is the NIS map being queried. For example, to look up the IP address corresponding to host pixel, you should enter the following ypmatch command:

```
# ypmatch jade hosts
100.0.0.2    jade
```

You can also use the ypcat command to have the entire map displayed on your monitor. In the following example, ypcat is used to look up the contents of the hosts map:

```
# ypcat hosts
198.53.237.20 emerald
198.53.235.10 jadeppp jadeppp
198.53.237.1  pixel pixel
198.53.235.1  netrixppp
100.0.0.10    salim #salim's dos machine
150.1.0.1     orbit #netrix second interface
127.0.0.1     localhost
100.0.0.2     jade wanrouter
100.0.0.1     netrix
```

How many master servers should you install? One should be enough. Having more than one master defeats the purpose for which NIS is being introduced: the centralized administration and management of commonly shared configuration and data files. Having more than one master server entails the manual synchronization of the databases (that is, maps) that they separately maintain.

There is no way of informing a master server about the existence of another master server for the same domain. If you want to have more than one server for reasons having to do with performance and redundancy, slave servers are a better deal than additional master servers. It is easier to manage them and to have their databases synchronized with the original replica maintained on the master server.

Setting Up Slave Servers

Before installing the slave server, you must ensure that the master server is running by checking for the ypserv daemon. To do that, log in to the host running the master server, and enter the following command:

```
# ps -ef ¦ grep ypserv
```

You must also ensure that the domain name is correctly established on the host on which the slave server is to be brought up. Using the domainname command, make sure that the domain name on both the master and the slave servers perfectly match.

Now, you can proceed with initializing the slave server. To propagate NIS database maps for the NIS master server to a slave server, the slave server should be bound first to a master server in its domain. To do that, enter the following command:

```
# /usr/lib/netsvc/yp/ypbind
```

To verify that the server is indeed bound properly, use ypwhich as in the following example:

```
# ypwhich
unicom
```

The initialization process is handled by the ypinit command, with the -s option and the name of a master server, as shown in the following example:

```
# ypinit -s netrix
```

In the preceding example, it is assumed that host netrix is already set up as, and is running, the NIS server (that is, the ypserv daemon). When used to initialize a slave server, ypinit does not prompt you for the names of other servers as it does when used to set up a master server.

Upon initialization, the slave server engages in the transfer of domain maps from the master server to its own /var/yp/domainname directory, which it must have created at an early stage of the process. ypinit handles map transfers by invoking the ypxfr program.

> **Note:** In the ypinit -s *servername* command, the server you specify does not necessarily have to be a master server. A slave server can be specified as well, as long as it has a stable copy of the NIS maps. Also, make sure that the server is running when ypinit -s is invoked on the new server.

Invoking the slave server is no different from invoking the master server. Here, too, ypserv is invoked by the S75rpc script only if the /var/yp/domainname is verified to exist on the host. For more details, see the previous sections.

The previous steps work if both the slave and the master are on the same network only. This is so because of the way ypbind behaves by default. As explained in the section "The Binding Process," when ypbind is invoked, it transmits a broadcast message in its search for a name server within its domain. This means that the host initiating the broadcast should be on the same broadcasting network as the servers; otherwise, it won't get its search satisfied, and the bind will fail. To remedy the situation and force ypbind to talk directly to a server of your choosing, independently of where that server is on the network, you can use the ypset command. You can specify the host by name, provided that NIS is not running, or by address, as in the following example:

```
# ypset 100.0.0.1
```

The preceding ypset command forces ypbind to bind to the server with IP address 100.0.0.1. Only if ypbind fails to hear from this server does it attempt other servers by sending out a broadcast message.

To verify that the NIS service is running properly, use the ypwhich command to verify that the server is indeed bound to the domain, and use the ypmatch command to check that queries are answered properly.

Setting Up the NIS Client

Now that all servers are initialized and operational, you can proceed with configuring the NIS clients. This task mainly involves minor modifications to some of the local files that you want to integrate with the NIS maps. When the modifications are completed, you can continue with the steps of establishing the domain name and bringing up the ypbind daemon.

It was explained earlier in the chapter that whenever NIS is started on the client, applications that are run no longer access most of the client's local files to obtain information. They instead resort to NIS maps located on the server to which the client is bound. Exceptions to this rule include files such as /etc/group and /etc/passwd. In these cases, the client might be configured such that local files are consulted first, before NIS maps are queried. To enable this search order, however, you need to add a plus sign (+) entry to each of these files. To allow applications to search the local /etc/passwd file before NIS is consulted, for example, just add the following entry to the end of the file:

```
+:*:0:0:::
```

Where you put the + entry determines when the NIS map is to be looked up should the local search fail. Including the + entry in the middle of the file, for example, makes an application issue an NIS lookup query if it fails to find a matching record in the first half of the file.

Those entries are conventionally referred to as marker entries because they mark the part of the file to integrate with the NIS maps. What has been said about marker entries is enough for the purpose of bringing up the client. Interested readers can refer to their manual pages for more details on these entries.

After marker entries are taken care of, continue with the setup process by establishing the domain and invoking ypbind as shown here:

```
# domainname unicom
# domainname
unicom
# ypbind
# ypwhich
netrix
```

Notice that, in the preceding illustration, both the domain name and the binding were verified, using the domainname and ypwhich commands.

NIS Maintenance

After you have brought up the NIS service, you will likely be required to make some changes to the setup, either by adding a new server or a new map, or by updating existing maps. In this section, some of the maintenance tasks are explained, including the following ones:

◆ Adding a slave server to the original set

◆ Modifying a standard map

◆ Propagating NIS maps

Adding a Slave Server to the Original Set

When a new master server is initialized, it creates the /var/yp/ypservers file, in which it maintains the names of all the slave servers that were entered in response to the prompts by the ypinit -m command. The file is stored in an NIS map format.

To add a new slave server, you must first convert the file contents into ASCII format and save them in a temporary file for editing. When the names of the new servers to be added to the original set are added to the file, the temporary file contents can be converted back to an NIS map format and stored in the ypservers file. The following steps summarize the process:

1. Log in as root to the master server, and make /var/yp your current directory.

2. Using the makedbm command, convert the contents of the ypservers file into ASCII, and have the contents saved in a temp file as shown here:

   ```
   # /usr/sbin/makedbm -u ypservers > /tmp/temp_file
   ```

   temp_file is any filename where you want the ASCII version of the ypservers saved.

3. Using your preferred editor, add the names of the new slave servers you want to add to the original set.

4. Finally, save the contents of the file *temp_file*, specified in Step 2, in an NIS map format in the ypservers file as shown here:

```
# /usr/sbin/makedbm /tmp/temp_file ypservers
```

To verify that ypservers is duly updated, enter the following makedbm command:

```
# /usr/sbin/makedbm -u ypservers
```

This concludes what must be done on the master server. The next thing to do, of course, is to set up the new slave server. For information on how to do that, refer to the section "Setting Up Slave Servers."

Modifying a Standard NIS Map

Modifying a standard map (refer to Tables 11.1 and 11.2) is a simple matter involving editing the ASCII version of the file in the /etc directory to make the necessary changes, and regenerating the updated NIS version. Remember, however, that any modifications to the maps must be carried on the master server. The following example illustrates how to modify the passwd map:

1. Log in to the master server as root.
2. Using an editor, make the necessary changes to the /etc/passwd file.
3. Make /var/yp the current directory, and enter the following ypmake command:

```
# ypmake passwd
```

The preceding ypmake generates an updated passwd map and puts it in the /var/yp/*domainname* directory. Also, it propagates it to the slave domain servers specified in the ypservers map.

Propagating NIS Maps

Propagating an NIS map involves replicating it on slave servers. Map propagation ensures that all servers, master and slaves, maintain a consistently distributed set of NIS maps. Propagation can be initiated by either the master server or the slave server.

Two commands are involved whenever a map is propagated: yppush, invoked on the master server, and ypxfr, invoked on the slave server. Whenever ypmake is used to update an existing map, yppush is called after a new updated map is generated. yppush reads the ypservers map in the /var/yp/*domainname* directory for the names of the slave servers. It then contacts ypserv on each server by sending it a request for ypxfr service. Upon acknowledging the request, the slave server invokes the ypxfr program to take care of the map transfer process.

As noted earlier, it is possible to have the transfer initiated by the slave server. This can be done either by virtue of scheduling map propagation processes through crontab or by directly invoking ypxfr on the command line on the slave server.

Scheduling *ypxfr* Using *crontab*

When invoked on a slave server to initiate a map transfer, ypxfr contacts the master server for the domain to which it belongs, requesting it to propagate the map if the master's copy was found to be more recent than the slave's copy.

Because some map files change more frequently than others, ypxfer was designed to handle one map at a time. For this reason, when scheduled through crontab to do map checks and transfers, one ypxfr entry must be included per NIS map. If, for example, you want ypxfr to check for updates on both the passwd and the hosts maps, you must include two ypxfr entries, each taking care of one map.

One precaution to observe, though, is to avoid scheduling ypxfr entries to execute at the same time. If you have more than one slave server, schedule similar entries so that they execute at different times. Otherwise, the master server might suffer degradation in performance whenever it engages in responding to multiple map propagation requests simultaneously. The degradation be can significant on networks with large map databases.

Following are several sample ypxfr entries in a crontab file:

```
0 0 1, 15 * * /usr/sbin/ypxfr passwd.byname
0 0 1, 15 * * /usr/sbin/ypxfr passwd.byuid
0 0 1 * * /usr/sbin/ypxfr hosts.byname
0 0 1 * * /usr/sbin/ypxfr hosts.byaddr
```

The first and second entries invoke ypxfr to check for passwd updates and have them transferred on the 1st and the 15th of each month. The third and fourth entries invoke ypxfr at half the frequency (only at the beginning of the month), because the hosts map does not change as frequently as user accounts do.

ypxfr optionally can be directed to obtain its updates from a slave server maintaining an updated version of the NIS maps. You can achieve this by using the -h option as in the following crontab entry:

```
0 0 1, 15 * * /usr/sbin/ypxfr -h host mapname
```

In this entry, *host* is the name of the server, with the map specified in *mapname*.

As was said earlier, ypxfr also can be invoked from the command line following the same command syntax discussed previously. One good reason for doing this is to recover the consistency of the server's NIS maps with those on the master server after it has been out of service for some time.

Summary

Network Information Service implementation involves setting up administration domains, referred to as NIS domains. An NIS domain is a logical grouping of hosts sharing the same set of standard UNIX administration files, such as /etc/passwd, /etc/group, and /etc/hosts. In setting up these domains, the system administrator can centralize the management of all resources in one host, known as the NIS master server.

When initialized, the master server generates non-ASCII NIS maps corresponding to the standard administration files. The relationship between the ASCII file from which the map is generated and the map files is not a one-to-one relationship. Taking /etc/hosts as an example, the corresponding hosts map files are hosts.byname and hosts.byaddr. After a master server has been initialized, you can bring it up by invoking the ypserv daemon. You can also invoke ypserv, at boot time, from the RPC startup script.

For reasons of robustness and better performance, a network administrator can bring up slave servers. A slave server obtains its data from the master server by virtue of scheduled map propagations using the ypxfr command. It is the responsibility of the network administrator to ensure that a map is propagated whenever he makes a change to it. Failure to do so risks introducing inconsistent NIS service.

After the client is brought up by the ypbind daemon, applications running on that host stop referring to most of the local administration files for information. A few files, however, are still referred to before NIS maps are consulted, and only if the application fails to find the information in that file.

NIS provides some troubleshooting and verification tools to help assess the performance of the service. Among those tools are the ypcat command, to list the contents of a particular map; the ypwhich command, which is helpful in determining whether the client daemon is bound, and to what server; and the ypmatch command, to look up a particular piece of information.

NIS service should not be confused with, and neither is it meant to replace, the Domain Name System, described in Chapter 10, "Setting Up the Domain Name System." NIS is a local service that maintains a flat database aimed at centralizing the management of administrative files across a group of local hosts. DNS, on the other hand, is a hierarchical and distributed database whose services are meant to span the Internet. It is mainly used to help locate Internet-wide services and resources. Organizations wanting to connect to the Internet must plan to implement DNS, independent of any NIS-related plans they might have.

CHAPTER

Setting Up Network File System Services

Introduction

In Chapter 7, "TCP/IP Applications Overview," the File Transfer Protocol (FTP) was introduced as one method of accessing resources hosted by remote file systems. By establishing an FTP session, a user could engage in file transfer operations with the remote host using commands such as get and put. TELNET was also introduced as another method of accessing remote resources.

Both FTP and TELNET, however, come with their self-imposed limitations and inconveniences. Taking FTP as an example, unless a file was transferred to the local host, the user could not process that file using local programs and shell commands. Even worse, users had to suspend, or exit, the FTP session to process the transferred file.

The Network File System service (NFS) circumvents the limitations imposed by other file system access methods. In contrast to FTP, TELNET, and RLOGIN, among other services, NFS provides the user with transparent access to remote file systems.

From the user's perspective, an NFS-accessible resource is treated in exactly the same way a local resource is treated. When set up, a remote file system will appear to the user as part of the local file system. As such, a user will be able to access this part without having to log in to the remote system and enter a password. This way, NFS-accessible resources become an extension to the local one.

Figure 12.1 presents a pictorial depiction of what this means. The shaded part of netrix's file system actually belongs to a disk on the remote host jade. Thanks to NFS, users logged in to netrix perceive it as a local resource that is accessible using commands such as cd and vi. As a matter of fact, some users might not have a clue about the underlying physical structure of their file system.

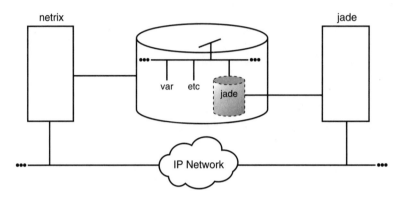

Figure 12.1. *NFS-accessible file systems become an extension of the local one. The shaded part of netrix's file system is physically located on a disk connected to host jade. To a user logged in to netrix, accessing /jade is indistinguishable from accessing any other directory native to the disk owned by netrix.*

The NFS service is based on the client-server model, in which the server owns and manages the shared file systems, and the NFS client accesses the file systems by mounting them from the server. NFS client-server interaction is based on a suite of procedures known as the Remote Procedure Calls (RPCs).

An insight into the concepts governing RPC is helpful in understanding NFS-related issues. Consequently, the chapter is split into two parts. The first part introduces RPC protocols, and the second one builds on the first part by discussing NFS, the concept and the implementation. Also included in the first part is an introduction to the External Data Representation (XDR) protocol, which RPC relies on for the unified representation of data objects.

Remote Procedure Call

RPC (RFC 1050, Developed by Sun Microsystem) is a session layer protocol underlying the client-server interaction mechanisms governing NFS among other network services, called RPC-based servers. (For simplicity, such servers will be referred to as RPC servers.)

> **Note:** Among RPC servers is the Network Information Service (NIS), covered in Chapters 6 and 11. For a complete listing of RPC servers supported by your host, view the contents of the first column of the /etc/rpc file. The contents of this file will be discussed later in the chapter.

RPC defines a transparent distributed computing service by which a process is split into two components. One component is local to the host, called the client. It uses the shared network resource and is responsible for communicating the procedure call to the remote server. The other component manages the shared resource, called the server. It processes the call upon receiving it and returns its result to the client.

RPC transparency stems from the apparent feel of how a remote procedure call is handled by a local application. RPC makes the procedure appear to be an extension to that application. Hence, a network programmer can treat RPC server procedures much like calls to local subroutines are treated.

Figure 12.2 and the following description depict the execution life cycle of an RPC request.

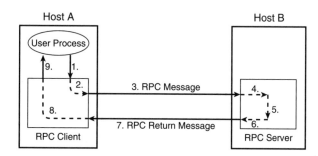

Figure 12.2. Execution life cycle of an RPC request.

1. The user process makes a call to an RPC call. Included in the call are the command arguments.
2. The RPC client packages the call and associated arguments in an RPC message. Procedure identification will be discussed shortly.
3. The client transmits the RPC message to the RPC server.
4. The RPC message is decoded by the server.
5. The identified procedure executes and returns the results to the server.
6. The server packages the results in an RPC return message.
7. The RPC return message is sent to the client.
8. The client decodes the return message.
9. The results are returned to the calling user process.

While the remote procedure is executing at the remote end (that is, the RPC server), the local user process waits for the return results the way it would have waited if the call had been made to a local routine. After receiving the return results, the process resumes executing subsequent instructions.

Transport Support

Being at the session layer, RPC mechanisms have to rely on a transport protocol for the exchange of RPC messages between the client and server ends of the service. There are currently two flavors of RPC: one version that works with TCP and UDP only, and another, a transport-independent version, that works with any transport the kernel supports. The latter version is known as Transport Independent RPC (TI-RPC). UNIX SVR4.2 supports this version and is currently capable of working with SPX (Novell's transport protocol) in addition to TCP and UDP. Discussion will, however, be restricted to UDP and TCP transport support.

Although both UDP and TCP are supported, most RPC servers rely on UDP, a *connectionless* transport protocol. This is mostly the case because RPC routines live a relatively short life cycle, making the overhead associated with the creation and termination of TCP connections unjustifiably high. For this reason, message sequencing and reliability checks are built into most of the RPC servers. TCP connections are commonly started in the event of a requirement to transmit large chunks of data.

In contrast to other TCP/IP services, such as TELNET, FTP, and DNS, RPC servers do not rely on well-known port numbers. They are, instead, dynamically assigned an available port number at boot time. As explained in the next section, RPC servers make the port numbers on which they are listening to services through the rpcbind daemon, known as the port mapper.

RPC Servers: Program Number, Port Mapper, Procedure Number, and Version Number

RPC is not restricted to NFS. As noted earlier, NIS is an example of another RPC server. For a complete list of RPC servers, you can view the contents of the /etc/rpc file. For brevity, only a sample of the file contents is presented here:

```
rpcbind       100000 portmap sunrpc rpcbind
rstatd        100001 rstat rup perfmeter
rusersd       100002 rusers
nfs           100003 nfsprog
ypserv        100004 ypprog
mountd        100005 mount showmount
ypbind        100007
walld         100008 rwall shutdown
yppasswdd     100009 yppasswd
sprayd        100012 spray
llockmgr      100020
nlockmgr      100021
statmon       100023
status        100024
ypupdated     100028 ypupdate
rpcnfs        100116 na.rpcnfs
pcnfsd        150001
```

Each row of this listing identifies the server by its formal name, followed by a program number and one or more nicknames.

Program Number and Port Mapper

Why is each RPC server assigned a program number? Because RPC servers listen to service requests on port numbers that are dynamically assigned at startup time, there arises a requirement for a mechanism by which the server can make its services available to the clients. RPC achieves this mechanism by assigning every server a unique program number and defining a port registry server that is responsible for the maintenance of program number-to-port number mappings. The server thus defined is itself an RPC server. It is called the port mapper, and the daemon supporting it is rpcbind.

> **Note:** There are two different port mapper daemons: portmap, which works with UDP and TCP transport protocols only, and rpcbind, which supports TI-RPC.

When an RPC server is assigned a port number for each of the transport protocols, it contacts the port mapper to register the ports at which it will be listening for requests. The UDP and TCP port numbers do not necessarily have to be identical, and neither do they have to be the same ones used by the server before it was last restarted. Port numbers are assigned to servers subject to availability.

Before a client requests an RPC service for the first time, it should contact the port mapper for the port number on which the associated RPC server is listening for requests. After a favorable response is obtained, the client caches the port number and uses it to contact the RPC server directly. Understandably, for clients to reach the port mapper, the latter must listen to port resolution requests on a well-known port number. The port number is 111.

Procedure Number

Each RPC server is composed of a number of procedures, in which each procedure handles a certain functionality of the service. NFS, for example, supports many procedures, including NFSPROC_READ, which a client uses to read from a file; NFSPROC_WRITE, to write to a file; and NFSPROC_REMOVE, to delete a file belonging to the NFS server. Every procedure is assigned a number, which the client passes in an RPC request to identify the procedure it wants executed by the server.

Version Number

Every implementation of the same RPC server is assigned a version number. A new implementation is always assigned a higher number. A new version of an RPC server is usually made to support earlier procedure implementations so that all versions are taken care of by a single server process.

It is not sufficient, therefore, that a client specifies the RPC program number, the procedure number, and the port number when passing an RPC request to the server. The client must also specify the version number that it supports. Unless the server and the client agree on a mutually acceptable version support level, the port mapper returns an error message complaining about version mismatch.

Hence, to uniquely identify a procedure to an RPC server, the client must specify the program number, the procedure number, the port number, and the version number.

Starting Up RPC Servers

RPC servers are started at boot time by the /etc/rc2.d/S75rpc script (check your vendor's documentation for the RPC startup script on your system) as the system is brought to run level two. rpcbind, the port mapper, is started first.

To find out which RPC servers are running on your host, the ports on which each is listening for requests, and the supported version numbers, enter the following rpcinfo command with the -p option:

```
# rpcinfo -p
   program vers proto   port  service
   100000    3   udp     111  rpcbind
   100000    2   udp     111  rpcbind
   100000    3   tcp     111  rpcbind
   100000    2   tcp     111  rpcbind
   150001    1   udp     958  pcnfsd
   100003    2   udp    2049  nfs
   100024    1   tcp    1028  status
   100021    1   tcp    1024  nlockmgr
   100026    1   udp    1029  bootparam
   100005    1   udp    1030  mountd
   200012    1   udp    2049
   100021    1   udp    1032  nlockmgr
   100005    1   tcp    1029  mountd
   100024    1   udp    1031  status
   100021    3   tcp    1024  nlockmgr
   100002    1   tcp    1030  rusersd
   100012    1   tcp    1031  sprayd
   100021    3   udp    1032  nlockmgr
   100020    1   tcp    1033  llockmgr
   100002    1   udp    1033  rusersd
   100002    2   tcp    1030  rusersd
   100012    1   udp    1034  sprayd
   100008    1   tcp    1032  walld
   100008    1   udp    1035  walld
   100020    1   udp    1036  llockmgr
   100002    2   udp    1033  rusersd
   100021    2   tcp    1024  nlockmgr
   100021    2   udp    1032  nlockmgr
```

Notice how each server is registered twice with UDP and TCP port numbers. Take a look at the first four lines of this listing. They should not lead you into thinking that rpcbind is invoked four times. What you see means that rpcbind is registered with the port mapper (that is, itself), it supports both version levels two and three, and the server is listening on UDP and TCP port numbers 111 for each version level.

External Data Representation

External Data Representation (XDR) protocol, developed by Sun Microsystems, works at the presentation layer of the OSI model and defines a machine-independent format for data representation. It is meant to reconcile differences in the way data is encoded internally on two different hardware platforms.

To understand the need for XDR, look at how Intel 80X86 processor architecture and Motorola's 680X0 represent integer data internally. Figure 12.3 shows the order in which the hexadecimal integer 5F3E68A9 is stored by both processors in memory. Intel 80X86 represents a 32-bit integer such that the high-order word is stored in a low-memory address, and the low-order word is stored in a high-memory address. Within each word, the high-order byte is also stored in a low-order memory address, and the low-order byte is stored in a high-order memory address. Contrast this with the reverse order that Motorola 680X0 uses to represent the 32-bit integer.

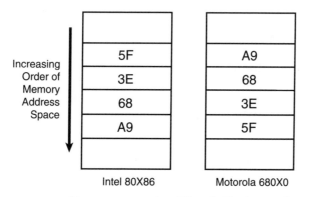

Figure 12.3. *Different processor architectures represent data differently. The diagram illustrates the difference between the Intel 80X86 process and the Motorola 680X0 rules of encoding a 32-bit integer.*

Unless something is done to reconcile these differences, among others, in data representation, exchanged data between the Intel and Motorola architectures might lead to erroneous interpretation of this data. XDR solves this problem by introducing a standard way to represent data objects. Unless this set of encoding rules defined by XDR is adopted by all communicating parties, no meaningful exchange of data is possible. A sender must format data to conform with XDR rules of representing it before transmitting it to the other end. When the data is received, the receiver must decode it and convert it back into a machine-specific representation that the receiver can process error-free.

XDR and RPC work together to provide the infrastructural support that NFS and other RPC-based applications need to operate based on a client-server setting. Whereas RPC allows for transparent access to distributed file systems by shielding differences at the logical level, XDR extends this transparency to the physical level by formalizing machine-independent ways to represent data on the wire.

Network File System: Concept and Setup

Network File System (NFS) allows user processes and programs *transparent* read and write access to a remotely mounted file system. Transparent access implies that programs would continue to work and process files located on an NFS-mounted file system without any modifications to their code. This is because NFS is cleverly designed to present remote resources to users as extensions to the local resources.

NFS follows the client-server model, in which the server is the system that owns the file system resource and is configured to share it with other systems. An NFS-shareable resource is usually referred to as an *exported* file system. The client is the resource user. It uses the exported file system as if it were part of the local file system. To achieve this transparency, the client is said to *mount* the exported directory to the local file system.

In Figure 12.4, /efs is the exported directory on host netrix (the NFS server). To access that directory from client jade, it must be mounted first. To do that, the administrator creates the /ifs directory to use as the mount directory and issues the appropriate mount command. Consequently, to access the file budget.rpt from host jade, the user must specify /ifs/reports/budget.rpt as the path to that file.

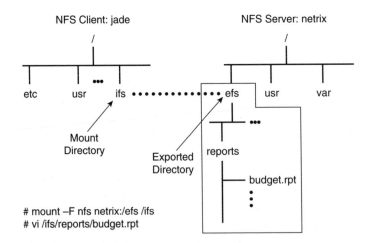

Figure 12.4. *The relationship between the NFS server and client file systems. To transparently access the file* budget.rpt *from host* jade, *the user mounts the exported directory* /efs *on NFS server* netrix *and specifies* /ifs/reports/budget.rpt *as the path to the command.*

NFS Daemons

Table 12.1 lists the server and client daemons that take care of NFS services. As can be seen from the table, some daemons run on both the server and the client, whereas others run exclusively on the server or the client. The table gives a brief description of each of the daemons, leaving details to upcoming sections.

Table 12.1. NFS client and server daemons.

Daemon	Description
nfsd	Is the NFS server daemon. It runs on the server and is responsible for handling and responding to client requests. As will be explained later, nfsd handles client requests by decoding RPC requests to determine the nature of the desired operation and submitting the call to the local I/O disk access mechanism for actual execution. nfsd is normally invoked when the system is brought up to run level three (file-sharing run level). For performance-related reasons, multiple instances of nfsd are invoked.
biod	Is the block input/output daemon. It runs on NFS clients and handles reading and writing data from and to the NFS server on behalf of the client process. Again, performance-related issues dictate that multiple instances of this daemon be invoked on the client.
mountd	Runs on the NFS server. It is responsible for handling client mount requests. In reference to Figure 12.4, when the command mount -F nfs netrix:/efs /ifs is issued on the command line on host jade, an NFS RPC mount request is sent by the client to the NFS server. Unless host netrix is running mountd, it will not be able to honor the request, and the mount is bound to fail. NFS servers run only one mountd.
lockd	Run by both the client and the server, this daemon handles file locks. On the client side, the daemon issues such requests, whereas the server's lockd honors those requests and manages the locks.
statd	Run by both the client and the server, this daemon maintains the status of currently enforced file locks. Its usefulness is particularly realized during server crashes because it helps clients reclaim locks placed on files after the recovery of the server.

Client Daemons	Server Daemons
biod	nfsd
lockd	lockd
statd	statd
	mountd

Although rpcbind is not listed in Table 12.1, the port mapper, of course, must also be running on the server. After all, NFS is an RPC server.

Setting Up the NFS Server

NFS is usually supplied as an optional extension to the operating system. System administrators are normally provided with the choice to have it installed at installation time. Unless you have installed the system yourself, you should check for the existence of this package on your system before you proceed with the actual setup. To determine whether NFS is installed, you can use the following pkginfo command:

```
# pkginfo
```

After you have decided which parts of the file system you want to share on the server with client hosts, you can proceed with setting up NFS.

To export a file system (rendering it shareable), you must use the share command. Following is the syntax of the command:

```
share [-F nfs] [-o options] [-d description] pathname
```

In this syntax,

-F nfs	Specifies the type of exported file system. UNIX supports many types of remotely accessible file systems. Examples of such file systems include RFS (Remote File Systems) and AFS (Andrews File System). This option can be omitted if NFS is the only distributed file system that your system supports.
-o options	Specifies restrictions that apply to the exported file system. Table 12.2 lists the options and gives a brief description of their effects.
-d description	Is a descriptive statement.
pathname	Specifies the pathname to export (or share).

Table 12.2. Options that can be included in -o options upon mounting an NFS file system.

Option	Description
rw=host[:host...]	Exports pathname as read/write to the listed hosts. If no hosts are specified, all clients, with exceptions stated using other options, are allowed the read/write access.
ro=host[:host...]	Exports the pathname as read-only to the listed hosts. If no hosts are specified, all clients, with exceptions stated using the rw= option, are allowed read-only access.
anon=uid	Assigns a uid for anonymous users when accessing pathname. By default, anonymous users are assigned a uid of user nobody. User nobody normally has the same access privileges as public.
root=[host[:host...]]	Allows root access privileges to the user from host. The user's uid has to be 0. Unless specified, no user is allowed root access privileges to pathname.
secure	Enforces enhanced authentication requirements before a user is granted access to an NFS-mounted file system.

> **Note:** Flavors of UNIX other than SVR4/SVR4.2 provide the export command, rather than share, to render exported file systems shareable. For details, refer to your vendor's documentation.

Taking the scenario depicted in Figure 12.4 as an example, the following share command allows host netrix (the NFS server) to export /efs with rw privilege to all clients, except for users from host saturn:

```
# share -F nfs -o rw,ro=saturn -d "Just an example" /efs
```

According to this share command, no root access privileges are granted to any of the NFS users.

The following share command, on the other hand, prevents all hosts but saturn from accessing the file system:

```
# share -F nfs -o ro=saturn /efs
```

Hosts other than saturn attempting to mount the /efs directory will fail and end up with the Permission denied message.

To grant root access from host jade, enter the following command:

```
# share -F nfs -o rw,root=jade /efs
```

To verify which file systems are exported, enter share without command-line arguments:

```
# share
-               /nfs    rw      ""
-               /efs    rw,ro=saturn    ""
```

Automatic Sharing

Unless a directory is occasionally shared to perform a specific task, after which the directory is unshared, it makes more sense to automate the sharing of exportable directories at boot time. To achieve automatic sharing, you must edit the /etc/dfs/dfstab file. In this file, you should include as many share commands as you need to take care of all the directories you want exported by the NFS server. The syntax that a share entry must follow is exactly the same as described previously. The following two share entries, for example, are extracted from the /etc/dsf/dfstab file on host netrix:

```
share -F nfs /nfs
share -F nfs rw,ro=satrun /efs
```

When the system enters run level three as it is brought up, the /etc/dfs/dfstab contents will be read, and its share entries will be executed. No longer will the system administrator have to issue both share commands manually.

The program that is called from the /etc/init.d/nfs script to export all the file systems specified in the dfstab file is shareall. You can use it on the command line as well to force sharing, especially after you make changes to the /etc/dfs/dfstab that you want to implement immediately.

Setting Up the Client

On the client side, a user has to issue the `mount` command before attempting access to the exported path on the NFS server. For example, to access the exported `/efs` directory on NFS server `netrix`, the user must first issue the following `mount` command:

```
# mount -F nfs netrix:/efs /ifs
```

The preceding command assumes that the user has already created the mount point directory (`/ifs` in the example). Otherwise, the mount attempt will fail.

As shown in Figure 12.4, `/efs` is the exported directory on host `netrix`, and `/ifs` is the mount directory. Once mounted, `/efs` or any directories below it can be accessed (subject to security restrictions) from host `jade`, using ordinary UNIX commands and programs.

Following is the complete syntax of the `mount` command:

```
mount [-F nfs] [-o options] host:pathname mountpoint
```

In this syntax,

`-F nfs`	Specifies the type of the file system to mount.
`-o options`	Specifies the mount options. Table 12.3 lists commonly used `options`.
`host:pathname`	Completely identifies the server and the resource directory being mounted. `host` is the host name of the NFS server, and `pathname` is the pathname of the exported directory on this server.
`mountpoint`	Specifies the pathname of the directory on the client through which the NFS-mounted resource will be accessed.

Table 12.3. Mount-specific options.

Option	Description
`rw ¦ ro`	Specifies whether to mount the NFS directory for read-only or read/write. The default is `rw`.
`retry=n`	Specifies the number of times `mount` should retry. This is normally set to a very high number. Check your vendor's documentation for the default value of *n*.
`timeo=n`	Specifies the timeout period for the mount attempt in tenths of a second. `timeo` is normally set to a very high number. Check your vendor's documentation for the default value.
`soft ¦ hard`	Specifies whether a `hard` or `soft` mount should be attempted. If `hard` is specified, the client relentlessly retries until it receives an acknowledgment from the NFS server specified in *host*. A `soft` mount, on the other hand,

Option	Description
	causes the client to give up attempting if it does not get the acknowledgment after retrying the number of times specified in the retry=*n* option. Upon failure, a soft mount returns an error message to the attempting client.
bg ¦ fg	Specifies whether the client is to reattempt mounting, should the NFS server fail to respond, in the foreground (fg) or in the background (bg).
intr	Specifies whether to allow keyboard interrupts to kill a process that is hung up waiting for a response from a hard-mounted file system. Unless interrupted, the process waits endlessly for a response, which in turn locks the session.

Should a soft-mounted file system fail to respond to an RPC request, the request will be retried by the client for the number of times specified in the retry=*n* option. If the *n* retries are exhausted without any success in getting an acknowledgment from the server, an error message is returned, and the client stops retrying.

If the affected file system was mounted for read/write access, this mode of behavior can seriously impact the integrity of applications that were writing to this file system before the interruption in service occurred. For this reason, it is recommended that read/write mountable file systems be hard mounted. This guarantees that the client will indefinitely retry an operation until outstanding RPC requests are honored, even in the event of an NFS server crash.

Unreasonably extended server failure might cause an application to be locked up indefinitely while waiting for a response from a hard-mounted file system. Hence, whenever a hard mount is desired, it is important that keyboard interrupts are allowed (by specifying the intr option) to kill the process so that a user can recover his login session to normal operation.

Following is a mount command that would be used to soft mount the /nfs/sales directory on the NFS server netrix, with read-only access. The mount point is /usr/sales on host jade:

```
# mount -F nfs -o soft,ro netrix:/nfs/sales /usr/sales
```

To verify that a file system is indeed mounted, use mount without any command-line arguments, as shown here:

```
# mount
/ on /dev/root read/write on Sat Feb 18 09:44:45 1995
/u on /dev/u read/write on Sat Feb 18 09:46:39 1995
/TEST on /dev/TEST read/write on Sat Feb 18 09:46:40 1995
/usr/sales on netrix.unicom.com:/nfs/sales read/write on Sat Feb 18 10:02:52 1995
```

The last line indicates the name of the mount directory, the name of the NFS server, and the name of the mounted file system.

Automatic Mounting

After a server is set up to share file system resources, clients can be conveniently configured to mount the server resources automatically at boot time, or whenever the system enters run level three. Configuring for automatic mounting involves editing a single file, which is vfstab in the /etc directory. vfstab can include information that is useful for automounting other distributed file systems such as Remote File System (RFS).

Entries in vfstab must follow this syntax:

```
special    fsckdev    mountpoint    fstype    fsckpass    automount    options
```

In this syntax,

special	Refers to the resource name in the host:pathname format, in which host is the name of the server, and pathname is the shared directory.
fsckdev	Is normally ignored, and therefore won't be addressed. A dash (-) character should be entered for ignored arguments. Refer to your vendor's manual for details.
mountpoint	Specifies the mount directory on the client host.
fstype	Specifies the type of the file system being mounted. To specify NFS, use nfs.
fsckpass	Does not apply to NFS-mountable file systems, and therefore will be ignored. Refer to your vendor's manual for details.
automount	Assumes one of two values: yes or no. A yes indicates that the file system is to be mounted whenever the system enters run level three.
options	Specifies the mount-specific options, such as ro, rw, bg, and fg.

To automatically mount the /nfs/sales directory of server netrix on the client's directory /usr/sales on host jade, the following mount entry should be added to the /etc/vfstab file:

```
netrix:/nfs/sales - /usr/sales nfs - yes soft,ro
```

After changes are made to the /etc/vfstab file, you can implement those changes either by restarting NFS as described in the next section or by using the mountall command on the command line. Before using mountall, however, you must ensure that file systems that are going to be affected adversely by the changes are first unmounted using the umount command. See the next section for details about starting and stopping NFS services.

Automatic mounting of the file system specified in the /etc/vfstab file is taken care of by the system whenever it enters run level three. Then, the mountall command executes from the /etc/init.d/nfs file, thus taking care of all the NFS-mountable file systems.

The Mounting Process

The flowchart in Figure 12.5 ties learned concepts together by depicting how the mounting process is handled by NFS. The flowchart examines the process from the client's end.

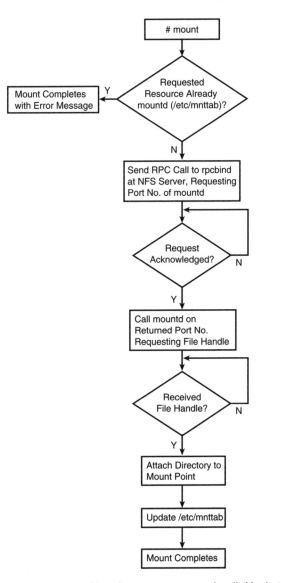

Figure 12.5. *A flowchart representation of how the mounting process is handled by the NFS client in relation to the server.*

When a mount command is issued, the /etc/mnttab is first checked to determine whether the requested resource is already mounted. If not, the client sends an RPC call to the port mapper, rpcbind, requesting the port number on which the nfsd is listening for requests on the network. The client then waits until its request is acknowledged. Next, the client issues an RPC call to mountd at the port number it received from rpcbind. This time, the RPC call requests that mountd send a file handle for the designated directory (see the following note for an introductory notion of the file handle). At this point, the server verifies that the requested resource is shareable and returns the requested file handle. The client then attaches the requested resource to the specified mount point. Consequently, /etc/mnttab is duly updated to include the newly mounted resource to the list of mounted file systems.

File Handle

For our purposes, it is enough to know that a file handle uniquely identifies a shareable resource. After being mounted, the client and the server exchange the file handle (fhandle) in the RPC request and response messages.

Starting and Stopping NFS Services

After all the necessary steps for automatic sharing and mounting of file systems are completed, you can start NFS operation on both the server and the client hosts.

To manually start NFS using the command line, use the following command:

```
sh /etc/init.d/nfs start
```

This command automatically starts the same set of NFS daemons independent of whether the command was invoked on a client or a server. By default, /etc/init.d/nfs start starts four nfsd daemons and four biod daemons. As will be explained later, starting multiple instances of the nfsd and biod daemons contributes to an overall improvement of the NFS service by enhancing the throughput of the file system. Some UNIX implementations go as far as invoking eight of each daemon by default.

The /etc/init.d/nfs script also starts all other daemons, including lockd, statd, and mountd. All NFS daemons are invoked on both the server and the clients because UNIX allows a host to assume both roles, server and client. While the system is a server to clients on the network, the system itself can be a client to some other servers.

The /etc/init.d/nfs script will work provided that your system is at run level three. To check the state of your system, enter the following who -r command:

```
# who -r
   .            run-level 3  Feb 19 10:40    3    0    S
```

To bring the system up to run level three, if it is not there yet, enter the following init command:

```
# init 3
```

To bring the system up to run level three by default at boot time, you must ensure that the /etc/inittab file includes the following initdefault entry:

is:3:initdefault:

Upon checking the /etc/inittab file, you might find the following entry instead:

is:2:initdefault:

If this happens to be the case, use vi or any other editor to change the run level from 2 to 3 in this entry. This guarantees that the system enters run level three when booted, a necessary condition for starting the NFS service on both the client and the server.

Figure 12.6 shows a flowchart summarizing the NFS startup process at boot time. When the system enters run level three, init executes the /etc/rc3.d/S22nfs script. The script, in fact, maintains a link to the /etc/init.d/nfs script mentioned earlier.

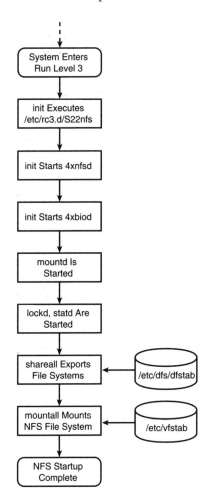

Figure 12.6. *Flowchart of the NFS startup process at boot time.*

The S22nfs script first invokes four instances of nfsd, the server daemon. These are necessary to process RPC requests coming from the clients. Then the script runs four instances of biod, the client daemons. Independent of whether the host is a client or server, all NFS daemons are invoked whenever NFS is brought up. Next, the mountd daemon, another server daemon, is started to process NFS mount requests.

Next, lockd, the lock manager daemon, and statd, the lock status monitor daemon, are started. Both daemons are required for both the server and the client. Now that all the daemons are running, the system checks /etc/dfs/dfstab for the list of resources to share. It consequently executes the shareall command to take care of sharing the identified resources. Similarly, /etc/vfstab is checked next, and mountall is called to take care of mountable file systems identified in the vfstab file.

> **Note:** If you are configuring a host as a client only, you can edit the /etc/init.d/nfs file to comment references to the daemons pertaining to the server only (to prevent them from running at boot time). You can do the same thing for hosts configured as servers only, by commenting references to client daemons.

Manual Unmounting and Unsharing of File Systems

Optionally, you can manually interrupt part of the service, whether to troubleshoot or reconfigure NFS on a host.

To selectively unmount a file system on a client, enter the following umount command:

```
# umount mountpoint
```

mountpoint is the name of the directory where the NFS file system is attached. Hence, to unmount, for example, the /efs directory of server netrix from the /ifs directory on client jade, enter this:

```
# umount /ifs
```

To unmount all NFS file systems, enter umount as many times as it takes to get the job done.

On the server side also, you can selectively unshare a currently shared resource. To do that, use the unshare command as in the following example to unshare /efs on server netrix:

```
# unshare -F nfs /efs
```

The -F nfs option is necessary only if more than one type of distributed file system (such as RFS and AFS) is exported by the server.

To unshare all the exported file systems, simply use the unshareall command.

NFS Automounter

Previous sections explained how to export and mount file system hierarchies. After a file system is mounted using the mount command, the mounted resource becomes immediately available to the user as long as the integrity of network operations is maintained. Unmounting an NFS resource takes issuing the umount command. Again, an unmounted NFS resource stays that way (that is, inaccessible) until the mount command is issued.

In this section, a dynamic mechanism for the mounting and unmounting of NFS file systems, called Automounter, will be explained. The Automounter, served by the automountd daemon, performs both functions (mounting and unmounting) as needed. This means that after automountd is configured properly, an NFS resource will be mounted only if needed. If the mounted resource is not accessed for a predetermined period after it has been last accessed, automountd unmounts it automatically.

These are the benefits of using the Automounter:

◆ *Reduced administrative overhead:* Using automountd relieves the system administrator from administering individual /etc/vfstab files on all workstations. This is especially applicable if Network Information Service tools for the centralized management and distribution of network host configuration are applied to NFS Automounter maps. Updating the Automounter's configuration files can be done on a single workstation and propagated to all hosts using the NIS programs explained in Chapter 11, "Setting Up the Network Information Service."

Another advantage of using the Automounter is that neither the administrator nor the user has to worry about creating the mount directories. The Automounter creates the required mount directories the first time they are needed.

◆ *Reduced risk of hanging the workstations:* As explained in previous sections, workstations normally hang in the event of an NFS server crash whenever a user attempts to access a resource which was mounted from that server. A hard mount might even lock up the workstation indefinitely. The Automounter unmounts file systems that were not accessed for a predetermined time (with a default of five minutes), which reduces the risk of hanging the workstation should the user attempt to access a crashed server.

◆ *Improved network performance:* The Automounter enables the administrator to specify multiple servers as possible sources for mounting a resource. If, for example, you have more than one NFS server offering identical file system resources on the network, then properly configured, automountd will be able to mount a resource from the first server to respond to its mount request. Hence, this provides a load-balancing feature, contributing to better overall performance.

◆ *Reduced workstation boot time:* Because automountd does not mount resources unless needed, booting a workstation becomes less time-consuming than relying on the boot process to mount resources specified in the /etc/vfstab file.

Automounter Operation

The automountd daemon can be automated to be invoked at boot time when the system enters run level three, or it can be invoked using the automount command. automount's behavior is based on a set of maps (that is, a database) that is normally maintained in the /etc directory. Only NFS resources described in these maps are dynamically mounted and unmounted by automount. automount does not reference the /etc/vfstab file for any of the resources it includes.

When invoked, automount mounts a daemon on each mount point instead of mounting actual NFS resources. When a user attempts to access a file or a command that crosses the remotely mounted directory, the daemon *intercepts* the access request and issues the necessary RPC calls to handle the request appropriately. This includes mounting the involved remote resource.

Network File System Architecture

Although the information presented in the previous sections is sufficient for configuring and bringing up NFS services on the network, the following discussion (dominantly theoretical) is needed for developing the insight necessary for the proper optimization and troubleshooting of the NFS service.

It's therefore recommended that you continue reading this part of the chapter. The remaining option, of course, is to skip it and continue with the upcoming chapter. You might want to come back to this section later, likely when troubleshooting NFS is discussed in Chapter 15, "Network Troubleshooting and Performance Tuning."

Network File System is a client-server application built on both XDR and RPC protocols (see Figure 12.7) for the presentation of data and the exchange of messages between the client and the server. It provides user processes with transparent access to files and file systems on a remote file server. This means that user applications should be able to access and process these data resources without modifying the applications. To the applications, resources appear to "belong" to the local disk and are therefore treated in exactly the same manner as local resources.

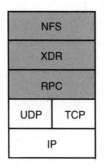

Figure 12.7. Protocol layering of NFS.

Figure 12.8 depicts the interrelationship between the various components of both the client and the server ends of the NFS service. As can be seen in the diagram, both server and client codes are embedded in the UNIX kernel. When NFS is installed, the operating system is extended to include function calls supporting the client code, the server code, and high-level I/O access code acting as a redirector of file access calls issued by user processes. It is the redirection mechanism that accounts for the transparency of NFS services. Whenever a user process issues a normal I/O call to access a file, the redirector passes the call to either local file access routines or the NFS client procedures for subsequent handling.

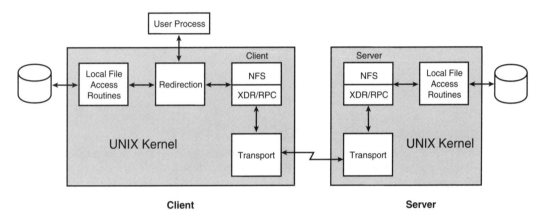

Figure 12.8. *Interrelationship between the various components of both the client and the server ends of the NFS service.*

Redirection is based on the path context of the file being accessed. If anywhere in the specified path there is an indication that the file being accessed resides below an active NFS mount point, NFS is delegated the job of retrieving the file data. For example, if a user logged in to `netrix` (see Figure 12.9) invokes `vi /home/alia/resume`, the file I/O call is passed on to the local file access routines. If the `/ifs/reports/sales.rpt` was instead specified, then because `/ifs` is a mount point on which the remote directory `/efs/reports` on host `jade` is mounted, the user call is redirected to NFS routines.

Whenever a file access call is passed to the NFS client, NFS generates the necessary RPC calls and delivers them to the NFS server by utilizing the underlying transport service (mainly UDP on top of IP). The server, on its part, decodes the RPC messages and handles the file access request by passing it on to its local access routines. The NFS daemon (`nfsd`) waits until the local routine returns with the requested data. The server then packages the data with the response and submits the RPC response to the transport provider for delivery to the client. The client consequently recovers the data and submits it to the requesting user process. At this time, the user process can proceed with executing the next instruction.

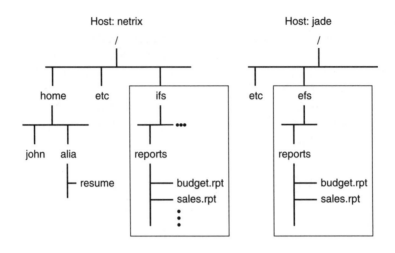

mount −F nfs jade:/efs /ifs

Figure 12.9. Host netrix *file system includes an NFS-mounted resource under the* /ifs *directory. The directory being mounted is* /efs *on host* jade. *A file access call that includes* /ifs *as part of the path raises a flag prompting UNIX to redirect the call to NFS procedures.*

While the NFS RPC call is handled, the user process has no means of telling whether its file access call is being handled by a remote NFS process. Even problems in obtaining the data in a timely fashion are perceived by the user process as local to system resources including the hard disk. A degradation in performance of the NFS server, for example, is perceived as a slow local disk. In the event of complete NFS failure, users attempting to open a file might end up with the not found error message on their screens.

Server and Client Daemons: Performance Issues

When NFS is brought up, the system starts multiple server and client processes. By default, UNIX SVR4 starts four biod daemons on the client and four nfsd daemons on the NFS server itself. As discussed next, the number of times each daemon is invoked impacts the performance of the service.

nfsd Daemon

When an nfsd server daemon receives an RPC request, it decodes its contents and schedules a kernel process for the subsequent processing of the requested file-access operation. It might take local access routines a while before the scheduled process is executed and the desired data is returned.

During this time, nfsd blocks other client requests, in which case the requests are kept waiting in a queue maintained by the server. This means that depending on the load put on the NFS server, clients might suffer degradation in performance as they try to access remote resources on that server. To circumvent this situation, an NFS server starts multiple instances of the nfsd daemon. This way, the server will be able to handle multiple independent client requests simultaneously. When a daemon is done executing a request, it waits in a queue for future ones or handles a request that might be waiting in the queue for an nfsd daemon to take care of it.

biod Daemon

The way client requests are handled by the kernel is tricky business. In the section "Network File System Setup," you were told that to provide full NFS client functionality to user processes, multiple biod daemons should be invoked, among other daemons. As a matter of fact, this requirement is not absolutely true. A client can even live to function without a single biod daemon! These statements might lead the intuitive reader to ask some questions: Does this mean that biod is *not* the client? If this is the case, then where is, and how do I invoke, the client? and finally, What part of the picture does biod fit, and what is the role it plays?

The biod daemon is not the client per se. It is more of a helper to the actual client, which it works with to improve the client's performance. The actual client, like the server component, is embedded in the kernel itself. Embedding the NFS code in the kernel will have been handled when the NFS package was installed, and it is implemented by extending the kernel system calls to include client-related calls. This explains why there is no requirement to invoke the client, because it comes up when the kernel itself is brought up.

When a user process accesses an NFS-mounted file system, it can issue one or a sequence of RPC calls to the NFS server to satisfy a certain requirement. For example, when ls is used to look up a directory on an NFS server, three RPC calls are made: to get the file attributes for the directory, to read the entries in the directory, and to look up the names and attributes for the files.

RPC calls are issued by a single client process one at a time. The client process will not issue another RPC until the current one completes and has been acknowledged by the NFS server. This mode of operation is satisfactory and well-paced for operations not involving storing or retrieving data from the NFS-mounted file system.

The storage and retrieval of data, however, such as block read/write operations, are inherently slow and can possibly lead to real bottlenecks in performance. Reading large chunks of data can significantly impair performance because user processes will have to wait prolonged times before a block read or write RPC completes. During the wait, operations that are less time-consuming, such as getting file attributes, cannot be issued.

So what does biod do to alleviate the performance problem? To start with, biod stands for block input/output daemon. When run, biod is employed by client processes to handle reading or writing large chunks of data, in *excess* of their immediate need, from or to the NFS-mounted file system. In other words, biod employs a caching mechanism with the purpose of reducing the client's reliance on across-the-wire transfers for reading or writing data to the NFS file system. The idea is that biod carries the task of getting data from the NFS file system and having it ready in memory for the client process before it is immediately needed by that client.

The first time a process attempts an NFS read, the process handles the NFS read request directly. The process issues the RPC call and goes to sleep until the requested data is returned. As noted earlier, the time the process spends sleeping, and therefore blocking subsequent requests, might be long. In anticipation of future read requests, however, and to avoid long sleep times, the client process schedules biod to read ahead, on its behalf, and cache large chunks of data from the NFS server. Thereafter, whenever the client process is required to read data, it will likely be able to return with data from cache instead of reading it across the wire from the NFS server. Thus, the read process completes more quickly, and the client will be able to execute subsequent calls more efficiently.

Why does the client process handle the first request itself? Again, the issue is performance related. You should think of biod as a friendly helper whose assistance should be sought only when needed. Whenever there isn't any readily available cached data, the client should be handling the read request itself because no performance gain would be realized by delegating the RPC to biod.

In fact, it might take biod longer to complete the call than it would take the client itself in this situation. The reason is that a client might not always find an idling biod whenever an NFS read or write requirement arises. When a client submits an RPC to biod, it is normally scheduled for completion depending on biod availability.

When writing data, biod is also relied on to perform delayed-writes. Instead of transferring data in small chunks to the server, the client process delegates to biod the responsibility of performing the transfers in large chunks using one write RPC each. biod keeps accumulating data in cache until enough is available for sending it in one shot to the server. Again, this process contributes to improved performance.

File Locking: *lockd* and *statd* Daemons

NFS is inherently a stateless protocol, meaning that its definition precludes support for network state maintenance information. It is left to clients to maintain such information in order to operate consistently across the network. It is the client's responsibility, for example, to provide all the necessary information to successfully write data to a file, including the procedure number identifying the action, the file handle identifying the affected file, the offset into the file, and the number of bytes to write to the file. To the NFS server, RPC calls are treated as self-contained unrelated requests, without respect to the order in which they were received.

The statelessness of NFS prohibited it from dealing with server and client crashes. In particular, NFS per se cannot support a network-wide file- and record-locking mechanism, a stateful functionality, which works homogeneously with native UNIX locking mechanisms.

To circumvent this weakness, two daemons, lockd (the lock manager) and statd (the status monitor), were introduced outside the periphery of the definition of NFS. Hence the distinction between NFS the protocol and NFS the product, the product including both the NFS protocol and additional daemons such as lockd and statd.

The lock manager (lockd) extends the kernel's capability to perform file- and record-locking operations to NFS distributed file systems. In other words, when lockd is running, it handles both local and remote locks. Local locks are submitted to local handling routines for enforcement. If, however, an application requests locking an NFS-mounted resource, the lock manager relays the request to its peer, via an RPC request, on the NFS server (see Figure 12.10). The server's lock manager responsibility is then to enforce the lock on the requested resource if no other lock is already in effect. Subsequently, the client's lock manager is informed of the action being taken. Whenever a lock request is honored, both lock managers, the server's and the client's, maintain status information about the lock until it is released.

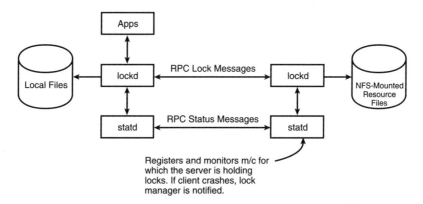

Figure 12.10. The interrelationship between the various locking daemons.

When a client makes its first lock request, the server's lock manager enters the name of that client in a special register and passes this information to statd, the status monitor. The status monitor relies on the register to monitor the status of concerned clients. The status monitor's prime functionality is to inform the lock manager of crash-related events.

Depending on where the crash occurs, a different approach is adopted for the reclamation of the locks that were established before the crash:

◆ *Client crash:* If the status monitor on the server detects a client crash, it informs the lock manager of the event. The status monitor has no means of telling whether the crash was due to actual client failure or some other failure on the network, such as a failing router separating them, or simply because the user turned off the power to the client machine. Consequently, the only way to handle a situation like this is to let the lock manager release all the locks it is enforcing on behalf of that client. Thus, it is left up to the client to reclaim lost locks after recovery.

◆ *Server crash:* Server crash recovery is a more delicate matter, affecting not only the server but potentially several tens, if not hundreds, of clients. Due to the statelessness of NFS, when the server crashes, there is no way for clients to tell what happened until the server is brought up again. Meanwhile, clients retain their local registry of the "enforced locks," where the server loses all its lock information.

Once recovered from a crash, the server's status monitor sends out notification of the reboot event to the affected clients. The notification is communicated to the client's status monitor, which in turn informs its local lock manager. As of the notification time, the server grants all clients a grace period during which they qualify to reclaim their lost locks. During this period (45 seconds by default), only lock reclamation requests are honored. Hence, it is up to the clients to try to reclaim all lost locks and to consequently recover the consistency in the NFS network service.

NFS Is Not for UNIX Only

Although NFS is most widely implemented on UNIX platforms, its services can be extended to include other environments, such as DOS, Novell NetWare 3.*x* and 4.*x* file servers, DEC VAX systems, and IBM VMS mainframes. A UNIX host, for example, can NFS-mount part or all of a NetWare file system supported by a NetWare file server. This adds another dimension to the *access transparency* that NFS provides to local processes. NFS not only has to hide the whereabouts of the remote file system, but also has to make differences between the file system supported by the client operating system and the NFS-mounted file system oblivious to the local process. To the local process, the file system structure appears to "conform" to the native structures that the operating system supports.

To provide this level of apparent homogeneity among different file systems, SUN Microsystems developed a high-level internal file system interface, the Virtual File System (VFS) (see Figure 12.11). VFS defines a set of generic file system operations that are independent of the file systems operating beneath the VFS interface itself. User processes interact with the desired file system (beneath VFS) via VFS generic calls. File system-specific calls are generated by VFS on behalf of the requesting process.

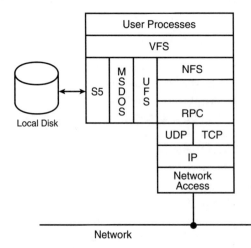

Figure 12.11. *The Virtual File System interface shields user processes from file system-specific details by allowing them to call a standardized set of high-level file system access calls. In turn, the VFS interface redirects the calls to the desired file system.*

Thanks to NFS, in a mixed environment, a DOS user, for example, perceives network resources as native to the DOS operating system, whereas a UNIX user perceives all resources, including DOS file servers, as native to UNIX.

Chapter 17, "UNIX on a Multiplatform Network," sheds more light on architectural requirements for integrating UNIX with other network resources.

Summary

Network File System (NFS) provides users with transparent access to remotely distributed file systems on the network. NFS achieves transparency by extending the UNIX kernel to include a suite of RPC calls, an XDR presentation protocol, and a redirection capability. In doing so, user processes need no modification whatever in order to access NFS-mounted resources. Whenever a user process references an NFS resource, the redirection capability forwards the request to the NFS client, which in turn issues the required RPC calls to the NFS server to get the request honored.

To share a resource with other hosts, the /etc/dfs/dfstab NFS file should be duly edited, and NFS should be started. Alternatively, using share, a resource can be shared from the command line. On the client side, the user must have the NFS resource mounted before it can be accessed. Mounting an NFS resource can be achieved by executing the proper mount command from the command line, or by updating the /etc/vfstab file and starting or restarting the NFS service.

NFS also supports an automounting feature, which, if implemented properly, allows for the dynamic mounting of resources on an as-needed basis. A resource that is not accessed for a predetermined period is also dynamically unmounted by the automounting capability. Configuring the Automounter involves writing automount maps, the details of which were covered in the chapter.

CHAPTER

Remote Access Utilities

Introduction

In Chapter 7, "TCP/IP Applications Overview," some of the most commonly used commands and TCP/IP services were introduced, including TELNET, FTP, and TFTP, among other services. This chapter serves as a supplementary extension to Chapter 7. It explains some of the interesting commands, commonly known as r-utilities, that add to your ability to access remote hosts on the network.

R-utilities were mainly created by the University of California in Berkeley. Although they were originally developed as a network version of some UNIX-specific commands, some vendors have managed to extend them to other environments. LAN WorkPlace for DOS, by Novell, for example, includes support for r-utilities that enables users to remotely copy files or execute commands from their DOS workstations on remote UNIX machines.

In particular, this chapter explains the following r-utilities:

rlogin	Provides remote login capability
rcp	Remotely copies files between hosts
rsh	Provides remote shell capability
ruptime	Displays network utilization statistics
rwho	Displays who is on the network

One common feature that r-utilities share is that if they are set up properly, authorized users should be able to use them to access remote resources without being required to enter a valid password. For this reason, the chapter starts with a discussion on how to secure access to those utilities such that only authorized users can use them, whether to remotely copy files, log in to the host, or remotely execute commands on the host.

Securing R-Utilities: */etc/hosts.equiv* and *$HOME/.rhosts*

Unless properly secured, r-utilities can become a security hazard to the network. Although it is convenient for users to be able to access resources on remote hosts without having to provide a valid password, if improperly secured, r-utilities can provide computer hackers with the means to break into your environment.

Securing r-utilities is based on the concept of *trusted hosts* and *users*. A trusted host is a host from which trusted users are granted access to the system without being required to enter a password. A trusted user normally means a user with the user accounts on both hosts: this host and the one from which the user is attempting to access this host.

For example, a user with mike for a login name on both hosts jade and netrix is said to be a trusted user (security allowing). Consequently, if host jade is a trusted host, mike can access host netrix without entering a password. If mike is not a trusted user, he will still be able to use all r-utilities, except for rcp, to access host netrix. He will be prompted, however, for a valid password. An unchallenged access to a system is said to be a *trusted access*.

Names of trusted hosts and users can be maintained in /etc/hosts.equiv and $HOME/.rhosts (that is, .rhosts in the user's home directory). hosts.equiv sets up permission for the entire host being accessed, whereas .rhosts is set up by each user to control access to her own logins. Each of these files has a different implication for system security.

/etc/hosts.equiv

/etc/hosts.equiv is used to maintain a list of trusted hosts and users that are allowed or denied trusted access to your system using r-utilities. Host and user names maintained in this file define system-wide trusted access.

Following is the syntax of /etc/hosts.equiv entries:

```
[+ ¦ -] [hostname] [username]
```

The + sign is used to designate a trusted host. The host being trusted is specified by *hostname*.

If the + is entered alone without a host name, every host on the network then becomes a trusted host. You should have no reason to have a + sign-only entry in the /etc/hosts.equiv file. It implies that any user on the network is a trusted user and can therefore be allowed access to the system without having to enter a password. Furthermore, the user does not have to own identical account names on both his system and the host being accessed. For example, a user can use the `rlogin` command with the `-l` option to specify any login name he is aware of.

Following is an example of a variation on the theme, whereby only users logging from host `netrix` are granted access to host `jade`:

```
+jade
```

Users coming from host `jade` must own similarly named user accounts on `netrix`.

If, however, you want to allow only user `pat`, logged to host `jade`, access to `netrix` while denying others trusted access, you must include the following entry in the `/etc/hosts.equiv` file:

```
+jade pat
```

To globally, or selectively, disable trusted access to your host, you can use entries that include the minus (·) sign. To globally disable access, include a minus sign with nothing else. Consequently, all users attempting access using r-utilities will be prompted for a password before their attempts are honored.

Following is an entry that discriminates against users coming from host `saturn`:

```
-saturn
```

This entry means that a user logged in to host `saturn` cannot be granted trusted access. Consequently, such users will be prompted to enter a valid password.

You can narrow denial to certain users coming from host `saturn` by following this example:

```
saturn -steve
```

This entry denies `steve`, coming from host `saturn`, trusted access to the system.

$HOME/.rhosts

The `/etc/hosts.equiv` file is normally used by the system administrator to define system-wide trusted access measures. The `.rhosts` file is normally used by users to grant trusted access to their account to other network users. For example, for user `pat` to grant trusted access to user `roy`, on host `jade`, he should include the following entry in the `.rhosts` file in his (pat's) home directory:

```
jade roy
```

As illustrated in this example, `.rhosts` entries assume the same syntax as in the `/etc/hosts.equiv` file.

To be effective, the `.rhosts` file must meet two criteria: (1) it must be owned by the superuser `root` or by the given account name, and (2) the file must not be available to public write access. Failure to meet either of these conditions causes the system to ignore the file and deny access to would-be trusted hosts and users.

It is important to keep in mind that whenever a trusted access is attempted, the system searches the /etc/hosts.equiv file first. If no matching record is found in this file, the system searches the $HOME/.rhosts file of the user on whose behalf the access is attempted. This means that /etc/hosts.equiv overrides .rhosts files. For example, if a user is disallowed access in the /etc/hosts.equiv file, the user will be denied access even if she is allowed access in the .rhosts file.

Remote Login: rlogin

Chapter 7, "TCP/IP Applications Overview," explained the use of telnet to log in to a UNIX host on the network. rlogin (a term that stands for remote login) is yet another utility that achieves the same functionality. On the server side, the superserver inetd listens to rlogin requests on well-known TCP port number 513 on behalf of the server daemon rlogind.

Whenever rlogind is handed a login request, it checks to see whether the user's host name is in either the /etc/hosts.equiv file or the $HOME/.rhosts file. If this is the case, rlogind grants the user access without prompting her for a password. Otherwise, the user will be prompted to enter a valid password.

The syntax for the rlogin command is as shown here:

```
rlogin hostname -l username
```

The hostname is the name of the remote system being attempted for access, and username is the login name used in this attempt. If username is left blank, rlogin defaults to the user's login name on the local host.

The main functional difference between rlogin and telnet is that rlogin is UNIX-specific, which allows a UNIX host to log in to another UNIX host. telnet, on the other hand, is not platform specific, and it allows a user to log in to other non-UNIX hosts from a UNIX or non-UNIX platform. This is because the TELNET application protocol is a TCP/IP standard, whereas RLOGIN is not.

Remote Shell: rsh

The remote shell command rsh enables a user to execute a single command on a remote host without having to log in. On the server side, the rshd daemon takes care of honoring rsh requests. Again, before being granted access, the user must be coming from a trusted host and must have the same username in the /etc/passwd file.

Following is the most common form of the rsh command:

```
rsh [ -l username ] hostname command
```

In this syntax, command specifies the command that the user wants executed on the remote host identified in hostname. Unless the -l option is used to specify a username different from the local username, rsh defaults to the local one.

When rsh is used to run commands on a remote host, it passes its standard input to the remotely executed command and returns standard output and standard error from the remote command to your local system. While doing that, rsh reads your terminal line by line, which renders it unsuitable to screen-oriented interactive applications, such as the vi editor, which read your terminal one character at a time.

> **Tip:** In an X Window System environment, rsh can be used to start a remote xterm session and have an interactive remote shell open on the local display. Following is an example of using rsh to invoke xterm on host netrix while redirecting its output to jade's display:
>
> ```
> $ rsh netrix /usr/X/bin/xterm -display jade:0
> ```

The rsh utility is helpful in many situations. For example, you can use it to occasionally print on printers attached to other remote systems, as shown here:

```
# rsh jade lp -d garfield sales.report
```

In particular, the author uses rsh to transfer data on a scheduled basis, using cron, every night from many hosts, to the host where the network administrator logs in for most of the day. An example of the data transferred is performance reports, as reported by the sar utility. This way, the network administrator has all the performance data conveniently stored on the same host. Following is an example of using rsh to run sar on remote host jade and having its output logged into a local file:

```
# rsh jade sar -a >> /hosts/jade/sar/reports
```

Remote Copy: rcp

rcp enables a user to transfer files between the local and the remote hosts, and between two remote hosts. A user enjoying trusted access status can conveniently use rcp to copy files across the network without entering a password. Also, users can use rcp to copy an entire directory, a convenience not available to ftp users.

The use of rcp, however, is mostly restricted to UNIX platforms. Both the source and the destination hosts must be running the UNIX operating system (read the following note for exceptions). In situations in which one of the platforms is non-UNIX, ftp is still the common method of file transfer.

> **Note:** LAN WorkPlace for DOS, by Novell, is an exceptional product that provides, in addition to native TCP/IP protocols and applications, the DOS equivalent of all the r-utilities discussed in this chapter.

The syntax of the rcp command is similar to that of the UNIX cp command. Optionally, you can prefix the source or the destination paths of involved file system resources by the host name. The host name and the path must be separated by a colon.

Following is the syntax of the rcp command:

```
rcp [ -r ] source destination
```

Both source and destination assume the format hostname:path. If the host name is left blank, rcp defaults to the local host. The -r option enables users to copy entire directories. In the following example, rcp copies the file forecast from the local host to remote host jade:

```
# rcp forecast jade:/apps/weather/forecast
```

Following is an example of using rcp to copy an entire directory between two remote hosts. The command is issued on the local host:

```
# rcp -r netrix:/movies jade:/movies
```

For this example to work, the user has to have trusted access status with both hosts jade and netrix and the write permission to the /movies directory on host jade.

ruptime and rwho

The ruptime and rwho commands provide information about users and hosts on the network. Both commands are served by the rwhod daemon, which listens for service requests on well-known UDP port number 513.

ruptime provides status information for every host on the network. For each host, ruptime prints a line on-screen displaying information about the number of users currently logged in to the host, its load, and the time elapsed since the host was last brought up. Following is an example of an output of ruptime:

```
# ruptime
jade          up 14+00:43,    1 user,   load 1.33, 1.99, 0.66
netrix        up     0:07,    0 users,  load 0.00, 0.00, 0.00
```

rwho lists the usernames of those users currently logged in to the network. The information includes the username, the host that the user is logged in to, the date and time of login, and the time elapsed since the user logged in to the host. Users idling for more than one hour are excluded from the report unless the -a option is included upon invoking rwho, as in the following example:

```
# rwho -a
maya    jade:tty01    Feb 19 07:49 99:59
alia    jade:ttyp0    Mar  4 10:24
tania   netrix:pts000 Mar  4 11:25 99:59
```

Rather than directly soliciting information from the servers on the network, both rwho and ruptime get their information from data logged by the rwhod daemon in the /usr/spool/rwho directory. This information is obtained by virtue of regular broadcasts that every rwhod daemon propagates on the network. Through these broadcasts, each `rwhod` daemon tells other `rwhod` daemons about the status of its local host and the users logged in to the host. When such a broadcast packet is received by a `rwhod` running on another host, the receiver logs the information pertaining to the sending host in the `/usr/spool/rwho/rwhod.hostname` file it creates, in which *hostname* is the name of the host originating the broadcast.

Following is a directory listing of the `/usr/spool/rwho` directory on host `jade`:

```
# ls /usr/spool/rwho
total 4
-rw-r--r--  1 root     other          108 Mar 04 11:30 whod.jade
-rw-r--r--  1 root     other          108 Mar 04 10:33 whod.netrix
```

When `ruptime` or `rwho` is entered on the command line, the command processes each file for the desired status information. Both commands rely on the time stamp on each file to determine whether the corresponding host has had its status information duly updated. Typically, if more than 11 minutes have lapsed since the status was last updated, the host is considered down by the local host, and no users are reported logged in to the host. Following is the output corresponding to a similar situation affecting host `netrix`:

```
# ruptime
jade            up 14+01:01,     1 user,   load 1.50, 1.23, 1.16
netrix          down     0:14
```

According to this output, host `netrix` has been down for the past 14 minutes.

Because of the way `rwhod` exchanges broadcast messages, network administrators are recommended to disable the `rwhod` daemon on their hosts. The recommendation particularly applies to large networks, where the regularity with which this activity takes place can introduce unnecessary traffic on the network, in addition to the CPU and disk I/O activities associated with logging the information into their respective files.

Note: To enable the `rwhod` daemon on startup, you should appropriately edit the `/etc/rc.inet` file to include the following line:

   `/usr/sbin/rwhod`

Summary

R-utilities represent network extensions to some UNIX commands, such as `cp` and `who`. R-utilities include the `rlogin`, `rcp`, `rsh`, `rwho`, and `ruptime` commands.

A feature common to all the r-utilities is that they allow access to remote hosts without requiring the user to enter a password. Users must have their accounts properly set up to use r-utilities.

Remote access setup information can be included in the /etc/hosts.equiv file or in the user's home directory on the remote host called $HOME/.rhosts. The former file defines a system-wide list of trusted hosts and users; the latter defines trusted hosts and users specific to the user in whose account trusted access can be attempted.

CHAPTER

♦

Special Servers and Services

Introduction

The TCP/IP protocol suite supports various special-purpose applications and services. Due to their nature, some of the applications are transparent to the users yet essential to the operation of their workstations.

Examples of special services are Reverse Address Resolution Protocol (RARP) and Bootstrap Protocol (BOOTP). Both are used for the central administration and distribution of IP addresses, as well as allowing diskless workstations to boot remotely from boot servers. Both RARP and BOOTP are discussed in this chapter.

Network printing and anonymous FTP access are two widely implemented services on TCP/IP networks. Network printing gives users the flexibility to print to any shared printer on the network, a convenient and time-saving feature of networks. Anonymous FTP access is becoming the norm for providing information on the Internet to public access. This chapter provides step-by-step procedures for setting up both services.

Reverse Address Resolution Server

In Chapter 4, "The Internet Layer and Routing," you were shown how before a host can send any user data to another host on the network, it has to resolve the destination IP address into a physical (MAC) address. You were also shown how the Address Resolution Protocol (ARP), operating at the data link layer, handles this requirement by propagating a broadcast packet on the local network requesting the host with the matching IP address to respond with its MAC address. The mapping thus obtained is then saved in the ARP cache for subsequent use for communicating user data to that host.

This section explains how the Reverse Address Resolution Protocol (RARP) handles the inverse requirement—that is, given the MAC address, how it would be mapped into an IP address. Such a mapping mechanism, known as reverse address resolution, has at least two applications:

◆ *Support for diskless workstations:* You have seen how UNIX hosts rely on locally stored TCP/IP files for networking configuration parameters such as the host's IP address, and the IP and address for the default router. At startup, those files are looked up by the boot process and are used to configure the network interfaces and applications. As the name implies, diskless workstations do not have the luxury of maintaining their configuration data locally. For this reason, they must rely on a mechanism by which they can be assigned an IP address whenever they are restarted.

◆ *Centralized distribution of IP addresses on large networks:* Depending on the size of the network, the individual administration and assignment of IP addresses to hosts on the network can become a tedious and time-consuming task. As hosts are moved around, their IP addresses might need to be changed. This is the case as the network subnetting structure changes.

In the case of subnetting structure changes, the changes might not be trivial at all, because they might require attending to every host for the subsequent reassignment of the new IP address. RARP can help in alleviating this problem by allowing the administrator to centrally manage, on an RARP server, any pool of IP addresses for their subsequent distribution to hosts whenever these hosts reboot. This way, IP address changes need to be implemented only on the RARP server whenever dictated by changes made to the network.

How RARP Works

The Reverse Address Resolution Protocol (RARP) is based on the client-server model, in which the client is the workstation or host requesting an IP address assignment, and the server is the host running the rarpd daemon.

On a diskless workstation, the client component is implemented in Programmable Read-Only Memory (PROM) on the network interface. The PROM includes a compacted implementation of the TCP/IP stack that allows the workstation to communicate RARP or BOOTP requests to the respective servers. At boot time, a diskless workstation has no idea about its own IP address, the IP address of the default router, the name server, and other parameters that are needed to render the workstation fully functional on the network.

As shown in Figure 14.1, at boot time a diskless workstation broadcasts on the local physical network an RARP packet requesting that it be assigned a unique IP address. Included in the packet is the MAC address of the requesting workstation. Of all hosts, only those running the rarpd daemon (that is, RARP servers) attempt handling the request.

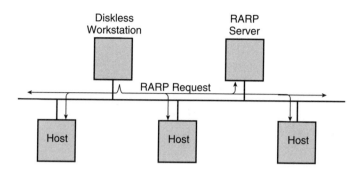

Figure 14.1. *At boot time, diskless workstations propagate an RARP request in which they elicit an IP address assignment.*

An RARP server responds to the request by consulting a database that contains one-to-one mappings between MAC and IP addresses. If a matching MAC address is found, the server encapsulates the corresponding IP address in an RARP response packet and sends it directly to the requesting station. Otherwise, the request is silently discarded.

RARP packets ride directly on Ethernet frames. For this reason, they cannot traverse networks across routers. Consequently, each subnet with diskless workstations attached to it must have at least one RARP server.

The /etc/ethers File

The /etc/ethers file contains the MAC-to-IP address associations. RARP servers use this file when responding to RARP requests. The /etc/ethers file must contain an entry for each of the workstations requiring RARP service.

The format of the /etc/ethers file is as shown here:

```
# MACaddress   hostname
#
00:80:c7:44:0d:7b     saturn
```

MACaddress is the physical (data link) address of the host, and hostname is the official name of the host as it appears in the /etc/hosts file on the server. When an RARP request is received, the server searches for a matching MAC address in the /etc/ethers file. If a match is found, the corresponding hostname is then used to find the corresponding IP address in the /etc/hosts file. The IP address is then sent directly to the requesting station in an RARP response packet.

Diskless Workstation Boot Process Using RARP

A diskless workstation needs more than the IP address to become fully functional after boot. In particular, it needs a bootfile and a kernel specific to its architecture, in addition to other TCP/IP parameters including the subnet mask, default router, domain name server, and so forth. None of these parameters is within RARP's reach. For this reason, the boot ROM on the network interface or diskless workstation normally contains implementations of TFTP, UDP, and IP protocols to assist it in continuing the boot process. Using TFTP, the workstation attempts to transfer all it needs for a successful boot.

The laddergram in Figure 14.2 depicts a flow of the events that take place from the time the diskless workstation starts booting until the kernel is read from the boot server and executed. As noted earlier, the client starts with an RARP broadcast requesting an IP address. The rarpd daemon matches the client MAC address with an entry in the /etc/ethers files, cross-references it with the /etc/hosts file, and responds with the corresponding IP address to the client.

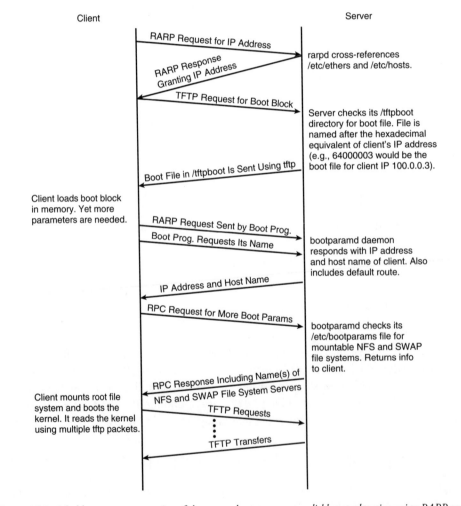

Figure 14.2. *A laddergram representation of the remote boot process on a diskless workstation using RARP service.*

Next, the client sends a TFTP request for a boot image block to continue booting the machine. On the server side, TFTP is taken care of by the tftpd daemon, which in turn is invoked by the inetd superserver daemon. As explained in Chapter 9, "Installing and Configuring TCP/IP," inetd listens on behalf of all the daemons, defined in the /etc/inet/inetd.conf file, on the network for service requests. In the tftpd case, inetd listens on well-known port number 69. The entry in /etc/inet/inetd.conf pertaining to the tftpd daemon should look like this:

```
tftp   dgram udp    wait    root    /usr/sbin/in.tftpd  in.tftpd -s /tftpboot
```

> **Note:** On most systems, the preceding line is disabled by the presence of a comment character (#) in front of it. To enable TFTP, you only have to remove the character.

The /tftpboot directory is where the boot server maintains the boot block files. Because clients might have different machine architectures, the boot server must maintain multiple bootfiles, one per client. To differentiate between the files, each file is named according to the following convention:

hexIPaddress.suffix

hexIPaddress is the hexadecimal equivalent of the IP address assigned to the client. The *suffix* can be anything. For example, if the client's IP address is 100.0.0.3, its corresponding bootfile as maintained in the /tftpboot directory could be 64000003.pc, in which pc denotes it as IBM PC compatible. After a request for a bootfile is received from a client, its corresponding bootfile is fetched in the /etc/tftp directory and transferred using the TFTP protocol to that client.

At this point, the client loads the boot block in memory and executes it. The boot program is responsible for locating the file system resources to mount its root file system and swap file system, and for locating the kernel to boot the machine into a fully functional state.

To start with, the boot program broadcasts a request for its IP address and its host name. But why request its IP address if it is already assigned one by virtue of the first RARP request that was broadcasted at the outset of the boot process? When the boot program executes, it loses track of the IP address obtained earlier, which forces it to rebroadcast the request. On the server side, the bootparamd daemon, an RPC boot parameter server, responds to the requests with the client's IP address and host name. bootparamd also includes information about the default route.

Next, the client broadcasts an RPC request for the remaining boot parameters that identify the file system resources to mount and read the bootable kernel. On receiving the request, bootparamd looks up its /etc/bootparams file for the requested information. /etc/bootparams is a database that has information about names of servers and pathnames of file systems that these servers make available to the diskless workstations. Following is a sample entry in /etc/bootparams:

```
sunrise root=saturn:/nfsroot/sunrise \
        swap=saturn:/nfsswap/sunrise \
        dump=saturn:/nfsdump/saturn \
```

The preceding parameters define the root, swap, and dump file systems for client sunrise. This information is conveyed by bootparamd to the client via an RPC response packet. Consequently, the client mounts its root file system from host saturn and reads the kernel via multiple TFTP transfers to boot the machine to a fully functional state.

RARP Drawbacks

There are a few problems with RARP, some of which render it unsuitable for large networks. Following is a summary of those problems:

◆ RARP relies on data link layer (MAC) broadcasts. This has the effect of preventing RARP broadcasts from crossing routers, which in turn confines the service to the boundaries of the local subnet segment. Consequently, you must bring up an RARP server on every segment of the network to accommodate all the dataless/diskless workstations.

◆ RARP servers provide only one piece of information: the IP address of the requesting client. Other information that is necessary for the success of the boot process—such as the name of the bootfile, the IP address of the default router, and the IP address of NFS servers—are obtained via more request broadcasts made on the network, thus imposing bandwidth loss due to these broadcasts. On a large network, such broadcasts might even slow the network, especially during peak hours when many users simultaneously turn on their workstations.

◆ Because RARP operates at the data link layer, it is not easy to develop applications on top of it.

These reasons led the TCP/IP developers to develop an alternative solution called the Bootstrap Protocol, commonly known as BOOTP, for booting diskless workstations. As explained in the next section, BOOTP circumvents all the previously stated problems and adds to the efficiency of the boot process.

Bootstrap Protocol: BOOTP Server

BOOTP protocol (RFC 951 and RFC 1048) is a high-level protocol that uses UDP for the purpose of the exchange of boot request/response messages between clients and servers. Unlike RARP messages, BOOTP messages can be forwarded across routers to extend their reach beyond the local subnet. Furthermore, BOOTP is well-equipped to provide more information than just the client's IP address.

A single BOOTP reply message can also include the name of the client, the name of the boot image file, the IP address of the routers, the IP address of the DNS servers, and so on. This feature has the advantage of reducing exchanged traffic between the client and host to a minimum. It also contributes to improving the overall efficiency of the boot process.

How Does BOOTP Work?

A diskless workstation can use the BOOTP protocol to boot itself only if the machine or the network interface has a built-in PROM containing a compacted implementation of TCP/IP. The implementation must include support for each of BOOTP, UDP, and IP protocols. On the server side, the `bootpd` daemon implements the BOOTP protocol. It is normally run by the `inetd` superserver (see Chapter 9, "Installing and Configuring TCP/IP," for more details on `inetd`). Following is the line that must be included in the `/etc/inet/inetd.conf` file to make `bootpd` manageable by `inetd`:

```
bootps dgram udp    wait   root   /usr/sbin/in.bootpd in.bootpd
```

> **Note:** As in TFTP's case, the preceding line might have been disabled by default. To enable it, you just have to remove the comment character (#) at the beginning of the line.

Consequently, `bootpd` will be started only when a `bootp` request is received by the server. By default, `bootpd` waits 15 minutes after it receives a request before exiting. The default can be changed to anything you like by using the `-t` *n* option, in which *n* is the number of minutes to wait for a new request after the last request is received before `bootpd` can exit.

When invoked, `bootpd` self-configures to use two UDP ports that it obtains from the `/etc/services` file. These are 67 for the server, and 68 for the client. If you check `/etc/services` to verify them, you will find them defined in two entries: `bootps` (for the server) and `bootpc` (for the client).

Figure 14.3 shows a laddergram depiction of the events that take place during a BOOTP-assisted boot process of a diskless workstation. The client, as expected, starts by sending a `bootp` broadcast requesting an IP address and any other information the responding server might have to assist it in booting properly. After the request arrives, `inetd` on the server invokes the `bootpd` daemon and hands it the request.

To properly respond to client requests, `bootpd` relies on a special database maintained in the `/etc/inet/bootptab` file. This file is the network administrator's responsibility to maintain. Included in the database are client-specific entries containing the IP address of the client, the pathname of the bootfile, and so forth. Hence, when handed a client request, `bootpd` looks up all the information in the client-specific entry in the `/etc/inet/bootptab` file, packages it, and sends it to the requesting client.

When the client receives the information, it self-configures to the assigned IP address, the assigned host name, the router addresses, and so on. It also notes in its memory the pathname of the bootfile for subsequent retrieval. Before proceeding to retrieve the bootfile, the client goes through verifying that the assigned IP address is uniquely its own. It does this by sending several ARP broadcasts (in the form of `ping` messages). If no other workstation claims the address, the client establishes its ownership of the address.

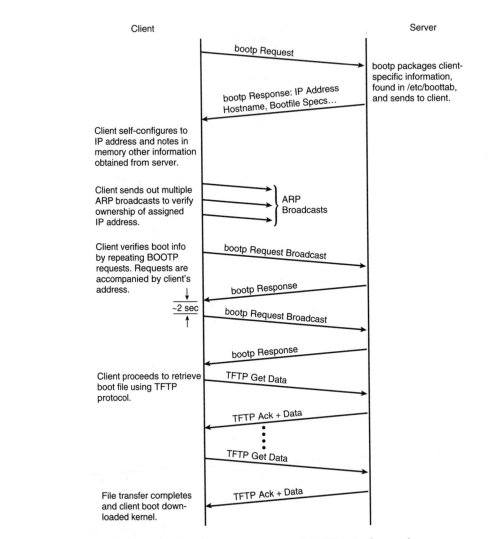

Figure 14.3. *Laddergram depiction of events pertaining to a BOOTP-assisted remote boot process.*

The client also verifies that the information that was obtained earlier is indeed the correct information. It does this by sending the server a directed boot request message (as opposed to the broadcast message it sent at the outset of the boot process). If the information thus obtained matches the information sent earlier, the client proceeds to the phase of retrieving the bootfile from the server. As in RARP's case, here too the client employs the TFTP protocol for handling the file transfer process.

On completion of the TFTP transfer of the bootfile, the file is booted to bring up the system.

/etc/inet/bootptab Configuration Database

As mentioned earlier, `bootpd` references a configuration database maintained in the `/etc/inet/bootptab` file when responding to `bootp` requests. One entry pertaining to each client is maintained in the database, which is labeled after the client's `hostname`. All the information needed by the client is maintained in this database. Following is the syntax of the `/etc/inet/bootptab` file:

```
hostname:tg=value...:tg=value...:tg=value...
```

In this syntax, `hostname` is the name of a `bootp` client, and `tg` is a two-character tag symbol. Tag symbols serve as constants assigned values describing resources that this `bootp` client might need in order to boot properly. Table 14.1 provides a complete listing of currently supported tag symbols and a description of the resource each can be assigned.

Table 14.1. Tag symbol list and description of information each symbol is assigned. See the manual pages of your system for details.

Tag	Description
bf	Pathname of the bootfile
bs	Bootfile size in 512-byte blocks
cs	Space-separated list of cookie servers
ds	Space-separated list of DNS servers
gw	Space-separated list of routers
ha	`bootp` client hardware address
hd	Bootfile home directory
hn	Host name to send
ht	Client hardware type (it can assume the value `ether` for Ethernet, `ieee802` for IEEE 802.3 Ethernet, `tr` or `token-ring` for Token-ring, and so on)
im	Space-separated list of impress servers
ip	Client IP address
lg	Space-separated list of log servers
lp	Space-separated list of LPR servers
ns	Space-separated list of IEN-116 name servers
rl	Space-separated list of resource location protocol servers
sm	Client subnet mask
tc	Table continuation
to	Time offset in seconds from UTC
ts	Space-separated list of time servers
vm	Vendor magic cookie selector

Only the most pertinent tag symbols will be touched on here. For more information, check your vendor's documentation.

As shown in Table 14.1, a client can obtain information from the boot server including its (the client's) IP address, lists of gateway addresses, DNS name servers, subnet mask, print and time servers, and bootfiles. It should be emphasized that a client might not need all the information described in this table.

In some environments, BOOTP is used to configure the client for network support only. In this case, there is no need for a bootfile, because the client might have its own local disk with UNIX installed on it. Such a client can therefore send a BOOTP broadcast requesting an IP address for itself and another for the default router only.

Except for two exceptions, the order in which the tag symbols can be arranged is immaterial to bootpd. The exceptions are that (1) the host name label must always be the first in the entry, and (2) the ht (hardware type) tag must always precede the ha (hardware address) tag.

Following is a sample entry pertaining to client artist on network 100.0.0.0:

```
artist:ht=ether:ha:0080c7440d7b:ip=100.0.0.15:sm=255.0.0.0:gw=100.0.0.1:ds=100.0.0.3:
```

When a server receives a bootp request from client artist, it is going to match the MAC address of the client with the value assigned to tag ha. Using this entry, the server packages all the information it contains in a BOOTP response message and sends the package to the client. As you can see, the entry includes only the information necessary for the client to self-configure for network support, because no bootfile specifications are included.

To include bootfile specifications, if client artist requires remote boot support, you should use the hd, bf, and bs tag symbols. hd specifies the home directory of the bootfile for that client, bf specifies the pathname of the bootfile, and bs specifies its size. The bf tag can specify a full pathname or a pathname relative to the home directory specified in the hd tag. Following is an example of a bootfile specification in an /etc/inet/bootptab entry:

```
artist:ht=ether:ha:0080c7440d7b:ip=100.0.0.15:sm=255.0.0.0: \
gw=100.0.0.1:ds=100.0.0.3:hd=/usr/boot:bf=boot.artist:bs=auto:
```

According to this entry, the full pathname of the bootfile specific to client artist is /usr/boot/boot.artist. Notice how instead of the bs tag being set to the size of the bootfile, it was set to auto. An auto setting forces the booptd daemon to calculate the size of the bootfile—a convenient feature.

There are quite a few parameters that all clients or a subset of the clients might have in common. Examples of these configuration parameters include the subnet mask, the default gateway, and the DNS name server. To save the tedium of having to enter these parameters in every client's entry, you can create template entries including all the parameters that are common to the clients. Using the tc (table continuation) tag, you can incorporate these settings into individual client entries.

Following is an example of such a template entry:

```
.default:sm=255.0.0.0: \ gw=100.0.0.1:ds=100.0.0.3:hd=/usr/
boot:bf=boot.artist:bs=auto:
```

Consequently, assuming that both clients artist and musical belong to the same subnet and have identical machine architectures, their client-specific entries in the /etc/inet/bootptab file become these:

```
artist:ht=ether:ha=0080c7440d7b:ip=100.0.0.15:tc=.default:
musical=ether:ha=001b3b21b260:ip=100.0.0.12:tc=.default:
```

By virtue of including tc=.default, bootpd expands both artist's and musical's entries to include the values assigned to the tag symbols defined in the .default entry.

You can include and use as many template entries as you want. On some systems, you can even create three-level template entries. The highest level would define parameters that apply to the entire network, the mid-level would define those that apply to clients sharing the same subnet, and the lowest level would be client-specific entries.

/etc/inet/bootptab is read by bootpd only once, at startup. Therefore, to force bootpd to read the configuration file, you should restart the inetd daemon after making changes to it. To restart inetd, enter the following two commands:

```
# sacadm -k -p inetd
# sacadm -s -p inetd
```

After inetd is restarted, bootpd will reread the /etc/inet/bootptab file upon receiving the first BOOTP request.

BOOTP Across Routers

One of RARP's major drawbacks is that it operates at the data link layer. This means that RARP requests and responses cannot traverse networks across routers. This limitation implies that to support diskless clients, you must bring up an RARP server on each segment that has such clients. BOOTP overcomes this limitation if the router separating the server from the clients is configurable to run what is known as a BOOTP relay agent.

Figure 14.4 illustrates what happens when a BOOTP relay agent (also called BOOTP forwarder) mediates communications between the client and the server. When brought up, the BOOTP relay agent listens to BOOTP request broadcasts on port 67. When it detects one, it includes the IP address of the interface on which the request was received in a special field in the BOOTP packet—the Gateway IP Address field. It then forwards the request *directly* to the BOOTP server.

The router's IP address serves two functions: (1) it makes the BOOTP server aware that the request is being forwarded, and (2) it prepares the BOOTP server to respond with a directed (*not* a broadcast) response. When the BOOTP server receives the request, it fetches the client-pertinent information, packages it, and sends the message back directly to the relay agent, not the client. The relay agent receives the response message and forwards it to the client.

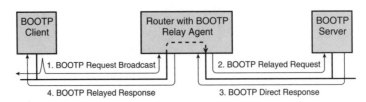

Figure 14.4. *BOOTP request/response interaction across a router supporting the BOOTP relay agent.*

Although mainly intended for deployment on routers, BOOTP relay agents can be implemented on hosts on the same network as the BOOTP clients as well, as shown in Figure 14.5. In a situation like this one, the relay agent still listens on port 67 (the `bootps` server port) to pick BOOTP requests. Whenever it receives a request, the relay agent still changes the Gateway IP Address in the request to its own IP address. It then forwards the packet to the router separating it from the server for direct delivery to the BOOTP server.

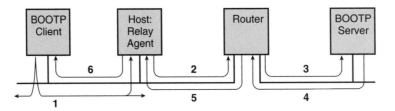

1) BOOTP Request.
2) Relay agent forwards request to router for delivery to BOOTP server.
3) Router delivers to BOOTP server.
4) BOOTP server sends response message to router for delivery to relay agent.
5) Router delivers to relay agent directly.
6) Relay agent sends response to client.

Figure 14.5. *BOOTP relay agents implemented on hosts on the same network as the BOOTP clients.*

It is possible as well that the server is several hops away from the BOOTP relay agent. Yet this should not affect the message exchange between the relay agent and the server, because the exchange is based on unicast transmission—not a broadcast—involving the IP addresses of both the server and the relay agent.

Why would someone bring up a BOOTP relay agent on a host, not a router? Depending on the number of workstations relying on the relay agent, if it's implemented on a router, the router might get too busy processing BOOTP requests and responses to perform its main function (that is, the routing function) efficiently. Some might think, "But the router is going to still be involved forwarding packets back and forth between the relay agent and the server." Although this is indeed the case, routing involves processing packets at the IP level, where relaying BOOTP requests/responses involves UDP and the process layer. Thus, more demand is placed on system resources.

Anonymous FTP Server

With the phenomenal growth in the popularity of the Internet, many of the organizations began offering a wide range of Internet services, including the distribution of software, information, technical support, and other services. Anonymous FTP access was among the earliest methods used to offer such services on the Internet.

Anonymous FTP access provides users who do not have an account with the FTP server with the ability to establish an FTP session with that server. Users use anonymous for user name, and their real identity for the password, as shown in the following sample connection session:

```
$ ftp netrix.unicom.com
Connected to netrix.unicom.com.
220 netrix FTP server (UNIX(r) System V Release 4.2) ready.
Name (netrix.unicom.com:salim): anonymous
331 Guest login ok, send ident as password.
Password:
230 Guest login ok, access restrictions apply.
Remote system type is UNIX.
Using binary mode to transfer files.
ftp> ls
200 PORT command successful.
150 Opening ASCII mode data connection for /bin/ls (0 bytes).
total 0
drwxr-xr-x   2 root      sys            96 Mar  7 11:37 bin
drwxr-xr-x   2 root      sys            96 Mar  8 11:28 dev
drwxr-xr-x   2 root      sys            96 Mar  8 11:28 etc
drwxrwxrwx   2 root      sys            96 Mar  7 11:41 pub
drwxr-xr-x   3 root      sys            96 Mar  7 11:42 usr
226 Transfer complete.
ftp> quit
221 Goodbye.
$
```

After a user is connected, she can transfer files from and to the FTP server. As shown in the preceding ftp session, the user can easily be misled to believe that she is at the root of the file system.

For reasons having to do with security, ftp designers included in the ftpd daemon the feature of forcing it to change the root of the file system to the home directory of a special account. The account name is ftp. Assuming that the home directory of the ftp account is /home/ftp, then whenever a user establishes an anonymous access session with an FTP server, the ftpd daemon uses chroot to change the root of the file system to /home/ftp for that user.

Setting Up an FTP Server for Anonymous Access

Setting up an FTP server for anonymous access involves creating the ftp user account and creating a minimized file system under the home directory of ftp. The directory must contain the necessary file system resources that make anonymous access functional. In particular, the following directories must be created:

◆ $HOME/etc

This directory must contain copies of /etc/passwd, /etc/group, and /etc/netconfig databases. The passwd and group databases are used to display user names and group names when files are listed. The netconfig file serves as a system file used to maintain information about networks connected to the host and available to the system. This database as well as the special files $HOME/dev/tcp and $HOME/dev/zero are necessary for the establishment of the data socket over which data will be exchanged. If any of $HOME/etc/netconfig, $HOME/dev/tcp, or $HOME/dev/zero is missing, the user ends up with the Can't create data socket (0.0.0.0,20): Bad file number error message upon attempting to exchange data with the server, as shown in the following listing:

```
$ ftp netrix.unicom.com
Connected to netrix.unicom.com.
220 netrix FTP server (UNIX(r) System V Release 4.2)
ready.
Name (netrix.unicom.com:salim): anonymous
331 Guest login ok, send ident as password.
Password:
230 Guest login ok, access restrictions apply.
Remote system type is UNIX.
Using binary mode to transfer files.
ftp> ls
200 PORT command successful.
425 Can't create data socket (0.0.0.0,20): Bad file
number.
ftp>
```

◆ $HOME/dev

Contains both special files /dev/tcp and /dev/zero. Both files have to be created using the mknod command as explained later.

◆ $HOME/bin

Contains a copy of the /usr/bin/ls command to allow ftp users to list directory contents.

◆ $HOME/usr/lib

Contains a copy of the /usr/lib/libc.so.1 library of routines.

◆ $HOME/pub

Short for public, is where files made accessible to anonymous users are usually kept. Subject to security constraints, users might also be able to upload files to this directory or any of the subdirectories below it.

Here is a self-explanatory depiction of the command sequence to follow to set up an anonymous FTP server:

```
# useradd -d /home/ftp -m ftp
# chmod 555 /home/ftp
# chown root /home/ftp
# mkdir /home/ftp/etc
# mkdir /home/ftp/dev
# mkdir /home/ftp/bin
# mkdir /home/ftp/usr
# mkdir /home/ftp/usr/lib
```

```
# mkdir /home/ftp/pub
# chmod 777 /home/ftp/pub
# cp /etc/passwd /home/ftp/etc
# chmod 444 /home/ftp/etc/passwd
# cp /etc/group /home/ftp/etc
# chmod 444 /home/ftp/etc/group
# cp /etc/netconfig /ftp/etc
# cp /usr/bin/ls /home/ftp/bin
# chmod 111 /home/ftp/bin/ls
# cd /home/ftp/dev
# major='ld -og /dev/tcp ¦ cut -f1 -d, ¦ cut -f7 -d" "'
# minor='ls -og /dev/tcp ¦ cut -f8 -d" "'
# mknod tcp c $majorr $minor
# major='ld -og /dev/zero ¦ cut -f1 -d, ¦ cut -f7 -d" "'
# minor='ls -og /dev/zero ¦ cut -f8 -d" "'
# mknod zero c $majorr $minor
```

By the end of this procedure, you should be able to establish an anonymous ftp session with the server. Also, the server will default the user to the /home/ftp directory and make it look as though it's the root of the file system.

Network Print Service

Network print service allows for the sharing of a limited number of printers among network users. Hence, by implementing network print services, a user no longer will be limited to the type and quality of printer tied directly to his machine. The user potentially has access to a range of printers and associated print qualities that exist on the network. From an investment perspective, network print service is a money saver compared to local printing, which requires that each host have a dedicated printer.

Figure 14.6 illustrates the concept of network printing. There are two network printers, quality (a laser printer attached to host saturn) and rough (a dot-matrix printer attached to host pixel), that network users should be able to print to regardless of where they are logged into. A user logged into host jade, for example, should be able to print to both printers.

Furthermore, the user should be able to print by issuing the same commands as he would have issued had the printers been directly attached to the host he is logged in to. This task involves configuring both the client host (for example, host jade) and the print server hosts (that is, where the network printers are attached) to allow enough level of interaction between them that user transparency in accessing remote print resources is achieved.

User transparency is achieved by creating print destinations (that is, queues) on both client hosts and server hosts. Granting access to a remote printer requires that an association be made between the local (client) print destination and the remote print destination. In Figure 14.6, for example, to allow users access to both remote printers quality and rough, the LP print service on host jade is configured to support two local print destinations, laser and daisy. Furthermore, the print service on host jade is configured to associate print destination laser with print destination quality on host saturn. Likewise, print destination daisy is associated with rough on host pixel.

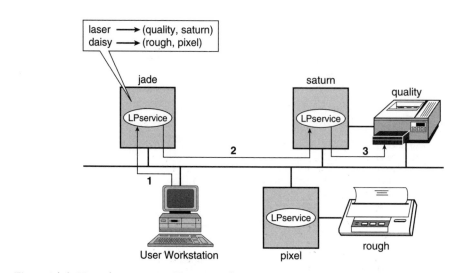

Figure 14.6. *Network print service. Host* jade *redirects print requests, sent to its printer destinations, to LP print service destinations* quality *and* rough *defined on host* saturn.

A user on host jade prints to printer quality by entering the following command:

```
$ lp -d laser filename
```

Notice how the user addresses the local printer name. The print service on host jade, if configured properly, looks up its associations to determine that it must send the print job to host saturn. The print service request must specify quality as the name of the printer to handle the job.

This section describes the underlying concepts and mechanisms for setting up the network print service. It is assumed that the reader is already familiar with UNIX print services. Also, it is assumed that the user is familiar with Service Access Facility (SAF), which was introduced in UNIX SVR4 as the means for configuring and administering access to local physical resources and network resources.

Configuring the Print Server

Configuring the print server involves the following steps:

1. Create local print service.
2. Create the listen port service (refer to Appendix A, "Service Access Facility," for information about SAF).
3. Register clients with the LP print service.

Creating Local Print Service

To set up and configure the LP print service, you follow the same steps you would normally follow if the printer were to be accessed locally. To start with, verify that the needed resources are available. Namely, verify that there is a free physical port (serial or parallel, depending on the type of printer interface), that there is an lp login on the host, and that the daemon lpsched (the print scheduler) is running on the system. If the lp login does not exist, create one using the sysadm utility or useradd command. To check on lpsched, enter the following command:

```
# ps -ef | grep lpsched
```

If lpsched is not reported as running, you should make it run by issuing the following command:

```
# /usr/lib/lp/lpsched
```

Next, using the /usr/lib/lpadmin command, create the print destinations. To create print destination quality corresponding to a PostScript printer on host saturn, for example, enter the following command:

```
# /usr/lib/lpadmin -p quality -v /dev/lp1 -T PS -b -IPS -mPS
```

This command creates print destination quality and defines the device special file /dev/lp1 as the file to take care of printing to the printer attached to the parallel port. Refer to the manual pages for details on the lpadmin command.

For security reasons, disable direct access to the /dev/lp1 port by issuing the following commands:

```
# chown lp /dev/lp1
# chmod 600 /dev/lp1
```

The first command changes ownership of the special file /dev/lp1 to login lp. The second one changes permissions on the file such that only login lp (that is, the scheduler) can write to the /dev/lp1 file.

You need to execute two more commands to render the printer accessible to users local to host saturn for the time being. Enter

```
# accept quality
```

to allow lpshed to accept print jobs destined for quality, and

```
# enable quality
```

to logically turn on printing to that destination.

In the following two subsections, the steps to render the printers shareable with other hosts and users on the network are depicted.

Creating *listen* Port Service

Being an across-the-wire service, network printing is accessible only via a `listen` port service as defined by SAF. Very briefly, a `listen` port service lies at the bottom of the SAF hierarchy of port control processes. It defines a process that controls and monitors access to applications and other network services. Another type of port service defined by SAF is the `ttymon` port service, which defines processes that control and monitor access to the local physical resources, such as serial ports.

Port service processes are themselves controlled by mid-level management processes called port monitors. Two port monitors are defined: `listen` and `ttymon`. Whereas `listen` controls port services delivering network access to services such as printing and remote file-sharing capabilities, `ttymon` controls processes running on local physical resources. Unless the port monitor process is running, access to associated resources is not possible. Finally, at the top of the hierarchy is the `sac` (service access controller) process. There is only one `sac` per system, and it is responsible for controlling and managing the mid-level processes (that is, port monitors). Figure 14.7 illustrates the hierarchy and the relationship between the various components of SAF.

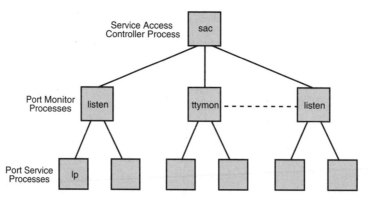

Figure 14.7. *Hierarchy of Service Access Facility (SAF) architecture.*

To bring up a print server on a host, the host must have an active `listen` port monitor and at least one `listen` port service. Normally, when UNIX is installed, your system is automatically configured to support a `listen` port monitor with port monitor tag `tcp`. Also, this port monitor is configured to support two print server-associated port services, with one taking care of System V clients and the other taking care of BSD clients. If they exist on your system, you do not have to bother creating and configuring them. To check for their existence, enter this:

```
# pmadm -l -t listen
PMTAG           PMTYPE          SVCTAG          FLGS ID     SCHEME    <PMSPECIFIC>
 .
 .
 .
tcp             listen          0               -    root   -         \x00020ACE
➥6400010000000000000000 - c - /usr/lib/saf/nlps_server #NLPS SERVER
tcp             listen          lp              -    root   -         - - p -
➥/var/spool/lp/fifos/listenS5 #
 .
 .
 .
```

Unless the listing on your screen includes the lines just shown, you must create one or both of the port services yourself. Following is what you would enter on host saturn to create the necessary print port service:

```
# pmadm -a -p tcp -s lp -i root -v 'nlsadmin -V' -m 'nlsadmin -o /var/spool/lp/fifos/
↪listenS5'
```

This command creates a port with service tag lp. Through this port, the listen tcp port monitor listens on the network for print requests coming from System V hosts only. Consult your manual pages for more information about SAF and SAF-associated commands and options, or Appendix A, "Service Access Facility," for a refresher on SAF.

To invoke the new port service, you should restart the port monitor controlling it. Following is the command needed to restart the tcp port monitor, which in turn starts the newly created port service lp:

```
# sacadm -x -p tcp
```

Registering Clients with LP Print Service

The last step in setting up the print server involves registering all the clients that the print server is authorized to service. Unless a client is registered with the print server, the client will have its print requests discarded.

Use the lpsystem command to register a client with the print server. lpsystem also enables you to define the communication parameters binding on the connection maintained between both the client and the server after the connection is established. Clients and associated parameters are kept track of in the /etc/lp/Systems database.

Following is the syntax of the lpsystem command:

```
lpsystem [ -t type ] [ -T timeout ] [-R retry ] [ -y "comment" ] clientname
```

In this syntax,

-t type specifies the type of the client; s5 stands for System V and BSD stands for Berkeley System Distribution.

-T timeout specifies how long the print server should wait after receiving the last print request before dropping the connection. timeout can be 0, n, or N, in which N is the number of minutes the connection idles. If timeout is set to 0, the connection is dropped as soon as the connection idles. If n is specified instead, the connection is never dropped after being established. For occasional printing, set this parameter to 0. If the frequency with which the client sends print jobs to this print server is high, you'd be better off setting timeout to n (that is, never disconnect). This way, both hosts will be saved the CPU time and the bandwidth that are wasted when the link must be relinquished and reestablished for every new service request.

-R *retry* specifies in minutes the time to wait before reestablishing an abnormally disrupted connection.

-y *"comment"* can be any meaningful comment.

clientname is the name of the host being authorized for the print service.

In the following example, host jade is registered on host saturn as a print service client (see Figure 14.6):

```
# lpsystem -t s5 -T n  jade
```

Consequently, whenever host jade is configured properly, it can start sending host saturn print jobs that it receives from users.

Configuring the Client

Setting up the client is very similar to setting up the server, except that when you create the printer destination, using the lpadmin command, you must associate the local printer destination with the names of the remote print queue and the host serving as print server.

Again, the first step is to verify that the client host has its listen port monitor configured to support network printing services. The following pmadm command does just that:

```
# pmadm -l -p tcp
PMTAG           PMTYPE          SVCTAG          FLGS ID      SCHEME   <PMSPECIFIC>
tcp             listen          0               -    root    -        \x00020ACE
➡6400010000000000000000 - c - /usr/lib/saf/nlps_server #
tcp             listen          lp              -    root    -        - - p -
➡/var/spool/lp/fifos/listenS5 #
tcp             listen          lpd             -    root    -        \x00020203
➡6400010000000000000000 - p - /var/spool/lp/fifos/listenBSD #
```

The first two entries pertain to System V client support, whereas the last one pertains to BSD client support. If any of these entries is missing, you should create the associated port service using pmadm.

Following are the three pmadm commands that might be needed to set up the listen port services properly for network printing:

```
# pmadm -a -p tcp -s lp -i root -v'nlsadmin -V' \
-m 'nlsadmin -o /var/spool/lp/fifos/listen5'

# pmadm -a -p tcp -s 0 -i root -v'nlsadmin -V' \
-m'nlsadmin -o /usr/lib/saf/nlps_server \
-A "\x02000ACE6400000100000000000000000"` -y "NLPS SERVER"

# pmadm -a -p tcp -s lpd -i root -v 'nlsadmin -V' \
-m 'nlsadmin -o /var/spool/lp/fifos/listenBSD \
-A /"x00203640000010000000000000000000"
```

The last pmadm command is required only if you are supporting BSD clients. Otherwise, you can ignore it.

The bold part of the hexadecimal address following the -A option in the preceding pmadm commands corresponds to the hexadecimal equivalent of the client IP address. On the author's system, x64000001 is the hex equivalent of 100.0.0.1. Hence, on different systems, this part should be different. Following is a time-saving tip that enables you to find this piece of information without the hassle of doing manual conversions.

Using the lpsystem -A command, you get the following response on your screen:

```
# lpsystem -A
020002033640000010000...
```

The eight digits starting with the 10th digit from the left correspond to the hex equivalent of the IP address of that system.

Next, you should create the local printer destination and have it associated with the print destination on the remote print server. To that, enter the following command:

```
# lpadmin -p clientprinter -s remote_printer!print_server
```

clientprinter specifies the name of the local print destination about to be created.

remote_printer identifies the name of the remote printer to which print jobs must be sent by lpsched whenever it receives user print jobs destined to the clientprinter destination.

print_server is the name of the host configured for network print services, and where the remote_printer destination belongs.

Hence, applying what has been explained to the scenario depicted in Figure 14.6, following is the lpadmin command that must be invoked on host jade (the client) to print to printer quality on host saturn:

```
# lpadmin -p laser -s quality!saturn
```

Three more simple steps are required before users logged in to the client can use network print services. To start with, the client must register the remote server with its print service as discussed in the preceding section. Next, the local printer destination must be allowed to accept print jobs. Finally, printing to the local print destination must be enabled. Applying these actions to host jade, following are the remaining commands to execute on that host:

```
# lpsystem -t s5 -T n saturn
# enable laser
# accept laser
```

Consequently, a user logged in to host jade can now send the file cookie.recipe to printer quality on host saturn by simply entering the following lp command:

```
# lp -p laser cookie.recipe
```

Notice how the user uses the name of the local printer destination, as though the printer is attached to the host he is logged into.

Summary

The network administrator has available various special services that could help in improving resource availability and ease of administration. Among these services, the TCP/IP protocol suite provides two methods (RARP and BOOTP protocols) for a client/dataless workstation to determine its network configuration parameters, and remotely booting the kernel from other servers on the network.

Both RARP and BOOTP require the client to have a PROM embedding a compacted implementation of TCP/IP protocols. After its network interface is configured, the client relies on TFTP for the purpose of transferring an image of the boot kernel from the server to its memory.

RARP suffers from major drawbacks, including the incapability to traverse networks across routers. And it is limited in the information it provides to the client. BOOTP remedies these drawbacks by having enough space in the packet to include in the response packet more than just the IP address for the client. It also, with the cooperation of so-called BOOTP Relay Agents, allows clients and servers separated by routers to exchange BOOTP request/response messages.

To enable users to make their resources publicly available, TCP/IP offers an "anonymous FTP" user access. It gives off-site users access to specially designated areas on the FTP server without entering a valid password.

Network printing has always been one of the main reasons why people have wanted networks. Network printing enables users to share a pool of printers with varying features and qualities without necessarily dedicating a resource to individuals. LP network print service setup and administration is achievable via the Service Access Facility (a unified interface for the common management of physical local and network resources).

CHAPTER

Network Troubleshooting and Performance Tuning

Introduction

Earlier chapters dealt with network concepts and configuration issues. The concern was how to set up a network and make it operational. This chapter deals with the problems as they are encountered during the post-installation and mature phases of the network. Being dynamic, network environments can be challenging to troubleshoot and maintain at a reasonable level of performance.

The diversity of network problems leaves the network administrator with no choice but to learn, and master, a comprehensive set of troubleshooting tools, and to gain good troubleshooting skills. This chapter presents you with the minimum set of these tools. It begins with introductory notions about troubleshooting methodology and approach.

Troubleshooting TCP/IP

Troubleshooting TCP/IP networks demands both a good understanding of the protocol suites and a methodology that builds on this understanding, using it to quickly narrow down the problems encountered on the network. Coupled with the methodology is the identification and skillful use of the TCP/IP diagnostic tools. A solid understanding of the interaction of various protocols is essential.

Troubleshooting Methodology

Troubleshooting, in general, passes through three phases of activity:

1. Gathering information.
2. Developing and executing a problem-specific troubleshooting plan.
3. Documenting the problem.

Information gathering involves two aspects: documentation and user-reported complaints and messages.

Documenting the Network Layout

Maintaining an up-to-date document about the network setup is a vital part of the troubleshooting process. Without documents describing the physical and logical layout of the network, trouble-shooting a network can become a frustrating exercise.

The physical layout should include the actual cabling scheme of the network, including floor plans showing the exact locations of user workstations, routers, bridges, and servers. The logical layout, on the other hand, normally includes information about servers, including the location of each server, its host name, its IP address, the purpose it serves, the configuration it supports, the user group that relies on the services of this server, and any dependencies this server might have on other servers. Having those details at your disposal eliminates lots of legwork, guessing, and checking, thus contributing to less downtime and a higher level of user satisfaction.

The documentation should also include details about the history of changes made to the network. Any change is worth documenting. Changes such as network segmentation, address changes, netmask changes, and addition or removal of servers are examples of what the document should cover. The troubleshooting history of the network should also be included. More than half of the problems encountered on a network are repetitive. Documenting those problems, and the solutions, provides a library of proven fixes that could be applied under similar circumstances in the future.

For these reasons, documentation should be regarded as a proactive exercise in troubleshooting networks. Developing the habit of documenting the network can quickly prove its worth, especially when having complete information would have reduced the time and effort involved in a repair.

Responding to Users

User-reported error messages and complaints are an important part of the information gathering process. Do not rely on secondhand information. You should be able to talk to the user directly and listen to what she has to say. If possible, go to the user's workstation and ask the user to try recreating the problem. It is much more accurate to see the problem and record the corresponding detailed error messages as they appear on the screen. While trying to accommodate the user's feedback on the nature of the problem, you should place a heavier emphasis on the objective information displayed.

A rule of thumb for most network troubleshooters to follow is to ask what has changed since the last time the network was well behaved. This question should not be difficult to answer if you maintain good documentation. Often, a slight uncoordinated change in a user's workstation, a router, or any other network service configuration lies behind abnormalities that did not exist before the change was made.

Developing a Troubleshooting Plan

Now that you have all the basic information you need, you can get started with the troubleshooting exercise. Effective troubleshooting, however, requires developing a plan for attacking the situation.

Although the troubleshooting plan you develop should be specific to the situation in question, it should aim at methodically narrowing in on the extent of the problem (that is, is it a user-specific, user group-specific, or network-wide problem?) and the network layers where you suspect the problem is likely to be (that is, is it at the physical, network access, internet, transport, or process layer?). Both objectives can be achieved by extensive testing and recreation of the reported problem.

Narrowing In On Problems

Recreating the problem should initially aim at isolating the extent to which the problem is affecting the user community. You need to find out whether the problem affects all users on the network, a group of users, or only one user. You can reach this conclusion by trying to recreate the problem on more than one or two workstations. The spread of the problem dictates the tools and the methodology you need in order to figure out the solution.

A problem affecting one user, for example, is likely to be something the user is doing wrong, or a configuration problem on his workstation. Consequently, using the proper troubleshooting tools, your efforts should be focused at the user's workstation level. This should not mean that the workstation is the only place to look for the bug. The bug might be due to a change made on the network that affects this particular user only (for example, duplicating the IP address of the workstation on a management hub—not an uncommon problem).

Using the proper troubleshooting tools (discussed in the next section), you should be able to further narrow in on the affected layers in the communication process. This helps focus your attention on that layer and the associated configuration (or misconfiguration) that might be adversely affecting the network. Nothing short of a solid understanding of TCP/IP will help you in this phase of the exercise. It requires the methodical testing of the layers, starting with the physical layer and walking through the layers, one at a time. Layer testing normally involves more than the "problematic" workstation. It can also include the servers, the routers, and the physical wiring connecting them.

A problem affecting a group of users dictates examining the factors along which those users are aligned. You might find, for example, that only users on a particular segment of the network are affected. In this case, you narrow the search to that particular segment. If, instead, the members of the identified group belong to different segments, they might be logically aligned to draw on a common network resource. The next step would be to find out the service they share exclusively, and figure out ways of resolving the problems pertinent to it.

As troubleshooting evolves, you should take notes to keep track of the observations you have made. Regularly reexamine your notes for clues and guidance. While doing so, never dismiss what might sound trivial or close your mind to an experience that might seem irrelevant. When you're armed with a solid understanding of TCP/IP, troubleshooting networks is primarily based on insightful observation and accounting for the *seemingly* "unrelated" and "insignificant" events. Often, an observation that was dismissed early in the troubleshooting process has provided the necessary clues about the nature of the problem.

Whenever the problem is resolved and the solution is identified, you should update your documentation to include a description of the problem encountered and a thorough depiction of the solution. The underlying rationale is twofold: (1) you keep track of the changes and problems, providing guidance when similar situations arise, and (2) independent of how thoroughly you test the solution, in some instances the solution itself becomes the origin of future problems. In such cases, proper documentation helps shed light on the suitability of the solution, in the context of the new and related problems.

TCP/IP Diagnostic Tools

As noted earlier, troubleshooting a TCP/IP-related problem requires a walk through the network layers in the hope that the culprit layer can be identified for subsequent resolution. Walking through the layers requires investigating different aspects at each layer. Because no single tool has these capabilities for all layers, UNIX provides different diagnostic commands matching the layer undergoing investigation. Table 15.1 lists the commonly used UNIX diagnostic commands in association with the categories of problem areas that are normally encountered on the network.

Table 15.1. A categorized listing of commonly used TCP/IP diagnostic tools.

Problem Category	Command Set
Reachability/Routing	ping
	arp
	ripquery
	traceroute
	netstat
	ifconfig
NFS-Related	rpcinfo
	nfsstat
	nfsping
	df
	showmount
DNS-Related	nslookup
	whois
	dig
TCP Connection-Related	trpt
	netstat

Many of the commands in this table were explained in previous chapters. In this chapter, they will be reintroduced in the context of diagnosing and troubleshooting TCP/IP networks. Some of the commands are included for information only and will not be explained.

Troubleshooting Reachability/Routing Problems

Reachability-related problems are normally manifested by the inability of the user to establish a connection, such as an ftp or telnet session, with other hosts on the network. Depending on the origin, these problems might exhibit themselves permanently or intermittently. A particular problem on the network can affect one host, a few hosts, or all hosts.

The following subsections will touch on some of the most common reachability-related problems. The purpose is twofold: (1) to introduce the tools required to troubleshoot situations and (2) to walk you through some of troubleshooting techniques you might need in real-life scenarios. Some of the problems presented in this chapter are based on real-life situations that the author faced at client sites.

Testing for Reachability

Whenever a connection-related problem is suspected, ping is the command you should use for a preliminary testing of reachability with remote hosts.

In its simplest form, ping takes the host name for an argument, as in the following example:

```
# ping jade
jade is alive
```

ping uses the ICMP protocol ECHO REQUEST to elicit an ICMP ECHO RESPONSE from a target remote host. A successful attempt is signaled by printing the *hostname* is alive message on the standard output. Otherwise, ping yields either the ping: unknown *hostname* message or the ping: no answer from *hostname* message. The first message implies a problem in resolving the host name to its IP address. The second implies a reachability problem—possibilities are physical failure, a routing problem, or the target host being down. If ping returns successfully, you can conclude that the problem has nothing to do with the lower layers. Instead, you should be looking for the problem in the higher layers—that is, the process/application layer protocols such as TELNET and FTP, depending on the nature of the failing service.

If you check the target host and it is not down, and ping cannot reach it, you should start looking for a physical failure or misconfiguration error along the path connecting the user's workstation to the target host. A good place to start is the network configuration of the user's workstation, using the ifconfig command.

Using ifconfig, information such as the IP address, netmask, and broadcast address can be verified, as well as the status of the interface.

Following is an example of using ifconfig for verifying the parameters for which the interface is configured:

```
# ifconfig el30
el30: flags=23<UP,BROADCAST,NOTRAILERS>
    inet 150.1.0.1 netmask ffff0000 broadcast 150.1.255.255
```

According to this output, the interface el30 is assigned the IP address 150.1.0.1, the netmask is 255.255.0.0, and the broadcast address is 150.1.255.255. Also, note that the interface is marked UP and is operational. You usually need ifconfig whenever you suspect that the interface is misconfigured with a duplicate IP address, wrong broadcast address, or wrong netmask. See Chapter 9, "Installing and Configuring TCP/IP," for a detailed treatment of ifconfig.

A misconfigured interface can give rise to intermittent, or permanent, communications problems. These will be exhibited in the form of an incapability to reach other hosts on the network, or timing out an already established connection.

If in the preceding example all the IP parameters were valid, yet you find that the interface is marked DOWN, then you should suspect the problem to be of a hardware nature local to the user's workstation, or somewhere in the cabling connecting it to the backbone or to the wiring concentrator. If your network is cabled using 10BASE-T wiring specifications, checking for the defective cabling component becomes a simple task. It involves replacing the cable from the user workstation to the RJ-45 connector, and the patch panel cable, one at a time. If nothing works, try connecting the workstation through an alternative circuit. The problem might well be in the RJ-45 connector itself. If this fix does not work, check the network interface. The quickest way to do this is to swap the network interface with another one that you know will work.

Aside from these suspect areas, there are a few other trouble spots to check. These are duplicate addresses, inconsistent subnet masks on the network, inconsistent broadcast addresses, and routing configuration problems.

Duplicate IP Addresses

Duplicate IP addresses have the effect of intermittently slowing an already established connection, timing it out, and disrupting it.

Remember that when a workstation wants to engage in data exchange with another workstation, or server, it first issues an ARP request that queries the network for the MAC address of the target server (see Chapter 4 for a detailed treatment of MAC addresses). The ARP request must carry the IP address of the target host. All hosts on the network pick up the ARP request packet and process it. Only one host, with the matching IP address, is supposed to return an ARP response packet including its MAC address. After the MAC address becomes available, the originating host proceeds to the packet exchange phase with the target host. To save bandwidth lost to ARPing, every host caches the ARP responses it obtains from the network.

To look up the contents of the ARP cache, enter the arp command with the -a option, as in the following example:

```
# arp -a
saturn (150.1.0.10) at 0:0:3:32:1:ad permanent
jade (100.0.0.2) at 0:0:c0:15:ad:18
pluto (150.1.2.1) at 0:0:c8:12:4:ab
```

This output does not mean that the host talked to only three other hosts. By default, ARP retains responses pertinent to hosts it talked to for the past four minutes only. Each entry includes the host name, IP address, and MAC address of that host.

What do duplicate IP addresses have to do with ARP? When an ARP request is sent out on the network, hosts with duplicate IP addresses will respond to that request if the IP address being queried matches the address being duplicated. If two hosts are sharing the same address, they will both respond, and the MAC that is received first by the ARP originator will be the one that is kept. Consequently, if the MAC address corresponds to an "impostor" host, the originating workstation won't be able to talk to the desired target server because the data frames will be carrying the wrong address.

If you suspect that duplicate IP addresses exist on the network, ask the user about the service or server he tries to access when the problem occurs. Most likely, the duplicate address is either that of the user's workstation or that of the host server to which access is being attempted. Consequently, you should be able to quickly determine which of the two IP addresses is being duplicated and redress the situation accordingly. The main tools you need in this exercise are the arp and the ping commands. arp helps you check the ARP cache, whereas ping is normally used to force ARP broadcasts.

To determine whether the IP address being duplicated belongs to the user's workstation, physically disconnect it from the network. Using another workstation, force an ARP request broadcast using the ping command. Be careful to use the IP address of the disconnected workstation, not its name, as the target host specification. If you get a response saying that *hostname* is alive, the next step would be to enter the arp -a command on the same workstation you used for pinging and note the MAC address of the responding host. That host must then be the one with the duplicate IP address. Those of you who maintain good documentation, including the MAC address corresponding to each host on the network, will be able to quickly determine the offending host and work on having it reconfigured for a different, and unique, IP address.

Should pinging fail in resulting in the *hostname* is alive message, you can conclude that the IP address being duplicated does not belong to the user's workstation. You can reconnect it to the network and proceed to the second phase of figuring out which host is duplicating the server's address.

Troubleshooting the server's address is a bit more tricky than troubleshooting the user workstation's address. This is because unless a downtime is scheduled during which users won't be provided access to the server, the server cannot be brought down or physically disconnected from the network. To determine whether the server's IP address is duplicated, and the MAC address of the host duplicating the address, attend to any workstation on the network and use it to perform the following tests:

1. Check the ARP cache table, using arp -a, for any reference to the IP address being investigated. If an entry exists, delete it. Deleting the entry ensures that a response obtained for an ARP request is cached. To do that, enter arp with the -d option. An example follows:

    ```
    # arp -a ¦ grep "100.0.0.10"
    pluto (100.0.0.10) at 0:0:c0:1a:b2:80

    # arp -d 100.0.0.10
    100.0.0.1 (100.0.0.10) deleted
    ```

2. Force an ARP request broadcast using the ping command. Again, use the IP address to denote the host, not its host name.

3. Check the ARP cache. You should be able to see an entry pertaining to the IP address being pinged. Note the corresponding MAC address, and compare it with that of the server. If the MAC addresses match, repeat the first two steps. You might have to recycle through them several times before a MAC address different from the server's is detected. Consequently, use the MAC address to track down the host supporting it, and take the necessary corrective measures to redress the situation to normal.

More About arp

When using arp -a to look up ARP's cache of IP-to-MAC address mappings, you might come across various types of status qualifiers—temporary, permanent, published, and incomplete—as in the following listing:

```
# arp -a
saturn (150.1.0.10) at 0:0:3:32:1:ad permanent published
jade (100.0.0.2) at 0:0:c0:15:ad:18 permanent
pluto (150.1.2.1) at 0:0:c8:12:4:ab
absent (169.22.45.2) at (incomplete)
```

If no status qualifier exists, the default is temporary. Temporary ARP entries are dynamically added to the host's cache by virtue of an ARP request/response exchange. These entries normally last four to five minutes before they're deleted.

An incomplete status is an indication of a failure to have the IP address resolved into a MAC address. This entry is normally removed after a few minutes.

An entry marked permanent implies that the entry has been added manually, and unless it's expressly deleted by the system administrator, it will stay in the ARP table. Normally, you would want to add entries pertaining to the hosts or servers that the user's workstation communicates with most often. This measure has the advantage of saving the bandwidth that would otherwise be lost to ARP request/response exchanges. Adding a permanent entry to the ARP cache takes the following form of the arp command:

```
# arp -s hostname MACaddress
```

For example, to permanently add the IP address-to-MAC mapping of host jade to the user's ARP cache, enter the following command:

```
# arp -s jade 0:0:c0:15:ad:18
```

An entry marked published qualifies the host to respond on behalf of the workstation whose IP address matches the one in this entry. In the preceding sample listing, the host includes a permanent published entry for host saturn. This means that this host is qualified to respond on behalf of saturn to ARP requests involving saturn's IP address. This is commonly adopted when the querying host and the target host belong to two different network segments separated by routers that are configured to suppress broadcasts. In this case, you designate a machine on each segment as an ARP server with the mandate of responding to ARP queries on behalf of hosts that are not attached to the same segment. To render this task manageable, arp can be forced to look up the contents of a file in which you can maintain all the published entries. The general format of the file is as shown here:

```
hostname MACaddress pub
```

Make sure that there is a matching entry for each host name in the /etc/hosts file.

To force arp to update the ARP cache using the contents of the file containing all the desired ARP mappings, enter the command including the -f option:

```
# arp -f filename
```

Consequently, when troubleshooting duplicate IP addresses, you should check the ARP files used to update the cache of ARP servers. They can potentially be the source of the duplication, or erroneous replies due to outdated data in the files.

Troubleshooting Routing Problems

If, after testing reachability from a user's workstation, you discover that you can randomly ping any host on the local network but not hosts on other networks across routers, the problem might be routing related.

Routing problems arise if any of the routing tables of communicating hosts, and intervening routers, is somehow corrupted or improperly set up. UNIX provides several simple-to-use, yet powerful tools to help in diagnosing and assessing routing-related errors and problems. The diagnostic command set includes netstat, ripquery, and traceroute, in addition to the basic connectivity-related commands such as ping, arp, and ifconfig, explained earlier in the chapter.

Figure 15.1 shows the layout of a network consisting of three local area networks (one Token-ring and two Ethernet) joined by routers R1 and R2. The Token-ring network connects the organizational network to the Internet via router R3. One day, I was called upon by the client authority to find out why users on LAN E1 were unable to reach the Internet while everybody else on LAN E2 and LAN TR1 had no such problem.

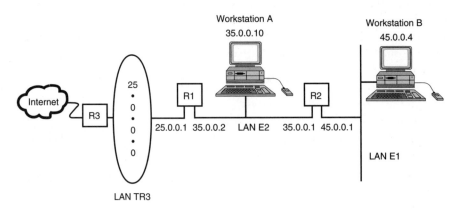

Figure 15.1. *Layout of an IP network that is experiencing communications difficulties.*

When you are faced with a similar situation (all users on one network segment are having the same problem) and you are new to the environment you are going to deal with, the first question that should come to mind is whether the users were able to connect to the Internet before this problem occurred. In my situation the answer was no, because this segment (LAN E1) was recently installed. To me, the answer immediately suggested a routing configuration error. The point is that asking the question helped me focus most of my energy and thoughts on tracking routing misconfiguration errors for subsequent elimination and correction. Otherwise, I would have followed other lines that would have wasted my time as well as the client's.

To start, I picked a workstation on LAN E1 and verified, using `netstat -r`, that the workstation's routing table maintained an entry for the default route. The default route was `45.0.0.1`, as illustrated here:

```
# netstat -r ¦ grep "45.0.0.1"
default                45.0.0.1          UG     0     0          ne2k0
```

What could I have done if the user's workstation did not have the default route configured in its routing table? I could have used the `route add` command as shown here:

```
# route add default 45.0.0.1 1
```

Refer to Chapter 4, "The Internet Layer and Routing," for a detailed examination of both commands.

Without being configured for the proper default route, the workstations on LAN E1 could not possibly communicate with the other networks beyond router R2. It is their only gateway to the outside world.

Next, using `ifconfig`, I verified the network interface configuration and verified that both the network interface in the workstation and the one in the router connecting to LAN E1 had the same network ID, netmask, and broadcast address. After I felt comfortable with the basic network configuration on the workstation, the next logical step was to carry out a few tests using `ping`. The idea was to determine how far `ping` can reach on the network. Initially, I `ping`ed a few hosts on the local network. There were no surprises. Next, I `ping`ed router R2's interfaces, `45.0.0.1` and `35.0.0.1`, without difficulty. Then I `ping`ed a workstation (workstation A, with the `35.0.0.1` address, in Figure 15.1) on LAN E2. Instead of getting the *hostname* is alive message, `ping` waited until it timed out and then put the no answer from *hostname* message on-screen.

The fact that the `35.0.0.1` interface responded to the `ping` command issued on the workstation implied that the problem lay somewhere beyond R2. If R2 was improperly configured, or if the forwarding of packets was somehow disabled, the workstation wouldn't have had its `ping` ARP request answered favorably. Furthermore, the failure of workstation B to get a response to its `ping` from workstation A confirmed that the problem was, at least partially, on LAN E2. The problem seemed to have something to do with the way routing was configured on workstation A and possibly all other workstations on the LAN E2. So I went to workstation A and, using `netstat -r`, looked up its routing table. This was the output:

```
# netstat -r
Routing tables
Destination     Gateway         Flags  Refs  Use    Interface
default         35.0.0.2        UG     0     0      ne2k0
35              35.0.0.10       U      1     61     ne2k0
```

A very simple routing table! According to it, packets destined anywhere on the network must be sent to router R1 at IP address 35.0.0.2. Of course, the next logical step is to check router R1's routing table to verify that R1 has the information necessary to reach LAN E1. What I would expect to see is an explicit route entry showing router R2 at address 35.0.0.1 as the route to LAN E1. Because R1 was, however, on a different floor, in addition to being a router box, not a UNIX host, I decided to use ripquery (see the following note for details on ripquery) from workstation A. To my surprise, ripquery never came back with the routing table information I was hoping to get. Upon calling the network administrator who takes care of the router, I was told that RIP (see Chapter 4) is being disabled on the router—a reason for ripquery not working properly. Unless RIP is active on the router or host being queried, RIP lookup requests issued by ripquery remain unanswered.

---

ripquery

The ripquery command enables the system administrator to query, from the local workstation, another host or router for its routing table. When issued, ripquery polls the target host for its routing table and displays it on the standard output. ripquery requires that the routing daemon (either routed or gated) be running on the host being queried. Otherwise, ripquery times out and exits silently. Here is an example of using ripquery to query host jade for its routing information:

```
# ripquery jade
84 bytes from jade(100.0.0.2):
       ???(198.53.235.1), metric 1
       ???(198.53.235.10), metric 1
       unicom(100.0.0.0), metric 1
       ny.unicom(198.53.237.0), metric 1
```

The output includes the number of bytes received from the remote host, as well as one entry per route that the host supports. Included in each entry is the route symbolic name if available (in the /etc/networks file), the route IP address, and the applicable metric.

The fact that RIP was disabled on R1 gave rise to the suspicion that R1 was not statically configured for route 45.0.0.0. Using a network management tool (you'll find more on network management systems in Chapter 16), I looked up the routing table and indeed found out that R1 had no route entry pertaining to LAN E1.

Do you see the problem? Whenever a workstation on LAN E1 tried to reach another workstation, or server, on LAN E2, its requests for service were able to cross R2 without difficulty. For the contacted host on LAN E2 to respond to the service request, it packaged its response in an IP packet and had it sent to the default router, which was found to be R1. While configured to support static routing, R1 was not configured to support the route to LAN E1. Upon receiving an IP packet from a host on LAN E2 that was destined to a host on LAN E1, R1 did not know what to do with it, and thus dropped it. Consequently, workstations on LAN E1 could not possibly hear from hosts they were trying to talk to on LAN E1 and LAN TR1, in addition to being unable to get onto the Internet.

To remedy the situation, all I had to do was install a static route to LAN E1 on router R1. This way, because all hosts on LAN E2 have router R1 defined as their default router, whenever any of them want to talk to another host on LAN E1, it delivers its IP packet to R2. This forces R2, in turn, to send an ICMP route redirect message to the sending host telling it to use R1 instead. Consequently, the host updates its routing table, as instructed by the ICMP route redirect message, and uses router R1 for future deliveries to hosts on LAN E1.

traceroute

Sometimes, you might be confronted with a routing problem involving too many routers separating two hosts. In this case, using the previous techniques will consume a lot of time, until you find where along the communication path the problem manifests itself. For this reason, and to help you quickly identify the trouble spot, UNIX comes equipped with the traceroute command.

traceroute, as the name implies, traces the route a data packet takes from one host to another on the network. Its output includes one line per router that the packet traverses. Included in each line is information about the hop count (that is, how far the reported router is from the workstation), the router name, the router IP address, and round-trip time in milliseconds. The maximum number of routers traceroute reports is 30.

To trace the route to a particular destination, you enter the traceroute command and the name of the target host, as in the following example:

```
# traceroute rome
```

Figure 15.2 illustrates how traceroute works. When invoked, traceroute issues up to 30 UDP packets, in sequential order, in which the first packet has its TTL field set to one (see Chapter 4 for details on TTL). Each subsequent UDP packet has its TTL field incremented by one. This means the first packet does not make it through any router. The first router that picks up the packet decrements TTL to zero. According to IP rules, the router ignores the packet (does not forward it) and prompts ICMP to send an ICMP time-exceeded message to the originating host. This message carries the identity (that is, the IP address) of the router that killed the packet. The second packet makes it through this router. Because its TTL was originally set to two, however, upon hitting the second router the packet gets killed. Again, the router prompts ICMP to send the time-exceeded message to the sending host.

This chain of events continues until the target host is reached. To elicit a response from the target host, traceroute destines the UDP packet to port 33434—an invalid port number. In response, the target host ignores the packet and prompts ICMP to send an unreachable-port message. When traceroute receives this message, it stops sending the diagnostic UDP packets.

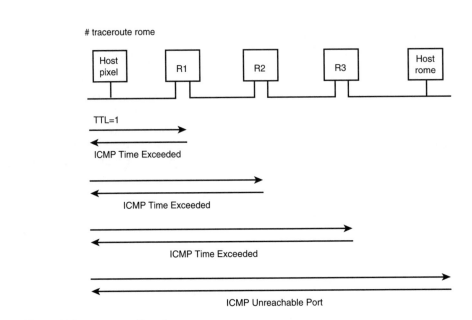

Figure 15.2. traceroute *flow of events.*

In the following example, traceroute is used to determine the intermediate routers leading to host rome:

```
# traceroute rome
traceroute to rome (148.53.27.11), 30 hops max, 40 byte packets
 1    198.237.53.1 (198.53.237.1)   5 ms   5 ms   4 ms
 2    198.235.54.2 (198.235.54.2)   6 ms   6 ms   4 ms
 3    143.22.45.9 (142.22.45.9)   11 ms   8 ms   7 ms
 4    169.48.1.158 (169.48.1.158)   28 ms   28 ms   24 ms
```

According to the output, four routers are separating host rome from the workstation where traceroute was issued. If there had been a problem in getting to host rome, the listing would have looked similar to the following example:

```
# traceroute rome
traceroute to rome (148.53.27.11), 30 hops max, 40 byte packets
 1    198.237.53.1 (198.53.237.1)   5 ms   5 ms   4 ms
 2    198.235.54.2 (198.235.54.2)   6 ms   6 ms   4 ms
 3    * * *
 4    * * *

        .
        .
        .
29   * * *
30   * * *
```

When traceroute cannot make it beyond a certain router, it prints three asterisks at each hop count until the count reaches the maximum of 30. According to the preceding output, traceroute packets could not make it beyond the second router (198.235.54.2). Consequently, you should be able to locate where traceroute failed to resolve the routing problem.

Logging Routing Problems

An additional measure you can take for tracking down routing problems is enabling tracing of routing problems on the suspect host. You can do this by including a log filename on the line that invokes the `in.routed` daemon in the `/etc/inet/rc.inet` file. An example follows:

```
/usr/sbin/in.routed -q /var/routerlog
```

> **Caution:** Be aware that this file can potentially grow to an astronomical size, especially if enabled on a busy network. It is strongly recommended that you turn off logging as soon as you are done troubleshooting the network.

Here is an example of the contents of a created, and updated, log file:

```
Tracing enabled: Action Tracing started: Mon Nov  7 06:47:06 1994


Mon Nov  7 06:47:06:
ADD dst 127.0.0.0, router 127.0.0.1, metric 1, flags UP state
➡PASSIVE¦INTERFACE¦CHANGED¦EXTERNAL timer 0
ADD dst 100.0.0.0, router 100.0.0.1, metric 1, flags UP state INTERFACE¦CHANGED timer
➡0
SIOCADDRT: File exists
ADD dst 150.1.0.0, router 150.1.0.1, metric 1, flags UP state INTERFACE¦CHANGED timer
➡0
SIOCADDRT: File exists

Mon Nov  7 06:47:06:
ADD dst 198.53.237.0, router 100.0.0.2, metric 2, flags UP¦GATEWAY state CHANGED
➡timer 0

Mon Nov  7 07:01:22:
➡ADD dst 213.23.1.0, router 100.0.0.2, metric 5, flags UP¦GATEWAY state CHANGED
timer 0

Mon Nov  7 07:04:11:
CHANGE metric dst 213.23.1.0, router 100.0.0.2, from 5 to 16

Mon Nov  7 07:07:07:
DELETE dst 213.23.1.0, router 100.0.0.2, metric 16, flags UP¦GATEWAY state timer 240
```

As shown in this listing, route additions, deletions, and changes are logged into this file, including the date and time the action took place. For more detailed traces, you can optionally include the `-t` option when invoking `in.routed`. The `in.routed` line in the `/etc/inet/rc.inet` file should then look like this:

`/usr/sbin/in.routed -qt /var/router.log`

Following is an example of the information in `router.log` when the `-t` option is included:

```
Tracing enabled: Action Tracing started: Sat Apr  8 10:09:05 1995
```

```
Tracing packets started, with action tracing on: Sat Apr  8 10:09:05 1995


Sat Apr  8 10:09:05:
ADD dst 150.1.0.0, router 150.1.0.1, metric 1, flags UP state INTERFACE¦CHANGED timer
➥0
SIOCADDRT: File exists
ADD dst 100.0.0.0, router 100.0.0.1, metric 1, flags UP state INTERFACE¦CHANGED timer
➥0
SIOCADDRT: File exists
ADD dst 198.53.235.1, router 198.53.235.10, metric 1, flags UP¦HOST state
➥PASSIVE¦INTERFACE¦CHANGED timer 0
SIOCADDRT: File exists
REQUEST to 150.1.255.255.0 Sat Apr  8 10:09:05:
REQUEST to 100.255.255.255.0 Sat Apr  8 10:09:05:
REQUEST from 150.1.0.1.520 Sat Apr  8 10:09:06:
REQUEST from 100.0.0.1.520 Sat Apr  8 10:09:06:
RESPONSE from 100.0.0.2.520 Sat Apr  8 10:09:06:


Sat Apr  8 10:09:06:
ADD dst 198.53.235.10, router 100.0.0.2, metric 2, flags UP¦GATEWAY¦HOST state
➥CHANGED timer 0
SIOCADDRT: File exists
ADD dst 198.53.237.0, router 100.0.0.2, metric 2, flags UP¦GATEWAY state CHANGED
➥timer 0
SIOCADDRT: File exists
RESPONSE from 100.0.0.2.520 Sat Apr  8 10:09:30:
```

As you can see from this listing, RIP packets are also traced and included. Depending on the nature of the problem, this information might prove to be helpful in sorting it out.

Diagnosing Domain Name Service

Domain Name Service (DNS) problems manifest themselves in the incapability of an application to contact another host due to DNS's failure to resolve the name of the desired host into an IP address. Error messages such as unknown host *hostname* or Host name lookup failure will show on the user's screen when a connection with that host is being attempted.

There are two equally capable tools you can use in troubleshooting DNS problems: nslookup and dig. Chapter 10, "Setting Up the Domain Name System," explained and illustrated the use of nslookup. A few more of its features will be introduced in this section. dig offers almost the same capabilities, with a difference: nslookup establishes an interactive session with named (that is, the DNS daemon); dig does not. Because of the similarity between nslookup and dig, it is left to the initiative of the interested reader to research the man pages for more details about using dig.

Looking for Trouble?

There can be many causes for DNS failures. Here is a short list of the most commonly encountered causes:

◆ *Typing errors:* Where do you start looking for the cause of DNS failure? If asked, 9 out of 10 experienced `named` administrators suggest that you start with the user. It is very common that users report problems arising mainly from typing errors. Hence, whenever a user complains about an application's failure to establish a connection due to name service lookup failure, you would want to go to that user's workstation and ask the user to try again. Note the way the user spells the remote host name. If the error persists, use the name as typed on the screen to carry out further investigation into the matter.

◆ *Mis-serialized database files:* It is not an uncommon mistake for system administrators to forget to increment the serial number of a `named` database file after updating it. Remember from Chapter 10 that unless a primary server's database serial number is incremented, a secondary server will neglect to make a zonal transfer to get the updates replicated on its host. Whenever a refresh is due, a secondary server matches the serial number of each database file it has in cache with that of its counterpart on the primary server. If the primary's serial number is not larger than the secondary's, the latter assumes that there is nothing new to transfer.

Mis-serialized database files will lead to one or both of the following problems:

◆ One problem involves inconsistent name resolutions, exhibited by conflicting answers to the same query, depending on the server responding to the query. This situation occurs mainly when, for example, the IP address on the primary server is changed, and because no zonal updates took place, the secondary server maintains the old information. This is an intermittent problem.

◆ The other problem is that some users will be able to establish connections with newly introduced servers, whereas others won't. Again, this depends on which server the user's workstation contacts for resolution. This problem arises from adding new records pertinent to servers recently attached to the network.

There is no direct way of comparing the serial numbers on both servers (the primary and the secondary). One indirect way is via an `nslookup` session. Following is a depiction of how to use `nslookup` to look up the serial number of a server's DNS database:

```
# nslookup
Default Server:  jade
Address:  0.0.0.0

> set type=soa
> pulse.unicom.com
Server:  jade
Address: 100.0.0.2

pulse.unicom.com
    origin = jade.pulse.unicom.com
    mail addr = root.jade.pulse.unicom.com
    serial = 1
    refresh = 14400 ( 4 hours)
    retry   = 3600 ( 1 hour)
    expire  = 604800 (7 days)
    minimum ttl = 86400 (1 day)
> exit
#
```

As shown, after invoking `nslookup`, you only have to set the type of the query to `soa` (that is, Start Of Authority) and enter the name of the domain or subdomain to which the query applies. In response, `nslookup` queries for, and displays, all the information maintained in the SOA record for that domain, including the serial number. Make sure that the server being queried is the secondary server. Next, compare the serial number you obtained from `nslookup` with the one maintained in the SOA record in the `named` database of the primary server. If they match, you should increment the primary server's serial number.

After the serial number is incremented, you must send the server a `SIGHUP` signal to force it to reload the database and update its cache with the new serial number. Failure to do so will cause the primary server to retain the old information and might cause the secondary server to again ignore zonal transfers, leaving you back where you started. It is not uncommon for novice DNS administrators to forget to signal the primary server after making changes to the DNS database. This is a mistake that affects all domain users, not only users of secondary servers. If left unsignaled, primary servers won't be able to update their caches with the changes. Secondary servers, as well as users, will continue to be served old data. Here is an example of sending the server a `SIGHUP` signal:

```
# kill -HUP namedpid
```

In the example, *namedpid* is the `named` process ID as reported by the `ps -ef ¦ grep named` command.

After the serialization problem is taken care of on the primary server, you need to restart `named` on the secondary server only if you are in a hurry to replicate the updates. You can also let the server wait until the next refresh is due. At that time, a zonal transfer will take care of the replication.

◆ *Period rules-related problems:* As administrators update the `named` database files, they sometimes forget to include the trailing period, or they mistakenly might include it where it does not belong. Unless the period rules (explained in Chapter 10, "Setting Up the Domain Name System") are strictly followed, your domain service is prone to name lookup failures. Make sure that you understand where the periods belong. The best thing to do to avoid problems arising from misplaced periods is to verify the validity of an update by testing it as soon as it is introduced, and as thoroughly as possible.

◆ *Missing PTR records:* Missing PTR records prevent name servers from reverse-resolving an IP address to its host domain name. Missing PTR records might remain unnoticed for quite some time, until a requirement for reverse resolution arises. Resulting errors usually occur when a user attempts to contact a remote host using applications that require reverse mappings. Applications such as rcp (discussed in Chapter 13, "Remote Access Utilities") allow access to users coming from workstations with names that are included in the `/etc/hosts.equiv` or `$HOME/.rhosts` files. Hence, before access is granted to the user, these applications reverse-map the IP address of the requesting workstation to match the *hostname* with the records maintained in the `hosts.equiv` or `.rhosts` files. A missing PTR record causes the authentication process to fail, and the user would consequently be denied access by the application.

Access denial messages might mislead a system administrator and put her on a path that is oblivious to DNS. Just remember to check your PTR records whenever a user reports security-related error messages. The check is simple to perform, and by doing it, you set yourself a step ahead in solving the mystery.

To check whether the reverse database file contains a PTR record corresponding to the workstation in question, start an nslookup session, query the server for the IP address of the workstation, and subsequently issue a reverse query, as in the following example:

```
# nslookup
Default Server:  jade
Address:  198.53.237.1

> wing
Server:  jade
Address:  198.53.237.1

Name:    wing.pulse.unicom.com
Address:  198.53.237.7

> 198.53.237.7
Server:  jade
Address:  198.53.237.1


Name:    wing.pulse.unicom.com
Address:  198.53.237.7

> exit
#
```

Here is an example of a failing nslookup query:

```
# nslookup
Default Server:  jade
Address:  198.53.237.1

> flyer
Server:  jade
Address:  198.53.237.1

Name:    flyer.pulse.unicom.com
Address:  198.53.237.16

> 198.53.237.16
Server:  jade
Address:  198.53.237.1

*** jade can't find 198.53.237.16: Non-existent domain
> exit
#
```

In this case, nslookup responds with Non-existent domain. To a novice, this message can be misleading. What it really means, in the context of this exercise, is that there isn't a PTR record for host flyer. Consequently, to redress the situation, you must edit the reverse domain database to add the required PTR record. For details on how to do this, consult Chapter 10.

◆ *Connectivity-related problems:* Expectedly, if the transport path connecting a user's workstation to its name server is broken, the workstation will no longer be able to have its name queries answered. Under such circumstances, users normally get timeout-type messages on their screens after waiting patiently to get connected to the desired host. Your only remedy, of course, is to diagnose connectivity on the wire as discussed earlier in the chapter.

What other resources can you possibly use to hunt for hints about the problems you are diagnosing? There are at least three places where you can browse for helpful information:

The /var/tmp/named_dump.db file
The /var/tmp/named.run file
syslogd log files

/var/tmp/named_dump.db

The /var/tmp/named_dump.db file is a dump file created when named is sent an INT signal as shown here:

```
# kill -INT namedpid
```

namedpid is the process ID of named, as reported by the ps -ef ¦ grep named command.

The dump file is an exact replica of named's cache. You would normally need to resort to dumping the cache when you suspect corrupted cache data behind the service problems that are emerging on the network. This is an example of what the contents of named_dump.db look like:

```
; Dumped at Sun Apr  9 17:49:54 1995
; --- Cache & Data ---
$ORIGIN in-addr.arpa.
100        IN    SOA    netrix.unicom.com. root.netrix.unicom.com.100.in-addr.arpa. (
           1 14400 3600 604800 86400 )
           IN    NS     netrix.unicom.com.
           IN    NS     jelly.unicom.com.
$ORIGIN 150.in-addr.arpa.
1          IN    SOA    netrix.unicom.com. root.netrix.unicom.com. (
           1 14400 3600 604800 86400 )
           IN    NS     netrix.unicom.com.
           IN    NS     jelly.unicom.com.
$ORIGIN 0.1.150.in-addr.arpa.
10         IN    PTR    saturn.unicom.com.
11         IN    PTR    pluto.unicom.com.
1          IN    PTR    netrix.unicom.com.
$ORIGIN 0.0.100.in-addr.arpa.
4          IN    PTR    maser.unicom.com.
2          IN    PTR    jade.pulse.unicom.com.
3          IN    PTR    laser.unicom.com.
1          IN    PTR    netrix.unicom.com.
$ORIGIN 0.127.in-addr.arpa.
0          IN    SOA    netrix.unicom.com. root.netrix.unicom.com. (
           1 14400 3600 604800 86400 )
```

```
              IN    NS       netrix.unicom.com.
              IN    NS       jade.unicom.com.
$ORIGIN 0.0.127.in-addr.arpa.
1             IN    PTR      localhost.0.0.127.in-addr.arpa.
$ORIGIN com.
unicom    IN      SOA      netrix.unicom.com. root.netrix.unicom.com. (
          3 14400 3600 604800 86400 )
              IN    NS       netrix.unicom.com.
              IN    NS       jelly.unicom.com.
$ORIGIN unicom.com.
maser     IN      A        100.0.0.4
saturn    IN      A        150.1.0.10
pulse     IN      NS       jade.pulse.unicom.com.
              IN    NS       wing.pulse.unicom.com.
      85081 IN      SOA      jade.pulse.unicom.com. root.jade.pulse.unicom.com. (
          1 14400 3600 604800 86400 )
pluto     IN      A        150.1.0.11
localhost IN      A        127.0.0.1
laser     IN      A        100.0.0.3
netrix    IN      A        150.1.0.10
              IN    A        100.0.0.1
$ORIGIN pulse.unicom.com.
wing      IN      A        198.53.237.7
jade      IN      A        100.0.0.2    ; 20
              IN    A        198.53.237.1
              IN    A        198.53.235.10
; --- Hints ---
```

By going through the lines, you should be able to compare this data with the contents of the actual disk database file and possibly discover the discrepancies, if any.

/var/tmp/named.run

Optionally, you can enable debugging on named. named supports nine levels of debug. The higher the level, the more events that are traced and logged in this file.

You can turn on the debugger either by restarting named with the -d *n* option, in which *n* specifies the debug level, or by sending named a USR1 signal, as in the following example:

```
# kill -USR1 namedpid
```

To bring debug to a higher level, reenter the command once per level. Following are the sample contents of named.run after debug was set to level one and host jade was pinged:

```
Debug turned ON, Level 1

datagram from 150.1.0.1 port 1038, fd 5, len 39
req: nlookup(jade.pulse.unicom.com) id 256 type=1
req: found 'jade.pulse.unicom.com' as 'jade.pulse.unicom.com' (cname=0)
req: answer -> 150.1.0.1 5 (1038) id=1 Local

To turn off the debug option, send named a USR2 signal as follows:

# kill -USR2 namedpid
```

syslogd Log Files

UNIX supports a syslogd daemon that, if enabled, reads and logs network-pertinent messages and debug information into files specified in the configuration file /etc/syslog.conf. syslogd listens on the network at UDP's well-known port 514.

You are advised not to configure and run syslogd unless you really must. This file can grow to a considerable size, thus wasting your disk space. Also, make sure that you kill the daemon and remove the file after you are done with it.

Here is a sample /etc/syslog.conf that should be sufficient for most needs:

```
#       @(#)syslog.conf    4.3 Lachman System V STREAMS TCP   source
#       SCCS IDENTIFICATION
*.info,*.debug                   /usr/adm/syslog
```

This file makes syslogd send all informational and debug messages to the /usr/adm/syslog file. Refer to the man pages for more information on configuring the syslogd daemon.

This file could be used to track down messages pertaining to named, among other messages, as illustrated in the following sample of syslog's contents:

```
named[1451]: restarted
Jan  8 07:19:16 jade named[1451]: /etc/named.boot: No such file or directory
Jan  8 07:19:56 jade named[1454]: restarted
Jan  8 07:20:16 jade.unicom.com named[1455]: No root nameservers for class 1
Jan  8 11:21:13 jade.unicom.com named[1455]: zoneref: Masters for secondary zone
➥1.150.in-addr.arpa unreachable
Jan  8 11:37:28 jade.unicom.com named[1455]: zoneref: Masters for secondary zone
➥100.in-addr.arpa unreachable
Jan  8 11:37:29 jade.unicom.com named[1455]: zoneref: Masters for secondary zone
➥237.53.198.in-addr.arpa unreachable
Jan  8 11:37:29 jade.unicom.com named[1455]: zoneref: Masters for secondary zone
➥unicom.com unreachable
Jan 10 08:41:22 jade syslogd: exiting on signal 15
Jan 11 03:58:16 jade syslogd: restart
Jan 11 03:58:17 jade pppd[190]: restarted
Jan 11 03:58:18 jade pppd[190]: bound to host 'localhost' port 911.
Jan 11 03:58:19 jade named[191]: restarted
 .
 .
 .
```

It can easily be deduced from the contents of this file that host jade was having difficulty reaching the servers for the domain unicom.com.

Diagnosing NFS

Being static in nature, when NFS is set up properly, it has little trouble working properly. As part of the real world, however, you would still expect to have a few problems with NFS, as with anything else in computer technology. Here is a list of problems you might encounter in your own environment, and ways of resolving them:

◆ *Hung servers:* Depending on how the NFS file system was mounted, client workstations will react differently to this situation. A hard-mounted file system causes a client to hang indefinitely as it attempts to complete an NFS operation. A soft-mounted file system, on the other hand, retries for the number of times specified in the retry=*n* parameter in the mount command. After that, the attempted NFS operation exits with an error message.

Sorting RPC service-related problems involves the rpcinfo command. Using rpcinfo, the system administrator can query the local and remote hosts for the RPC services they are running. If you suspect a hung server, issue rpcinfo using the -p option and specify the name of the host being queried, as in the following example:

```
# rpcinfo -p netrix
   program vers proto   port  service
   100000   2   tcp     111   rpcbind
   100000   2   udp     111   rpcbind
   100008   1   udp    1036   walld
   150001   1   udp    1037   pcnfsd
   150001   2   udp    1037   pcnfsd
   100002   1   udp    1038   rusersd
   100002   2   udp    1038   rusersd
   100005   1   udp    1042   mountd
   100005   1   tcp    1026   mountd
   100003   2   udp    2049   nfs
   100024   1   udp    1046   status
   100024   1   tcp    1027   status
   100020   1   udp    1051   llockmgr
   100020   1   tcp    1028   llockmgr
   100021   2   tcp    1029   nlockmgr
   100021   1   tcp    1030   nlockmgr
   100021   1   udp    1055   nlockmgr
   100021   3   tcp    1031   nlockmgr
   100021   3   udp    1056   nlockmgr
   100004   2   udp     925   ypserv
   100004   2   tcp     926   ypserv
   100004   1   udp     925   ypserv
   100004   1   tcp     926   ypserv
   100007   2   tcp    1032   ypbind
   100007   2   udp    1061   ypbind
   100007   1   tcp    1032   ypbind
   100007   1   udp    1061   ypbind
   100009   1   udp    1015   yppasswdd
```

rpcinfo -p probes the port mapper (rpcbind) on the specified host for the names of the registered services, their program numbers, their versions, and the UDP and/or TCP ports they support. A hung server causes rpcinfo to timeout and report an error message. In this case, go to the console of the suspect server and restart NFS.

◆ *Connectivity problems:* A basic connectivity problem usually results in the rpcinfo: can't contact portmapper: RPC: Miscellaneous tli error - An event requires attention error message. TLI (Transport Layer Interface) errors occur when the transport path connecting the client to the server is seriously damaged. The possibilities are a hardware problem on the local machine, the remote machine, the router (if any), or the cable. In this case, just resort to the reachability troubleshooting techniques explained earlier in the chapter.

◆ *RPC service-version mismatch:* A mismatch in the RPC service-version between a client and the server might prevent the client from getting the desired service. Even if a file system mounts "successfully," the client might still fail to get its service requests honored by the server. To diagnose this situation, use the following rpcinfo command syntax to verify the version of the suspect service:

```
rpcinfo -u hostname program [version]
```

or

```
rpcinfo -t hostname program [version]
```

In this syntax, u stands for UDP and t stands for TCP transport. *program* specifies the name of the service, and *version* is the version you want verified. Here is an example:

```
# rpcinfo -u netrix nfs 2
program 100003 version 2 ready and waiting
```

If you do not specify the version, rpcinfo displays a listing of the versions that are running and supported. It also includes intermediate versions that might not be supported, as in the following example:

```
# rpcinfo -u nlockmgr
program 100021 version 1 ready and waiting
rpcinfo: RPC: Procedure unavailable
program 100021 version 2 is not available
program 100021 version 3 ready and waiting
```

As shown, only versions 1 and 3 are supported. Version 2 is reported as unavailable and therefore unsupported.

◆ *Wrong run level:* If the server is not at run level three, network users will not be able to mount NFS file systems from that server. You can easily waste time looking for the problem in all the wrong places. During NFS setup, a system administrator might manually bring the system to run level three. Forgetting to update the initdefault entry, in the /etc/conf/init.d/kernel file, with the correct run level (that is, 3) after NFS was properly set up might lead to bringing the system up to any level but level three the next time it is booted. To check the level at which the system is run, enter the who -r command as shown here:

```
# who -r
    .         run-level 3  Apr 11 20:27     3    0    2
```

It does not hurt to check /etc/conf/init.d/kernel, ensuring that the default run level is set right, as shown here:

```
is:3:initdefault:
```

Network Performance Tuning

The previous part of this chapter examined some of the problems you can encounter on the network. Depending on their severity, some of these problems have the effect of preventing the network from delivering part or all of the services it supports. Corresponding to every problem, certain remedies and courses of action were suggested.

This section discusses problems that impact the network performance if they arise. They might not have the fatal impact on the ones examined in the previous sections, but they might still prove to be a costly affair in the long run. These problems have more to do with performance than with network service stoppage, partial or total.

Performance primarily implies the speed at which a service is reliably delivered to the network user. In the following few pages, an attempt is made to highlight some of the common areas for improving network performance. The discussion is not meant to be exhaustive, because network performance tuning is an art by itself, deserving an exclusive treatment in a separate book.

Improving overall network performance involves dealing with far too many components making up the network. For this reason, only the most eminent issues will be explored—with suggestions for remedies that might contribute to better response times.

Network Congestion

Network capacity to carry data is limited by the bandwidth that the underlying data link technology is capable of supporting. A 10BASE-T Ethernet network, for example, supports 10 Mbps. Most networks designed to operate satisfactorily a few years ago might not be able to deliver the same trouble-free level of performance now. There are many factors that can contribute to this degradation. On one hand, the user community might have grown since then. Also, the nature of applications and the demands these applications put on the network in terms of transmission capacity have changed considerably. This is due to the ever-increasing sophistication in functionality that software applications continue to provide.

Considering all of these factors, it should be easy to imagine that the traffic will continue to add to the network over its lifetime. Consequently, you should expect performance-related problems and be prepared to deal with them.

Performance-related problems are normally perceived by users as slow response time. Assessing network performance can be reasonably achieved using the netstat command. netstat provides the network administrator with various statistics helpful in pinpointing the trouble spot for subsequent handling. In following the discussion, a few features of netstat will be introduced in the context of resolving network congestion-related problems.

Among the primary uses of netstat is checking for routing information (using the -r option, explained in Chapter 4) and the local network interface statistics. To display the local interface statistics, use netstat with the -i option, as in the following example:

```
# netstat -i
Name  Mtu   Network     Address       Ipkts  Ierrs  Opkts  Oerrs  Collis
e3B0  1500  198.53.237  jade.pulse.un  12683  0      10683  0      148
lo0   8232  loopback    127.0.0.1      271    0      271    0      0
ppp0  296   198.53.235  198.53.235.10  0      0      0      0      0
```

In this example,

- ◆ Name refers to the name of the local interface.
- ◆ Mtu stands for the maximum transmission unit—that is, the maximum size of the data frame that the interface can support. Being an Ethernet interface, the e3B0 (a 3com 3C503 network interface card) can support a maximum of 1500 bytes.
- ◆ Network refers to the network that the interface is attached to.
- ◆ Address refers to the IP address assigned to the network interface. The host name will be displayed, if available, rather than the address, unless the -n option (for numerical output) is used with the -i option.
- ◆ Ipkts is the number of packets received on the local interface.
- ◆ Ierrs is the number of erroneous packets received.
- ◆ Opkts is the number of packets the interface sent on the network.
- ◆ Oerrs is the number of errors encountered when data is being transmitted to the network. Oerrs does not include the number of collisions reported under Collis.
- ◆ Collis is the number of collisions the interface detected when transmitting to the network.

Obviously, the error and collision rates are what you should be concerned about. High error rates might indicate a failure in the cabling system, as well as high collision rates on the network. In particular, a high input error rate might be due to deformed packets on the network as a result of electrical problems arising from a defective cable. A defective interface card might also be corrupting packets on their way out to the network. Similarly, a high output error rate might be attributed to failures in the local interface or the cable connecting it to the network. It might also be due to excessive collisions taking place on the network, explaining the sluggish response users are reporting.

Collision rates higher than 5 percent are unacceptable on Ethernet networks. The collision rate is equal to the number of collisions (Collis) divided by the number of the output packets (Opkts).

A high collision rate shouldn't imply that the network is saturated with the aggregate traffic generated by all hosts on the network. High collision rates might be due to defective network interfaces jabbering on the network. Hence, it is a good idea to verify the physical sanity of the network before you "establish" the need for extra bandwidth.

It is worth the effort to try running netstat -i on as many randomly selected hosts as you can. If the collision rates (that is, the percentages, *not* the absolute figures reported by Collis) are within 5 to 10 percent, then chances are that you need to have a serious look at your network. You should consider introducing traffic optimization and isolation strategies using bridges, routers, and Ethernet switches. Chapters 3 and 4 include detailed discussions about bridges and routers.

If the collision rates reported by different hosts vary significantly, this might, again, imply defective hardware. You should then start checking the hardware pertaining to the host that reported the highest collision rate.

You might, on the other hand, reach the conclusion that the network topology needs to be reconsidered in light of the changes in network usage patterns taking place over the years. This means that a close study of the current usage patterns is required. The study should include the nature of the services being delivered, and the load each service puts on every segment of the network. Consequently, planned changes to the network topology should take into consideration the current network usage patterns.

For example, diskless clients and their file servers should be placed on the same network segment wherever possible. Diskless clients introduce heavy network traffic compared to workstations with local hard disks. Hence, placing a bridge between a few diskless clients and their file server might impose a heavy load on that bridge, causing it to drop a considerable number of packets at peak usage times. Using a router, instead, might worsen the situation due to the additional delay that is introduced by the network layer having to process the routing information carried by each packet.

RARP service is one more example of an application that should be taken into serious consideration when planning the new network topology. RARP broadcasts do not span the network across routers. They operate at the data link layer, a factor that renders them unroutable.

In summary, unless existing applications and usage patterns are taken into consideration, network repartitioning might prove to be a costly affair accompanied with more problems than it planned to solve.

Tuning NFS

Routine monitoring and performance tuning of NFS services contribute to improving response time on client workstations, and reduced network traffic due to potential timeouts and retransmission.

nfsstat is the UNIX command for monitoring and collecting NFS-pertinent statistics. With no options, nfsstat provides performance statistics for both the server and the client sides of the service. Optionally, you can use the -s option to request the server's statistics, or the -c option for requesting the client's statistics only. Following is an example execution of the netstat -s command:

```
# nfsstat -s

Server rpc:
calls       badcalls    nullrecv    badlen      xdrcall
120         0           0           0           0

Server nfs:
calls       badcalls
117         0
null        getattr     setattr     root        lookup      readlink    read
3   2%      27 23%      0   0%      0   0%      64 54%      0   0%      8   6%
wrcache     write       create      remove      rename      link        symlink
0   0%      0   0%      2   1%      0   0%      0   0%      0   0%      0   0%
```

```
mkdir       rmdir      readdir    fsstat     access
0   0%      0   0%     8   6%     5   4%     0   0%
```

As seen, nfsstat includes RPC-level statistics and NFS-level-per-procedure statistics. For the purpose of this section, it is sufficient for you to understand what the RPC statistics stand for, and to use them in making the necessary tune-ups for the delivery of better performance.

calls	Is the total number of RPC NFS service request calls received by the server. The number includes all requests received from all clients.
badcalls	Is the total number of rejected NFS service requests. Included in the tally are requests attempting unauthorized access to server resources.
nullrecv	Is the total number of times an nfsd daemon was idle after completing the processing of a service request. Normally, as soon as an nfsd daemon is done processing a request, it checks the service queue for more requests to process. An empty queue causes nfsd to increment nullrecv.
badlen	Is the number of RPC request packets found to be of bad length. Normally, bad length means shorter than the supported minimum packet size. Packets might be deformed while enroute to the server by electrical failure or excessive collision on the wire.
xdrcall	Is the number of RPC calls received by the server that were found to have a defective XDR header.

Of these figures, you need to concern yourself with the last three. If both badlen and xdrcall are high (approximately .5 percent), there is a serious electrical problem on the network. Check the network wiring, bridges, routers, and network interfaces and connectors for electrical faults. Eliminating electrical problems reduces bandwidth wasted due to retransmissions caused by packet damage on the network.

A high nullrecv means that the nfsd daemons in the server are spending a considerable part of their time idling. To improve the server's performance, you should have only the number of daemons required to keep nullrecv from incrementing. CPU cycles spent on supporting idling daemons might as well be saved for other, more productive processes.

Now, take a look at the client's statistics. Using nfsstat -cr enables you to get only the RPC-level statistics, without the NFS per-procedure call data.

```
# nfsstat -cr

Client rpc:
calls       badcalls    retrans    badxid     timeout       wait        newcred
318         273         1095       0          1368          0           0
```

In these statistics,

calls	Is the number of calls made to all NFS servers.
badcalls	Is the number of calls that returned an error. badcalls increments every time the client times out before receiving a response to its request from the NFS server. Included in the tally are user-generated interrupts. Interrupts are allowed if the file system was mounted with the intr option. See Chapter 12, "Setting Up Network File System Services," for mount options.
retrans	Is the number of retransmitted requests. A request is retransmitted when the client fails to receive a response within the timeout period.
badxid	XID is the field in the RPC request that uniquely identifies it. With every new request, this field is incremented by one. Retransmitted requests keep the same XID until the request is serviced. There is always a chance that a server will respond to a request after the timeout period. Meanwhile, the client might have retransmitted the request. Being connectionless, NFS does not keep state information identifying the status of the services it renders to its clients. Consequently, the server responds to the same request. The client, upon checking the XID, determines whether the response is a duplicate of an earlier one. If so, the response is discarded and badxid is incremented.
timeout	Is the number of timeouts experienced by the client, due to lack of response from the NFS server.
wait	Is the number of RPC requests that had to wait because the client was busy.
newcred	If secure RPC is implemented, this indicates the number of times clients were re-authenticated by furnishing new credentials. Otherwise, this field will always be zero.

If the number of retransmissions is more than 5 percent, this is an indication of a problem worth attending to. Retransmissions occur due to one or any combination of reasons, including a slow or overloaded NFS server; a congested network; or hardware problems on the client, the server, or anything else in between. To narrow down the real cause, you should correlate retrans, badxid, and timeout in the nfsstat report.

If the number of retransmissions and timeouts is high, you would expect the number of reported packets to be equally high. This is so because a client should, under ideal network conditions, receive an equal number of responses from the servers to the number of retransmitted requests. With that in mind, if the number of badxid packets is considerably less than the number of times the client timed out (that is, timeout), the network is congested and is dropping packets. This condition can be further confirmed by using the netstat -i command. Under these circumstances, an Ethernet network, for example, should report a high collision rate.

What if badxid and timeout tallies are roughly equal? This implies that one or more NFS servers are either overloaded or slow. Consequently, you might consider adding more memory to the machines hosting NFS services, or replace the hard disks with faster ones, or maybe move the service to machines with more processing power.

A temporary measure to reduce the number of retransmissions arising from timeouts due to slow server response is to mount the file system with a larger timeo value (see the mount options in Chapter 12). A longer timeout period allows the server more time to respond before the client is forced to retransmit its request. Adjust timeo in reasonable increments. After each adjustment, monitor the NFS statistics and verify that both badxid and timeout tallies are dropping in unison until they level off. Again, under ideal network conditions, they should drop to zero. Real-life networks are bound to suffer, however, from minimal collision rates, congestion levels, and a few other problems that are bound to induce a corresponding minimal rate of retransmissions. The best way to make the measurements is to reset the NFS statistics right after you mount an NFS file system with an adjusted timeo parameter. This can be done by entering the following nfsstat -z command:

```
# nfsstat -z
```

Instead of displaying a cumulative report, a subsequent nfsstat -rc command will, therefore, report statistics relative only to the time when the last mount was performed.

Another suggestion to consider is reorganizing the exported file systems on the slow NFS server. If, by any chance, all the diskless clients are serviced by the same disk in a multidisk system, you should try to distribute the load on as many disks as possible.

Increasing the number of nfsd daemons can be equally helpful in improving the performance of NFS. Increasing the number of daemons beyond a certain limit can, however, have a counter-effect on performance. This is due to the overhead associated with the time the CPU spends in managing the daemons.

Summary

Troubleshooting TCP/IP networks demands a good understanding of the protocol suite and the skillful use of the UNIX troubleshooting tools. To troubleshoot the network, the administrator has to base his approach on a methodology that enables him to walk through the layers using the proper tools to nail down the suspect layer. The chapter introduced the diagnostic tools and the layers to which they apply. After the suspect layer is identified, the search for the offending element becomes an easier task to handle.

Network performance tuning is concerned with ensuring that network users are provided with the optimum response time that the network can potentially handle. Rather than dealing with the day-to-day problem of diagnosing and troubleshooting, network performance tuning deals with the means to improve on every aspect of the services that exist on the network. Mainly, performance is affected by the network usage patterns currently dominating the network. It is also affected by the network topology, the server response times, and the nature of the applications running across the wire. This chapter introduced a few of the concepts and the suggestions that network administrators have to be aware of to tune the network for delivering the desired performance.

Network Management Using SNMP

Introduction

As networks grow in size and complexity, the task of maintaining the network becomes more complex and time-consuming. Networks grow in many different ways. Over time, more hardware is normally introduced. Hardware can include workstations, servers, routers, bridges, and the like. Geographically, some organizations have networks that span the city, the state, or even the globe. Managing such complex and large dynamic environments demands more than just diagnostic tools. Equally important is to have the tools that enable the network administrator to centrally, from a single workstation, have access to all the data pertinent to network performance and configuration. Those tools should provide the capability of reaching a node, regardless of its physical proximity to the administrator's management station. In the networking industry, these tools are referred to as the network management tools.

Simple Network Management Protocol (SNMP) lays the foundation for TCP/IP management tools. Besides providing some unparalleled diagnostic capabilities, it enables the skilled network administrator to proactively avoid problems on the network and to anticipate necessary changes to keep the network operational at an uncompromising level of performance.

This chapter starts with a conceptual overview of network management systems as defined by SNMP. Next, UNIX SVR4.*x* configuration and startup are presented. The chapter then closes with a discussion about using SNMP tools for network troubleshooting and proactive network administration.

SNMP Management Concepts

SNMP (RFC 1157) network management is based on the client/server model (see Figure 16.1) that many TCP/IP applications are based on. The server, which is referred to as the management *agent*, is implemented in software or firmware in what are known as *network elements*. By definition, a network element can be any network-attached device such as a UNIX host, router, bridge, or wiring hub.

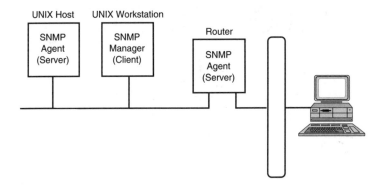

Figure 16.1. *The relationship between SNMP components. The server is the agent, whereas the client is the network manager.*

The agent's responsibility is to collect and track information pertaining to the status and configuration of the device (that is, element) being managed. Depending on the nature of the device, tracked data can span the physical layer up to any higher layer. On a router, for example, the agent tracks information at the physical, data link, and network layers. On a bridge, the network layer is not implemented. Consequently, only the physical and data link layers are tracked for information. Hence, in addition to physical and data link statistics, the router's agent tracks IP protocol statistics such as packets forwarded and packets discarded. To save bandwidth and minimize the impact of running network management systems on the network, agents do not report tracked data unless specifically requested to.

The client is normally implemented in application software that is brought up most often on a UNIX workstation dedicated to this task. The station is referred to as the *management station*. The client software is referred to as the *manager*. Using the manager, a network administrator can issue queries to agents about the status of network-attached devices. For example, a query can be issued to a router to verify the status of the links it is attached to, or for information about its routing configuration. The device being queried can be anywhere on the network—that is, sharing the subnet with the manager or on an entirely different subnet across WAN connections.

SNMP is composed of three basic building blocks: the protocol, the Structure of Management Information (SMI), and the Management Information Base (MIB).

Protocol

The SNMP protocol is a very simple protocol composed of four basic operations for the exchange of data between the manager and the agents. Data is packaged and transmitted in what are known as Protocol Data Units (PDUs). These are the operations:

get
: Can be a request to the agent or a response to a request from the agent to the manager. A get request asks the agent to retrieve and send data pertaining to one or more of the parameters being tracked. A get response is a packet carrying the requested data.

get-next
: Is a request for data pertaining to a parameter after the one specified in the request packet. A series of get-next requests can, therefore, be used to browse through information maintained by the agent.

set
: Is used to set a certain parameter to a certain value. Not all parameters can be set using the set request. Routing information parameters such as next hop or cost are examples of parameters that can be set. The MAC address of an interface card, on the other hand, is a read-only parameter that cannot be changed.

trap
: Is a critical message the agent sends to the management station whenever the agent detects a serious event. An example of a serious event triggering a trap message is an unauthorized attempt to query the agent for information, or a link failure.

SNMP uses UDP for transporting PDUs between the manager and the agents. An agent listens on well-known port 161 for requests, whereas the manager listens on well-known port 162. Why use a connectionless unreliable transport service? Why not use TCP? Because SNMP requests and responses require one packet each, establishing a TCP connection before packet exchange adds considerable overhead. It takes at least three packets to establish a TCP connection. Furthermore, if the network is corrupting packets, this might involve much more bandwidth loss to retransmissions arising from attempts to establish the connection. Using UDP, if the packet does not make it from the first attempt, there is always a chance that it will make it in subsequent ones without incurring any overhead.

Structure of Management Information

Given the range and variety of the SNMP management data, there arose the need to define a skeleton for grouping and identifying the information that SNMP is required to maintain. Structure of Management Information (SMI, RFC 1155) provides this frame. It defines the SNMP types of data, as well as a hierarchical organizational structure to which management data must adhere.

SNMP defines basic types of data from which composite types can be constructed. One example of a data type is integer. This data type can take any numerical value, such as the maximum transmission unit (MTU), or it can be used to describe the status of an interface by assuming one of two values, in which one value indicates that the link is down, and the other value means that the link is up. IpAddress is another example of an SNMP data type. IpAddress is defined to be four bytes in length, each representing a byte of the IP address. Interested readers are referred to RFC 1155 for details. A third example is the object identifier data type. It represents the fundamental concept underlying the organization of management data. For this reason, it is detailed in the next subsection.

Object Identifier Tree

Central to SNMP is the object identifier data type. An object identifier is a tag that agents and managers use to uniquely refer to a particular object. Object identifiers are assigned in a tree fashion resembling the UNIX file system (see Figure 16.2). The value of an identifier is a dot-separated sequence of numbers that describes a specific traversal order of the tree. For example, management data pertaining to IP protocol is grouped at the `ip(4)` object level. Consequently, it is referred to as `1.3.6.1.2.1.4`. Also, as shown in the diagram, objects are assigned textual names. As such, the IP object can be referred to as `iso.org.dod.internet.mgmt.mib.ip`. Only numeric sequences are included in SNMP messages. Textual references are meant to make messages more readable.

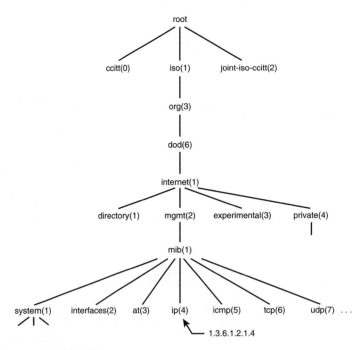

Figure 16.2. *Organization of the OID tree.*

The organizing tree of object identifiers is referred to as the object identifier tree. For simplicity, though, it will be referred to as the OID tree. The OID tree groups management data into logically related object sets. As shown in Figure 16.2, the root of the OID tree has no numeric label. Below the root, three children are defined: `ccitt(0)`, `iso(1)`, and `joint-iso-ccitt(2)`.

Below the `iso(1)` level, the `org(3)` level is defined and is allocated for international organizations. Below `org(3)`, the U.S. Department of Defense is assigned the `dod(6)` node. Organizations are delegated the authority to manage their own nodes—that is, define and maintain lower-level nodes in the tree as the need dictates. It is the organization's responsibility to ensure the uniqueness of the OIDs it assigns to objects it defines.

One more word about OIDs. An OID node can represent either a leaf node or a logical grouping of two or more nodes below it (known as a group object). The leaf node represents the actual management data of interest. An example of a leaf node object would be the `udpInDatagrams(1)` (numerically represented as OID `1.3.6.1.2.1.7.1`; see Figure 16.3). This leaf object maintains the number of UDP datagrams delivered to user processes.

Together with the other leaf objects—`udpNoPorts(2)`, `udpInErrors(3)`, and `udpOutDatagrams(4)`— `udpInDatagrams(1)` is grouped and defined under the `udp(7)` object. Consequently, to get UDP performance data, the manager should traverse the OID tree to the `udp(7)` node level. This is very similar, once again, to the UNIX file system, in which filenames are leaf node representations of the resource to which a user wants access. Directories or subdirectories represent a level below which logically related files are maintained.

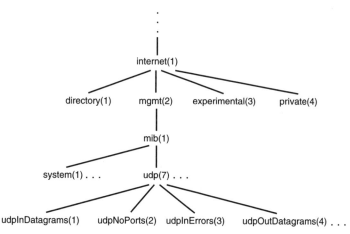

Figure 16.3. *The relationship between leaf objects (or nodes) and group objects in an OID tree. The shown part is the* `udp(7)` *part of the tree.*

Management Information Base

The Management Information Base (MIB) defines the standard objects that any SNMP implementation should support. In other words, MIB defines the database of information that any

SNMP-compliant agent should maintain. Originally, SNMP defined MIB-I, specified in RFC 1156. Another more comprehensive MIB was later defined, called MIB-II, which is specified in RFC 1213. MIB-II is a superset of MIB-I, because it supports all MIB-I objects in addition to the newly introduced ones.

As shown in Figure 16.4, MIB objects are divided into logically related groups of objects below the mib(1) node in the OID tree. Examples of these groups are system(1), interfaces(2), at(3), and ip(4). Each of these nodes defines a subset of the management information that the SNMP agent should maintain. Notice how each protocol of the TCP/IP suite is taken care of separately by one of the nodes defined at the mib(1) level. The ip(4) node, for example, defines numerous objects that take care of IP-related events such as ipForwDatagrams, which describes the number of IP datagrams for which an attempt was made to forward, and ipInDiscards, which represents the number of datagrams that were discarded because of insufficient memory buffer space.

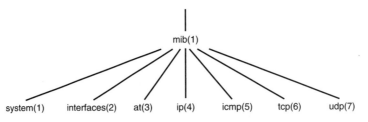

Figure 16.4. *Organization of MIB under the mib(1) node in the OID tree.*

In addition to the per protocol group, MIB defines the system(1) and the interfaces(2) groups. The system(1) group maintains information about the network node such as sysUpTime, representing the time since the agent was brought up on that device; sysLocation, representing the physical location of the device; and sysContact, representing the name of a contact person and means of contacting that person. The interfaces(2) group defines only one variable, the ifNumber, an integer representing the number of network interfaces.

Traps

All the MIB management data maintained by the agent is provided to the manager upon the manager's request. However, SNMP defines critically abnormal events that the agent must notify the manager with as soon as they are detected. Critical event notification is implemented in what SNMP defines as trap messages. Table 16.1 lists the seven types of supported traps.

Table 16.1. Types of SNMP trap messages.

Trap Name	Description
coldStart	The agent is undergoing initialization.
warmStart	The agent is undergoing re-initialization.
linkDown	The link (that is, an interface) underwent a change in state from an up to a down state.

Trap Name	Description
linkUp	The link (that is, an interface) underwent a change in state from a down to an up state.
authenticationFailure	An authorized attempt was made by a manager to query the agent for information. This event is normally reported upon failure of the manager to provide a valid community name to the agent. See the next section for details.
egpNeighborLoss	The agent has detected the failure of a neighboring EGP router.
enterpriseSpecific	This is a vendor-defined event.

Authentication

Network managers can poll agents for information subject to providing a valid community name/ IP address pair to the polled agent. The community name serves as a password that agents require before they can honor any request for management data. When configured, both the agent and the manager have to be set to use the same community name. If the agent receives an invalid community name/IP address pair in an SNMP request, it sends an authenticationFailure trap message to a manager or to a specific group of managers.

Setting Up SNMP on a UNIX Host

UNIX SVR4.*x* implements both components of SNMP: the agent and the manager. The agent is implemented in the snmpd daemon. The manager is implemented in an SNMP command set that enables the user to monitor the status of any device on the network in which an SNMP-compliant agent is deployed. A UNIX host can even monitor itself if it has the snmpd daemon running.

The SNMP agent is started when the system enters a multiuser state (that is, run levels two or three). Upon startup, it reads three agent-specific configuration files: /etc/inet/snmpd.conf, /etc/inet/snmpd.comm, and /etc/inet/snmpd.trap.

Note: Recent versions of UNIX (for example, UnixWare 2) maintain the snmpd files in the /etc/netmgt directory.

/etc/inet/snmpd.conf

The information maintained in the /etc/inet/snmpd.conf file is used by the SNMP agent to update the system(1) group of MIB objects (see Figure 16.4). The system(1) node defines four variables that should be supported by the /etc/inet/snmpd.conf file. Table 16.2 shows the correspondence between the variable names as defined in the OID tree and the variable names as set in the configuration file.

Table 16.2. Correspondence between the `system(1)` group MIB variables and the `snmpd.conf` file variables as implemented by UNIX.

`system(1)` *MIB Variable*	`snmpd.conf` *Variable*
`sysDescr`	`descr`
`sysObjectID`	`objid`
`sysContact`	`contact`
`sysLocation`	`location`

When UNIX is installed, normally both `descr` and `objid` are set for you, so you don't have to worry about them. Only two variables should consequently be modified: `contact` and `location`. Following is a sample `snmpd.conf` file:

```
# /etc/inet/snmpd.conf
descr=UNIX System V Release 4.2
objid=Lachman.1.4.1
contact=Raymond Doucette rdoucette@unicom.com
location=64-200 Owl Dr., Ottawa, ON. K1V 9P7
```

As you can see from the contents of this file, the `contact` variable specifies the name of the person that should be returned by the agent if queried for `sysContact` MIB variable. You would normally include the name of the UNIX system administrator. You can include other information, such as the person's phone number and E-mail address, to be used in emergencies arising from system malfunctions.

The `location` variable defines the physical location of the host. Again, whatever you include here will be returned by the agent if queried for the `sysLocation` MIB variable.

Authentication/Community File */etc/inet/snmpd.comm*

The `/etc/inet/snmpd.comm` file maintains a list of the hosts that can have access to the agent's database and in what capacity. Access is granted subject to the host's providing a valid community name as set in this file. Following is a sample listing of an `/etc/inet/snmpd.comm` file:

```
#
# community    address         access
#
private        198.53.237.2    read
operators      198.53.237.14   write
public         0.0.0.0         none
```

As shown, each line in the file is a separate access record. The first column specifies the community name that the host with the IP address in the middle column must provide to the agent in order for the agent to grant this host the type of access specified in the last column. The following access rights are the only ones the SNMP agent can recognize:

read   Users coming from the host specified in the IP address field can only query the agent for MIB data. Any attempt to make changes is blocked by the agent.

write   Users coming from the host specified in the IP address field are granted full read/write access privileges. Consequently, attempts to make changes to read/write MIB variables are allowed by the agent. For example, the privileged user can make changes to the routing table of the host being accessed.

none   Users coming from the host specified in the IP address field are not allowed any access privileges.

Looking at the records one at a time, the first record grants host 198.53.237.2 read access to the SNMP database subject by supplying private for the community name to the agent. The second record provides the host 198.53.237.14 write access to the database, again subject to supplying operators for the community name. The last record is a special one. According to it, all hosts (except, of course, for the hosts described in the first two records) are denied any access rights. The IP address 0.0.0.0 is the key to granting or preventing public access to the database.

It is worth noting that the /etc/inet/snmpd.comm file is used by the SNMP agent to authenticate host (*not* user) access attempts. This means that any user on an authorized host who knows the proper community names can potentially use this knowledge to make changes to MIB-writable MIB variables. You can prevent this from happening by changing the permissions on the SNMP management commands so that only root or a trusted group can have access to them.

Traps File *letclinetlsnmpd.trap*

The /etc/inet/snmpd.trap file specifies the name of the addresses of the hosts to whom the agent must send its trap messages (see Table 16.1 for a list of trap messages). The agent sends trap messages upon detection of critical events that are worth the immediate attention of the manager. Following is a sample listing of the /etc/inet/snmpd.trap file:

```
#
# community     address        udp port
#
critical        198.53.237.4    162
private         145.23.2.10     162
```

Each line in the file is a separate record indicating the IP address of the host running the manager software, the UDP port number on which the manager is listening for trap messages, and the community name that the agent must include in the datagram carrying the trap message. A manager discards a trap message if not accompanied by a valid community name.

SNMP Commands

UNIX supports a handful of SNMP commands that enable the network administrator to browse the MIB variables on any system or SNMP-compliant device attached to the network. Table 16.3 summarizes the purpose of each command.

Table 16.3. Common SNMP Commands.

Command	Description
getone	Retrieves a set of individual variables using SNMP get request.
getnext	Retrieves a set of individual variables using SNMP get-next request. It returns the object appearing in the database immediately after the object specified.
getid	Retrieves the variables sysDescr, sysObjectID, and sysUpTime from the system(1) group.
getmany	Retrieves groups (system(1), interfaces(2), at(3), and so on) of variables.
snmpstat	Retrieves, in human readable formats, the contents of various network-related data structures.
getroute	Retrieves routing information.
setany	Sets a read/write MIB variable using SNMP set request.

These commands are not as user friendly as you might want. To be able to use most of them, you need to know more about the MIB variables. In particular, you need to understand how MIB variable instances are identified—a subject that is beyond the scope of this chapter. However, in the following few paragraphs, you'll find examples illustrating the usage of these commands. The objective of these examples is to familiarize you with those commands and give you a head start in this area. More details about identifying and using the MIB variables are available in the appropriate RFCs mentioned earlier.

getone

The getone command allows for the retrieval of specific MIB variables. The syntax is shown here:

getone *hostname* ¦ *hostaddress community variable*

Here is an example of using getone to obtain the total number of UDP datagrams received by host netrix:

getone netrix udpInDatagrams.0

```
Name: udpInDatagrams.0
Value: 8
```

getnext

The getnext command allows for the retrieval of the next MIB variable in any MIB group. Following is the syntax of the getnext command:

getnext *hostname* ¦ *hostaddress community variable* ¦ *objectgroup*

As shown, the syntax allows for specifying either a variable name (for example, `ipForwarding.0`) or the name of an object group (for example, the `ip` object group of variables). The first of the following examples specifies the `ip` object group, in which case the value of the first element in the group (that is, `ipForwarding.0`) is returned. The subsequent `getnext` commands browse and retrieve the values of the variable next to that specified in the `getnext` command:

```
# getnext netrix public ip

Name: ipForwarding.0
Value: 1
# get netrix public ipForwarding.0

Name: ipDefaultTTL.0
Value: 255
# getnext netrix public ipDefaultTTL.0

Name: ipInReceives.0
Value: 34
# get netrix public ipInReceives.0

Name: ipInHdrErrors.0
Value: 0
```

getid

The `getid` command retrieves a subset of the `system(1)` group of MIB. In particular, it reports the `sysDescr`, `sysObjectID`, and `sysUpTime`, in which the first two are derived from the `snmpd.conf` file discussed earlier. Here is a sample execution of the `getid` command:

```
# getid netrix public
Name: sysDescr.0
Value: UNIX System V Release 4.2

Name: sysObjectID.0
Value: Lachman.1.4.1

Name: sysUpTime.0
Value: 4199744
```

`sysUpTime` reports the elapsed time since the SNMP agent (that is, the `snmpd` daemon) was started—*not* the time since the workstation or server was brought up.

getmany

The `getmany` command retrieves sets of MIB variables pertaining to any of the MIB groups: `system(1)`, `interfaces(2)`, `at(3)`, `ip(4)`, and so on. When any of the MIB groups is specified, `getmany` retrieves and displays all the variables defined in that group. Following is the syntax of the `getmany` command:

```
# getmany hostname¦address community MIB_group
```

In this syntax, *MIB_group* is any of the OID nodes at `mib(1)` level (see Figure 16.2). Here is a sample output of the `getmany` command:

```
# getmany netrix public system
Name: sysDescr.0
Value: UNIX System V Release 4.2

Name: sysObjectID.0
Value: Lachman.1.4.1

Name: sysUpTime.0
Value: 4235271

Name: sysContact.0
Value: Raymond Doucette rdoucette@unicom.com

Name: sysName.0
Value: netrix

Name: sysLocation.0
Value: Computer Arts Department

Name: sysServices.0
Value: 72
```

For brevity of output, the system(1) group was chosen. If you want to, try some of the more interesting ones, such as ip(4) and tcp(6). Notice that when a group is specified, the relative OID number in parentheses shouldn't be included.

Summary

Network management tools provide LAN managers with the ability to remotely diagnose and troubleshoot problems arising on the network. A skilled administrator can even use these tools to predict upcoming problems. He can then plan to circumvent the problems before they materialize into serious situations that could impact user productivity by inflicting degradation in network performance, which can possibly lead to extended downtime.

Simple Network Management Protocol (SNMP) is the protocol that underlies most of the network management tools. SNMP is based on the client/server model. The server is what is commonly referred to as the management agent. It is deployed on the node being managed, such as routers, bridges, wiring hubs, and UNIX hosts. The agent's responsibility is to collect information pertinent to the node and make it available upon request to the managing station (that is, the client). The managing station can be a UNIX host where the management application is being run.

UNIX SVR4.*x* ships with built-in support for the SNMP protocol. This support includes an SNMP command set that could be used in place of the sophisticated management tools that exist in the market. The efficient use of these commands requires a thorough knowledge of the SNMP protocol and its internals. This chapter summarized the command set and highlighted its use in diagnostic and troubleshooting situations. By themselves, the commands are far from satisfactory for unveiling trouble on the network. For this reason, it is strongly recommended that you use commercially available SNMP management applications, especially on large and geographically dispersed networks.

CHAPTER 17

♦

UNIX on a
Multiplatform Network

Introduction

> **Note:** This chapter was coauthored by Patrick T. Gilligan.

The ever-increasing demand on sophisticated productivity tools has made it hard for a single platform to satisfy all user requirements at an acceptable level of satisfaction and performance. For this reason, it is becoming fashionable to provide users with access to resources hosted by hybrid platforms sharing the same network. A UNIX user can, for example, be provided access to a high-quality printer serviced by the NetWare operating system, whereas a DOS user is provided with a terminal emulation session to a UNIX host to bring up an application that would not run on his DOS machine.

This chapter provides a conceptual overview of some of the existing exciting technologies for integrating hybrid platforms on the same network. In particular, the NetWare operating system, Windows NT, and X Window technologies will be exposed in the context of achieving transparency in user access to any resource independent of the actual client platform the user is attempting the access from.

Obviously, one chapter cannot include all the "how to" details. Such details are available in the user and administrative manuals accompanying the products and platforms of interest.

This chapter is composed of two major sections. The first section provides an overview of the operating systems being considered for platform integration. The second section provides a conceptual understanding of what architectural elements each of the platforms includes in order to make transparent integration with other platforms realistic.

Technical Overview of Select Platforms

The following discussion introduces two operating system platforms: NetWare Operating System and Windows NT.

NetWare Operating System

Developed in the early 1980s by Novell Inc., NetWare OS is the most commonly deployed network operating system (NOS) for DOS-based environments. It enables DOS users to share a host of services, including file services, print services, and a wide range of other communication services.

Unlike UNIX and some other operating systems, NetWare OS maintains a server-centric view of how network services are shared and managed. UNIX on the desktop comes with built-in networking capabilities providing for file transfer service and print service, among other services, at the desktop level. This means that UNIX hosts and workstations can be configured to allow for the cross-sharing of file and print services. As shown in Figure 17.1, the two UNIX workstations, saturn and pluto, can be configured such that host saturn has part of its file system exported to the user on host pluto, and vice versa. The same thing applies to other network services such as printing, TELNET, and FTP.

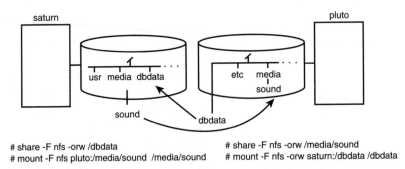

Figure 17.1. *UNIX workstations can be configured to cross-share resources on the network. Hosts* saturn *and* pluto *cross-share parts of their file systems using NFS. See Chapter 12 for details on the commands shown.*

NetWare OS is not a desktop operating system that a user can operate directly at the console. It is a NOS (network operating system) that is specifically designed to manage central repositories of file and print services, among others. Figure 17.2 illustrates the concept. As shown, NetWare OS is brought up on a machine (normally powered with high-end CPU, superior disk access, and faster I/O) that is designated as the file server.

A NetWare file server is normally equipped with a huge disk space that is used as the central data repository which DOS users on the LAN can share. Using administrative tools, the administrator configures the file system for desired security measures, including file system access rights. As shown, no two network users in a strictly NetWare environment can talk directly to each other. All users communicate only with the file server. Consequently, users can share only the data that is maintained on the server's disk. Other network services are also shared similarly. The NetWare server is, therefore, delegated the responsibility for managing system services' security and for coordinating multiple user requests for managed resources.

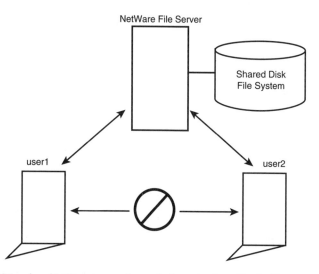

Figure 17.2. *On NetWare-based LANs, users can share only the services hosted by the file server. Direct interaction between two DOS users is not supported by NetWare OS.*

Another important feature that is supported by NetWare network operating systems is the concept of distributed network services. A NetWare-based LAN can be designed to aggregate all network services such as file, print, and communication services in one file server. This approach has disadvantages, creating a central point of failure and performance degradation. By supporting distributed network computing, network services can be implemented on multiple servers. LAN services can be split vertically among multiple servers to end up with a server per type-of-service (that is, a communications-only server, a file service-only server, a print service-only server, and so on). Another approach is to split services horizontally among the server community so that each server is handling its fair share of various services (that is, every server is configured to support more than one type of service). Again, subject to security restrictions, DOS users can communicate service requests to one or more server.

One of NetWare's noted features is its modularity. At a minimum, the core operating system supports file services only. If desired, the server can be made to support other types of services by the addition of software programs in the form of what Novell calls NetWare Loadable Modules (NLMs).

Adding print services, for example, is accomplished by loading one NLM (PSERVER.NLM) on the server. Adding dial-in/dial-out communications services requires, on the other hand, a host of NLMs. The same thing applies for all other services. Loading and unloading NLMs on a Novell server is characterized by two features: (1) there is no requirement to recompile the operating system as more NLMs are introduced or removed, and (2) most NLMs can be loaded and unloaded on the fly while the server is in full operation, causing minimal disruption to the user community.

Native NetWare Network Protocols

The protocol stack on which NetWare OS relies for the delivery of network services is commonly referred to as IPX/SPX. IPX, or Internetwork Packet eXchange protocol, is a network layer protocol (see Figure 17.3). Like IP, IPX is a connectionless routing protocol that delivers routing services on the network. SPX stands for Sequenced Packet eXchange protocol, a connection-oriented transport protocol that shares many of the features of TCP.

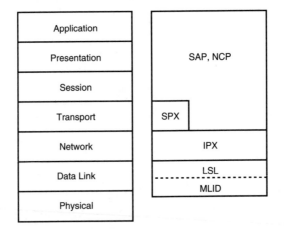

Figure 17.3. *NetWare native protocol stack and OSI.*

At the data link layer, NetWare supports most of the common MAC technologies, including all flavors of Ethernet, Token-ring, FDDI, and ATM, to name a few. As shown in Figure 17.3, this layer is implemented by two components, Multiple Layer Interface Driver (MLID) and the Link Support Layer (LSL). The next section takes a detailed look at the purpose of dividing the data link layer in this fashion.

NetWare Core Protocol (NCP) embodies the session through the application layers of the OSI model. It provides NetWare's core functions, including file and print services. It is also responsible for services such as file locking and synchronization. On the file server, NCP is implemented in the core operating system itself. On the workstation, it is implemented in a software program called NETX.EXE or VLM.EXE. The DOS user should load the program after loading a few other network-related programs that take care of the data link and network layer services.

The Service Advertising Protocol (SAP) is, as the name implies, an advertising service that announces existing services on the network. Whenever a service is brought up on a server, be it a print service, file service, communication service, or such, SAP propagates messages on the network announcing that service among others at the configurable rate (the default being one announcement per minute). This is how all servers and client workstations become aware of the existing services that consequently become available to the user community. There is no protocol similar to SAP in the TCP/IP protocol suite. TCP/IP network applications do not advertise their services.

Organization of NetWare File Systems

Under NetWare, disk space is divided into volumes. A volume constitutes the major division of the NetWare file system. It can be configured to represent a part of a disk (that is, a disk can be split to contain more than one volume) or span a maximum of 32 hard disks. In either case, NetWare OS treats the volume as a fundamental entity for organizing disk space. Consequently, unlike under UNIX, users reference NetWare volumes individually, with each volume having its own root.

At the time of creation, a NetWare volume is assigned a unique name that can be used to reference it. It is mandatory that one volume is assigned the SYS: volume name. On the SYS: volume, NetWare system, public, and login utilities, as well as print queues, are maintained (see the following note).

Note: Under NetWare 3.1x, print queues are maintained exclusively on the SYS: volume. NetWare did not allow system administrators the flexibility of moving the print queues to other volumes. Depending on the printing load, print queues could potentially grow to huge temporary directories that might impact disk space utilization on the SYS: volume. Under NetWare 4.x, things changed for the better by allowing the creation and movement of print queues on any volume deemed more suitable to the environment needs.

At the volume level, the organization of the file system closely follows that of the DOS file system—directories at the root, below which subdirectories and files can be created and maintained. Shown in Figure 17.4 is a file server with two volumes, SYS: and APPS:. Volume SYS: is mounted on one physical drive, whereas APPS: is mounted on two drives. There is an advantage to allowing a volume to span multiple disks. Volumes running short of disk space can be expanded without requiring major work reorganizing the file system. This means that files and directories can continue to grow in size across the physical limits imposed by the supporting drives.

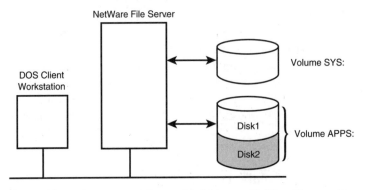

Figure 17.4. *A volume can be made to span more than one hard drive on a NetWare file server. Users perceive a particular volume as one logical entity, each referenced by a unique name.*

To simplify matters, DOS users make use of a MAP command that assigns letters to the volumes. These letters can be used in the same way as they're used to reference local disk drives. In the following example, MAP is used to assign drive letter J to the SYS: volume:

```
C:\> MAP J:=SYS:
```

Thereafter, the user can use the letter J: to reference the volume as though a DOS drive is being referenced. Better still, MAP can be used to reference any logical part of the directory structure on that volume. The following example shows how to map a drive letter to reference the path SYS:PUBLIC\DOS:

```
C:\> MAP N:=SYS:PUBLIC\DOS
```

Drive mappings are normally included in system and personal login scripts so that users get a consistent view of the way file system resources are referenced by applications. Including drive mappings in the login scripts also reduces the tedium associated with entering multiple MAP commands every time the user logs in to the server.

NetWare Multiprotocol Support

Starting with version 3.*x*, NetWare OS included support for multiprotocol stacks on top of the same network interfaces. This support was motivated by Novell's desire to respond to the ever-rising user demand for transparent access to other platforms and networks, including TCP/IP, AppleTalk, and OSI.

Multiprotocol support enables loading and delivering of services pertaining to any combination of the supported stacks—that is, a NetWare server, for example, can be configured to route TCP/IP packets in addition to routing its native IPX packets using the same interfaces. This way, the NetWare server is functioning as an IP router, routing IP packets emerging on UNIX workstations and other TCP/IP-compliant devices, in addition to delivering file and print services to DOS users (see Figure 17.5).

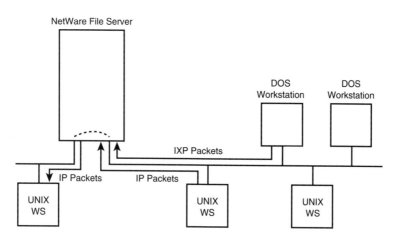

Figure 17.5. *A NetWare file server can be configured to support multiple protocol stacks on the same interfaces. In this scenario, the file server is configured to behave as an IP router routing IP packets between UNIX workstations in addition to providing file and print services to the DOS user community.*

The key to NetWare's support for multiprotocol stacks is what is known in NetWare terminology as the Open Data-link Interface (ODI) technology. ODI subdivides the data link layer into Multiple Layer Interface Driver (MLID) and Link Support Layer (LSL). MLID directly drives the network interface card plugged into the server. Inserting LSL between MLID and the network layer makes the driver independent from the actual protocol stack that the interface driver carries in its frames. Hence, when MLID receives a packet from the network, it has no idea where to deliver the encapsulated data field (that is, the network layer packet). Instead, MLID invariably delivers the data field to the LSL layer.

Above LSL, more than one protocol stack can be deployed (see Figure 17.6). When it receives a packet from the MLID driver, LSL behaves like a telephone switchboard that is well-equipped to identify packets with the corresponding protocol stack. Based on this identification, IP packets are delivered to the TCP/IP suite, whereas IPX packets are delivered to the IPX/SPX suite. It is then left to the individual upper layers to decide how to handle packets they receive from LSL. An IP packet that needs routing, for example, is resubmitted to the data link layer for delivery to the network out of the proper interface, whereas an IPX packet that includes a file service request is passed up the layer hierarchy to NCP for processing.

Overview of Windows NT

In 1993, Microsoft unveiled its next generation of operating system, Windows NT. This was to be the foundation Microsoft would use to build a new generation of client/server technology applications such as SQL Server, SNA Server, and Systems Management Server. Windows NT initially suffered from a bit of an identity crisis. This was in part because of the user interface in NT, which looked very much like Windows 3.1, and perhaps even because of the word "Windows" in its name. People initially made all comparisons of Windows NT to Windows 3.1 as though this were the next "upgrade" from Windows 3.1.

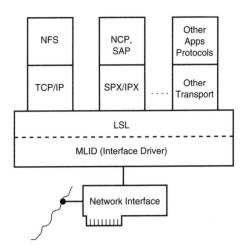

Figure 17.6. NetWare implementation of multiprotocol support. Open Data-link Interface (ODI) technology subdivides the data link layer into the Multiple Link Interface Driver (MLID) and Link Support Layer (LSL).

After the "hood" has been lifted, however, and the internals and features of this extremely powerful operating system are exposed, there is no mistaking Windows NT for Windows 3.1. In fact, if a comparison to a current operating system is to be made, it would be more appropriate to compare it to UNIX. This section will try to give you an appreciation for some of the features and internals of Windows NT. However, this is merely an overview to explore its architecture and network integration capabilities.

Before looking at the architectural components of NT, it is helpful to compare the two Windows NT products and define their purpose and where they fit into an enterprise computing environment.

Windows NT Server and Workstation

Windows NT is available in two versions, the Windows NT Server and the Windows NT Workstation products. Both are built on the same core 32-bit, multitasking, multithreaded Operating System, both are Symmetrical Multi-Processor (SMP) aware, and both run on not only Intel processors but also various RISC-based processor versions (DEC Alpha, MIPS R4000, PowerPC, and Intergraph Clipper). The primary differences between the two versions of this operating system are the built-in services over and above the standard OS and the number of users that are able to connect to services running on the machine.

Note: Symmetrical Multi-Processing means that the operating system can run on a computer with more than one CPU. An SMP operating system can dispatch a thread that requires CPU attention to any free CPU. This contrasts with Asymmetrical Multi-Processing operating systems, which require that the operating system run on a dedicated

CPU, with user processes and threads running on the remaining CPUs. SMP operating systems can run on any free CPU or across all available CPUs.

Windows NT Workstation is for the computer user who requires a high-power 32-bit graphical workstation for running computational-intensive applications such as application development tools, as well as technical, engineering, and financial applications.

NT Workstation is intended for those environments where UNIX on a graphics workstation was typically used or where the highest performance and reliability for mission-critical applications are required. Its built-in networking capabilities allow for file and print services as well as client/server-type application services to be offered to other NT Workstations and other Microsoft clients. The NT Workstation is also intended to be a more superior client to the Windows NT Server product than DOS or regular Windows-based platforms.

Note: A service running on Windows NT is a process that runs regardless of whether anyone is logged on to the computer; it is analogous to a system daemon on UNIX.

Windows NT Server has additional services and capabilities beyond the Workstation product that allow it to be more of an enterprise server. The Server product has greater capabilities for the administration and control of user accounts and other servers for small to large networks, with practically no limit on the number of servers that can be administered as a single entity. This product is intended to compete with other network server products such as Novell NetWare, Banyan VINES, and IBM LAN Server. Even though this product is intended as a network server for file and print services, or as a platform for client server applications, it is a nondedicated Network Operating System, and it can be used as a personal operating system exactly the same way as can a Windows NT Workstation.

Both products also have built-in capabilities to interoperate in the UNIX environment in both client and server capacities. These services will be explored in more detail toward the end of the section.

To gain an appreciation for the capabilities of this operating system, parts of the core operating system architecture, with an emphasis on the networking architecture, are explored on the next few pages. To get an appreciation for the potential for extending this technology into other environments (including UNIX), a couple of examples of other environments are given where it seemed logical, in order to emphasize the importance of a component. It is important to keep in mind that the primary purpose of the section is to explore some of the similarities to UNIX as well as the integration technologies built into NT.

Overview of Networking Architecture

This overview of the Networking architecture of NT is intended to give a simple comparison of NT's networking components to the OSI reference model (Figure 17.7). It's also intended to show the components and interfaces that allow NT to fit into existing environments such as UNIX, as well as the capability to be easily extended to accommodate new environments.

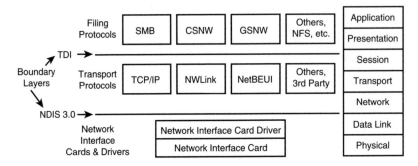

Figure 17.7. *Windows NT's networking architecture is divided into three primary components. The illustration compares these components to the OSI reference model.*

Boundary Layers

NT provides the capability to interoperate in many different network environments concurrently, in both a client and a server configuration. Windows NT networking components are organized into three modules: the *Filing Protocols*, the *Transport Protocols*, and the *Network Interface Adapter and Driver* layers. These three modules will be discussed in more detail later, but of significant importance are the two *boundary layers* separating the three modules.

These boundary layers are known as the Transport Device Interface (TDI), which separates the filing protocols from the transport protocols, and the Network Device Interface Specification (NDIS), which separates the transport protocols and the network adapter drivers. These layers are actually application programming interfaces that provide a division between layers. They therefore reduce the dependencies between the three primary layers so that new components can easily be added and existing modules can be replaced without affecting modules at adjacent layers.

Microsoft's SMB Filing Protocol

This section provides a brief overview of the file and print services built into Windows NT to provide network access to Microsoft clients. It also shows how these file and print services interact with NT's local file systems.

Windows NT's standard services for providing file and print services between NT clients are called the *Workstation* and *Server* services (remember that a service on NT is like a system daemon on UNIX). The Workstation service is the client end of Microsoft's *Server Message Block* filing protocol, used for communicating with Windows NT Servers or other SMB-compliant server products such as LAN Manager, DEC Pathworks, IBM LAN Server, Windows for Workgroups, and LAN Manager for UNIX. The Server service is the server end of the SMB filing protocol, which responds to SMB requests from any SMB client (DOS, Windows for Workgroups, Windows 3.1, OS/2, Windows NT, and so on).

> **Note:** Throughout this section, the terms "Microsoft networking" and "SMB clients and servers" are used synonymously.

Both the Workstation and the Server services reside on each NT Workstation or NT Server product, so any of these operating systems can play the role of client or server at any time (peer to peer). The Server component of an NT Workstation, however, is restricted to 10 inbound concurrent connections (clients), whereas there is no restriction on the number of inbound connections to an NT Server or the number of outbound connections on either version of the operating system.

One of the principle design goals of NT was that networking would be a core component of the operating system and not an add-on. This is evident in the method in which NT's Workstation and Server components were implemented in the NT architecture. Both of these services reside in the I/O manager component of Windows NT as file system drivers, parallel to the FAT (File Allocation Table), the HPFS (High Performance File System), CDFS (Compact Disc File System) and the NTFS (New Technology File System) drivers for accessing local disk resources. The benefit of incorporating these services in this manner is that network I/O can be handled for network resources in the same way it is handled for local disk resources (see Figure 17.8).

NT makes disk resources available to clients by creating *shares* on the directory structure. For example, Figure 17.9 presents a directory structure on an NT Server partition in which some directories need to made available to network clients.

The administrator makes directories available to clients by creating shares. Shares are a way of "exporting" a portion of the directory structure so that they can be accessed by clients of NT. The administrator can share the directory by using Windows NT's graphical File Manager utility, or by using a command-line utility called Net Share.

The following example demonstrates publishing the Applications directory on a file server called Kim as a share called Appl. There is also a remark or a description of the share called *application software* that the clients will see when they are browsing for network resources.

```
C:\>NET SHARE appl=c:\applications /R:"Application software"
```

Now the shared directory is available to NT, OS/2, DOS, or other SMB clients by the use of graphical network resource browsing utilities such as the Windows File Manager. It's also available from a character-based interface by issuing the following command:

```
C:\>NET USE h: \\kim\appl
```

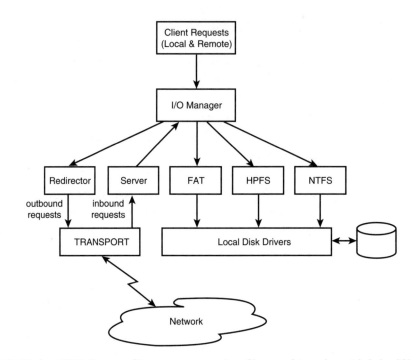

Figure 17.8. *Windows NT Redirector and Server components exist as file system drivers along with the local file system drivers in Windows NT's I/O Manager.*

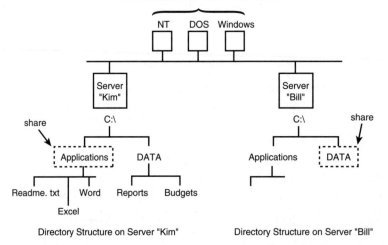

Figure 17.9. *Windows NT uses a concept similar to NFS shares to "export" portions of its directory structure to SMB clients.*

H: is the local drive letter that will be assigned to the network resource, \\KIM is the name of the server that holds the resource, and APPL is the shared resource created by the NET SHARE command previously.

Case Sensitivity

Windows NT is case-insensitive on the command line (unlike UNIX). Note that, as a demonstration, KIM appears in both uppercase and lowercase characters in this discussion.

Now the client can access the `c:\applications` directory on the server called KIM by referencing the drive letter H:. In the preceding command, the name `\\KIM\APPL` is the method by which a server and its resources are accessed using the SMB filing protocol. This is called the *Universal Naming Convention* (UNC). These kinds of commands can be made a permanent part of the user's environment by entering the same command into a logon script, or the Microsoft client software can automatically preserve these connections as a *Persistent connection* as the user is defining them.

In Windows NT, you can access remote resources by pointing to the share name on the server by directly using the UNC name. Following is a list of some standard DOS-like commands executed from a Windows NT command prompt:

```
C:\>DIR \\KIM\APPL

C:\>TYPE \\KIM\APPL\README.TXT

C:\>MD \\KIM\APPL\NEWDIR

C:\>COPY \\KIM\APPL\README.TXT    \\BILL\DATA\README2.TXT

C:\>\\KIM\APPL\EXCEL\EXCEL.EXE
```

NTFS Local File System

The local disk partitions under Windows NT can be formatted using various file systems (mentioned previously), and directories can be shared on all the file systems (including the CD-ROM file system and even the floppy disks, for that matter). However, the NTFS file system offers the greatest degree of power and flexibility. Even though the local file systems are not network components, it is worth taking a short side-trip to see a couple of the features of NTFS that add support and functionality to the network environment.

This file system not only has built-in capabilities to support NT's filing requirements with support for 255 character filenames, file level permissions, and auditing, but it also has extremely powerful capabilities for extending partitions across multiple drives.

An NTFS partition can be extended whenever a partition becomes full and more disk space is required. Or a partition can be created spanning multiple drives, called a *volume set*. This special partition can span up to 32 drives of different drive technologies (IDE and SCSI) and can accommodate a theoretical maximum partition size of 16 E (exabytes).

Note: NTFS uses 64-bit file pointers, which explains this rather large partition size (or file size, for that matter) of 16 exabytes (2^{64} or 18,446,744,073,709,551,616 bytes).

Windows NT's disk partitioning technology also includes support for several levels of the *RAID* specification, specifically RAID 0, RAID 1, and RAID 5. RAID level 0, which is support for *stripe sets*, defines a disk partition scheme that allows a single partition to span from 2 to 32 drives allowing the multiple read/write heads in the partition to write files in *stripes* across the multiple disks, thus achieving faster reads and writes from the concurrent action of the multiple read/write heads. The only down side to this partition type is the lack of protection if one drive fails.

> **Note:** RAID (Redundant Array of Inexpensive Disks) is a system developed in 1987 at the University of California at Berkeley to provide methods of creating large virtual disk partitions out of several hard disks. It also specifies various *fault tolerance* mechanisms to keep a system running if a single hard disk fails.

NT also supports RAID 1 (NT Server only), which is disk mirroring and duplexing. In RAID 1, a partition is mirrored with another partition on another drive. The system duplicates all data on the mirror drive; should one drive fail, the remaining good drive can take over all subsequent file I/O. The difference between mirroring and duplexing is that in mirroring, the two mirrored partitions are on separate drives attached to the same controller card, whereas in duplexing, each disk is attached to a separate controller card, adding another level of redundancy to hardware that could fail.

Another level of RAID support (only found in the NT Server product, not Workstation) is called RAID 5. This partition scheme behaves very much like the stripe set described previously, except for a built-in fault tolerant mechanism. In RAID level 5, the data is again laid down in stripes across multiple drives (see Figure 17.10), but on every stripe, the file system driver calculates *parity* information based on the actual data being saved in that stripe. If one drive fails, NT can keep running by regenerating the missing data from the parity information present on each stripe.

Microsoft also designed NTFS to support the filing requirements of other operating systems. In addition to the features mentioned previously, such as RAID, file-level permissions, file-level auditing, and so on, NTFS supports some UNIX file naming characteristics such as case-sensitive filenames, symbolic links, hard links, file ownership, and long filenames up to 255 characters.

This represents a brief overview of the default file and print services that are included with Windows NT, as well as the importance of some of the features present in the NTFS file system that support some of the network features. The end of the section will demonstrate additional components that can be installed to provide integration with other environments.

IPC Mechanisms for Distributed Processing

Windows NT also has excellent support for distributed applications, applications that are split into two components: a client component and a server component. The goal in distributed applications is to move the bulk of the processing for the application onto a more powerful server component. Applications such as Microsoft's SQL Server, SNA Server, and Lotus Notes are just a few examples of distributed applications.

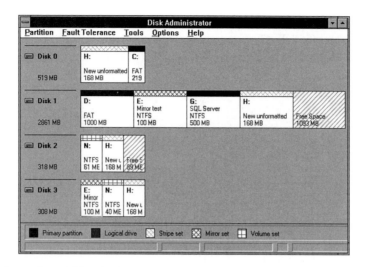

Figure 17.10. The Windows NT™ Disk Administrator utility, used for creating and removing disk partitions. This figure demonstrates the capability for various partition types to span multiple drives. For example, a new "strip set with parity" partition type has been created, indicated by drive letter H:, which spans the four hard disks in this system. Partition N: originated on disk 2 but was extended to disk 3 when more disk space was required. Partition E: demonstrates a mirrored partition between disks 1 and 3. (Screen shot reprinted with permission from Microsoft Corporation.)

A distributed application requires a component called an *Inter Process Communications* facility to link the two components of the application so that they can work as one. Windows NT provides several of these IPC mechanisms with the operating system to provide a communications method for these types of applications. Windows NT can be used as the client or server component for distributed applications—in fact, NT's own administration utilities use IPC mechanisms for remotely administering servers and workstations.

Windows NT can support distributed applications running either entirely on computers running only NT, or with either the client or the server components running on other operating systems such as UNIX.

Multiprotocol Support

Windows NT supports several transport protocols out of the box for networking with other Microsoft networking products, as well as for providing interoperability with other environments such as UNIX or NetWare.

The transport protocols included in the package are TCP/IP, NWLink, NBF, and DLC. Third parties can develop other transport protocols for NT. For example, the Banyan Vines client for Windows NT includes Vines IP as a carrier for the Banyan redirector, and Digital Equipment Corporation makes the DECnet protocol available with the Pathworks client for NT.

The Transport Device Interface eliminates dependencies between filing protocols and the transport protocols. Thus, Windows NT networking, or clients and servers using the Server

Message Block filing protocol, is not dependent on any one transport protocol. A server can have TCP/IP, NWLink, and the NetBEUI transport protocols loaded concurrently (see Figure 17.11) and service a wide variety of clients, some using NetBEUI, others NWLink or TCP/IP.

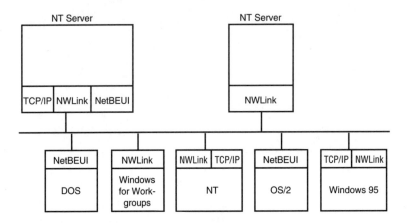

Figure 17.11. *The Windows NT Servers are responding to various clients, each using different transport protocols to transmit the SMB requests to the server. Clients can use any (or all) of the protocols listed, and the way they interact with the server does not change.*

NetBEUI Frame Protocol (NBF)

NBF, or the NetBEUI Frame protocol, is the 32-bit transport protocol included in Windows NT as a compact, fast transport protocol for carrying SMB filing protocol messages between Microsoft-compatible clients and servers.

NBF provides both *connection-oriented* and *connectionless* services to client and server applications, but its main drawback has been its lack of routing capabilities. Therefore, even though it can be used on any Microsoft networking product for client and server interaction, it is included mainly for backward compatibility with older LAN Manager clients as new NT servers are added to existing LAN Manager networks or as LAN Manager servers are upgraded to Windows NT Servers.

NWLink

NWLink is the Microsoft 32-bit IPX/SPX-compatible transport protocol that supports both the CSNW and the GSNW services (discussed in the section on filing protocols) for interacting as clients or for providing gateway services to Novell NetWare servers. This is not the only reason for using NWLink, as mentioned in the preceding section. NetBEUI, which was Microsoft's former default protocol in its networking products, lacked the capability to be routed from one network to another. The NWLink protocol provides a compact, routable, 32-bit transport protocol for the Server Message Block filing protocol.

This protocol makes an attractive alternative to TCP/IP, which formerly was Microsoft's only solution for providing a routable transport for its network products. For an environment that does not require some of the spin-off benefits of TCP/IP, such as the capability to connect to other environments, and where TCP/IP's additional administration requirements are undesirable, NWLink is an ideal solution for providing transparent routing between clients and servers.

> **Note:** TCP/IP has additional configuration requirements. However, Windows NT TCP/IP includes a feature to dynamically distribute TCP/IP configurations to clients. This feature will be described in the following section.

Besides providing a 32-bit protect-mode transport protocol for carrying file and print services to other Windows NT (as well as Windows for Workgroups and Windows 95) and Novell NetWare servers, NWLink can also be used for distributed applications. When the NWLink protocol is used on an NT Server running a distributed application such as Microsoft's SQL Server, even non-Microsoft clients can access the services of the SQL Server without additional software. A Windows NT client using NWLink can also access similar services running on a Novell NetWare server, or even a Novell UnixWare server, without additional software installed.

TCP/IP

TCP/IP, in the current version of Windows NT, has been significantly enhanced over previous versions. The reasons for implementing TCP/IP on NT are threefold. One of the most obvious reasons is for providing a connectivity solution to other environments such as UNIX and the Internet (this topic will be expanded on later in the chapter). Another purpose for using TCP/IP on NT is to set up the NT machine as a *multihomed* computer or as an IP router. This multi-homed computer can join two or more IP networks passing traffic from any host computers using TCP/IP and requiring access to one of the connected networks. The other reason for implementing TCP/IP is to provide a routable transport protocol for Microsoft networking (SMB filing protocol).

Most connectivity applications that use the TCP/IP transport protocol are written to the *Sockets* API, which is simply a set of instructions that can be accessed by an application to request services of a transport protocol. Microsoft networking uses the *NetBIOS* API to access the services of the transport protocol. To provide transparent access between NT Servers and clients using TCP/IP, a method had to be developed to use the NetBIOS API to give instructions to the TCP/IP protocol. This has surfaced as something called *NBT*, or *NetBIOS over TCP/IP*. It is documented in RFC 1001/1002.

All computers in a Windows NT network are known by a name. These names are NetBIOS names, so when a client is trying to find a server, it does so by referencing its NetBIOS name (the server name component of a UNC name described earlier is referencing a NetBIOS name). Of course, any computer using TCP/IP must also have the typical IP configuration data, such as IP address, subnet mask, and default gateway. But one of the reasons for the NBT API is so that NetBIOS names used in Windows NT commands can be resolved to IP addresses.

The DHCP Service

One significant enhancement made to TCP/IP in Windows NT Server is an addition to the protocol suite called the Dynamic Host Configuration Protocol (DHCP). DHCP is meant to relieve the anxiety endured by network administrators brought on by the myriad potential problems associated with manual configuration of TCP/IP.

DHCP practically eliminates the need for a network administrator to ever visit a workstation again (at least as far as TCP/IP issues are concerned). DHCP runs as a service on a Windows NT Server. From the DHCP graphical administration utility, the administrator defines a series of *scopes*. A scope is simply a range of IP addresses that can be given to clients on a particular subnet on the network. The administrator can configure multiple scopes, one for each subnet, on one DHCP server. There is no need to have a separate DHCP server on each subnet. As part of the scope, the administrator configures various TCP/IP configuration parameters, such as the subnet mask, the default gateway, DNS servers, and any other parameters appropriate for a particular scope of addresses, or for the entire network.

When TCP/IP is installed on what will become a DHCP client (DHCP clients can include clients as well as other servers), no options are configured. The station is simply configured as a DHCP client, and when it boots, it requests an address from a DHCP server. The DHCP server downloads the IP configuration along with any other parameters defined in the scope, and the client can then use TCP/IP. The beauty of DHCP is that if a configuration option changes or if one was overlooked before, the administrator can simply make that change at the DHCP server, and all clients automatically receive that new option the next time they boot (or manually request updates). On a network with hundreds or thousands of nodes, this update can take minutes rather than weeks.

Although DHCP is a new feature in the NT Server operating system, it is an implementation of the Internet standard RFC 1541. DHCP is actually an extension to the BOOTP protocol discussed in Chapter 14, "Special Servers and Services." For IP routers to be able to forward DHCP messages, and hence allow DHCP servers to service clients from any subnet, they must be able to act as a *BOOTP Relay Agent* (RFC 1542).

DLC

The DLC (Data Link Control) protocol is, as its name implies, a Data Link Layer protocol. It has limited capabilities and is intended for a couple of very specific purposes. The DLC protocol has no network layer or transport layer component. It therefore cannot be used as a transport protocol to carry the filing protocol messages of any of the supported networks.

DLC is intended to give Windows NT Workstations or Servers access to Hewlett Packard Jet Direct printers. These printers are directly connected to the network with their own network interface card. NT can print directly as a single client to these types of printers, as well as on behalf of other clients in a print server capacity. The second purpose for this protocol is for accessing IBM SNA networks. With a 3270 terminal emulation application and the DLC protocol, a client can make a connection to an IBM mainframe.

Network Device Interface Specification (NDIS)

The Network Device Interface Specification is a standard, originally developed by Microsoft and 3Com, to allow multiple network adapters and multiple transport protocols to coexist in a single computer. This interface also allows transport protocol components to be completely independent from network adapter drivers. Companies that develop transport protocols can write them to the NDIS standard and know they will automatically work with NDIS-compliant network adapter drivers.

NDIS consists of a small piece of code called a *wrapper*. The NDIS wrapper looks like a network adapter card driver to transport protocols, and it looks like a transport protocol driver to the network adapter driver. Hence, an NDIS-compliant TCP/IP protocol stack will pass the same information to a Token-ring network interface driver as it will for an Ethernet network interface driver.

Windows NT supports the NDIS version 3.0 specification. This version allows an unlimited number of network adapters in a single computer, and an unlimited number of transport protocols that can be bound to a single card.

Windows NT Printing

The Windows NT print architecture is broken into a client and a server component. Print support includes NT print servers accepting print requests from other NT Workstations and Servers; from other SMB clients, such as DOS, Windows, and OS/2; and from UNIX clients. Windows NT can also be configured as a print client to UNIX and other environments.

When Windows NT is acting as a print server to other SMB clients, those clients must have the appropriate printer drivers installed locally so that a print job can be completely formatted before the job is sent to the print server. This is really no different from the print support available in any current network operating system's print environment. However, it makes for a rather inconvenient situation when a user wants to send an occasional print job to network printers other than the default printer, because drivers must be installed and configured before the job can be printed.

The Windows NT print environment has some enhanced capabilities, however, when an NT client prints to an NT print server (either NT Workstation or Server). When an NT print client selects a network printer attached to an NT print server, the print server dynamically sends a copy of the printer driver to the workstation. The application on the client workstation can then use the print driver to format and send print jobs to this particular printer and can simply discard the driver when the session is finished. With this extremely simple method, users literally "point and shoot" at printers they need access to, without having to install print drivers or call administrators to install print drivers for them. Benefits are also seen when print drivers need to be updated, because they need to be updated in only one place, rather than on all workstations.

Windows NT users who want to connect to another Windows NT printer can do so by browsing the available network printers through Windows NT's Print Manager utility. Or they can do so from the command prompt by issuing the following command:

```
C:\>NET USE LPT1: \\NTSERVER\PRINTERNAME
```

From the command prompt, and from most clients, the usage of the redirection of a local parallel port, as demonstrated in the preceding line, is necessary not only in Microsoft networking but in many environments. Windows NT, however, can directly connect to printers on other computers without the need to redirect from local print ports. Therefore, the maximum number of printers you can connect to concurrently is not dictated by the number of parallel ports you have, and there is basically no limitation on the number of print connections you can have.

Windows NT also includes the capability to send and receive print jobs to and from the UNIX environment. By installing a network component called TCP/IP Printing, NT has the capability to act as an LPD print server to UNIX clients. UNIX clients can use their standard method of printing, either through applications or from a command line using the LPD command as long as they know the host name or IP address of the NT print server and the name of the printer itself. With TCP/IP printing installed, NT can also send print jobs to any printer with its own network interface card, directly attached to the network, as long as the interface card supports TCP/IP.

When NT is sending print jobs to UNIX, it can also do so through regular applications, or from a command prompt. Again, the same information about the UNIX print server is required: either the IP address or host name of the server, and the name of the printer. NT also includes the LPD command for sending print jobs to UNIX (or other NT print servers using TCP/IP), as well as an LPQ command for checking the status of print queues from the command line.

The following two examples demonstrate using these two commands. First, the LPD command is used to send a file called readme.txt to a print queue called LASER, on the host computer called BILL. The computer BILL could be UNIX or NT—the command works the same. The second command demonstrates using the LPQ command to check the status of the same print queue.

```
C:\>LPD -S bill -P laser readme.txt
```

```
C:\>LPQ -S bill -P laser -L
```

In its capacity as a printing client to UNIX, NT also can act as a UNIX print gateway on behalf of its own SMB clients that would otherwise not be able to print to UNIX printers. Clients send print jobs the same way they would for any NT shared printer, using any transport protocol they have in common with the gateway computer. Figures 17.12 and 17.13 illustrate the discussed concepts.

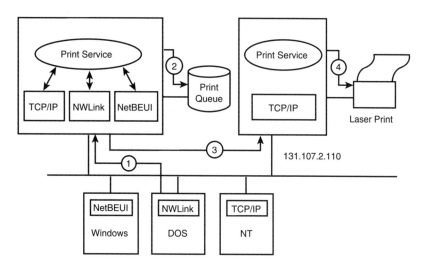

Figure 17.12. *NT clients access the Windows NT printer by connecting via a* NET USE *command as described previously or by using the graphical utilities. This works with any transport protocol they have in common with the NT print server. Windows NT simply takes the print jobs and forwards them to the UNIX printer using TCP/IP.*

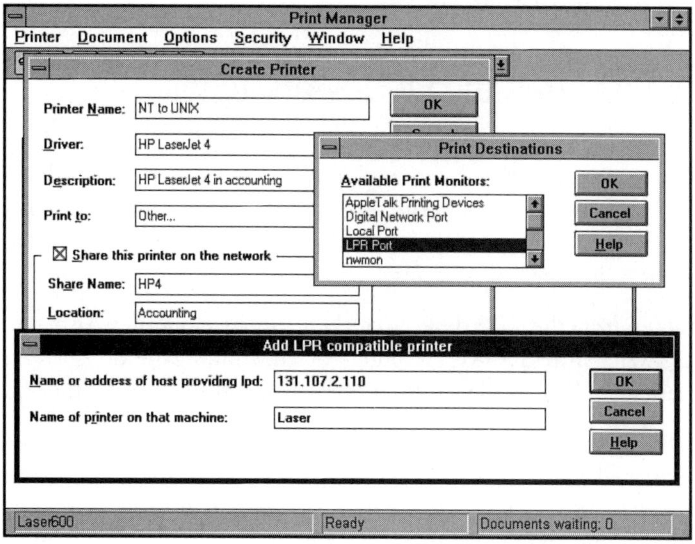

Figure 17.13. *The configuration screen of the Windows NT™ Print Manager application. It shows the setup of the UNIX print gateway, including the destination IP address of the UNIX host, and the name NT will use to make the UNIX printer available to its own clients (HP4). (Screen shot reprinted with permission from Microsoft Corporation.)*

Platform Integration Technologies

The preceding section surveyed both NetWare OS and Windows NT. Because both platforms support the TCP/IP protocol stack, both operating systems can provide routing services to hosts, including UNIX hosts, providing TCP/IP network services. This functionality falls short of achieving the higher goal of integrating resources pertaining to all hybrid network operating systems and desktop platforms and making them available to all users alike. Namely, the objective is to enable, for example, a UNIX user to make use of NetWare and Windows NT file and print services. Likewise, a DOS user should be able, in addition to accessing the NetWare and Windows NT Server, to access UNIX file and print services.

This section looks at some available options for achieving this objective. In particular, the following areas are those that are tackled in the upcoming pages:

♦ Accessing UNIX from the DOS workstation using TCP/IP

♦ Available NetWare options for integrating NetWare and UNIX file and print services

♦ Windows NT available options for integrating Windows NT and UNIX file and print services

♦ X Server technology as an integration solution

Accessing UNIX from the DOS Workstation

The ever-increasing processing power of PC computer technology, coupled with its ever-falling costs, provides many users enough motivation to consider accessing UNIX hosts right from their DOS desktops. They want an option that provides them with simultaneous access to both environments without having to abandon one for the sake of establishing a session with the other—a flexibility that ordinary terminals lack.

UNIX host access from the DOS desktop can be achieved in one of two ways: (1) by using terminal emulation software (either DOS or Windows based) running on top of a serial connection or (2) by implementing TCP/IP at the workstation, which is the subject of the current discussion.

Many TCP/IP software implementations are available for the DOS workstation. In addition to providing users telnet access to UNIX, most of these implementations provide other TCP/IP access methods such as ftp, rcp, and rsh services—far more features and better performance than serial communications terminal emulation access methods.

Implementing TCP/IP on the DOS workstation involves the following steps:

1. Install a network interface card in the PC. The interface card must be set up properly, ensuring that its hardware settings do not conflict with existing hardware. The interrupt request number, the port I/O address, and the memory address must be unique to the network interface card.

2. Install the TCP/IP software according to the vendor instructions.

3. As with UNIX hosts, DOS workstation running TCP/IP must be assigned unique IP addresses. See Chapter 4, "The Internet Layer and Routing," for details on IP address structures and assignments.

4. Unless DNS service is set up on your network, you must create a hosts file on the PC as directed by the TCP/IP software vendor. Include in the file the host name-to-IP address associations pertaining to all hosts to which the user wants access.

5. If DNS service is set up on your network, you must update the DNS database to include the newly set up DOS workstation. In particular, this task involves updating the named.hosts with a host name-to-IP address mapping, and the named.rev file with the reverse mapping. Refer to Chapter 10, "Setting Up the Domain Name System," for details on updating the DNS database.

6. If RARP service is set up on the network and the PC is configured to rely on the RARP server for address assignment, you must duly update both /etc/ethers and /etc/hosts on the RARP server. Look in Chapter 14, "Special Servers and Services," for details on updating the RARP server database.

Note that this level of integration provides the user with simultaneous access to both DOS and UNIX from the DOS workstation. A UNIX user is not provided an equivalent access. Depending on the identified needs of the user community, this might as well be an acceptable solution. It is also worth mentioning that this level of integration is not taking place at the file system level.

This solution assumes that the user is well versed in UNIX user commands and TCP/IP utilities to be able to make use of UNIX resources on the network. To the DOS user, establishing a connection with UNIX does not grant her transparent access to the resources or the ability to freely copy and manipulate files using DOS commands. Neither does the user have the ability to invoke a DOS application to process a UNIX host-resident data file, let alone print to UNIX shared printers. All of these limitations make alternative solutions based on integrating file systems more appealing.

PC NFS Client

A better level of integration can be achieved by installing on the DOS workstation any of the commercially available PC NFS client implementations, such as LAN WorkPlace NFS Client from Novell or PC/NFS from ftp software.

PC NFS products are mostly client-only implementations of the NFS suite. This means an NFS client product provides the client mechanisms extending the DOS user's local resources to include remote file systems that are exported by UNIX hosts. The NFS client on the workstation enables the user to perceive file systems mounted from UNIX hosts as additional drives that can be accessed using DOS conventions.

Figure 17.14 illustrates the NFS client concept as applied to the DOS workstation. In the figure, a DOS workstation is shown to include one local hard disk only, which is commonly referenced as DOS drive C:. With the NFS client installed, the DOS user perceives the UNIX exported file system as another local drive that can be referenced using another drive letter, such as D:. As such, users will be able to transparently invoke DOS programs and data files directly from the UNIX host. This therefore eliminates the need for the user to learn the UNIX operating system in order to take advantage of UNIX network available resources.

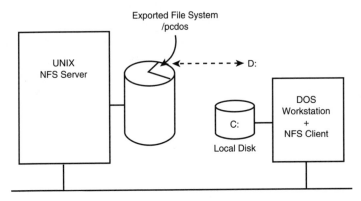

Figure 17.14. *With NFS installed on the workstation, the DOS user perceives an exported file system as an additional disk that can be accessed using DOS conventions.*

Some NFS client implementations go even farther by providing DOS users with network printing capabilities. Accordingly, a user will be able to redirect printing out of local LPT or COM ports to UNIX shared printers on the network.

Installing DOS NFS Client

Installing the NFS client on the DOS workstation is vendor specific. To provide you with a feel of what is being involved, an overview of installing LAN WorkPlace NFS Client by Novell is presented in the following few pages.

The installation program INSTALL.EXE comes on a single disk with other programs and utilities. Before you run INSTALL.EXE, the workstation should be already configured to run the TCP/IP protocol suite. The installation is a straightforward process, involving responding to a few prompts with the necessary information that INSTALL.EXE needs in order to configure the NFS client properly. You should be prepared to enter the IP address of the UNIX NFS server.

At the end of the installation, both the CONFIG.SYS and the AUTOEXEC.BAT files are modified to accommodate NFS drivers and client programs. Of particular interest are the two NFS programs run from AUTOEXEC.BAT, assuming that the TCP/IP suite was run before those programs were loaded. These are the programs:

LWPRPC.COM   When run, this program makes the Remote Procedure Call protocol memory resident.

LWPNFS.COM   This program is a network redirector. When run, LWPNFS.COM inserts itself between the DOS operating system and the application code. Depending on the context of the path being referenced, the redirector submits the call either to DOS for processing or to the NFS server in the form of an RPC request. In Figure 17.15, for example, a function call referencing a path including C: as the drive being accessed is passed to DOS OS. On the other hand, a function call referencing D: would be packaged in an RPC request and submitted to the NFS server across the wire. At this stage, LWRPC.COM takes over communication of the request to its RPC peer on the NFS server.

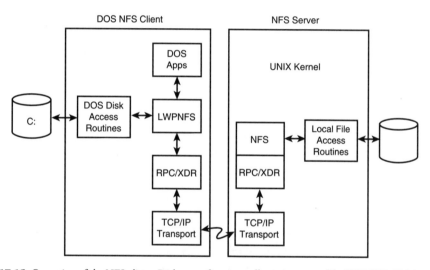

Figure 17.15. *Operation of the NFS client. Disk access function calls are intercepted by LWPNFS.COM and fielded to the appropriate mechanism, depending on the disk drive letter being specified.*

In addition to its redirection capability, LWPNFS.COM performs data read-ahead and write-behind operations in a fashion similar to the biod daemon on UNIX clients. Data is read from, and written to, the NFS server in large chunks. Separate read and write buffers are maintained on the client for this purpose. The size of the buffers is tunable using command-line parameters with LWPNFS.COM. The read-ahead caching mechanism contributes to better performance by ensuring that data is readily available to user processes before it is requested.

Further improvement in performance is also achieved by the write-behind mechanism. It ensures that data pertaining to several write requests is sent to the server in one large packet instead of being sent in several smaller packets—hence contributing to better disk I/O performance on the NFS server.

On the server side, UNIX is equipped with a pcnfsd daemon, which authenticates DOS NFS clients and their users, as well as provides support for network printing. pcnfsd is started with other NFS daemons whenever the system enters run level three and requires no configuration; neither does it support any command-line options.

In addition to the pcnfsd daemon being started, the NFS server must be configured to share its file systems with the DOS clients. Chapter 12, "Setting Up Network File System Service," explained how to share file systems using the share command. In the following example, share is used to export the /pcdos file system to DOS host name muffy:

```
# share -F nfs -o rw=muffy /pcdos
```

You can also update the /etc/exports file, as explained in Chapter 12, to ensure that the shared file systems are exported upon reboot of the server.

This concludes the installation and configuration overview of the LAN WorkPlace NFS Client. To bring up the server, the DOS workstation needs to be rebooted, making the new CONFIG.SYS and AUTOEXEC.BAT take effect. Next, an overview of using LAN WorkPlace NFS Client is presented.

Using LAN WorkPlace NFS Client

To transparently access an NFS file system, the DOS user needs to reference it using a drive letter as per DOS path access conventions. Assigning a disk drive letter to the remote file system (called drive letter mapping) is achieved using the NET LINK command. In the following example, this command is used to map drive letter F to the /pcdos shared file system on host jade:

```
C:\> NET LINK F: \\jade\/pcdos pat password
```

Notice how both the user name and the password are required to authenticate the user for NFS access. When authenticated, the user will be able to reference the NFS file system using the designated letter (F: in the preceding example). Consequently, the user will be able to use DOS applications and traditional DOS commands such as COPY and EDIT to manipulate data files maintained on the NFS server.

There are two limitations to dealing with files maintained on the NFS server:

Data file formats   Plain text files are formatted differently under DOS and UNIX. An end-of-line under DOS is marked by two control characters: carriage return and line feed. Under UNIX, an end-of-line is marked by the line feed control character only. Consequently, before a file can be used by DOS applications, the user must ensure that the file is formatted to DOS conventions. Otherwise, he might need to use the UNIX2DOS utility to convert the file to a DOS-compliant format.

Namespaces

Whereas NFS allows filenames to be up to 255 characters in length and to include any printable character, DOS namespace is restricted to the familiar 8.3 naming conventions. A filename cannot exceed a total of 12 characters including the name, the extension, and the dot separating them. Consequently, when a user performs a directory listing using the DOS DIR command, NFS filenames not meeting DOS conventions undergo conversion by the NFS client. This results in names that might be significantly different from their original versions. Another restriction arising from name conversion is that only those paths including subdirectories with valid DOS filenames not requiring conversion are supported by the NFS client.

As mentioned earlier, DOS NFS clients support network printing from the DOS workstation. This is achieved by redirecting the output of any of the LPT or COM ports on the PC to a UNIX shared printer. To do that with LAN WorkPlace NFS Client, use the NET LINK command as depicted here:

```
C:\> NET LINK LPT1: \\jade\nwprinter pat password
```

This command redirects the LPT1 parallel port to network printer nwprinter on host jade. Consequently, whenever the user issues a print command to the LPT1 port, LWPNFS.COM intercepts the print function call and redirects it to host jade for printing on printer nwprinter.

NetWare Integration Solutions

The following subsections cover the topic of NetWare integration solutions.

NetWare NFS

Novell's NetWare NFS product transparently integrates UNIX systems with NetWare file servers. It provides UNIX users access to NetWare file system resources from their native operating system. It also includes support for bidirectional printing services, allowing both UNIX and NetWare clients (mostly DOS users) to share one common pool of network printers. As such, a NetWare user can print to a UNIX printer, and a UNIX user can print to NetWare printers.

NetWare NFS is implemented in compliance with the applicable TCP/IP RFCs (see Chapter 12 for the actual RFC numbers). This means that when deployed on a NetWare platform, the file server is perceived by UNIX users as a traditional NFS server.

By behaving as a native NFS server, NetWare NFS enables UNIX and DOS users to share all, or portions, of the file system resources using their native command set. Neither is required to learn a new command set.

NetWare NFS Architecture

As shown in Figure 17.16, NetWare NFS capitalizes on NetWare OS multiprotocol support. The product packages a suite of NetWare Loadable Modules (NLMs) that take care of the NFS application protocol suite and some other additional TCP/IP services such as FTP, BSD's Line Printing Daemon (LPD), and an X Window client that enables an X server user to remotely monitor the status of the file server.

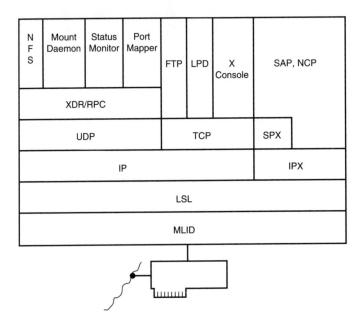

Figure 17.16. *NetWare NFS architecture.*

Because NFS protocols were explained in Chapter 12, no further detail is provided here. Instead, the discussion focuses on highlighting how some of the differences in semantics between the file systems (NetWare and NFS) are resolved. Also, bidirectional printing between UNIX and NetWare is discussed.

NFS and NetWare file systems define different semantics for organizing and managing files and directories. Under NFS, each file and directory has a set of associated attributes such as permissions defining access rights, owner ID, and file size. NetWare, on the other hand, defines a more comprehensive set of attributes, including access rights and flags that enable the system administrator or user to protect a file from being named, hide a file, or inhibit file deletions.

Another difference is manifested in the naming conventions that each of the file systems supports. Under NetWare, files and directories can assume names compatible with DOS naming conventions (that is, the 8.3 rule). NFS, on the other hand, supports file and directory names up to 255 characters. Also, some of the characters supported by NFS cannot be used under NetWare in naming files.

One way to resolve these differences is to implement some sort of a translation mechanism that arbitrates simultaneous access to a file by both DOS and UNIX clients. Translation mechanisms, however, can very quickly prove taxing in terms of performance as the load on the file server increases in direct proportion to the number of users and processes running on the server.

Among NetWare's strong features is its support of multiple namespaces in their native format. Among supported namespaces are DOS, NFS, OS/2, MAC, and OSI's File Transfer and Access Method (FTAM). The comprehensiveness of multiple namespace support allows hybrid clients on the same network to share the same file and directory resources available on the NetWare file server. To simplify matters and deliver reasonable performance, NetWare designers chose to support multiple directory entries per file. The number of entries depends on the number of deployed namespaces (see the sidebar below, titled "Multiple Namespace Support").

The NetWare file system organization is based on two structures, the File Allocation Table (FAT) and the Directory Entry Table (DET).

NetWare OS uses FATs to access files on the server volumes. A FAT maintains pointers to the various blocks of files that physically reside on the volume. Depending on its size, a file might reside on one or more blocks of disk space. The block size, which is configured at installation time, can be set to 4K, 8K, 16K, 32K, or 64K. Also, different volumes can be configured to support different block sizes.

DET occupies a special area of the volume where all NetWare file attributes and access rights are maintained by the server. At a minimum, the NetWare OS maintains one directory entry per file. Corresponding to every additional namespace, an additional directory entry per file is also created. Additional entries take care of the file attributes as defined by the native namespace. Hence, by adding NFS namespace, for example, an additional directory entry for every file on that volume is created. This entry maintains the full set of NFS file and directory attributes, in addition to the already existing default entry that maintains NetWare and DOS file attributes. This in turn cleverly eliminates the need for the more time-consuming translation process between the different namespaces. Depending on the client, NetWare OS presents the data file and its attributes to that client by directly accessing the pertinent directory entry maintained on the volume.

Multiple Namespace Support

Namespace support is subject to loading a special NLM with a name ending with the extension .NAM. NFS.NAM, for example, is the NLM that supports NFS namespace. Also, at the file server's console, a special command must be entered, only once in the server's NFS support life cycle. The console command is ADD NAMESPACE. Following is an example of adding NFS namespace to the volume UNIXVOL on the file server:

```
:ADD NAMESPACE NFS TO VOLUME UNIXVOL
```

As mentioned earlier, this is a one-time command that has to be issued on the file server's console. In addition, the NFS.NAM module must have been loaded on the file server. Loading it is a simple matter of entering the following command:

```
:LOAD NFS.NAM
```

Unlike ADD NAMESPACE, the NFS.NAM module must be loaded every time the server is restarted.

NetWare Exported File Systems and Security

Being compliant with the RFCs defining NFS, NetWare NFS is fully capable of providing all the features that traditional UNIX NFS servers provide. In particular, NetWare NFS enables the system administrator to export full or portions of NetWare volumes. Also, the administrator has control over the file server security.

As shown in Figure 17.17, the NetWare file server TATTOO supports two volumes, SYS: and APPS:. At the root of volume APPS:, operating system specific directories (UNIXAPPS and DOSAPPS) are created to maintain applications pertaining to UNIX and DOS users. In this example, a NetWare file server administrator might decide to export the path APPS:UNIXAPPS and potentially the APPS:SHARED directory, where data shared by both DOS and UNIX users is maintained.

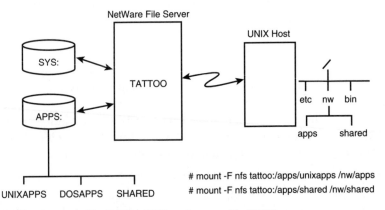

Figure 17.17. *Only paths exported by NetWare NFS can be accessed by UNIX users.*

A NetWare administrator can also restrict access to exported file systems to specific hosts, again similar to traditional NFS servers. Using the appropriate administrative tools, the names of the trusted hosts can be entered, as well as the operations (that is, read, write, and root access) that these hosts are allowed to perform on the exported paths.

Restrictions can be narrowed further to include the names of the users coming from those hosts who might have access to those paths. NetWare NFS controls user access by mapping NFS user and group IDs to NetWare user and group names. This means that, using the proper tools, the system administrator can establish a mapping between a UNIX user and an existing NetWare account name, implying that the UNIX user will have identical access rights to the equivalent NetWare account to the exported paths.

Mounting NetWare File Systems on UNIX Clients

After NetWare NFS is installed and configured on the file server, a UNIX user can access the exported file systems by first mounting them. To do so, the UNIX user needs to apply what he already uses to mount the remote UNIX NFS file system. The following example illustrates an instance of using the mount command on the UNIX client to mount the path APPS:UNIXAPPS from the file server TATTOO:

```
# mount -f NFS tattoo:/apps/unixapps /apps
```

The example assumes that the /etc/hosts file or the DNS server's database are updated with the appropriate host name-to-IP address mappings of the NetWare file server.

Bidirectional Print Services

Integrating UNIX and NetWare platforms extends beyond the file system boundaries to include network print services. NetWare NFS (the product) includes the necessary NLMs that allow both UNIX and NetWare environments to share the same pool of print resources. By virtue of this support, a NetWare client will be able to print to a UNIX shared printer, and a UNIX user can equally print to NetWare shared printers.

On a network, two UNIX hosts can share print resources by deploying BSD's Line Printing Daemon protocol. Figure 7.18 illustrates the interaction taking place between an LPD client (host A) and an LPD server where the physical printer is attached.

Setting up LPD print service requires the system administrator to configure the lpd daemon to send print jobs it discovers in its local spool area to the lpd daemon on host B. For host B to honor clients' print job requests, the system administrator should have created and updated the /etc/hosts.lpd file with the names of the hosts authorized to make such requests.

As shown in the following figure, when an LPD client discovers a print job in the local spool directory, it proceeds to establish a TCP connection with the remote server. Subject to security restrictions, the print job is then sent to the server, which in turn can send the job to the printer. If the printer is busy, the lpd server keeps the print job in its local spool directory until the printer becomes available.

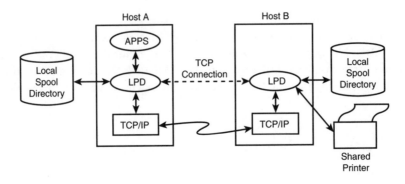

Figure 17.18. *Interaction between the LPD client and server.*

NetWare NFS implements the LPD daemon in two NLMs, PLPD.NLM and LPR_GWY.NLM. The former NLM provides the server's functionality allowing UNIX hosts to send print jobs to NetWare printers; the latter one provides the client's capability to submit the NetWare file server print jobs, on behalf of its clients, to UNIX network printers. Figure 17.19 illustrates the interaction between UNIX and NetWare when print services are being exchanged. The diagram shows a UNIX client printing to a NetWare printer. The same interaction applies if the roles are reversed.

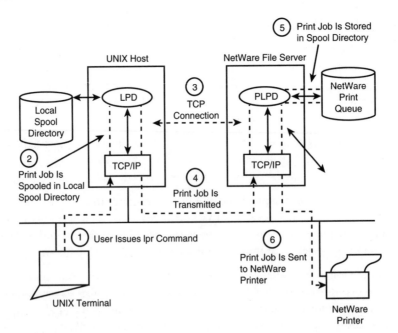

Figure 17.19. *UNIX-to-NetWare print service.*

Access Control

Bidirectional printing between UNIX and NetWare platforms is governed by the same access control mechanisms that are normally deployed between LPD clients and servers on an exclusively UNIX network. UNIX clients can print only to NetWare queues that are made available to the LPD daemon by the system administrator. Also, access restrictions can be narrowed to preclude all but so-called "trusted hosts." Furthermore, the administrator has the option to allow all users coming from trusted hosts, or to allow only some users while precluding all others.

NetWare-to-UNIX printing can be controlled in an almost identical fashion, whereby a UNIX host can honor only those requests coming from trusted hosts, both UNIX and NetWare. It also can be configured to accept requests from certain users only.

Windows NT Integration Technologies

Windows NT includes software to facilitate integration into many diverse environments. This built-in software, coupled with a network architecture that is wide open to the development of third-party network clients and other types of add-on software, provides for an extremely powerful desktop operating system and a network operating system.

The remainder of this section provides a brief overview of the connectivity software included with Windows NT, with an emphasis on UNIX integration from both client and server perspectives.

Client Service for NetWare and Gateway Service for NetWare

If you review the Windows NT network architecture diagram (Figure 17.7), you will notice two components at the filing protocol level that were included in the diagram but not discussed. These filing protocols are the Client Service for NetWare (CSNW), included with Windows NT Workstation, and the Gateway Service for NetWare (GSNW), included with Windows NT Server. These two products are built-in add-ons to NT that represent the client side of Novell NetWare's NetWare Core Protocol (NCP) filing protocol, allowing the NT Workstation and Server products to access file and print services on a NetWare server. This further enhances NT's capabilities for integrating into a hybrid environment of not only UNIX, but NetWare as well.

> **Note:** NCP, when referring to NetWare client and server interaction, is synonymous with the functionality of Microsoft's SMB filing protocol.

This product is not a Novell product; it is a 32-bit service developed by Microsoft and built into both NT platforms. Using this service, an administrator of an NT network can concurrently administer a Novell Network using the standard network administration tools from the NetWare server. It also means that a user can access the same files and printers from an NT Workstation as they can access from a DOS or standard Windows client.

These services are known by different names on the NT Workstation and Server products to reflect the capabilities inherent in each platform. The NCP service on the NT Workstation is known as the CSNW (Client Service for NetWare) to reflect its capabilities as a NetWare client, as described previously. The NCP service on the NT Server product, however, is known as the GSNW (Gateway Service for NetWare). The GSNW has all the same capabilities as its NT Workstation counterpart, except that it has the capability to act as an NCP gateway to applications and data stored on the NetWare servers for Microsoft SMB clients such as NT Workstations, Windows for Workgroups, DOS, or Windows 3.1 (using only MS network client software).

MUP and MPR

In discussing integration technologies from the perspective of Windows NT, it is interesting to see not only how well Windows NT accepts client (and sometimes server) software from other environments and vendors into its own environment, but also how NT presents these many diverse environments to the user. It's also interesting to see how a user faced with the need to access resources in an environment unfamiliar to her own can do so with very little effort.

Windows NT enables users to access the file and print resources, from virtually any supported network environment, the same way users access native NT resources or, more precisely, SMB resources. This transparency is extended to not only the built-in support for NetWare servers, but also third-party software such as the Banyan Vines redirector, or various NFS clients that are available from many vendors (some to be listed at the end of the section).

Figure 17.20 presents a high-level part of NT's networking architecture that has not been presented yet. These components sit above the filing protocols already discussed. They are the method applications used to access the services of the various redirectors. This example assumes that the two client redirectors already discussed, Microsoft SMBs and the CSNW (NetWare NCPs), are installed, as well as the Banyan Vines client for NT (available from Banyan). The important additions to note in the diagram are the components at the top, called the *Multi-UNC Provider* (MUP) and the *Multi-Provider Router* (MPR).

Recall from a previous discussion that an NT client had the capability to access another NT server's shared resources directly using UNC names or by connecting a drive letter, such as H:, to a UNC path. Because of the MUP component, this kind of flexibility can be extended to both NetWare servers or Banyan Vines servers, or others, by the use of these commands:

```
C:\>DIR \\NTSERVER\SHARE
```

```
C:\>DIR \\NetWare\VOLUME
```

```
C:\>DIR \\SERVICE@GROUP@ORGANIZATION\DIRECTORY
```

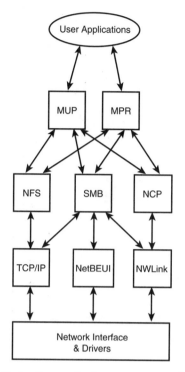

Figure 17.20. *Access methods available for client applications to access network services from multiple environments.*

The first command is being directed to an NT Server, the second is to a NetWare server, and the third is to a Banyan Vines server. If drive letter connections were required for these disk resources, you could have used the various operating system's native commands —for instance, NetWare's MAP command, or Banyan's SETDRIVE command. But you could also do all three by using NT's NET USE command:

```
C:\>NET USE F: \\NTSERVER\SHARE
```

```
C:\>NET USE G: \\NetWare\VOLUME
```

```
C:\>NET USE H: \\SERVICE@GROUP@ORGANIZATION\DIRECTORY
```

The MUP's responsibility here is to accept any UNC pathname (\\server\share) and find an underlying redirector (or filing protocol) that will accept it (redirectors "register" with the MUP at start time), regardless of the number of redirectors installed. Also, in the preceding example, standard filing procedures such as copying, deleting, moving, and renaming can be performed transparently across the three environments (for example, COPY G:*.* H:).

The preceding discussion assumes that all applications have to use UNC names, either with or without a drive letter to access network resources, which is not the case with Windows NT. NT includes a 32-bit network access API that applications can take direct advantage of, called the Windows NT Win32 API. Applications that take advantage of this (such as NT's File Manager or Print Manager) make calls directly to the Win32 API. The other component displayed in Figure 17.20 is called the MPR (Multi-Provider Router). The MPR accepts requests from any application making calls through the Win32 API, and it presents the applications with a consistent interface even when multiple redirectors are installed. Client redirectors like the ones described previously (NT's, CSNW, Banyan's or one of the many NFS clients available) include a component called a *provider* that informs the MPR that services through this redirector are available. Figure 17.21 demonstrates the user interface of a Win32 application (NT's File Manager) presenting the user with a "browse list" of file servers from the Banyan, Microsoft, NetWare, and NFS environments.

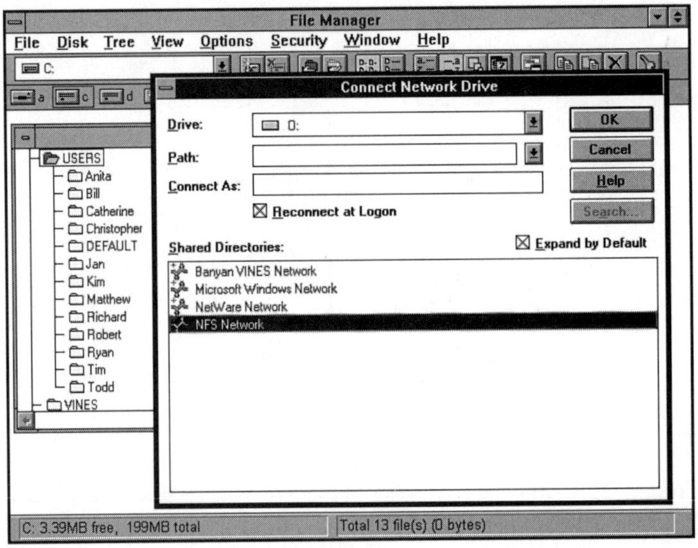

Figure 17.21. *The Windows NT™ File Manager application accessing the services of multiple networks concurrently. (Screen shot reprinted with permission from Microsoft Corporation.)*

The user can now easily browse resources on all four completely different environments from one application (one screen). A unified logon to the four environments is also possible. As new clients are developed for NT, those resources will automatically appear on this interface as well.

UNIX Integration

The preceding discussion might lead you to believe that integration with UNIX would require third-party software. Although it is true that an even higher level of integration can be achieved between Windows NT and UNIX using third-party products, such as NFS products, Windows NT includes many services and connectivity applications for providing integration to UNIX. Most of these are installed by default when the TCP/IP protocol is installed on NT. As a client to UNIX, NT includes TCP/IP applications and utilities such as FTP, TELNET, RCP, RSH, REXEC, PING, NETSTAT, TRACERT, FINGER, and ROUTE (the functionality and usage of these utilities are the same as were discussed in previous chapters), as well as the print utilities LPR and LPQ, discussed in the preceding section.

These TCP/IP applications are for the most part "Client side" only. Microsoft also provides an FTP server that UNIX clients can access with their own FTP client software. Internet users accessing Microsoft's FTP server on the Internet (FTP.MICROSOFT.COM), are connecting to the Windows NT FTP server service.

DNS and WINS

Another service NT can provide to UNIX clients is a DNS service. Microsoft's DNS service works in a similar fashion to the DNS discussed in Chapter 10, with one interesting modification. To describe this feature, it is helpful to reflect briefly on one of the previous sections on Windows NT multiprotocol networking with the TCP/IP protocol.

Remember that Microsoft networking on TCP/IP required a method to resolve NetBIOS computer names to IP addresses. On local networks, this is not very difficult, and clients can actually do their own name resolution. When a Windows NT client, however, tries to access a Windows NT server that is on the other side of a router, it is a considerably different situation. To handle this, the Windows NT Server product includes a service called WINS (Windows Internet Name Service).

WINS is simply an online directory of what servers are available (by NetBIOS name) and what their associated IP addresses are. This is actually a relatively easy service to implement; any server that should be known in this database is configured as a WINS client. On startup, the servers simply report to the WINS server, and the WINS server registers them in the database. Then, any Microsoft TCP/IP client (NT Servers and Workstations, DOS, Windows, or Windows for Workgroups) can use this centralized dynamic registry to find remote servers.

This might look very similar to the UNIX DNS service discussed in Chapter 10, "Setting Up the Domain Name System." That's because it provides very similar services to Windows NT clients. For Microsoft networking clients configured to use the WINS service for NetBIOS networking, WINS also functions as a DNS server to resolve IP addresses of host names referenced while using sockets-based utilities and applications.

One major difference between the WINS and DNS services is that entries are added and removed dynamically from the WINS server, whereas the DNS entries must be manually entered or removed. UNIX clients can take advantage of the dynamic nature of the WINS database (see Figure 17.22) by using Windows NT's DNS service. NT's DNS service has the capability to point to the WINS database. Therefore, any UNIX client that is using the services of NT's DNS is having its requests routed to the WINS service, running on either the same server or a remote server.

Note: Windows NT's DNS service is included with the Resource Kit for Windows NT, an additional product. It is not included in the standard package.

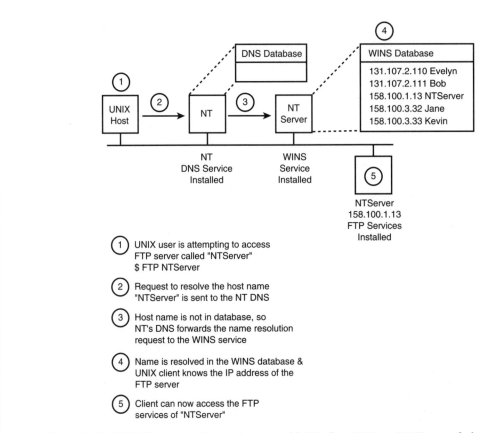

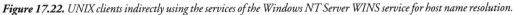

Figure 17.22. UNIX clients indirectly using the services of the Windows NT Server WINS service for host name resolution.

Third-Party NT Integration Software

In discussing interoperability between Windows NT and UNIX, it is important to mention some of the third-party products that are available for this purpose. There are many kinds of products available that further enhance integration between Windows NT and UNIX. Among the various products that are available from other companies are FTP servers and clients, TELNET servers and clients, and X Window servers and clients, as well as NFS server and client software. A few examples of some of these products are listed here:

NFS Product	Company
Chameleon32 NFS	NetManage
PCNFS for NT	Intergraph
Diskshare for NT	Intergraph
NFS for NT	Beame & Whiteside

X Window Product	Company
PC-Xware for NT	Network Computing Devices
MultiView/X	JSB Corporation
eXcursion	Digital Equipment Corporation

One other notable product that really deserves its own category in this section is a product called Portage from Consensys. This product is actually a full implementation of UNIX System V Release 4.2 running on top of Windows NT.

X Window

It is common to find more than one type of hardware platform running UNIX on the same network. It is also common to find different flavors of UNIX running on the same hardware platform. For many users, this compounded diversity prevented them from sharing applications on the network. This is mainly because most of the applications are specific to the hardware and software platforms they run on.

This difficulty presented both the academic and the vendor communities with the challenge of developing a technology that would make applications interoperable between different platforms across the network. Put differently, it presented them with the challenge of providing users with the ability to integrate network application resources regardless of the platforms on which they run. This challenge coincided with yet another one posed by the rising demand on GUI interfaces, primarily promoted by the plethora of shrink-wrapped MS Windows applications available to the DOS user.

In search of a solution to these challenges, the Massachusetts Institute of Technology (MIT) developed the X Window system in the mid 1980s. The promise that this technology manifested triggered an ever-rising interest in the vendor community for subsequent adoption and further development. X Window system is now taken care of by a consortium, known as X Consortium, of academic and vendor establishments that share the interest in pushing X to meet the ever-increasing user demand for better applications interoperability and GUI interfaces.

The X Window system provides a network graphics engine that enables a user to start an application on a remote host while collecting its output on her own physical display unit. This functionality is identical to starting a terminal emulation session using TELNET. An X Window session, however, provides the user with graphical capabilities that TELNET and other character-based terminal emulation solutions fall short of providing. Furthermore, using X Window, a user can even start multiple sessions on different hosts and manage to have the outputs displayed in separate windows on the same display device.

Although X Window was originally developed to meet the needs of the hybrid UNIX environments, one of X Window's greatest features is its portability to other platforms, such as DOS, Macintosh, and mainframe environments. This is due to the architecture on which X is based. Accordingly, right from the DOS workstation, for example, a user can invoke applications running on hybrid operating system and hardware platforms. And using capabilities such as cut-and-paste, the user can easily integrate data from those applications in one document or spreadsheet, a feature that further enhanced X Window's popularity as a trusted solution for integrating hybrid environments.

The Architecture of X

X's platform independence is derived from the mechanism and model that underlie its foundations: the X protocol and the client/server model.

Figure 17.23 illustrates the client/server model on which X is partly based. The X client runs on the host where user applications are invoked, whereas the X server runs on the user's workstation. This is a confusing concept because network users have always perceived, and duly so, their end of the connection as the client's end and the remote host as the server's end.

Under X, the client handles all data processing aspects for an application, except for the I/O interaction that it delegates to a server process. The X server process could be running on the same machine, a remote graphical terminal, or a graphical workstation across the network—that is, where the actual graphical resources reside. As shown in the figure, an X client issues messages to the server requesting it to carry I/O-specific commands that result in painting the user's display with the application output. Having said that, it is clearly implied that an X server presents applications with a virtual display unit that they can manage. The display server maps I/O primitives, passed to it by X applications, to physical actions on the actual display unit.

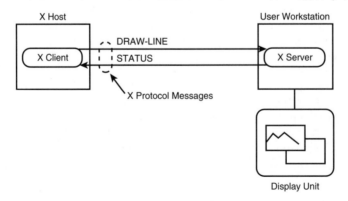

Figure 17.23. *The X Window system architecture. An X client and server exchange messages using an X protocol mechanism.*

As shown in Figure 17.24, an X client can be shared by more than one X server. In the figure, two clients, a UNIX user and MS Windows user, are shown to be sharing the same X client application simultaneously. This is possible because the client application runs at the client host, which in this diagram might be a mainframe bearing no relation to the platforms on which the X servers are running.

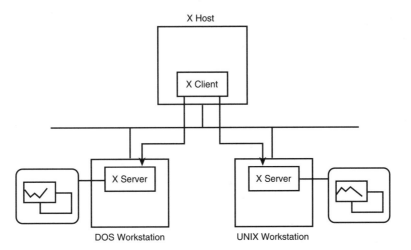

Figure 17.24. *X servers on hybrid platforms sharing the same client. The X client could be running on a mainframe while the X servers are running on DOS or UNIX workstations.*

Instead of making the I/O message exchange between the X server and client dependent on the hardware or operating system platform on which X is being brought up, the X Window designers chose to base it on a protocol mechanism called X protocol. In doing so, X's interoperability between hybrid platforms was guaranteed. Also, vendors and developers of X applications were insulated from platform-related concerns and specifics, which eased the path to porting their implementations.

Another important aspect of X protocol is its transport independence. There are current implementations, such as eXceed/W for Windows by Hummingbird Communications LTD, that run not only on TCP/IP but also on other popular transport protocols, such as Novell's IPX/SPX, DECnet, and dial-up protocols. This further enhances X Window's capabilities as a feasible choice for integrating complex environments.

Figure 17.25 depicts an X server that established three X sessions, one using TCP/IP, another using DECnet, and yet another with a mainframe across a dial-up link.

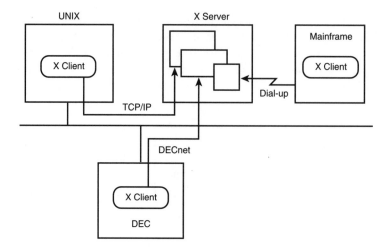

Figure 17.25. *In a multiprotocol environment, an X server can establish multiple sessions with hybrid platforms on top of different transport protocols.*

Summary

No single platform or transport protocol can fulfill the ever-increasingly sophisticated user needs. This led many environments to deploy hybrid platforms in which each was deemed best at responding to the particular needs of production. Hybridization manifested itself in diversity in hardware, operating systems, and network platforms.

This chapter gave an overview of the various networking technologies and some of the relevant products for providing interoperability between the various and hybrid components that exist on many networks today. In particular, multiprotocol support, NFS, and the X Window system were visited in the light of integrating multiplatforms. An overview of network operating systems such as NetWare OS, and Windows NT technologies were also covered. The concern was to demonstrate how different NOS vendors approached network integration and interoperability between hybrid platform, and to inform the reader of the opportunities that exist in the market for achieving the integration objective.

Appendix

Service Access Facility

Introduction

Service Access Facility (SAF) is a new administrative tool that was introduced with UNIX SVR4. SAF was intended to provide a comprehensive set of tools, with a uniform interface, for the purpose of creating and administering local and network physical resources. Examples of such resources include printing (local and network printing) and serial communications-related services.

Prior to SVR4, administrators had to use different tool sets when dealing with different resources. LP print service, for example, required different commands than those required to configure and manage a serial port for remote login. Although these tools are still supported for reasons of backward compatibility, SAF is intended as a convenient replacement.

This appendix provides an overview and command-level treatment of SAF. It supplements Chapters 9 and 14, which reference SAF without providing much detail.

Service Access Facility Hierarchy

As shown in Figure A.1, SAF defines a three-level hierarchy of processes:

◆ Port service processes, defined at the bottom of the hierarchy.

◆ Port monitor processes, defined in the middle of the hierarchy. A port monitor controls one or more port service processes.

◆ The service access controller process, at the top of the hierarchy. It controls one or more port monitor processes.

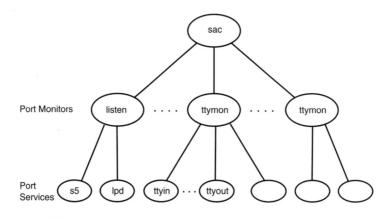

Figure A.1. *SAF's three-level hierarchy.*

Port Services

Port service processes, defined at the bottom of the SAF hierarchy, are responsible for controlling and monitoring access to applications through physical ports such as serial and network interfaces. Through the serial ports, port services provide users with remote login capabilities using either direct links or dial-in/dial-out capabilities.

Port services that control serial ports are known as `ttymon` port services. Across-the-network services such as network printing, NFS file service, or remote login are controlled and managed through network-specific port services, referred to as `listen` port services.

SAF enforces a one-to-one mapping between instances of port services and the physical ports they support. One port service cannot control more than one physical port, and no single port can be controlled by more than one port service. To render the port services conveniently distinguishable from each other, every instance of port services is assigned a name, called the port service tag. You should assign meaningful names to port services. Names that convey the nature of the service being supported by the associated physical port are the best. If, for example, a serial port is dedicated for dial-out purposes, a suggested tag would be `dialout`.

Note: Port services are not actually represented by running daemon processes. Each service is kicked off in response to an incoming request that's handled by the port monitor. The idea was to not have a separate `getty` running for every port, waiting for logins.

Port Monitors

A port monitor, defined in the middle of the hierarchy, is responsible for controlling and monitoring a set of related lower-level port service processes. Currently, only two types of port monitors are defined, listen and ttymon. listen is responsible for network-associated service processes, and ttymon is responsible for serial communications-associated processes.

Port monitor type ttymon replaces getty and uugetty, the two familiar programs that are used to control dial-in/dial-out access, as well as direct connection to terminals. To enable this access, system administrators used to include a line similar to the following one in the /etc/inittab file on the host:

```
co:2345:respawn:/etc/getty tty01 sc_m
```

Under SAF, both getty and uugetty are still supported—that is, administrators can continue using them in the accustomed way. Using SAF, however, is the preferred method of deploying and administering these services.

The advantage of using SAF as opposed to using getty processes is that by using a single ttymon port monitor, you aggregate the administration of all physical port services at the port monitor level. Using port-monitor administrative tools, you can enable or disable a set of tty ports instead of having to carry out these tasks individually. You can be selective and turn on or off one or two of a set of port services that are controlled by that port monitor.

Another advantage is derived from the uniformity in using these same administrative skills and applying them to other types of port monitors including listen. They can also be applied to the types that would be introduced in the future by UNIX vendors and application providers. Hence, there is a minimal demand on the learning curve as the new monitor types are introduced to your environment.

Port monitor listen uses the underlying TCP/IP protocol stack to provide across-the-wire services. Examples of services provided through listen port monitors are network printing (discussed in Chapter 14) and remote file sharing, including NFS (discussed in Chapter 12) and RFS.

There is no limit on the number of port monitors a system administrator can create. For this reason, each port monitor must be assigned a tag (that is, a name), referred to as the port monitor tag. Port monitor tags are useful for referencing the port monitor being administered, using port monitor-specific commands.

Service Access Controller (SAC)

The Service Access Controller (SAC) process, implemented in the sac daemon, operates at the top of the hierarchy. It is responsible for all port monitors that are defined on the system. Only one sac per system can be running. Unless the sac daemon is running, no port monitors can run, and consequently, all port services on the system are disabled.

The sac daemon is started at boot time by the init process whenever the system is brought up on run levels two, three, or four (that is, multiuser states) as signified by the following /etc/inittab-pertinent entry:

```
sc:234:respawn:/usr/lib/saf/sac -t 300
```

The -t 300 option tells sac to routinely poll all port monitors every 300 seconds for services. You can set the poll period by changing the number of seconds to whatever you deem more suitable to your environment.

SAF Administrative Files

Setting up SAF involves creating and updating a SAF-specific configuration and administration database that is maintained in the /etc/saf subdirectory, as shown in Figure A.2. Using the proper command tools, you will be able to update files maintained by this database.

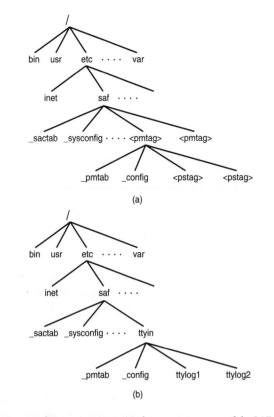

Figure A.2. SAF-specific supporting directory structure: (a) the generic structure of the SAF directory and (b) an example showing the SAF directory hierarchy corresponding to a system including support for a ttymon port monitor with the tag ttyin, which in turn supports two port services with tags ttylog1 and ttylog2.

Under SAF, a distinction is made between sac-specific, port-specific, and port service-specific configuration and administrative files, as well as command tools.

SAC Configuration and Startup Files

When invoked by init, sac reads and implements the contents of both the _sysconfig and the _sactab files, which are stored directly under the /etc/saf directory (see Figure A.2). The first file defines the environment governing all SAF-associated resources (that is, port monitors and port services).

When brought up, the sac daemon first reads the _sysconfig file to self-customize its own environment before invoking any port monitor processes. It is important to realize that unless the environment is overridden by port-specific or port service configuration files, the environment defined in _sysconfig applies to all SAF components. Using vi or your preferred UNIX editor, you can modify the contents of the _sysconfig file.

After the SAF environment is set up, the sac daemon reads and executes the contents of /etc/saf/ _sactab. This file defines which port monitors sac is to start up. SAF provides system administrators with the sacadm command to modify the contents of the /etc/saf/_sactab file. sacadm can be used to create new port monitors, enable or disable them, check their status, and delete them. As will be explained later, administrators are required to use port monitor-specific administrative commands in command substitution mode. Port monitor listen's administrative command is nlsadmin, whereas ttymon's is ttyadm.

Port Monitor Configuration Files

SAF defines two files per port monitor: _config and _pmtab. Both files are maintained by SAF in a subdirectory of /etc/saf named after the port monitor tag (see Figure A.2a). As an example, a ttymon port monitor was assigned ttyin for a tag. The subdirectory /etc/saf/ttyin was created, and the administrative and configuration files pertinent to this port monitor are maintained in it (see Figure A.2b).

_config defines environment settings that apply only to the port monitor in question. Before the invocation of a port monitor, sac fetches the corresponding /etc/saf/pmtag/_config file and customizes that port monitor's environment according to the file's instructions. The instructions contained in this file can override or add to those found in the SAF-wide /etc/saf/_sysconfig file. The file is optional. Like _sysconfig, port monitor-specific files can be modified using any UNIX editor.

The sac daemon invokes a port monitor after its environment has been customized. Upon startup, the port monitor in question reads the _pmtab file stored in its own home directory (the /etc/saf/ pmtag directory). This file's functionality is similar to sac's /etc/saf/_sactab. It defines the port services that a port monitor is to start and control. For example, if the ttyin ttymon port monitor was configured to support dial-in and login to the system through both the COM1 and the COM2 ports, it is the responsibility of `ttyin`'s port monitor to deploy the processes that control access to both ports. For this to happen, the administrator must have already created two pertinent entries in the `/etc/saf/ttyin/_pmtab` file by using the appropriate administrative commands.

Port Service Configuration Files

Port services have no home directories of their own. There is only one optional configuration file per port service. This file is maintained in the home directory of the port monitor controlling the port service. The configuration file is named by the port service tag and can be edited using UNIX editing utilities. A port service configuration file is similar in functionality to its predecessors, `_sysconfig` and `_config`. It is used to add to or override the environment settings defined by `_sysconfig` and `_config` for the port monitor controlling it.

The port monitor determines whether there is a port-specific configuration file before invoking a port service. If there is one, the environment is customized, and then the service is invoked. Otherwise, the port monitor proceeds directly to invoking the service in question and begins monitoring it.

In Figure A.2b, two files, `ttylog1` and `ttylog2`, are shown. They represent port services with tags `ttylog1` and `ttylog2`. The contents of these files may not be identical. Keep in mind that these files are optional, and their number might not tell you how many port services are being administered by the controlling port monitor.

SAF Startup Procedure

Figure A.3 shows a flowchart illustrating the SAF startup process from the point the system enters a multiuser run level to when the port service gains control of the physical port.

When the system enters a multiuser run level, `init` executes the following entry in the `/etc/inittab` file:

```
sc:234:respawn:/usr/lib/saf/sac -t 300
```

This entry forces `init` to invoke sac and to respawn it whenever necessary (that is, if sac for some reason should die).

After sac is started, it checks its home directory (`/etc/saf`) for the `_sysconfig` file. If the file exists, sac customizes the SAF environment by executing `_sysconfig`. Next, sac reads `/etc/saf/_sactab` to identify the port monitors to be invoked and controlled. Before the invocation of the port monitor, its home directory (`/etc/saf/`*pmtag*) is checked for the optional port monitor-specific configuration file `_config`, which is then used by sac to add to or alter the SAF environment for that particular port monitor. sac then proceeds to invoke the port monitor.

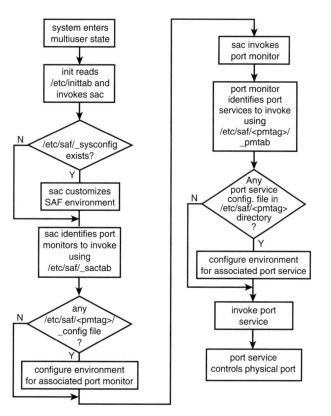

Figure A.3. *The SAF startup procedure.*

After the port monitor is invoked, it checks its home directory for the startup file _pmtab, which defines the port services it is to activate. Before starting any of the port services, it checks and runs any optional port service-specific environment configuration files. Finally, port services are started and each of them is delegated a physical port to control.

Setting Up SAF

Being hierarchical, SAF setup procedures start at the top of the hierarchy and pass by the mid-level (involving port monitors) on the way to configuring the bottom, represented by port services. At each level of the hierarchy, SAF provides a distinct set of tools that the administrator should use for configuring or checking the status of the SAF operation at that level.

Setting Up *sac*

Fortunately, there is not much to setting up sac. Just make sure that the sac-pertinent entry shown in the preceding section is in the /etc/inittab file. Also, make sure that it is running before you proceed to the next two phases of setting up the port monitors and services. To do that, enter the following command:

```
# ps -ef ¦ grep "sac"
```

Setting Up Port Monitors

You should lay out plans before you proceed to set up the port monitors. Decisions such as what types of port monitors are needed, and how many of each type, should have already been made.

Do not forget the purpose each port monitor is expected to serve. For example, if you are planning to provision your system to support dial-in/dial-out access, you might want to consider the number of ttymon port monitors. Depending on the total number of supported physical ports, you might end up with two or more port monitors. Also, you might want to consider dedicating some ports for dial-out access only, others for dial-in access only, and the rest for dial-in/dial-out access. This scheme requires a minimum of three ttymon port monitors. Segregating port services by type and making each category belong to one port monitor gives you the flexibility of the collective management and administration of these ports.

Port monitors can be created, administered, and managed using the command sacadm and port monitor type-specific administrative commands. These commands are nlsadmin for listen port monitors and ttyadm for ttymon port monitors. Both ttyadm and nlsadmin are used with sacadm in command substitution mode as explained in the following text.

> **Tip:** Often a vendor will have port monitors already set up to use its products. For example, a ports board vendor will add its own port monitor to listen to its ports. Also, GUIs that come with SVR4.2, such as Dialup Setup, will create these port monitors automatically. You are *strongly* encouraged to use a GUI to set up port monitors whenever possible. It's hard to create port monitor entries from scratch with either the command line or using vi. It's better to use the GUI, then modify it in the file later to make small corrections.

Here is the syntax of sacadm for creating a port monitor:

```
# sacadm -a -p pmtag -t type  -c "pm_cmd"  -v version [ -f d¦x ] \
[ -n count ] [ -y "comment" ]
```

In this syntax,

-a	Stands for create port monitor.
-p *pmtag*	Specifies the port monitor with the tag *pmtag*. Port monitor tags can be anything you choose. You should, however, consider assigning a port monitor a tag that conveniently describes the nature of the services the port monitor is rendering to the user community. A port monitor tag such as ttyin, for example, would be suitable to designate the ttymon port monitor controlling dial-in-only access port services.
-t *type*	Specifies the type of port monitor undergoing creation. *type* can be either listen or ttymon.
-c "*pm_cmd*"	Specifies the command that sac must execute to bring up this port monitor. Depending on the type, *pm_cmd* can be either of /usr/lib/saf/ttymon or /usr/lib/saf/listen.
-v *version*	Specifies the version of the port monitor. Better still, you can use the port monitor type-specific administrative command with the -V option in command substitution mode to provide consistently accurate information. The following two examples illustrate doing so for both port monitor types:

```
# sacadm -a ... -v `nlsadmin -V` ...
# sacadm -a ... -v `ttyadm -V` ...
```

[-f d¦x]	Specifies the state to which the port monitor must be brought. d means that sac should put the port monitor in a disabled state after invocation, and x means that the port monitor can be started only by the system administrator. When started by the administrator, the port monitor sac takes over controlling the port monitor. If no action is specified, the port monitor is started and enabled by sac whenever sac is invoked.
-n *count*	Specifies the number of times sac should attempt invoking a port monitor that is failing to respond favorably. The default value is zero.
-y "*comment*"	Can be conveniently used to describe the nature of the services this port monitor is rendering to the user community.

As an example, to provide users with local login access to the system via the tty serial ports, a ttymon port monitor is required. To create the port monitor, a sacadm command similar to the following one is required:

```
# sacadm -a -p ttyin -t ttymon -v `ttyadm -V` \
-c"/usr/lib/saf/ttymon" -f d -n 2 -y "Dial-in only"
```

This command creates a ttymon port monitor with port monitor tag ttyin. It also specifies that sac can make two attempts to invoke the monitor should it fail to respond initially, and that the port monitor should be put in a disabled state upon invocation. Notice the use of 'ttyadm -V' in command substitution mode for the determination and passing of the version of the port monitor to the sacadm command.

When sacadm is used to create a port monitor, a supporting entry is added to sac's administrative file, /etc/saf/_sactab. Here are the contents of the /etc/saf/_sactab file as they appear on the author's system after creation of the ttyin port monitor using the preceding sacadm command:

```
# VERSION=1
tcp:listen::3:/usr/lib/saf/listen -m inet/tcp0 tcp 2>/dev/null     #
inetd:inetd::0:/usr/sbin/inetd     #internet daemon
ttyin:ttymon::0:/usr/lib/saf/ttymon     #
```

It can be concluded that looking up the contents of this file helps in verifying that the port monitor is indeed taken care of by sac. This file listing includes an entry pertaining to the new ttyin port monitor. Also, the entry includes all the parameters entered on the command line in colon-separated format such that the first field refers to the *pmtag*, the second refers to the port monitor type, the third refers to the state in which the port monitor is started (d or x), the fourth specifies the retry count, and the fifth specifies the full pathname of the command to use to invoke the port monitor. The last field includes the comment entered using the -y option.

In addition to updating the _sactab file, sacadm creates two supporting directories:

◆ /etc/saf/pmtag, where the optional _config file is maintained, as well as the port monitor's administrative file _pmtab. In _pmtab, the port monitor keeps track of the port services it has been configured to invoke and monitor. Optional port service configuration files belonging to this port monitor's management are also maintained in this directory.

◆ /var/saf/pmtag, where the file log is maintained. In log, SAF logs all system messages pertaining to the port monitor.

Accordingly, if you were to check the system's directory structure after the preceding sacadm command was entered, you would expect to see both directories /etc/saf/ttyin and /var/saf/ttyin.

Managing Port Monitors

Port monitor management includes tasks such as status checking, as well as enabling, disabling, and removing port monitors.

Port Monitor Status

To check the status of supported port monitors, use the sacadm command with the -1 option as in the following example:

```
# sacadm -p ttyin -l
PMTAG    PMTYPE    FLGS    RCNT    STATUS      COMMAND
ttyin    ttymon    d       2       DISABLED    /usr/lib/saf/ttymon #Dial-in only
```

The status field in this example shows the port monitor as DISABLED. Depending on when you check the status, you might see one of the following five values:

STARTING	Indicates that sac is in the process of starting the port monitor. This state is a transition between NOT RUNNING and ENABLED or DISABLED.
ENABLED	Indicates that the port monitor is running and is accepting service requests.
DISABLED	Indicates that the port monitor is not running. Consequently, it is denying service requests.
STOPPED	Indicates that the port monitor is in the process of being shut down. This is a transition between ENABLED or DISABLED and NOT RUNNING.
NOT RUNNING	Indicates that the port service is not running and that none of the associated port services is currently accessible.

Enabling, Disabling, and Removing a Port Monitor

Using the sacadm command, you can enable, disable, or remove port monitors. Before taking this action, bear in mind that all associated port services will be affected. If a port monitor is disabled, for example, all port services supported by that port monitor become disabled.

Following is an example of using sacadm to disable the ttyin port monitor:

```
# sacadm -p ttyin -d
```

To enable it, enter this:

```
# sacadm -p ttyin -e
```

And to remove it, enter this:

```
# sacadm -p ttyin -r
```

Setting Up Port Services

SAF provides the pmadm command for creating, administering, and managing port services. Using pmadm involves using the port monitor-specific administrative commands: ttyadm for the ttymon port monitor or nlsadmin for the listen port monitor.

Following is the syntax of the pmadm command for creating a port service:

```
# pmadm -a -p pmtag -s svctag -m "pmspecific" \
-v version [ -fd¦u ] -y "comment"
```

In this syntax,

-a	Stands for create a port service.
-p *pmtag*	Specifies the port monitor under which the port service is being created.
-s *svctag*	Specifies the service tag to assign to the port service being created.
-m *"pmspecific"*	Specifies port monitor-specific (by port monitor type) command-line parameters. Normally, these parameters are passed to pmadm using port monitor-specific administrative commands, such as ttyadm or nlsadmin, in command substitution mode.
-v *version*	Specifies the version of the port monitor under which the port service is being created. Use either ttyadm or nlsadmin with the -V option in command substitution mode to pass this information to pmadm.
[-fd¦u]	Specifies whether the port service is to be started in a disabled state (-fd) and/or whether a utmp entry is to be created (-fu). To specify both, enter -fdu.

Following is an example of using pmadm to create a ttymon port service:

```
# pmadm -a -p ttyin -s s01 -v `ttyadm -V` -fd \
-m "`ttyadm -d /dev/term/01 -l 9600 -s /usr/bin/login \
-p "Saturn Welcomes All Aliens!, Please Login:"`"
```

By virtue of this command, a ttymon port service is being created under the ttyin port monitor. The service is assigned s01 for a service tag. It is configured to support login service access through the /dev/term/01 device special file (that is, COM2). The -l 9600 option specifies the supporting line settings entry in the /etc/ttydefs terminal line setting database file. The -p parameter in the ttyadm command specifies the prompt a user attempting access through the COM2 port should get. In this example, upon connecting to the host, the user gets the Saturn Welcomes All Aliens!, Please Login: prompt.

Notice how the ttymon's administrative command, ttyadm, was used to specify all port monitor-specific options, including the device special file, the line settings entry in /etc/ttydefs, the program to invoke whenever access to the system is attempted via the designated port, and the prompt message.

When the s01 port is created, an entry is made in the /etc/saf/*pmtag*/_pmtab file identifying the port service and the command-line parameters with which the port service should be invoked by the governing port monitor. Upon invocation, the port monitor starts monitoring the designated port for service requests. Upon receiving one, it invokes the program specified in the -s option in the port monitor-specific administrative tool to take care of the request. In the example, /usr/bin/login is the program that the port service is going to invoke upon detecting a service request on the COM2 port.

Managing Port Services

Like sacadm, the pmadm command is equipped with the command-line options enabling you to check for the status of port services, enable them, disable them, and remove them.

Port Service Status

To check the status of a port service, enter the pmadm command with the -l option as depicted in the following syntax:

```
# pmadm -l -p pmtag -s svctag
```

Applying this to the s01 port service, created previously, you get this:

```
# pmadm -l -p ttyin -s s01
PMTAG     PMTYPE     SVCTAG    FLGS ID    SCHEME    <PMSPECIFIC>
ttyin     ttymon     s01       u    -     login    /dev/tty01 bhr 0 /usr/bin/shserv 60
2400
➥ldterm SVR4.2 login: - - - - #
```

If no service tag is specified, pmadm -l reports the status of all port services governed by the port monitor specified in pmtag. Here is an example:

```
# pmadm -l -p ttyin
PMTAG     PMTYPE     SVCTAG    FLGS ID    SCHEME    <PMSPECIFIC>
ttyin     ttymon     s01       u    -     -         /dev/term/01 - - /usr/bin/login -
9600 -
➥Saturn Welcomes All Aliens!, Please Login: - - - - #
ttyin     ttymon     s00       u    -     -         /dev/term/00 - - /usr/bin/login -
9600 -
➥Saturn Welcomes All Aliens!, Please Login: - - - - #
```

If no port monitor is specified, pmadm reports the status of all port services pertaining to all port monitors.

The status of a port service is reported under the FLGS heading in pmadm's output.

Enabling, Disabling, and Removing a Port Service

Port services can be enabled, disabled, or removed using pmadm with the -e, -d, or -r options, respectively. Following is an example of enabling a port service:

```
# pmadm -p ttyin -s s01 -e
```

To disable s01, enter this:

```
# pmadm -p ttyin -s s01 -d
```

To remove s01, enter this:

```
# pmadm -p ttyin -s 01 -r
```

The *ttymon* Port Monitor

Port monitor ttymon is invoked by sac as the system enters a multiuser run state. ttymon is a mid-level process in the SAF hierarchy. It is responsible for the invocation, management, and control of port services configured to support services through the tty communication ports.

Whenever started, ttymon reads the administrative _pmtab file in its home directory, /etc/saf/ *pmtag*, and invokes all the port services identified in this file. Similarly, when it is stopped or disabled, all port services defined in the _pmtab file are also affected.

Like its predecessors, getty and uugetty, ttymon performs tty-related functions such as setting terminal modes and line speeds over connections established through the communication ports that the associated services support.

Although both getty and uugetty are still supported by UNIX SVR4.x, using ttymon is the preferred method of establishing and managing tty ports. Following are the reasons why this is so:

◆ Applying SAF administration skills to the management of tty-associated services requires little extra learning on behalf of the system administrator. This is due to the uniformity of the SAF management concepts and skills applied to all port monitor types.

◆ SAF allows for the collective management of related port services. Using port management commands, a system administrator can collectively invoke, enable, or disable all port services that are governed by the same ttymon port monitor—an unachievable task if getty or uugetty were to be used.

◆ ttymon supports a new autobaud feature that, if employed, automatically determines the line speed of the hardware to ports supervised by the ttymon port monitor.

◆ ttymon is not limited to providing login services—a limitation of both getty and uugetty. It is configurable to provide any service through ports it supervises.

◆ Also, on a large system, there can be many fewer daemon processes running, because there isn't a separate process running for each port being monitored.

---

ttymon in Express Mode

SAF supports a so-called express mode invocation of ttymon. Rather than being invoked by sac, under this mode, ttymon can be invoked by init. Place an entry to this effect in the /etc/inittab file. Following is an entry that exists in the /etc/inittab file normally found on each UNIX SVR4.x system:

```
co:12345:respawn:/usr/lib/saf/ttymon -g -v -p "Console Login: " -d /dev/console
➥-l console
```

The intent is to let init start ttymon and give it control over the console as soon as the system is brought up. This makes the console available to the administrator regardless of the run level of the system.

ttymon Port Monitor Administrative Command

Using sacadm and pmadm, a system administrator can create and manage both the port monitor and its associated port services. Both commands are useful for the currently supported port monitor types (listen and ttymon). However, to gear these commands toward administering a specific type of port monitor, UNIX introduced port monitor-specific administrative commands that should be used in command substitution mode: the sacadm and pmadm commands.

SAF provides ttyadm as ttymon's administrative command. This command was used on two occasions on previous pages without being introduced. Both examples are included here for the sake of explaining the options that ttyadm supports. The first command creates the ttymon port monitor ttyin, and the second one creates a port service, s01, under ttyin's administration:

```
# sacadm -a -p ttyin -t ttymon -v `ttyadm -V` \
-c"/usr/lib/saf/ttymon" -f d -n 2 -y "Dial-in only"

# pmadm -a -p ttyin -s s01 -v `ttyadm -V` -fd \
-m "`ttyadm -d /dev/ter/01 -l 9600 -s /usr/bin/login\
-p "Saturn Welcomes All Aliens!, Please Login:"`"
```

Following are the options of the ttyadm command:

-V	Forces ttyadm to report the version of the port monitor being managed.
-d /dev/term/##	Specifies the device special file corresponding to the physical tty port associated with this port monitor. Notice the deviation from the original way of referring to these special files. Under getty and uugetty, special device files were referred to in the /dev directory as /dev/tty##, in which ## refers to the tty port number (for example, tty01 means COM2). Under SAF, device special files are maintained in the /dev/term directory and are referred to as /dev/term/## (for example, /dev/term/01 stands for COM2). Both conventions, however, are still supported. You can still configure a tty port in the original method by specifying /dev/tty## when using getty or uugetty.
-b	Configures the associated port for bidirectional flow of data.
-r *count*	Specifies the number of times ttymon should attempt to restart a failing port service.
-t *timeout*	Specifies the time, in seconds, that the port monitor is required to wait for input on the port before closing it.
-p *"prompt"*	Specifies the prompt string to be written to the port whenever a user request is detected.
-i *"message"*	Specifies the message to print to the port when it is in a disabled state.

-l *ttylabel*   Specifies the desired record in the terminal line settings database /etc/ttydefs. This file is similar in functionality to /etc/gettydefs. The second file is still supported by UNIX SVR4.*x*. /etc/ttydefs records specify the desired communication parameters and line settings that should govern the connection a user establishes through the associated physical port. The label specified in this option can itself be part of a hunt sequence, which allows ttymon to cycle through alternative records until a record compatible with the line settings of the user's end of the connection is found. Refer to your man pages for details on /etc/ttydefs. The *ttylabel* usually represents the baud rate and sometimes the parity.

-s *program*   Specifies the full pathname of the program to invoke in response to the service request on this port.

All the parameters specified are maintained in the /etc/saf/*pmtag*/_pmtab administrative file for the port service being created.

Summary of Operation

When invoked, the ttymon port monitor consults its administrative database file, /etc/saf/*pmtag*/_pmtab. It then initializes and monitors its port services. Among other governing parameters, _pmtab includes the *ttylabel* specification that applies to each port service (and therefore physical port). Hence, upon initializing the port, ttymon sets the line speed and other connection parameters corresponding to the specified label and writes the prompt, which is also maintained in the _pmtab file, to the associated port.

A user attempting to connect to the system through the port with nonmatching line settings normally presses the break key once or twice. When ttymon detects a break signal on the port, it hunts to the next *ttylabel* noted at the end of the current entry in the /etc/ttydefs file. Only when a non-break key is detected does the ttymon port monitor invoke the program specified in the _pmtab administrative file. This program is the same one specified using the -s option in the ttyadm command when the port service was created. In the example given in the preceding section, it is /usr/bin/login.

The *listen* Port Monitor

Port monitor listen is invoked by the service access controller (that is, the sac daemon). listen provides access to network applications over any transport service provider, including but not limited to TCP/IP. Among the network applications that listen supports are network printing, and file sharing services such as NFS. Also, the listener supports terminal login sessions.

A listen port monitor is capable of invoking, monitoring, and managing multiple service ports, with each assigned a user service process. When invoked by sac, a listen port monitor reads its administrative file, /etc/saf/pmtag/_pmtab, containing information about which ports to monitor and what service (that is, network user process) is associated with that port. Consequently, listen initializes its ports and monitors them for incoming connection requests. When a request is detected on a service port, listen identifies and authenticates the user requesting the connection, and it invokes the service associated with that port.

Like ttymon port monitors, listen port monitors are made distinguishable by assigning port monitor tags (pmtag). Each listen port service is also distinguished by being assigned a unique service tag (svctag).

Port Service Addresses

Although under ttymon's management, there is a direct one-to-one association between available physical ports (for example, COM ports) and port services, this is not the case for listen port monitors. A listen port monitor listens on the same network interface (the same physical network port) for incoming service requests on behalf of all the service ports it supports. There arises the need for an addressing scheme that allows the port monitor to distinguish between the services being requested through the same interface. By assigning each network service a unique address, listen can invoke the service associated with the address included in the client request.

Here is the format of listen port service-associated addresses (see Figure A.4):

◆ Family address (4 hex digits): It is always set to 0x0020.

◆ Port address (4 hex digits): It is the port service-specific address, and it is unique to one port service. For example, the listen port service address assigned to LP System V network print service is 0x0ACE, whereas BSD's is 0x0203.

◆ IP address (8 hex digits): It is the IP address assigned to the network interface on the system, and on which listen is monitoring the network for requests. Using the lpsystem -A command (see Chapter 14), you can find the hex equivalent to the dotted decimal IP address assigned to the host.

◆ Reserved (16 hex digits): It is reserved for future use.

Family Address (4 digits)	Port Address (4 digits)	IP Address (8 digits)	Reserved (16 digits)

Figure A.4. listen's port service address format. Addresses are expressed in hexadecimal notation.

Here is an example of a complete listen port service address:

```
02000ACE640000030000000000000000
```

This address pertains to the LP System V network print service (0x0ACE) resident on the host with IP address 100.0.0.3 (0x64000003). Consequently, System V clients are expected to accompany their network print requests to this address so that the listener, upon detecting them, can invoke the associated process and submit the requests to it.

listen Port Monitor Administrative Command

nlsadmin is listen's specific administrative command. Like ttymon's ttyadm command, nlsadmin is used in command substitution mode with the sacadm and pmadm commands for the purposes of creating and managing port monitors and their associated port services.

In the following subsections, nlsadmin is presented in the context of creating and managing listen port monitors and port services.

Creating a *listen* Port Monitor

Here is the syntax of the sacadm command used to create a listen port monitor:

```
# sacadm -a -ppmtag -t listen -c "command" -v `nlsadmin -V` [ -n count ] \
[ -fd¦x ] [ -y "comment"
```

The meanings of the command-line options were explained earlier in the appendix. Notice in particular the use of the -t listen option to specify a listen port monitor. Also, notice the use of nlsadmin -V in command substitution mode to pass the version of the port monitor being created to the sacadm command.

In the following example, sacadm is used to create a listen port monitor with the port monitor tag tcpsvc:

```
# sacadm -a -t listen -p tcpsvc -v `nlsadmin -V` -c "/usr/lib/saf/listen" -n2
```

Consequently, an entry is added to sac's administrative database /etc/saf/_sactab pertaining to the tcpsvc port monitor just created. After startup by sac, /usr/lib/saf/listen is invoked as the program taking care of requests sent to this port monitor.

Creating *listen* Port Services

Creating a listen port service involves the use of both the pmadm and the nlsadmin command. Following is the syntax of pmadm for creating a listen port service:

```
# pmadm -a -p pmtag -s svctag [-i id] -v `nlsadmin -V` \
-m "`nlsadmin options`" -y "comment"
```

All the options have the same meanings as were explained earlier in the chapter.

Here is an example of using pmadm and nlsadmin for creating a new port service:

```
# pmadm -a -p tcpsvc -s lpd -i root -v`nlsadmin -V` \
-m "`nlsadmin -o /var/spool/lp/fifos/listenBSD -A\x0020203640000030000000000000000`"
```

This command creates a listen port service under the tcpsvc port monitor. The port service tag is lpd; it takes care of responding to print service requests coming from BSD workstations. Note the use of the port service address, described earlier.

Managing *listen* Port Monitors and Services

You can use both sacadm and pmadm to verify the status of listen port monitors and services, respectively. They can also be used to enable, disable, and remove port monitors and services. For details, consult the earlier section "The ttymon Port Monitor."

Summary

Service Access Facility provides UNIX system administrators with a uniform interface for the creation, administration, and management of local and network peripheral resources.

SAF defines a hierarchical organization of resource processes. At the top of the hierarchy is the service access controller, implemented in the sac daemon. sac is invoked by init as the system enters any multiuser run level. In turn, sac invokes middle-level processes called port monitors, which are defined in sac's administrative database, /etc/saf/_sactab. Each port monitor is assigned a set of related port services (the bottom-level processes) for subsequent control and management.

There are two types of port monitors: listen and ttymon. Port monitor listen runs on any reliable transport protocol and provides users access to network resources such as LP network print and remote file sharing services. Port monitor ttymon replaces the traditional uugetty and getty capabilities. It provides users with access to local resources through the physical tty ports.

Corresponding to every port monitor, SAF creates a supporting home directory, /etc/saf/*pmtag*, in which *pmtag* is the port monitor tag. In this directory, the port monitor administrative file, _pmtab, is maintained, in addition to optional per-service configuration files. Also, the directory /var/saf/pmtag is created so that system messages pertaining to the port monitor can be maintained in the log file.

I

Index

PLUG YOURSELF INTO...

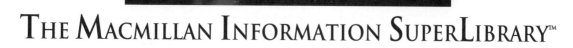

MACMILLAN INFORMATION SUPERLIBRARY™

THE MACMILLAN INFORMATION SUPERLIBRARY™

Free information and vast computer resources from the world's leading computer book publisher—online!

FIND THE BOOKS THAT ARE RIGHT FOR YOU!

A complete online catalog, plus sample chapters and tables of contents give you an in-depth look at *all* of our books, including hard-to-find titles. It's the best way to find the books you need!

● STAY INFORMED with the latest computer industry news through our online newsletter, press releases, and customized Information SuperLibrary Reports.

● GET FAST ANSWERS to your questions about MCP books and software.

● VISIT our online bookstore for the latest information and editions!

● COMMUNICATE with our expert authors through e-mail and conferences.

● DOWNLOAD SOFTWARE from the immense MCP library:
  - Source code and files from MCP books
  - The best shareware, freeware, and demos

● DISCOVER HOT SPOTS on other parts of the Internet.

● WIN BOOKS in ongoing contests and giveaways!

TO PLUG INTO MCP: → WORLD WIDE WEB: **http://www.mcp.com**

GOPHER: gopher.mcp.com

FTP: ftp.mcp.com

GET CONNECTED
to the ultimate source of computer information!

The MCP Forum on CompuServe

Go online with the world's leading computer book publisher! Macmillan Computer Publishing offers everything you need for computer success!

Find the books that are right for you!
A complete online catalog, plus sample chapters and tables of contents give you an in-depth look at all our books. The best way to shop or browse!

➤ Get fast answers and technical support for MCP books and software

➤ Join discussion groups on major computer subjects

➤ Interact with our expert authors via e-mail and conferences

➤ Download software from our immense library:
  ▷ Source code from books
  ▷ Demos of hot software
  ▷ The best shareware and freeware
  ▷ Graphics files

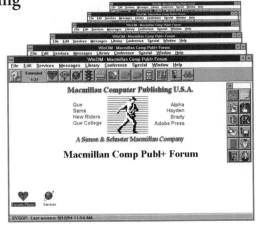

Join now and get a free CompuServe Starter Kit!

To receive your free CompuServe Introductory Membership, call **1-800-848-8199** and ask for representative #597.

The Starter Kit includes:
➤ Personal ID number and password
➤ $15 credit on the system
➤ Subscription to *CompuServe Magazine*

Once on the CompuServe System, type:

GO MACMILLAN

for the most computer information anywhere!

 **MACMILLAN COMPUTER PUBLISHING**

▤ **CompuServe**

Add to Your Sams Library Today with the Best Books for Programming, Operating Systems, and New Technologies

The easiest way to order is to pick up the phone and call
1-800-428-5331
between 9:00 a.m. and 5:00 p.m. EST.
For faster service please have your credit card available.

ISBN	Quantity	Description of Item	Unit Cost	Total Cost
0-672-30402-3		UNIX Unleashed (Book/CD)	$49.99	
0-672-30705-7		Linux Unleashed (Book/CD)	$49.99	
0-672-30540-2		Teach Yourself the UNIX C Shell in 14 Days	$29.99	
0-672-30553-4		Absolute Beginner's Guide to Networking, 2E	$22.00	
0-672-30501-1		Understanding Data Communications, 4E	$29.99	
0-672-30542-9		X Window System Programming, 2E (Book/Disk)	$39.99	
0-672-30586-0		Teach Yourself Perl in 21 Days	$29.99	
0-672-30448-1		Teach Yourself C in 21 Days, Bestseller Edition	$24.95	
0-672-30594-1		Programming WinSock (Book/Disk)	$35.00	
0-672-30655-7		Developing Your Own 32-Bit Operating System (Book/CD)	$49.99	
0-672-30667-0		Teach Youself Web Publishing with HTML in a Week	$25.00	
0-672-30737-5		World Wide Web Unleashed, 2E	$35.00	
		Shipping and Handling: See information below.		
		TOTAL		

❏ 3½" Disk

❏ 5¼" Disk

Shipping and Handling: $4.00 for the first book, and $1.75 for each additional book. Floppy disk: add $1.75 for shipping and handling. If you need to have it *now*, we can ship product to you in 24 hours for an additional charge of approximately $18.00, and you will receive your item overnight or in two days. Overseas shipping and handling adds $2.00 per book and $8.00 for up to three disks. Prices subject to change. Call for availability and pricing information on latest editions.

201 W. 103rd Street, Indianapolis, Indiana 46290

1-800-428-5331 — Orders   1-800-835-3202 — FAX   1-800-858-7674 — Customer Service

Book ISBN 0-672-30584-4

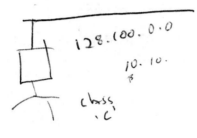

128.100.0.0

10.10.

class
'c'